SUPREME LEADERSHIP
IN MODERN WAR

This edited volume focuses on civil-military relations before and during great power conflicts and comprises historical case studies of the modern supreme leadership.

It aims to provide a guide for the future by shining a light on what worked and what failed in the civil-military relationships that steered great powers during the last era of rapid global change. While future civil-military relationships will have to adapt to the current global environment, the past remains, as always, a prelude. Thus, crucial concepts that underpin all such relationships are eternal and are waiting to be drawn out by historians trained to examine and present them to those who can put them to immediate good use. This volume demonstrates the relevance of history in every chapter, as readers will see parallels to today's problems throughout every case study. The world is entering an age of great challenges, many of which require nations – particularly the most powerful – to establish civil-military relationships capable of navigating dangerous currents without a repeat of the calamities reminiscent of the last century. Each chapter focuses on a particular civil-military relationship as it developed before and during a great war. The editors have gathered leading experts on each of these periods to produce a concise but thorough essay on each relationship's intricacies.

This book will be of much interest to students of military and strategic studies, military history, and international relations, as well as professional military colleges and policymakers.

James Lacey is Horner Chair of War Studies and a Professor of Strategic Studies at the Marine Corps University, Quantico, USA. He is author/editor of over a dozen books.

The late **Williamson Murray** was Professor Emeritus of History at Ohio State University, USA, and author/editor of over twenty books.

Cass Military Studies

Civil-Military Cooperation in International Interventions
The Role of Soldiers
Agata Mazurkiewicz

Contemporary Military Reserves
Between the Civilian and Military Worlds
Edited by Eyal Ben-Ari and Vincent Connelly

Military Strategies of the New European Allies
A Comparative Study
Håkan Edström and Jacob Westberg

Proxy War in Yemen
Bernd Kaussler and Keith A. Grant

Understanding Battlefield Coalitions
Edited by Rosella Cappella Zielinski and Ryan Grauer

Supreme Leadership in Modern War
Civil-Military Relations During Competition and War
Edited by James Lacey and Williamson Murray

For more information about this series, please visit: https://www.routledge.com/
Cass-Military-Studies/book-series/CMS

SUPREME LEADERSHIP IN MODERN WAR

Civil-Military Relations During Competition and War

Edited by James Lacey and Williamson Murray

Routledge
Taylor & Francis Group

LONDON AND NEW YORK

Cover image: Roosevelt, Stalin, and Churchill on portico of Russian Embassy in Teheran, during conference–Nov. 28 - Dec. 1, 1943, U.S. Signal Corps, LOC

First published 2024
by Routledge
4 Park Square, Milton Park, Abingdon, Oxon OX14 4RN

and by Routledge
605 Third Avenue, New York, NY 10158

Routledge is an imprint of the Taylor & Francis Group, an informa business

British Library Cataloguing-in-Publication Data
A catalogue record for this book is available from the British Library

Library of Congress Cataloging-in-Publication Data
Names: Lacey, Jim, 1958- editor. | Murray, Williamson, editor.
Title: Supreme leadership in modern war : civil-military relations during competition and war / edited by James Lacey and Williamson Murray.
Description: Abingdon, Oxon ; New York, NY : Routledge, 2024. | Series: Cass military studies | Includes bibliographical references and index.
Identifiers: LCCN 2023021678 (print) | LCCN 2023021679 (ebook) | ISBN 9781032451541 (hardback) | ISBN 9781032451534 (paperback) | ISBN 9781003375630 (ebook)
Subjects: LCSH: Civil-military relations--Case studies. | Command of troops--Case studies. | Military policy--Case studies.
Classification: LCC JF195 .S86 2024 (print) | LCC JF195 (ebook) | DDC 355.3/3041--dc23/eng/20230629
LC record available at https://lccn.loc.gov/2023021678
LC ebook record available at https://lccn.loc.gov/2023021679

ISBN: 978-1-032-45154-1 (hbk)
ISBN: 978-1-032-45153-4 (pbk)
ISBN: 978-1-003-37563-0 (ebk)

DOI: 10.4324/9781003375630

Typeset in Galliard
by KnowledgeWorks Global Ltd.

*To the memory of a great historian and friend,
Dr. Williamson Murray, who passed only a day after
approving the final proofs for this work.*

CONTENTS

LIST OF CONTRIBUTORS

Holger Afflerbach is a Professor of Modern European History at the University of Leeds. He published widely on the First World War. Among his books are a biography of Erich von Falkenhayn, a study of the Triple Alliance, an edition of sources from the German Headquarters in World War I, and recently the book On a Knife Edge. How Germany lost the First World War.

Richard Frank is the author of *Guadalcanal: The Definitive Account of the Landmark Battle*, which won the General Wallace M. Greene Award from the U.S. Marine Corps. His second work, *Downfall: The End of the Imperial Japanese Empire* (1999), received the Harry S. Truman Book Award. The first volume of his narrative history trilogy about the Asian-Pacific war, Tower of Skulls, was recently published.

John Gooch is an emeritus professor of international history at the University of Leeds UK. His recent book *Mussolini's War: Fascist Italy from Triumph to Collapse* was awarded the Duke of Westminster's Silver Medal by the Royal United Services Institute.

Alexander Hill is a Professor in Military History at the University of Calgary, Canada, and specializes in Soviet military history. His *The Red Army and the Second World War* was published in 2017, to which *The War on the Eastern Front: The Soviet Union 1941–1945 – A Photographic History* published in 2021 is a useful accompaniment.

James Lacey holds the Horner Chair of War Studies at Marine Corps University. Among many other works, he is the author of *Rome: A Strategy for*

Empire, Moment of Battle, The First Clash, Great Strategic Rivalries, Gods of War, and *The Washington War*.

The late **Williamson Murray** was professor emeritus of history at Ohio State and was the author of a wide selection of articles and books, including, with Allan Millett, the acclaimed *A War to Be Won: Fighting the Second World War* and with James Lacey, *Moment of Battle* and *Gods of War*.

Michael S. Neiberg is Professor of History and Chair of War Studies at the United States Army War College in Carlisle, Pennsylvania. His latest book is *When France Fell: The Vichy Crisis and the Fate of the Anglo-American Relationship* (2021), which won the 2022 Society for Military History Book Prize.

Brooks D. Simpson is a Foundation Professor of History at Arizona State University. He is the author of *Let Us Have Peace: Ulysses S. Grant and the Politics of War and Reconstruction, 1861–1868*, and *Ulysses S. Grant: Triumph over Adversity, 1822–1865*, editor of *The Civil War: The Third Year Told by Those Who Lived It*.

Richard Toye is a Professor of Modern History at the University of Exeter. His books include *Rhetoric: A Very Short Introduction* (2013), *The Roar of the Lion: The Untold Story of Churchill's World War II Speeches* (2013), and *Winston Churchill: A Life in the News* (2020).

Steven E. Woodworth, Texas Christian University, is the author of *Nothing but Victory: The Army of the Tennessee, 1861–1865*.

Christopher Yung is the Dean of the Marine Corps War College and is the author, editor, and contributor to numerous books, articles, and monographs on China's naval and military power. Prior to coming to Marine Corps University, he was a Senior Research Analyst at the Center for Naval Analyses.

1

INTRODUCTION

James Lacey

In 2008, Dr. Williamson Murray and I wrote The Joint Operational Environment for the now-defunct Joint Forces Command (JFCOM), a document that the Department of Defense (Joint Staff) continues to issue on a periodic basis.[1] The document aimed to give policymakers an idea of what the global environment would look like almost two decades after its publication. The hope was the document would act as a foundation for developing new operating concepts for the employment of military force in the 21st century. As the draft made its way through several layers of review, a few of our sections were dropped. One of those deleted sections addressed the fact that, since the end of the Cold War, we had been on a strategic hiatus, likely to last another decade. After that, we would face a new strategic paradigm.

The commander of the defunct Joint Forces Command (JFCOM), after ordering this section deleted, commented that he was involved in strategy development every day, implying that Dr. Murray and I did not know what we were talking about. What he overlooked was that while he may have been regularly conducting strategic planning, it was always to meet the pressing requirements of the moment. We were trying to tell policymakers and strategic planners to look out a decade or more and start planning for the radically different world that was already clearly on the horizon, one in which China presented a greatest geopolitical challenge than the United States and its allies had faced since World War II ended. This they manifestly did not do.

Ten years later, having lived through the nation's failure to plan and adapt to the looming China threat, the same senior leader who ordered the deletion from our earlier document, wrote in the National Defense Strategy (2018): "Today, we are emerging from a period of strategic atrophy .... "[2] Belatedly,

DOI: 10.4324/9781003375630-1

the United States and its allies realized they are locked in a strategic competition as intense as any in history, and are now playing catch-up as the nation tries to create strategic plans for the world the 2008 Joint Operational Environment predicted. Creating and executing the strategy required for a prolonged competition with another great power, one that may include periods of military conflict, will require a level of cooperation between our most senior political and military leaders that is typically only seen when the nation is involved in a major war.

Ongoing postmortems of America's recent conflicts in Vietnam, Iraq, and Afghanistan, have already exposed rifts between the nation's military and political leadership that do not bode well for future relations between the two. Historians will eventually sift through all of the evidence and lay out the specifics of where both sides of our political and military leadership and institutions failed each other. What will likely become increasingly clear is that our problems in recent conflicts are rooted in a clash of cultures, where neither side fully comprehends the overarching concerns of the other. This situation must be immediately repaired, as while our past conflicts have wasted vast amounts of blood and treasure, that loss pales in comparison to what will be at stake if our current competition with China erupts into war.

This book aims, through a series of historical case studies detailing the conduct of such relations during great state conflicts, to inform policymakers and strategists as to how civil-military relationships were managed in prior competitions and conflicts. This topic was first addressed in the groundbreaking works of Samuel P. Huntington's *The Soldier and the State*, and Morris Janowitz's, *The Professional Soldier.* Since these works were published, social and political scientists have continued working in the field.[3] Unfortunately, historians, with the exception of Eliot Cohen's *Supreme Command: Soldiers, Statesmen, and Leadership in Wartime*, have failed to produce any surveys of the broader field.[4] Even Cohen's, otherwise, excellent work suffers from several limitations: it only covers four persons, all of his subjects are leaders of democracies, each case study is told from the perspective of only the civilian leader, and finally, we learn nothing about how the civil-military relations were managed by the other warring party – the enemy.

Supreme Leadership in Modern War builds on Cohen's work, by presenting ten case studies, all written and authored by experts in the subject and the period. Moreover, these studies present each relationship from the perspective of both the politicians and the generals involved. By relating the civil-military relationship from both sides of several conflicts, this work showcases models of civil-military relations that do not appear in other works. Why is this important? Well, to gather real insights into how Chinese or Russian civil-military relations may develop over the course of a great-state conflict, one must examine how other tyrannical or non-democratic governments – Hitler, Stalin, Mao – handled relations with their military leadership during wartime.

This broader perspective also allows us to closely examine Cohen's key findings to see if they hold up as universal truths. For instance, Cohen calls Samuel Huntington to task for his presentation and acceptance of the "normal" theory of civil-military relations, which Huntington defined as "objective control." Cohen interprets Huntingdon as claiming that the: "healthiest and most effective form of civilian control of the military is that which maximizes professionalism by isolating soldiers from politics, and giving them as free a hand as possible in military matters." Thus, Huntington creates a sharp divide between the military and political spheres that cannot be violated by either side without ruinous consequences.

The problem with Huntington's ideas about objective control, as Cohen rightfully points out, is that no such state of affairs has ever existed, at least when great states are fighting one another. But Cohen goes too far when he boldly states: "The difficulty is that the great war statesmen do just those improper things – and, what is more, it is because they do so that they succeed."[5] He builds his case through his four case studies – Abraham Lincoln, Georges Clemenceau, Winston Churchill, and David Ben Gurion – all of whom meddled incessantly in military affairs and operations. But there is a problem here; for their opponents – Jefferson Davis, The Kaiser, Adolf Hitler, and the Arab political leadership in 1948, were also notorious meddlers, and they all lost. Thus, political meddling, in and of itself, does not present a universal method for assuring success.

In fact, political and military leadership are so intertwined, in wartime, that it is impossible to create spheres that are totally the domain of either politicians or soldiers. How could it be otherwise, for as Clausewitz points out: "… war is not merely an act of policy but a true political instrument, a continuation of political intercourse …"[6] Moreover, if it is impossible for politicians to refrain from meddling in military operations, it is just as impossible for senior military officers to divorce themselves from politics. In fact, doing so often leads to a disastrous outcome Huntington warns about. The secret, of course, is to achieve a prudent balance, which is only found when both sides respect the expertise and capacity of the other. This volume does not, in fact, it cannot define that balance, which is unique to every situation. It does, however, provide expert examinations of how previous leaders either discovered that often elusive proper balance and attained military success, or failed to do so and saw matters go awry. Therefore, this book abstains from providing a set of rules, in favor of establishing guideposts for future leaders to employ as a foundation for their own approaches to civil-military relations.

This volume begins with the American Civil War, as this was really the first major conflict to take place as the Industrial Revolution was starting to hit full stride. As such, many of the military problems and technologies employed remain crucial ingredients in current or potential conflicts, adding a degree of comprehensibility for the modern reader. Consideration was given to adding the wars of the Napoleonic era to the start of the volume. In the end, though, it was deemed uninstructive as Napoleon was arguably the final true example of the embodiment of political and military leadership melded into a single person. Hence, there was no separate military and civilian leadership that needed to come to terms with one another – Charles-Maurice de Tallyrand-Perigord excepted. Some later political leaders (Hitler and Stalin) took similar control of their military establishments. Still, neither ever took the field to direct active operations in the Napoleonic tradition, preferring to dictate from afar and then leaving it to the military professionals to execute their designs. Moreover, as the Industrial Revolution went into hyperdrive in the mid-19th century – particularly in such areas as transport, communications, and the scale of industrial plant – the character of war and the global social-political context of conflict radically changed. Thus, it became clear that current policymakers and military leaders would most profit from a focus on eras and events with more immediacy to our own time. A decision was also made to end this study with the Korean War, as it was the last war in which great powers directly engaged each other in battle.[7]

Historians may study history for the pleasure of revealing a previously hidden past. But for policymakers, strategists, and generals, history is employed to mine it for lessons of practical value. This is particularly true of wartime histories and biographies, where one hopes to discover clues as to how to manage nations and armies through the stress of war. For such professionals, any other use of history is often considered mere storytelling. But history never provides an easy-to-use checklist available for immediate employment for current policymakers. The impacts of contingent circumstances on every aspect of any great endeavor, such as war, make that impossible. Historians, mostly leave this type of analysis to political scientists who excel at teasing out single points of reference to study, while discarding or "controlling for" all of the surrounding messiness of real-world situations. Unfortunately, such messiness is a fact of life that historians cannot ignore. No wartime leader has ever been able to focus on one variable to the exclusion of all else, nor will that ever be the case.

Still, history can lay out guideposts enabling future leaders to steer a steadier course through a chaotic geopolitical maelstrom. For, there remains only two methods of practical learning. The first is through personal experience, which is often painful and costly. The other is through the deep study of the experience of others. The latter helps to build the mental templates that leaders can reference in any situation, and which are particularly useful in a crisis. Without such mental templates, every situation is novel, and every possible way forward is an unknown and incalculable risk. But humans, placed in any situation, will always apply heuristics to make sense of whatever they are witnessing or dealing with. Such mental shortcuts allow the brain to reach quick and apparently reasonable solutions without overloading and shutting down. Unfortunately, just because a mental template is wrong or not applicable to the situation at hand, will not stop a policymaker from employing it. The human brain will use whatever is available, no matter how inappropriate, to provide the context needed to make a decision. Moreover, once employed these heuristic narratives become certainties upon which a cascade of future decisions are built upon. As the saying goes, nothing is quite as dangerous as something one knows to be true but is not. If this work helps to establish new mental templates or corrects misperceptions in the reader's current narrative of past events, it will have done its job.

Lessons from the Past

Shared Vision

By far the most crucial lesson one can derive from these essays is the crucial importance of both the civil and military leadership possessing an agreed-upon common vision. In example after example, the lack of such vision is the strongest predictive factor as to what endeavors will be plagued by troubles and eventual ruin. In our, first historical case study, Lincoln spent the first three years of the Civil War looking for a general who shared his vision of how to win the war and who could comprehend the battlefield in its strategic entirety. Until he brought General Grant east to command all the armies of the Republic, Lincoln had endured repeated failures by generals that were highly regarded until they took the mantle of high command, whereupon they fell flat on their faces. Brooks Simpson attributes the success of the Lincoln-Grant team to their having a shared strategic vision and contrasts this to every other senior general whom Lincoln had tried. Even his Chief of Staff, Henry Halleck, was never able to "set forth more than a vague vision of how military operations would meet strategic goals," and no other commander Lincoln tried out in the Eastern Theater seemed capable of thinking about any facet of the war beyond considering what General Lee was plotting.

So, what was the Grant difference? According to Brooks, before Vicksburg fell, Lincoln prized one thing above all in Grant, an impression that he shared with a wounded General Daniel Sickles after the Battle of Gettysburg: "He isn't shrieking for reinforcements all the time. He takes what troops we can safely give him … and does the best he can with what he has got. And if Grant only does this thing down there – I don't care much how, so long as he does it *right* – why, Grant is my man and I am his for the rest of the war!" Two days later, Grant accomplished that "thing down there" and captured Vicksburg. Proving one more thing to Lincoln, Grant not only got on with business with what he had but he also won. The Confederate army captured at Vicksburg was the second such complete victory Grant had won. He would go on to smash another Confederate army to the brink of disintegration at Chattanooga, and then received the surrender of another field army at Appomattox Courthouse.

One cannot underestimate how crucial Grant's desire to fight and his capacity to win even under trying circumstances, such as at Shiloh, impacted Lincoln's decision to bring him aboard as his senior military commander.

However, there were other tremendous differences between Grant and all of his predecessors that Lincoln hugely appreciated. For one, in contrast to previous commanders in the eastern theater, Grant took the time to explain his thinking to Lincoln; in turn, the president set aside his tendency to engage in armchair strategy. One has only to compare this to the antics of General George McClellan, Lincoln's first general in chief of the Union army, who when Lincoln and Secretary of State, William Seward, came to his home for a discussion about war plans, refused to see him and retired to his bedroom. But what could one expect from a general who privately referred to Lincoln as "nothing more than a well-meaning baboon," and to Seward as an "incompetent little puppy." But McClellan had many other failings, he courted the opposition political party, he had a set of war aims that were not amicable to Lincoln, he was incapable of coordinating military efforts in several theaters simultaneously, but most crucially, he could not provide the military victories Lincoln hungered for.

Lincoln was, therefore, delighted to have a general capable of seeing the entire picture of a war fought on multiple fronts and who could conceptualize employing all Union armies in coordinated offensives. As the launch date for the campaign approached Lincoln wrote Grant: "The particulars of your plans I neither know, or seek to know." Grant, in turn, was delighted with the support he received, telling Lincoln that he assumed responsibility for whatever came next: "Should my success be less than I desire, and expect, the least I can say is, the fault is not with you."

Both leaders were a bit disingenuous in their comments, as the idea that Lincoln allowed Grant a free hand during 1864 is pure fiction: Grant operated under military and political restraints imposed by a president who was seeking reelection. Grant knew and accepted that his plans needed to conform to presidential priorities, especially in an election year; moreover, in assigning generals to carry out this plan, Grant understood the political necessity of giving important commands to several generals, including Benjamin F. Butler, Nathaniel Banks, and Franz Sigel, who were considered influential among various major voting blocs crucial to Republican fortunes in the 1864 elections. At no point during the campaign was Grant giving total autonomy!

That the Lincoln-Grant teams worked is due to the fact that both men shared an overall strategic vision for the conduct of the war, despite some tensions over the particulars. As they got to know each other on a personal level, their communications improved, and growing mutual respect turned into a friendship. Lincoln was not above nudging his general or reminding him of what was at stake, and Grant, unlike most generals, took the hints. Grant's empathetic awareness of Lincoln's political as well as military concerns and his willingness to accommodate them instead of railing against the restraints thus imposed, was essential to his overall success. But just as Lincoln sometimes played military strategist, Grant played politician, usually with equal (if not greater) skill.

As Brooks Simpson reminds us: "The two men walked together on why to fight the war and how to fight it, eventually accepting emancipation and the destruction of slavery as necessary to the achievement of a meaningful and lasting victory. A shared vision, Lincoln's eventual trust in Grant, and Grant's willingness to accommodate presidential concerns fostered a superior working relationship that saved the republic and crushed the Confederacy."

While it took Lincoln three years to settle upon Grant, Confederate President Jefferson Davis gave General Robert E. Lee command of the South's most important army early in the conflict. This was not by choice but by necessity. In June 1862, the Union Army, after a tedious march up the Yorktown Peninsula, was before the gates of Richmond. When toward the end of the Battle of Fair Oaks, the commander of the Confederate army, General Joseph E. Johnston, was wounded, President Davis found himself in immediate need of a competent new commander. Lee was then acting as the President's military adviser and was already with the army. With no better choice immediately available, Davis appointed Lee to command what would be soon renamed the Army of Northern Virginia.

As Stephen E. Woodworth points out, "It was not that Davis did not trust Lee, but that he valued him in his advisory role in Richmond and thought him best suited for that duty." As the president mentioned on more than one occasion, "only the extreme necessity of the hour moved him to spare Lee from the valuable tasks he was performing at the capital." Despite his initial hesitation, Davis maintained Lee in command, initiating what Woodworth calls one of the most successful command relationships in military history. Their collaboration kept Virginia and the southeastern United States in Confederate control through three years of intense conflict. "When the Confederacy finally tottered to its demise in the spring of 1865, Lee's Virginia was the last remaining militarily viable enclave that national forces overran. Its prolonged, stubborn resistance was partially attributable to the effective collaboration of the Confederate president with his top Virginia general."

But this relationship was not without its flaws, and these flaws were a crucial reason for the Confederacy's eventual defeat, a result that was not inevitable. Lee was by instinct a gambler. As Davis's aide stated: "… if there is one man in either army, Confederate or Federal, head and shoulders above every other in audacity, it is General Lee! His name might be Audacity. He will take more desperate chances and take them quicker than any other general in this country, North or South: and you will live to see it, too." Often, Lee would take these gambles and compel Davis to adopt a more daring strategy than he was comfortable with. For instance, Lee's note informing Davis of his plans to invade Maryland in 1862 arrived on September 7, too late for Davis to do any-thing to influence or countermand Lee's plans, as the Confederate army was already across the Potomac and entering Frederick – only days away from the fateful Battle of Antietam. Similarly, when Lee proposed an 1863 invasion that eventually culminated at Gettysburg, Davis only reluctantly went along, and then only after Lee strenuously opposed sending any portion of his army to re-trieve sinking fortunes in the west. In response to Davis's final plea to consider sending some of his army west, Lee proposed instead: "I think it all-important that we should assume the aggressive by the 1st of May." Lee was making an almost unfathomable argument that a victory in the east would do more to break Grant's stranglehold on Vicksburg than sending more forces west to help turn the tide in that theater. Rather than risk a rift with his preeminent wartime commander, Davis acquiesced to Lee's strategic views.

Unfortunately, for the Confederate cause, both of Lee's invasions of the North were a failure. Although Lee arguably won a tactical victory at Anti-etam, the entire campaign was a strategic catastrophe, as Lee's forced retreat into Virginia was enough of a Union victory to allow Lincoln to release the Emancipation Proclamation, which radically changed the strategic context of the war. As for the Gettysburg campaign, Lee's battlefield defeat, coupled with the fall of Vicksburg the following day, buoyed Union morale and hopes for an ultimate military victory. Just as crucially, Lee had expended vast resources and thousands of irreplaceable soldiers for no gain.

As Woodworth points out, after Gettysburg, the Davis-Lee relationship changed. Davis remained eager to strike blows at their enemies, but he was more willing to resist "Lee's seemingly instinctive urge to take large risks to go for the enemy's throat, even if it meant staking all on the results of a single campaign." As Lee saw it the path to ultimate victory required battlefield vic-tories. But Davis was increasingly inclined to view battlefields as places where one also risked defeat, which was contrary to his growing belief that the politi-cal objectives of the war could be won by not losing.

Davis never lost confidence in Lee as a battlefield commander, but he was increasingly disappointed in Lee's lack of strategic acumen. Lee's strategic vi-sion of a conflict that spanned more territory than Europe from Paris to Mos-cow, never went far beyond Northern Virginia. Lee, in fact, never gave up his belief that the war going to be won by a great battlefield victory fought within fifty miles of the Potomac River. Even, as Sherman's army tore the economic guts out of the deep South, Lee remained fixated on his singular battle with Grant. As for Davis, as he considered himself a master military strategist, he resisted, until almost the end of the war, the appointment of a commander in chief who could coordinate the southern military effort across multiple theaters.

As Woodworth points out, "Throughout the final twenty months of the war, Lee's operations never again gave Davis the disquiet they had in the summers of 1862 and 1863, and the partnership operated smoothly." But the partnership was as limited as it had always been. Lee remained fixated on the Army of the Potomac, and Davis let him be. In the meantime, the war was lost in the West. Lee never possessed the vision to see and fight the war on a continental scale, and Davis never had the political strength or will to force his best battlefield commander to expand his strategic horizons.

Without, a common strategic understanding, military operations wander into aimlessness, where battles are fought for the sake of appearing to do something. Worse, if your enemies possess an appropriate strategic vision they will eventually profit from your exhaustion. This was clearly apparent when, in 1918, when General Erich Ludendorff launched a series of massive German offensives against the Franco-British defenses. By this time in the war, Germany's civil-military leadership no longer had a clear vision of how to win the war, or even what objectives they were fighting for. This failure infected the army all the way down to the level of operational planning for the upcoming "war-winning" offensive. So, when asked by Crown Prince Ruprecht of Bavaria – commander of the forces tasked with the first of these offensives – what the operational objectives of such an attack would be, Ludendorff replied: "We will punch a hole in it. Then we will see what happens." This is a battle without strategic or political purpose. In the end, the German army captured huge swathes of militarily valueless terrain, at the cost of having dozens of its first-line combat divisions decimated. When the Entente powers eventually counterattacked, the Imperial German Army buckled, forcing a German surrender on harsh terms.

Not developing a shared vision or taking too long to do so is a pattern often repeated. For instance, General George Marshall was ecstatic after the January 1943 Casablanca Conference that he finally had a set of strategic aims, priorities, and political objectives. Note, by the time of the Casablanca Conference, America had already been at war for a year without anyone giving the military forces – already fighting all over the world – any strategic direction, beyond the vague principle of "Germany first." Still, the Allies' enemies were in a far worse position. Against all reason, Japan's and Germany's leadership kept their armies fighting long after there was any chance of strategic gain and ultimately saw their countries substantially destroyed and overrun.

Who Is in Charge?

In every major conflict, there is always an internal struggle over who is in charge – the civilian or the military leadership. As we will repeatedly see in these case studies, generals like to believe they are just plain military professionals with no interest in politics. At best, this is a polite fiction. At the very least, generals need to keep attuned to the political concerns of the civilian leadership, or they risk a diversion between national political aims and the employment of military efforts. As Marshal Ferdinand Foch wrote in 1918, "As for the notion so vociferously proclaimed by [Foreign Minister Stephen] Pichon and Georges Clemenceau, that a general works on one side of a barrier and the politicians and diplomats on the other, there is nothing more false, or, one can even say, absurd. War is not a dual object, but a unity; so for that matter is peace …. The two aspects are clearly and inseparably linked." This makes it incumbent upon politicians to keep the nation's military leadership informed on policy matters, particularly shifts in policy, or risk uninformed generals acting at their own discretion.

Typically, though, the military leadership, in a major war, goes far beyond merely keeping abreast of political concerns and priorities and begins taking an active role in political affairs. When there is a shared political-military vision this is rarely troublesome. When there is no such vision, problems arise. Sometimes such trouble can be avoided when there is a strong political leadership to keep politically ambitious generals in check. Lincoln, for instance, fired General McClellan, his most politically meddlesome general. In another case, Lincoln's comments to General Joseph Hooker, one of a succession of failed Army of the Potomac commanders, clearly demonstrate that he was certain of his ability to check generals who strayed into political territory, writing: "I have heard, in such way as to believe it, of your recently saying that both the Army and the Government needed a Dictator. Of course, it was not for this, but in spite of it, that I have given you the command. Only those generals who gain successes, can set up dictators. What I now ask of you is military success, and I will risk the dictatorship."[8] Still, popular generals can give even secure statesmen a reason to pause. Even Lincoln hesitated to bring Grant east until several trusted advisers assured him that the general had no immediate political aspirations.

When we look at France in World War I, we have a different situation, one where we find supremely confident and capable political and military leaders – Georges Clemenceau and Ferdinand Foch, respectively. As Michal Neiberg points out: "It is hard to imagine either man wanting to spend much time seated next to the other, had it not been for their shared desire to prosecute the war against Germany to its fullest. Personally, they could hardly have been more different. Professionally, they each jealously guarded what they saw as their exclusive role in the civil-military system. Neither was ever reluctant to push back at any perception that one or the other was encroaching on the other's primary sphere of concern." In the end, the relationship held together because in a "total war each man recognized when it was time to leave the other's sphere alone." Clemenceau was happy to have a general whose fighting spirit matched his own and made happier and more secure by the fact that Foch apparently had no political ambition. That did not mean that Foch was apolitical, as he clearly assisted Clemenceau, who was not yet France's Prime Minister, to bring down his superior, Marshal Joseph Joffre, and later Foch did the same to Joffre's replacement General Robert Neville. Still, in the end, "Each saw in the other a fellow patriot whose differences from his own beliefs could surely be forgiven in the mutual quest to win the war."

It was Clemenceau who likely first said that war is too important a business to be left to generals, a statement reflecting his core belief that deciding on strategy was a job for the civilian leadership. To make the point as clearly as he could, he told Foch that the Supreme War Council would be led by the prime ministers, with the generals providing only advice. At an early meeting, Foch began to answer a question from Lloyd George, only to have Clemenceau grab his arm and say "Be quiet. I am the representative of France." Foch often found himself offering the political leadership on the Supreme War Council his best military advice, only to see it disregarded by Clemenceau because he was offering the wrong political options.

On the other hand, Germany, in World War I, provides an example of what can go wrong when weak political leadership cannot control its generals, and when generals come to believe that war is too important to be left to politicians. As Holger Afflerbach makes clear, the Reich possessed no strong wartime political leader, like Britain's Lloyd George or France's Clemenceau, or even somebody like the much missed Bismarck. Without such a leader Germany attempted to make do with a cumbersome political machine, where dissenting "power centers" (*Herrschaftszentren*) constantly fought one another to push forward their preferred policies.

Germany did have Kaiser Wilhelm II, but he was a dangerous combination of bombast and weakness, who often complained that his generals were keeping him in the dark. A stronger leader could have checked the worst instincts of various power centers and harnessed them to a common cause. But in the absence of such a leader, "polycratic chaos" ensued, where competing power centers rivaled each other for influence in the decision-making process. Moreover, if such a leader had existed or arose there was still no vision or common cause for him to direct everyone toward. For, at the root of Germany's problems was that it went to war without any proper political goals. What it had, instead, was an elaborate military plan – The Schlieffen Plan – for directing early operations, but without any idea as to what political outcome this plan was supposed to accomplish. As the war went on no true vision arose, leaving Germany caught in what, David Stevenson calls the "war trap." In such a trap, wartime governments find it politically impossible to conclude the war without gains that justify the sacrifices, even if such gains are no longer possible.

With no political goals in sight, the door opened for military leaders – Marshal Paul von Hindenburg and General Erich Ludendorff – to assume control of both the military and political spheres of the war. In doing so, they insisted on the one policy they understood, a total military victory with politically based strategic outcomes to follow. It was this quest for total victory, that eventually led to the decisions that ruined the German economy, as the generals demanded the maximum amount of war materiel possible, and, thereby, collapsed the civilian economy, which remained the foundation of the war effort. The myopic pursuit of total victory also led to the atrocious decision to renew unrestricted U-Boat warfare, which brought the United States into the conflict on the side of Germany's enemies.

In the end, Germany never found that single indispensable man who could control the politics and the military. As one of Germany's top generals, Erich von, Falkenhayn, wrote after the war: "The right thing to do is to have a supreme authority over warfare and politics, whether his name be Emperor, President or Prime Minister (Lloyd George). It has only to be the right man." For Germany that "right man" never arrived, and the results were disastrous.

In Great Britain, the right man did arrive in the person of David Lloyd George, who came to the fore as Minister of Munitions, in the wake of 1915's shell crisis, when the frontline armies ran out of artillery ammunition. This position provided the springboard for him to become Prime Minister, replacing Herbert Henry Asquith, who was described by one diplomat as a spent force. Once in office, he discovered that the military had a clear vision for the war – the clear and decisive military defeat of the Central Powers – and all they needed was for the politicians to provide soldiers and munitions, while otherwise staying out of the way. It was the same strategic vision the German military leadership had imposed on German politicians. This was unacceptable to Lloyd George who, for the remainder of the war, was engaged in a bitter struggle to bend the military to his political will.

At first, he failed miserably, as the British commander in France – Douglas Haig – with the full support of the Chief of the Imperial General Staff William Robert Robertson, managed to keep military operations in France walled off from political interference. As Robertson told Geoffrey Dawson, editor of *The Times*, on the eve of the Somme campaign, anything that could be done to keep politics and politicians out of the War Office would be "for the good of the country." The generals believed they had the answer but based on the butcher's bills for their repeated frontal offensives, Lloyd George did not believe them.

Still, the generals were often able to thwart the Prime Minster, as he was reluctant, at first to do what he considered necessary. He could have fired Haig and Robertson but did not do so, supposedly because he despaired of finding anyone better. One gets the impression though that he did not believe he had the political power to try and remove the generals and also survive in office. Either that or he lacked the courage for a showdown. Lloyd George did consider ordering a shutdown of the massive blood-letting that took place in 1917 at Passchendaele, but as he basically admitted in 1918, he lacked the courage to take a strong stand against the attack, telling his Dominion partners: "The Military Authorities would have insisted that they had been on the point of breaking through, that the enemy was demoralized, and at the last moment they had been stopped by civilian politicians." It was an admission of weakness, as Lloyd George, believed it would have taken all of the political capital he possessed to call off the generals and even then, it likely could have backfired. It was not until the middle of 1918, that Lloyd George managed to maneuver Robertson out of his job, and place Haig under tighter control. Great Britain paid a high price for letting what should have been an unequal dialogue, one where politicians held sway. Instead, the generals were permitted to dictate strategic policy objectives for much too long.

We can leave it to Churchill to give the most interesting and erudite viewpoint on the civil-military relations of the war, a viewpoint he took with him into the next war, writing about Douglas Haig, who succeeded French as commander of the BEF:

> "Inflexible, rigorously pedantic in his assertion of the professional point of view, he nevertheless at all times treated the Civil Power with respect and loyalty. Even when he knew that his recall was debated among the War Cabinet, he neither sought to marshal the powerful political forces which would have come to his aid, nor failed at any time in faithfulness to the Ministers under whom he was serving." Haig never threatened resignation even when he knew the government was weak. On the other hand: "Amid patent ill-success he never in his own technical sphere deferred to their wishes, however strongly those wishes were supported by argument, by public opinion – such as it was – or by the terribly unfolding facts."[9]

In the next war – World War II – Hitler and Stalin demonstrated the pitfalls that ensue when the pendulum swings too far in the other direction and a powerful civil authoritarian leader thoroughly dominates the military. In both cases, the results were disastrous, the different outcomes during the war were the result of how both men adapted to the stress of conflict. Russia undoubtedly came perilously close to destruction in 1941 and 1942, when Stalin was both setting strategic direction and making operational battlefield decisions. Stalin, who apparently could not accept that the war's early debacles were a result of his catastrophic decisions, declared that they were the product of a lack of political will and reliability among Red Army commanders. Thus, there was a requirement for the reintroduction of the dual command system of the Civil War era, where units from the front level down to the tactical level required both commissars and military commanders with equal authority. Stalin believed such dual command would prevent unauthorized withdrawals and helped fortify the will of army commanders who – in Stalin's mind at least – were the reason for the defeats of 1941 and 1942.

As time passed, Stalin increasingly trusted the competence and advice of his military commanders. By early October 1942, Stalin removed the dual command structure and placed military officers back in sole command. The commissars remained in position as advisers and to report on potential political subversives. But Stalin's gesture was a sign of his increasing confidence in the abilities of military officers. Moreover, as the war progressed, Stalin consulted ever more widely – often face-to-face. Even though, as the principal decision maker, he had far greater authority to decide as he pleased than either Franklin Roosevelt or Winston Churchill, he was increasingly willing to listen to and accept the recommendations of military leaders.

By mid-war, Stalin fully trusted in the competence of his military advisers and willingly accepted the opinions of those commanders who made up the inner circle of military decision-making, with Georgii Zhukov certainly being *primus inter pares.* Zhukov was certainly the most capable and prominent of Stalin's military advisers. Thus, he was the one, Stalin – who was always paranoid about threats to his power and position – feared. By broadening the number of military leaders whom he consulted and accepted advice from Stalin kept Zhukov from dominating decision-making as the war progressed. But as Evan Mawdsley has succinctly pointed out "Stalin selected effective subordinates…, but he made his own decisions."[10] Even Zhukov came to accept that by the second half of the war Stalin had learned much about military strategy, even if he lacked a level of understanding of operational matters that might have reduced Soviet losses. But what Stalin always understood better than any of his generals were the political dimensions of the war. He was willing to accept high losses to make sure that when the war ended the Red Army dominated Eastern Europe. Stalin knew, from the beginning, where the Red Army was when the war ended, where the Red Army would stay after the peace.

When we compare Stalin's approach to that of his fellow dictator, Adolf Hitler, we note a stark difference in approach. The key similarity was that both men totally dominated the military leadership, but as Stalin increasingly trusted in the military abilities of his generals, Hitler became ever more mistrustful of his generals.

As Williamson Murry points out, Hitler lost no time assuming military power, starting with the early removal of Field Marshall Werner von Blomberg as head of the War Ministry, which was then renamed the *Oberkommando der Wehrmacht* (*OKW*, high command of the armed forces). As his immediate subordinate in the *OKW*, Hitler appointed Wilhelm Keitel, a particularly obsequious, pro-Nazi general, who would slavishly do Hitler's bidding to the war's end. From its creation, the *OKW* was little more than a collection of office of clerks that allowed Hitler to pass his orders and intentions along to the service chiefs and their staffs. To head the army, Hitler chose another pro-Nazi general, Walther von Brauchitsch, providing that general with a substantial donative so that he could divorce his wife and marry a second time. Brauchitsch proved a perfect choice, as he was incapable of standing up to Hitler.

As for a vision, there was only the wildest setting of future goals, none of which bore any reality to Germany's strained economy and financial position could support. It was a perfect example of allowing ideology to trump reality. It is worth noting that all of the generals who claim to have opposed Hitler's military plans made such claims after the war. During the war, Hitler's grandiose ideas were rarely opposed. That was not, however, true when it came to operational planning and execution. At least at the start of the war, many generals could stand up to Hitler and propose operational plans. When Hitler overruled the generals on operational matters, military commanders often did as they pleased anyway. Many times, the generals got away with this clear insubordination, as the Germans were winning the war. But as defeats piled up, Hitler began replacing generals who would not toe the line, and he became increasingly wary of military advice.

After the Russian Stalingrad offensive, Hitler actually fired Field Marshal Wilhelm List, commander of Army Group A, the southern wing of Army Group South, and took direct command of that army group until late November, despite his remaining in Prussia. Thus, in terms of the German high command, Hitler, in the months after the start of the Stalingrad disaster, directly commanded OKW, the OKH, much of Army Group South, and all of Army Group A. In late summer Keitel's deputy, General Alfred Jodl, returned from a visit to Army Group South warning about emerging difficulties. For his troubles, he was almost sacked. General Franz Halder, was sacked, to be replaced by General Kurt Zeitzler, who had little to recommend him except enthusiasm and loyalty to Hitler.

By 1943, the framework for the German high command had become settled. The *OKW*, led by Keitel and Jodl was responsible for passing along Hitler's orders to the theater commanders in the Mediterranean and northern France. The *OKH*, under Zeitzler, and after July 20, 1944, Heinz Guderian, was responsible for the Eastern Front. There was virtually no cooperation between the two headquarters and a good deal of competition for resources. Everything ran through Hitler. In effect, there was no German high military command, although Hitler continued to fire and replace generals and admirals. The result was a continual series of awful military decisions followed by defeats and collapse.

Churchill's approach is an instructive counterpoint. For almost the entire war, Churchill was both Prime Minister and the Minister for War, and thus heavily involved in every major military decision and many of the lesser ones. But he did not dictate in the manner of Hitler or Stalin. Instead, he argued, wheedled, and cajoled. When dealing with Churchill nothing ever seemed settled. One would leave a debate with Churchill in the afternoon thinking he had been won over, only to have the Prime Minister return to the debate again that evening, this time attacking from a new angle and with different debating points. His methods drove his Combined Chiefs to distraction, particularly his Chief of the Imperial Staff, Field Marshal Alanbrooke.

As Richer Toye tells us, on the face of it, Churchill's and Alanbrooke's blazing rows appear like the epitome of civil-military crisis – a seemingly deranged politician and a furious Brass Hat battling it out hammer and tongs. But the reality was more complex and interesting. Clearly, the differences between Churchill and Alanbrooke were real and substantial. They concerned not only the details of specific military operations but also broader strategy. At the same time, their shouting and fist-shaking should not distract attention from the many assumptions they in fact held in common. They both shared a central shared vision on how to defeat Germany and what the world should look like when the war ended. In general terms they also agreed upon strategic priorities and how to go about achieving them. Their disputes were over the operational details.

In the end, the Churchill-Alanbrooke relationship was *difficult but functional*. Alanbrooke and the Chiefs of Staff, in the face of considerable provocation, offered robust responses to Churchill's excesses without ever straying into insubordination. Churchill, for his part, tested the ideas of his military advisers to destruction, but in the end bowed to their guidance, never overruling them on a point on which they had reached consensus. This can be compared to President Roosevelt who overruled his Joint Chiefs of Staff over a dozen times during the war. At the same time, those clashes may have been exacerbated by Churchill's determination to exert civilian control over the military, combined with his uncertainty, based on his past experiences, of whether he could actually do so. Remember, Churchill had been at the highest levels of civilian leadership in the First World War. In the First World War, Lloyd George was always at issue with Haig and Robertson, although he never involved himself with them in a frontal battle. But in this latter case [World War II], civil-military differences were settled by frank and often fierce disagreement, rather than by the devious expedients to which Lloyd George had such frequent recourse.[11]

Churchill once wrote about how difficult it was to overrule generals because of the public perception of them.

The foolish doctrine was preached to the public through innumerable agencies that Generals and Admirals must be right on war matters, and civilians of all kinds must be wrong. These erroneous conceptions were inculcated billion-fold by the newspapers under the crudest forms. The feeble or presumptuous politician is portrayed cowering in his office, intent in the crash of the world on Party intrigues or personal glorification, fearful of responsibility, incapable of aught save shallow phrase-making. To him enters the calm, noble, resolute figure of the great Commander by land or sea, resplendent in uniform, glittering with decorations, irradiated with the lustre of the hero, shod with the science and armed with the panoply of war. This sturdy figure, devoid of the slightest thought of self, offers his clear far-sighted guidance and counsel for vehement action -or artifice or wise delay. But his advice is rejected; his sound plans put aside; his courageous initiative baffled by political chatterboxes and incompetents.[12]

Churchill had too much first-hand knowledge of the folly and incompetence of generals to ever allow them to conduct the war according to their own designs. To make sure that never happened, John Gooch tells us that Churchill created a combined battle headquarters under the direct supervision of the head of government – himself – through which he could exercise continuous direct and personal control over the formulation of military policy and the conduct of military operations.

Churchill's contemporary in America, President Franklin Delano Roosevelt, took a more hands-off approach to running or guiding the war. In Roosevelt's view, he and he alone established strategic policy. He considered his generals and admirals mere technicians, and they, for the most part, were happy to be seen that way, and even act in the manner Roosevelt prescribed for them. Roosevelt only laid down the law on matters he considered of crucial policy interest, otherwise, he allowed his Joint Chiefs to get on with the planning and execution of the conflict. Where Alanbrooke was in conference with Churchill almost every day and sometimes many times each day, Army Chief of Staff General George Marshall sometimes went weeks without ever speaking to Roosevelt.

Hands-off does not, however, mean Roosevelt had no interest, or that the generals were given carte blanche, particularly early in the conflict. Roosevelt made his weight felt in setting overall strategic guidance, and was guided in doing so by a half-dozen foundational ideas[13]:

1. The Anglo-American coalition must be maintained, as well as the survival of Great Britain as a major power after the war.
2. Germany was enemy number one, and Atlantic operations took precedence over the Pacific.
3. The Soviet Union must be given all possible aid and kept in the war until the Axis powers were defeated.
4. The Axis must be forced to accept unconditional surrender.
5. China must be kept in the war.
6. To assure a lasting post-war peace the world must have an international organization consisting of the wartime allies – the United States, the Soviet Union, Great Britain, and China.
7. The complete and unstinting support of the American people must be maintained throughout the conflict.

As long as Marshall and the Joint Chiefs were designing operations aimed at securing Roosevelt's grand strategic objectives, FDR ruled with a light hand. But when Marshall and the Chiefs diverged from these core ideas, the president never hesitated to make his power felt and bring them up short. Throughout the war, Roosevelt was the strategic architect: Chairman of the Joint Chiefs Admiral William Leahy was the man who explained Roosevelt to the other Chiefs, and the Chiefs to Roosevelt; while the other three Joint Chiefs, including Marshall, were mere draftsmen for the military operations that secured FDR's vision.

For instance, when Marshall and Chief of Naval Operations Admiral King became frustrated with British intransigence over the rapid opening of a second front in Northern Europe they proposed switching America's main effort from Germany to Japan. Thus, the Joint Chiefs forwarded a memorandum to the President, who was at Hyde Park, asking permission to, as Secretary of War Henry Stimson put it, "turn our backs on them [the British] and take up our war with Japan."[14] Marshall and King concluded by asking the President to send an ultimatum to Churchill warning him that "if the United States is to engage in any operations other than the forceful, unswerving adherence to full BOLERO [the codename for the build-up for an invasion of Northern Europe] plans... we should turn to the Pacific."[15]

At Hyde Park, Roosevelt, after carefully reading the memo, called Marshall's and King's bluff. Telephoning the War Department, the President demanded that the Joint Chiefs dispatch to him "at once, by airplane, a comprehensive and detailed outline of the plans for redirecting the major effort of the United States to the war against Japan – including the effect of such a decision on the Soviet and Middle East fronts during the balance of 1942." Roosevelt also demanded definite plans for the remainder of 1942 and tentative ones for 1943, concluding by emphasizing that "it is of highest importance that U.S. ground troops be brought into action against the enemy in 1942."[16] He was able to quickly call the Chief's bluff, as he knew none of what he was demanding was available or had even been properly considered.

Roosevelt then received a second memo further detailing Marshall's position while he was still at Hyde Park. This time he rejected it out of hand. The next day, FDR ordered Hopkins, King, and Marshall to depart immediately for London and get everything sorted out. To make sure he got what he wanted Roosevelt prepared a detailed letter of instruction for the three men.[17] In it, the President spelled out that he was unalterably opposed to an all-out effort in the Pacific against Japan. Roosevelt also asked his representatives to keep three cardinal principles in mind – speed of decision on plans, unity of plans, and attack combined with defense but not defense alone. But it was the middle paragraph that ensured everyone knew what they had to come home with: "It is of the highest importance that U.S. ground forces be brought into action against the enemy in 1942." In short, if SLEDGEHAMMER [the codename for the immediate invasion of Northern Europe] was out, don't come home without a new plan – the invasion of North Africa. After the war Marshall said that his job would have been much easier at the start had he realized that leaders of a democracy at war must be seen to be doing something major every year.

Changing Visions

Once a war erupts, its course is always an open question. Starting with the battlefield, where chaos, confusion, and chance reign supreme, outcomes are often unknowable. As Napoleon quipped, "God is on the side of the big battalions," meaning it is usually much safer to bet on the side with overwhelming force and military power. But a safe bet is not a sure bet. Few could have predicted the prolonged Finnish stand during the Winter War (1939–1940) or Ukraine's continuing resistance against Russian attacks as this work is being written. In great state wars, there is even less capacity to foresee the final political outcome, even when it becomes clear which side will win the military conflict. For instance, World War II in Europe arguably began when Germany invaded Poland, as neither Great Britain nor France was willing to let a totalitarian power occupy a country at the center of Eastern Europe. The war, however, ended with a different totalitarian power – the Soviet Union – occupying Poland. What had been a reason for going to war – the initial defining vision and objective of the war – was quietly abandoned during the course of the conflict as the Western military powers acquiesced to Stalin's domination of Central Europe.

Clearly, war has its own calculus, and as it changes, so does the art of the possible. In 1945, there was no longer any political will to enforce the goal of a free Poland, if it meant fighting the Red Army. In another instance, during the Korean War, the shock of the Pusan Landings broke the back of the North Korean military, suddenly opening up more expansive war aims. In a remarkably short period, the United Nations' strategic objectives went from saving South Korea to the reunification of the entire Korean peninsula. Then, Chinese intervention created another massive change in the conflict calculus, one in which the United Nations was now willing to accept the prewar status quo. In the Korean case, the shift in political objectives led to an irreplicable rift between the political and military leadership, resulting in General Douglas MacArthur's dismissal. It is worth noting here, that this was an unusual type of civil-military crisis, as President Truman dismissed his field commander – MacArthur – with the full support of the Joint Chiefs of Staff.

Shifting political objectives happen with such regularity in the war that their occurrence should be presumed by both political and military leaders at the start of any future conflict. Such shifts will, in fact, become more likely in future conflicts than it has been for the past two centuries, as weapons of mass destruction make the pursuit of maximal gains, such as the conquest of Germany and Japan in World War II, a gamble with global suicide as the possible final result. With maximal gains off the table, future conflicts will revert back to the cabinet wars of an earlier era, with states fighting over more limited objectives. Of course, just because an objective is limited does not mean it will not require a massive mobilization. For instance, the Seven Year's War in Europe was fought over who would ultimately control the relatively unimportant province of Silesia, yet, before it ended, all of Europe's great powers were or were approaching total mobilization. Similarly, the NATO nations, faced with a limited conflict in Ukraine are revving up their arms production capacities to levels not seen in many decades, while Russia inches toward full mobilization. Finally, It does not take much imagination to envision a local conflict over Taiwan leading to a massive expansion of the military-industrial complexes of the two most powerful states on the planet.

What wars over limited objectives do provide, however, is a lot of room to change political objectives. As such conflicts are, by definition, not existential, one or both sides will often be willing to settle for something other than their original objectives. Ensuring a state's civilian and military leadership shares a common vision at the start of a conflict is already a difficult proposition. Maintaining a shared vision through the tumult of war, but as new political objectives drive requirements for new military objectives as well as new warfighting approaches will be exponentially more difficult.

Supervision

Even when political and military leaders share a common ultimate goal, it does not mean that there has been any meeting of the minds as to how to get there. Only a fool of a politician would give the military a goal to accomplish and then get out of the way as the professionals undertook military operations to accomplish the stated task. As Michael Neiberg points out, generals can often make the right military decision, only to belatedly discover it was the wrong political one.

In fact, the consequences of military affairs distancing themselves from political goals are often dire. Organizing a theater for active operations on the scale required for a great state conflict is a Herculean task, one that will consume every ounce of time and bit of energy a commander possesses. There is virtually no time left for the serious study of other concerns. For instance, When MacArthur was asked, post dismissal, about Truman's concerns over his actions in Asia, eliciting a Soviet reaction in Europe, he replied that it was none of his concern, as he was a theater commander.[18]

But politicians can never look at just one theater of operations. They must always be concerned with a much larger picture, where any military operation will impact both domestic politics and global affairs. To make sure military leaders are toeing the policy line, civilian leaders have historically developed a few workable solutions.

As an example, during the Civil War, Lincoln employed several methods. Some were as simple as speaking directly to a large number of generals and getting their viewpoints of the war and of each other. But too many generals used these opportunities to condemn their immediate superiors and for self-aggrandizement, both of which, in the early years of war, Lincoln was all too happy to entertain. Later in the war, Lincoln would send trusted representatives to various commands to check up on a number of matters that concerned him and then report directly back. The most famous of these, of course, is Charles Dana, whom he sent west to report back on Grant's campaigns.

In the late 1980s, this approach was taught in US professional military education as the "directed telescope," which advocated the systematic employment of trusted advisers both to keep track of the activities of subordinates and to force them in the right direction if they begin to veer away from the leadership's intent. Examples abound of the effective use of such techniques to control the sprawling activities involved in executing a major conflict. Roosevelt, for example, employed the inspectors of the Bureau of the Budget to look into every facet of the war effort. These inspectors were so thorough and seemingly ubiquitous that they became known as "Roosevelt's Gestapo." Hitler, of course, had the true Gestapo to keep everyone within his prescribed lines, just as Stalin used the NKVD (forerunner of the KGB) for the same purposes.

Stalin also used his rough equivalent of the American Joint Staff – Stavka – to help keep military operations in line with policy. After 1941, multi-front co-ordination was carried out by Stavka representatives that were part of a machinery that both informed Stalin about what was going on at the front and ensured that what had been decided upon centrally was indeed being carried out. This apparatus relied not only on the big-name Stavka representatives to fronts or groups of fronts – with Zhukov frequently leaving Moscow to carry out such a role – but also lesser representatives of the General Staff – the so-called Officers of the General Staff posted down as low as divisional level as required.[19] Until mid-1944, even when Zhukov and Vasilevskii were Stavka representatives at the front, these Stavka representatives did not have the authority to change plans decided upon in Moscow without consulting Stalin first – to the extent that, according to Vasilevskii, even the transfer of a single division from one front to another required Stalin's approval.[20]

The Cost

Both political and military leaders endure a high emotional cost during war. This cost manifests itself in many ways, and few persons have the capacity to lead a nation in war or through an arduous military campaign without it impacting their emotional state. President Lincoln, reportedly complained after the blood repulse of the Army of the Potomac at Fredericksburg: "No general yet found can face the arithmetic, but the end of the war will be at hand when he shall be discovered."[21] Lincoln finally found generals who could stand up to the brutal math of war and continue going – Grant, Sherman, and Sheridan – but not before enduring three bloody years of searching. Until they were found, Lincoln endured the harrowing emotional costs of bloody battles without any progress toward winning the war. In fact, if the length and intensity of this ruinous trial had any upside it was that it gave Lincoln a clear opportunity to see and test generals for their fitness to withstand the crucible of high command and win victories.

Roosevelt, on the other hand, began World War II with an established Joint Chiefs organization and, except for adding Admiral William Leahy to the roster, finished with those he had started with. In the future, civilian leaders are unlikely to be as lucky as Roosevelt. If Eliot Cohen's "unequal dialogue" in which generals must follow the dictates of the civilian leadership is going to be effective civilian leaders must always be on the lookout for superior military leaders as it is revealed in the most brutal arena possible. Because, until military leaders of sufficient competence are moved into positions of authority and those who have failed are pushed aside, a nation's civilian leaders will likely have to endure a massive loss in blood and treasure without any path to victory.

The stress of war must be dealt with even by the strongest personalities: Churchill had his alcohol and painting; FDR would retreat to his stamp collection for countless hours and enjoyed cocktail events every Friday, where all discussion of the war was forbidden; even a sociopathic paranoid like Stalin would often invite his murderous cronies to movie nights at his dacha.[22] Military leaders have other ways of dealing with stress, MacArthur reputedly spent two hours almost every afternoon watching a movie, Marshall went horseback riding, and it was well known that Grant was much easier to live with if operations were slow enough for his wife to join him at his headquarters encampment.

All wars take a toll. For those directly in the path of war, either soldiers or civilians, the toll is harsh and marked by death, ruined lives, and wonton destruction of homes and livelihoods. As wars drag on a high cost is also demanded of politicians and generals directing such wars, often from afar. This cost, which is rarely as physically destructive as that experienced in the fighting, manifests itself in a form of mental exhaustion that often incapacitates senior leaders to the point where they are incapable of making difficult decisions. Few persons can maintain their emotional equilibrium as wars drag on and the costs mount. Anxiety and other forms of mental distress often begin to inhibit leaders' cognitive abilities and impact their capacity to make hard decisions. Military leaders who can no longer stand the strain can usually be replaced, as the bench is often deep enough to find qualified replacements. The same is not true of political leaders, who are often close to irreplaceable in wartime. This is particularly true in authoritarian states, where rulers have spent most of their lives removing all potential rivals from the political arena.

Apply Lessons

The United States, its allies, and coalition partners only recently ended almost two decades of military engagement in Iraq and Afghanistan. One of the constant refrains heard during these long conflicts is the necessity of what the military called "campaigns of learning." At times it appeared as if both conflicts were one long campaign of learning. I witnessed the start of one such a campaign during the initial invasion of Iraq, when field commanders were bewildered by the sudden appearance of black and green flags outside of nearly every house along the invasion route. Many wondered aloud if the local population was displaying support for Al Qaeda. It took a few days before the troops on the ground learned that the locals were actually displaying their support of the Shia branch of Islam, which had been suppressed by Saddam Hussein, whose power rested upon his Sunni followers. Thus, the first campaign of learning started almost immediately as officers focused on understanding the political, cultural, and social maelstrom coalition forces had suddenly and without adequate preparation plunged into.

Many other campaigns of learning were to come. First, the military studied the local environment, but that was not sufficient to head off a widespread insurgency. Only after the insurgency had begun did military officers drag out the writings of previous counterinsurgency masters – Roger Trinquier, David Galula, Robert Thompson, etc. – looking for hints on how to deal with what they were facing on the ground. When they tired of reading advice from "experts" who had decisively lost their own conflicts, a new campaign of learning began., This one was focused on what a host of new counterinsurgency experts – David Kilcullen, John Nagl, Carter Malkasian, Seth Jones, etc. – had to say on the matter. The Army even put out a new field manual – FM 3-2-25 Insurgencies and Counterinsurgencies, which went unread by the vast majority of the force, who were clearly tired of hearing ideas that were demonstrably not working. Still, the campaign of learning droned on without ever touching upon what was truly wrong. From the very start of the conflicts in Iraq and Afghanistan the civil-military relationship was broken. As the original vision and definition of victory – toppling Saddam's regime and destroying Iraq's weapons of mass destruction arsenal – was faulty, it was incumbent on both parties in the civil-military relationship to enact a new vision. This never happened.

As early as 2003, General David Petraeus, then commanding the 101st Airborne Division, famously quipped "tell me how this ends." This, of course, is the fundamental question in any conflict, and it is, therefore, disturbing to find a senior battlefield commander without any idea as to what the ultimate goal he was fighting to achieve was. Petraeus's question would haunt America's senior leaders for most of the next two decades. During that time, the US military was engaged in a war the generals did not want to fight but never dared say so. Even the 2008 surge, which brought the Coalition as close to a military victory as it was to get, was the product of an outside analyst – Fred Kagan – and then forced upon a reluctant military. Later, when senior officers in Afghanistan demanded a similar surge, they told the Obama administration that such a surge would lead to victory; they were either naïve or lying.

Any military officer who had ever taken the time to study war, particularly the irregular wars we were fighting, knew two things from the start of our involvement in Iraq and Afghanistan. First, local populations hate foreign troops in their midst, and will never stop trying to eradicate them, whether through political means or an active insurgency. Second, and this is crucial, no insurgency in the modern era has ever been defeated if it has an outside sponsor and a safe haven it can use for logistics, training, planning, and to regroup in if things go badly on the battlefield. Yet, no military adviser, tasked by law to give his or her best military advice to the nation's civilian leadership, ever told the President of the United States that the nation was engaged in an unwinnable conflict.

The result of this failure was a premature withdrawal from Iraq, which opened the door for an ISIS takeover of a large portion of the country and a reintroduction of US combat forces to defeat them. Worse, in Afghanistan, where we were buying strategic stalemate at minimal cost, our precipitous withdrawal allowed the Taliban to retake the country.

If one asks who is to blame for this civil-military failure, it is easy to see pick out the civilian leadership as there were only four presidents – George W. Bush, Barrack Obama, Donald Trump, and Joseph Biden – throughout the entire saga. But who was the military adviser these presidents had to work with? Since the 2001 attacks on the World Trade Center, there have been seven different Chairmen of the Joint Chiefs of Staff. But, by law, the Chairman is only a military adviser with very limited command authority. So, the reality is that the Commander of United States Central Command (CENTCOM) actually possesses the military command authority to give orders throughout the entire region. But since 2001 there have been ten different CENTCOM commanders, making it difficult to pin the blame on any one general. But it does not end there, as both Iraq and Afghanistan had four-star commanders of their own. They were all equal in rank to the CENTCOM Commander and had authority over all day-to-day operations in their countries. Moreover, they were all in direct regular contact with the President. Since 2001, there have been three four-star and one three-star American generals commanding in Iraq, and six four-star commanders in Afghanistan.[23] Clearly Presidents Bush, Obama, and Biden, never found their General Grant. But, then again, they were never given the chance to do so, as no savior general ever broke free of the pack.

No book can provide all the answers on how to best conduct civil-military relationships in the future. But the case studies presented here do provide future senior leaders with examples of what has worked in the past, as well as the pitfalls that have led to disaster. As this introduction concludes I would like to add one key item worthy of note. In a successful civil-military relationship, there is no requirement for either party to like the other. What is necessary, however, is that each has a measure of respect for the other. In every successful case study in this book, there is a point where each side sees something in his counterpart that creates that reservoir of respect allowing them to continue working together through the many dozens of serious disputes that arise along the way. At the same time, when that mutual respect is missing the result is always disastrous.

If someone were to ask me what lies at the heart of the civil-military trouble in America's recent history, I would credit it to a profound lack of respect each side has for the other. When I was a junior army officer I remember attending a mandatory social occasion, where every officer was warned upon entry that the President of the United States was not to be a topic of discussion during the evening and that anyone who did not toast the President when the ritual toast was offered would be punished. That was a few decades ago, but my impression is that the situation has not mended and may be much worse. If it is not fixed, the nation's next conflict will likely start with a series of disasters. Hopefully, his book offers pathways toward the mending that is required.

Notes

1 The original can still be viewed online, at: https://www.jcs.mil/Portals/36/Documents/Doctrine/concepts/joe_2008.pdf?ver=2017-12-30-132024-953
2 The original Joint Operational Environment is still posted: https://dod.defense.gov/Portals/1/Documents/pubs/2018-National-Defense-Strategy-Summary.pdf
3 For an excellent summary of the debates through several decades, see: Peter D. Feaver, "Civil-Military Relations," *Annual Review of Political Science*, Volume 2: 211–41 (volume publication date June 1999): and, Peter D. Feaver, *Armed Servants, Agency, Oversight, and Civil-Military Relations* (Cambridge: Harvard University Press, 2005).
4 Eliot Cohen's *Supreme Command: Soldiers, Statesmen, and Leadership in Wartime* (New York: Free Press, 2002).
5 Cohen's *Supreme Command*, p. 5.
6 Carl Von Clausewitz, Eds., Michael Howard and Peter Paret, *On War* (Princeton: Princeton University Press, 1976), p. 87.
7 For those looking for a truly excellent works primarily focus on recent geopolitical leadership challenges, see: Lawrence Freedman, *Command: The Politics of Military Operations from Korea to Ukraine* (Oxford: Oxford University Press, 2022).
8 Roy P. Basler (Ed.) *The Collected Works of Abraham Lincoln*. Volume 6 (New Brunswick: Rutgers University Press, 1953), pp. 79–80.
9 Winston S. Churchill, *Great Contemporaries* (New York: G.P. Puttnam's Sons, 1937), pp. 193–94.
10 Evan Mawdsley, "Stalin: Victors are not Judged," *The Journal of Slavic Military Studies*, Volume 19, Number 4 (2006), p. 719.
11 Lord Templewood, "Alanbrooke and Churchill," *The Spectator*, February 22, 1957.
12 Winston S. Churchill, *The World Crisis 1916–1918 Part I* (London: Thornton Butterworth, 1927), p. 244.
13 Ibid., p. 78. By the middle of 1943, FDR's interest in China waned, as Stalin promised to join the war against Japan after German was defeated, and the Capture of the Marianna Islands made it possible to bomb Japan without airbases in China. I have added the seventh point to Greenstein's original six.
14 Stimson Diaries, Friday, July 10, 1942. For a complete copy of the memorandum see: King and Whitehill, *Fleet Admiral King*, pp. 398–99.

15 Lawrence Guyer, *The Joint Chiefs and the War in Europe, Section III*, p. 122. The entire memo is reproduced in Appendix E to Chapter III.

16 Ibid.

17 The entire memo is reproduced in Appendix F to Chapter III in Guyer's, *The Joint Chiefs and the War in Europe, Section III*. Another copy is available in: The President's Secretary's File (PSF), 1933–1945: Box 4 (FDR Library).

18 Freedman, *Command*, p. 18.

19 See Alexander Hill, *The Red Army and the Second World War*, pp. 379–80.

20 A.M. Vasilevskii, *Delo vsei zhizni. Kniga pervaia. Izdanie shestoe* (Moscow: Politizdat, 1989), p. 211.

21 William O. Stoddard, Inside the White House in Times of War (New York: Charles L. Webster & Co, 1890), p. 179.

22 Jackie Mansky, The True Story of Stalin's Death, *Smithsonian Magazine*, October 10, 2017. See: https://www.smithsonianmag.com/history/true-story-death-stalin-180965119/

23 American generals only became the senior commanders in Afghanistan in 2007. Prior to that date there was a succession of general from different coalition partners in command.

2

LINCOLN, GRANT, AND THE SECRETS OF THEIR SUCCESS

Brooks D. Simpson

On Tuesday evening, March 8, 1864, people flocked to the White House to attend President Abraham Lincoln's weekly reception. The crowd was somewhat larger than usual in anticipation that the nation's most famous military hero, Ulysses S. Grant, might make an appearance. It was about half past nine: as the president was greeting visitors in the Blue Room, the crowd began to buzz. Grant had arrived. Lincoln strode forward, extending his hand. "Why, here is General Grant! Well, this is a great pleasure, I assure you!"[1]

That was the first time the president and the general who together were to guide the United States to victory in the American Civil War had met. Over the next thirteen months, they finally completed what Lincoln at Gettysburg called "the unfinished work" of securing reunion through victory, with slavery all but destroyed completely (as it would be by the end of 1865). In years to come historians would commit much time and energy to telling and retelling the story of how Lincoln found his general and how they together brought the war to a successful conclusion.

As that story goes, Lincoln went through general after general for command of the Army of the Potomac; he also sorted through various names in seeking success elsewhere. All along he took a protective interest in a fellow Illinois transplant, a man by the name of Ulysses S. Grant, who seemed to do nothing but win, despite rumors that he was a mindless drunkard who barely evaded disastrous defeat on several occasions. At long last the president "found" the general he had protected and defended for so long, put him in top command, and then watched as that general led the United States to victory in subduing the Confederate insurrection, although it came at great cost in human life and property. They were the ideal team, always on the same

DOI: 10.4324/9781003375630-2

page, and the only question was whether Lincoln was far wiser than he let on with his folky jokes and observations.

As with all such narratives, there are some elements of truth contained within, but there are also some assertions that do not stand up under examination. For example, although the United States embraced several strategic objectives that shifted during the conflict, especially regarding slavery and the treatment of enemy civilians and their property, the closest thing it possessed to a strategic plan until the spring of 1864 remained a statement of the obvious that did not long remain confidential and never attained the status of a planning document that guided operations. Moreover, of Grant's predecessors as general in chief, only Winfield Scott even went this far in sharing in private correspondence what soon became publicly broadcast as the Anaconda Plan, about which much is known and more is misunderstood.

Neither George McClellan nor Henry Halleck ever functioned as a true general in chief directing military operations and setting forth overall strategy. Indeed, the chain of command remained undeveloped and did not support systematic interservice cooperation at the highest level between the army and navy, rendering planning haphazard and sporadic. It was not until Grant took over as general-in-chief in 1864 that there was some semblance of order and cooperation when it came to strategic planning. Even then there was improvisation.

Nor should we continue to hold dear the notion of the inevitability of the Lincoln-Grant partnership. Through the first two years of Grant's military service during the Civil War, Lincoln solicited input about Grant's generalship, habits, and support of administration policy, and the general's critics freely shared their opinions with a chief executive who showed a tendency to place too much credence in initial reports. For all the talk about the president's political talents, these narratives overlook the degree to which Grant exhibited a deftness in dealing with his civil superiors. Traditional accounts overlook the game of chess which took place during the winter of 1863–1864 when Lincoln weighed whether to offer Grant the top spot with the revived rank of lieutenant general. The notion that the president gave his new commanding general a free hand during 1864 is pure fiction: Grant operated under military and political restraints imposed by a president who was seeking reelection. They eventually forged a working partnership that included a growing friendship that facilitated the eventual success of Grant's strategy.

The formation of the Lincoln-Grant team reminds us of the way in which the United States defined and implemented strategy evolved over the course of the conflict. Grant's rise to overall command offers a case study of the issues faced by subordinate commanders in the absence of oversight, as well as how generals made their way through a welter of rivalries, intrigue, and political concerns. His relationship with Lincoln during the first two years of the conflict was far from perfect, and his rise to high command was far from inevitable. At the same time, Lincoln struggled to figure out how to work with the military. In some instances the president oversimplified the problems facing his generals in the field; he was susceptible to giving undue credence to complaints from subordinates, especially those who claimed they could have done a better job than their superior officers; and he was not above ridiculing some of his generals in ways unbefitting a chief executive, although in most cases, a literature largely favorable to the sixteenth president cites such comments as examples of his humor and wit.

Nor did the generals who preceded Grant as general-in-chief prove equal to the responsibility of the position, refraining from ordering subordinates into action or framing military plans that went beyond the manifestly evident in seeking to subdue the Confederate insurrection. It was left to Lincoln and Grant to devise a system of overall command in which armies sought to secure strategic objectives through unified and coordinated action. While the result did not quite approximate the "modern system of command for a modern war" celebrated by T. Harry Williams in *Lincoln and His Generals* (1952), it was a marked improvement over what had preceded it.[2]

Strategic Problems

In the spring of 1861, the United States military had no overall plan to subdue the Confederate rebellion. No one had seriously considered the contingency; there were no planning exercises. Even the much-ballyhooed "Anaconda Plan" was little more than a mere outline offered by Winfield Scott in correspondence with George B. McClellan, when McClellan outlined an impractical invasion of western Virginia. Scott's plan was as much political as it was military, designed to surround the Confederates and cut off their efforts to secure supplies from Europe while doing as little harm to the Confederate interior as possible to facilitate a capitulation followed by a rapid restoration of preexisting circumstances—in short, restore the Union and leave slavery untouched.

As Lincoln's private secretaries John Hay and John Nicolay later put it, Scott's proposal was "premature and therefore necessarily incomplete," remaining "in the shape of a purpose, rather than a defined project."[3] Many people assumed that a series of decisive victories by US forces, followed by the capture of the Confederate capital at Richmond, Virginia, a mere one hundred miles from Washington, DC, would crack civilian support for the Confederacy and lead to peace and reconciliation, although Scott's call for the slow strangulation of the Confederacy through depriving it of much-needed supplies and food presaged a more time-consuming approach.

Scott would not prevail in the debate over strategy, although elements of his plan seemed to be reflected in the course of events over the next four years. The imposition of a blockade actually preceded his proposal, while a plan to seize control of the Mississippi materialized under far different circumstances. His successor as general in chief, George B. McClellan, framed a plan focusing on the creation of a large army that, under his direct command, would wield overwhelming force as it marched through the Confederacy, starting with Virginia—a plan free from considerations of logistical support required on such a large scale. Elsewhere his recommendations were vague and remained undeveloped as well as unsupported once he replaced Scott as general in chief on November 1, 1861, following his most successful campaign of the war— that of displacing his superior officer.

During the first several years of the war US military planners rarely coordinated operations between the three major theaters of the conflict—the eastern theater, broadly defined as the land east from the Appalachian Mountain chain to the Atlantic coast; the western theater, which extended westward from the Appalachian Mountain chain to the Mississippi River valley; and the trans-Mississippi West, which extended westward from the western theater to the Pacific coast. Those definitions would change as Union forces progressed southward into the Confederate heartland, especially during the last year of the conflict. To these three theaters, one must add the operations of the naval forces on the coasts of the Atlantic Ocean and the Gulf of Mexico as well as the various riverine squadrons that played such a key role in the western theater, although they were never formally part of a unified approach to military operations directed from the top down but depended on cooperation at the scene of operations.

Geography shaped Union strategy in all three theaters, but the impact seemed most apparent in the Western theater. Reestablishing control of the Mississippi River was a prime objective evident to anyone who looked at a map; that the Tennessee and Cumberland rivers offered avenues of invasion that could also outflank Confederate strongholds along the Mississippi was equally obvious. The Lincoln administration's desire to target East Tennessee, a haven for white southern Unionist sentiment, proved difficult logistically given the comparatively rugged terrain in that region. Kentucky's posture of neutrality through early September 1861 prevented any offensive operations southward. Aside from forays into Missouri, therefore, there was little Union military planners could do in the region until Kentucky's fate was determined.

Grant, who struggled to secure a commission during the first two months of the conflict, first exercised field command in Missouri as colonel of the 21st Illinois. Over time his superiors expanded his authority, but his elevation to brigadier general of volunteers resulted from the efforts of his hometown congressman, Elihu B. Washburne, who urged Lincoln to put Grant's name forward at the end of July 1861. Within the week the Senate confirmed the promotion. It was not until September that Grant gained prominence. Having learned that Confederate forces had violated Kentucky's neutrality on September 3, Grant moved quickly to cross the Ohio River and seize Paducah, Kentucky, three days later, securing control of the head of the Tennessee and Cumberland Rivers. Two months later he directed an ill-defined raid against a Confederate encampment at Belmont, Missouri, across the Mississippi from Confederate fortifications at Columbus, Kentucky. Grant's attack earned early success until Confederate reinforcements crossed the Mississippi and counter-attacked, driving Grant's men back to their river transports.

These early actions presaged the course of Union military operations in 1862, although efforts to coordinate offensive operations proved futile. The best way to oust the Confederates from Columbus and thus open the Mississippi as a pathway for the invasion was to outflank it to the east by moving southward along the Tennessee and Cumberland rivers and into Tennessee, threatening the state capitol at Nashville.

The setback at Belmont revealed some of the difficulties involved in a direct strike down the Mississippi. In later years many people took credit for this flanking approach, but it was apparent to many observers. The actual movement did not get underway until news reached Grant's superior, Henry W. Halleck, that Confederate reinforcements were headed westward to block any such invasion. Grant and Flag Officer Andrew Hull Foote led a combined army-navy operation that advanced along the Tennessee River to capture two flimsy Confederate fortifications, Forts Henry and Heiman, located at the Kentucky/Tennessee line, on February 6.

Grant then took matters into his own hands, informing Halleck that he would march eastward to Donelson and take it with Foote's assistance. Both sides hurried reinforcements to the area, with Halleck panicking at the thought that Grant, whom he did not hold in high regard, might be headed for disaster. When Confederate artillery drove Foote's gunboats away, Grant prepared for a drawn-out siege. Fortunately for him, a failed Confederate breakout attack compromised Donelson's defenses, rendering Confederate defeat inevitable. In reply to a request for terms from Confederate commander Simon Buckner, Grant declared: "No terms except unconditional and immediate surrender will be accepted, I propose to move immediately upon your works." Such stirring language on top of the garrison's capitulation made Grant a hero, secured his promotion to major general of volunteers, and gained him the nickname of "Unconditional Surrender" attached to his first initials.

Grant's victory fundamentally shaped military operations in the Mississippi River Valley for the next eighteen months. West Tennessee was rendered vulnerable to US advances. Nashville soon fell; Union forces steamed southward along the Cumberland and Tennessee rivers, with the next targets Memphis and Corinth, Mississippi. Halleck picked a fight with Grant over bureaucratic irregularities in the aftermath of Donelson, effectively removing his victorious subordinate from field command.

Halleck's antagonism gained the attention of the Lincoln administration. The president had next to nothing to do with Grant to this point, aside from expressing some concern about the charges of a disgruntled officer who had been removed by Grant after meddling with securing river transportation for men and supplies. Pleased with Grant's successes at Paducah, Henry, and Donelson, the president now had to intervene in an unseemly squabble. Out went a telegram to Halleck directing him to prove his charges. Halleck, who had just been successful in his quest for overall command in western Kentucky and Tennessee, dropped his complaints about Grant and directed him to assume command of his army in the field at Pittsburg Landing along the Tennessee River. There Grant was to wait in place until a second Union army under the command of Don Carlos Buell arrived, whereupon the united force would push southward to attack the Confederate Railroad junction in Corinth, Mississippi.

Accounts of Halleck's generalship that focus on his animus toward Grant overlook his short-lived achievement in unifying operations in the Western theater with an actual plan to advance. However, the Confederates could also see what Halleck intended to do. General Albert Sidney Johnson and his leading subordinate, Pierre G. T. Beauregard, decided to strike at Grant before Buell's arrival. The result was the battle of Shiloh, where Johnston's army crashed into Grant's forces west of Pittsburg Landing. Not anticipating such an attack, Grant had failed to fortify his position, believing that it was more important to drill the raw recruits who had joined his three more experienced divisions.

It did not help that the subordinate Grant entrusted with keeping tabs on perimeter security, William T. Sherman, was anxious to overcome reports that he had gone insane with worry about the potential of a Confederate attack in Kentucky in 1861 that would overwhelm his undersized command, and it did not help that Halleck had directed Grant to avoid aggressive contact with the enemy that might have detected and perhaps even disrupted Johnston's advance. Grant directed a fighting withdrawal to the steamboat landing, where he established a solid line of defense as he awaited reinforcements. They began to appear as combat ended for the day with Johnston lying dead and his successor Beauregard not sure what to do next. The following morning Grant and Buell launched a series of attacks that drove the Confederates from the field. Halleck arrived days later, and in his deliberate style prepared to embark upon his advance against Corinth.

Grant came under criticism in the wake of Shiloh amid reports that he was unprepared, caught by surprise, and perhaps even intoxicated, leading to what at the time was a staggering casualty list that shocked many observers. However, when Lincoln through Stanton inquired as to the accuracy of such reports, Halleck defended Grant. He decided that the best way to keep Grant around while entrusting him with little responsibility was to make him second-in-command of the newly unified force, which combined Grant's, Buell's, and John Pope's armies.

Grant chaffed under Halleck's supervision to the point of seeking a transfer or even leaving the army altogether, but over time the chorus of criticism subsided. That Grant did not hold Sherman accountable for poor perimeter security was a wise decision given Sherman's political connections (including a brother who was a US senator and a father-in-law who remained an influential political sage). Although Sherman grew closer to Grant at this time, he still considered Halleck a superior general and noted that Grant was experiencing the vicissitudes of public opinion. Meanwhile, Halleck finally made his way to the outskirts of Corinth: Beauregard's evacuation of the city as in late May preempted Halleck of any chance to strike a decisive blow.[4]

Having united three armies under his command to take Corinth, Halleck now decided to disperse them. Some of his men would assist Union operations in Arkansas, while Buell's army would march eastward toward Chattanooga, Tennessee, as the first step in securing East Tennessee (a cherished Lincoln objective). There would be no advance southward into Mississippi, no effort to seize Vicksburg, which effectively conceded to the Confederates control of a large stretch of the Mississippi River (so much for the Anaconda Plan as offering meaningful guidance to operations). Grant would remain in West Tennessee on occupation duty, although at least he had his old command back.

At this moment the Lincoln administration made a significant decision that promised to refashion the management of the war effort. After relieving McClellan of his responsibilities as general in chief in March (and having at that time given Halleck an enlarged sphere of responsibility in the west), Lincoln, Secretary of War Edwin M. Stanton, and several other officers in Washington attempted to oversee military operations through the establishment of a "War Board" with minimal success, especially against Stonewall Jackson in the Shenandoah Valley. In June Lincoln sought to remedy these shortcomings.

First, Lincoln directed Pope to come east to take command of the newly established Army of Virginia, with orders to advance southward over land against Richmond and protect Washington from any future Confederate offensives (although by now Jackson had joined Lee outside Richmond). He next ordered Halleck to come to Washington to assume the position of general in chief. Given the success of US forces in the West under Halleck's command (especially by Grant), this seemed a logical measure that rewarded success. As Halleck departed for Washington, however, he abandoned any notion of continuing what was a de facto theater command by failing to name a successor, preferring to complete the dissolving of his army into its constituent parts. Arriving in Washington, he became so focused on what to do in Virginia with McClellan's Army of the Potomac and Pope's Army of Virginia that he paid less attention to the forces he had dispersed throughout the Western theater. Nevertheless, the position of general in chief had been reconstituted. The question remained whether Halleck was equal to the responsibility. He was not.

Halleck's most important decision as general in chief was his first, in which he ordered McClellan to abandon his position along the James River, from where it still posed a threat to Richmond, and to unite with Pope in northern Virginia. He reached this decision when it became apparent that McClellan would not advance without significant reinforcements, echoing a demand he had made for months. Yet in shifting McClellan northward Halleck relieved Lee of the need to keep at least a portion of his army in the Richmond defenses, allowing the Confederate general to move north to smash Pope before McClellan's divisions could arrive. The resulting Second Manassas campaign came close to doing just that, as Lee hit a partially reinforced Pope hard at the end of August, while McClellan speculated that perhaps the best course to pursue was to "leave Pope to get out of his own scrape"—a sign of just how bad things were.

Halleck collapsed under the pressure of high command: he would never fully recover, preferring to advise and criticize rather than direct. The general-in-chief became the chief adviser and confidant to his favorites, such as Sherman, although over time he even warmed to Grant when faced with the possibility of lesser generals managing campaigns. But whatever hope had existed that Halleck would exercise command effectively and vigorously faded after Second Manassas, meaning that the position of general in chief continued to fail to give overall direction and coordination to the war effort. At least Halleck was no longer looking over Grant's shoulder: before long he would be of use to Grant in fending off a Lincoln-supported initiative involving one of Grant's chief critics, John A. McClernand.

Move on Vicksburg

Throughout the summer and early fall of 1862 Grant largely stayed on the defensive in West Tennessee and northern Mississippi. In September he tried to snap up a Confederate force under the command of Sterling Price at Iuka, Mississippi, but a series of mishaps foiled his efforts: a new subordinate, William S. Rosecrans, was left to battle Price. Several weeks later Rosecrans repulsed Price's effort to recapture Corinth: however, Grant and Rosecrans could never get on the same page regarding the pursuit of Price's army, leaving it to escape. Grant and Rosecrans grew to despise each other as they took turns pointing fingers at who was responsible for missed opportunities, a situation ending only when Halleck ordered Rosecrans to replace Don Carlos Buell as commander of the Army of the Ohio, which Rosecrans renamed the Army of the Cumberland.

No sooner had Rosecrans left for his new command than Grant slowly became aware of yet another threat to his military future, this time orchestrated in part by Lincoln himself. Grant eyed a potential advance southward into Mississippi with Vicksburg as his ultimate destination. Even as he was pondering how to proceed, however, he began to hear that he was not the only general with an interest in the city. John McClernand had taken a leave of absence from Grant's army and went to Washington, where he met with Lincoln (and even journeyed with the president to visit McClellan's army in early October in the wake of the Antietam campaign). He proposed to raise his own force, composed of Midwestern regiments, and use it to take Vicksburg with the assistance of the Navy. Coming in the wake of an encounter with a general who seemed loathe to move at all, Lincoln found McClernand's proposal meritorious and approved it with the proviso McClernand could only operate with forces Grant was willing to spare—fine print McClernand overlooked. Halleck, who cared little for McClernand, finally shared news of the plan with Grant, but only after the latter had raised questions due to rumors circulating about McClernand's project.

Such difficulties demonstrated just how confused overall supervision of military operations had become in Washington. Grant hurriedly hatched a plan of campaign that used some of the forces supposedly raised by McClernand in a two-pronged operation against Vicksburg, with Sherman entrusted to venture down via the river while Grant marched southward into central Mississippi. The Confederates stopped first Grant, then Sherman: by the time McClernand arrived on the scene, the best he could do was to implement Sherman's proposal to ferry his command up the Arkansas River and take Arkansas Post, a move that resulted in success but complicated operations against Vicksburg proper. Grant, supported by Halleck, reasserted direct control of the forces under his command and installed McClernand as a corps commander, leaving McClernand to complain to Lincoln that he had been undermined. He was surprised to learn that the president did not intend to do anything about it; however, rather than grouse about being betrayed by the president, McClernand set to work to discredit Grant with Lincoln with an eye to taking his place.

When Grant arrived at his army's encampment across the Mississippi River from Vicksburg along the Arkansas/Louisiana border at the end of January 1863, he concluded the best course to pursue was to move southward, cross the Mississippi below Vicksburg, and then turn north to take the city. The roads and levees would not be dry enough to support such a move until April. It would not do, however, to sit and wait. Grant dismissed Sherman's recommendation that the army returns north to Memphis with the observation that such a move would look too much like a retreat, an admission of defeat, and a reason for the president to remove him, leaving McClernand in charge.

For several months Grant kept his men occupied. They dug canals in an unsuccessful effort to divert the course of the river away from Vicksburg, opening up a chance to strike at the city directly. Grant had heard that Lincoln was interested in such endeavors, although the president in fact dismissed them but never shared his sentiments with the general. Grant's men also attempted to make their way through the Yazoo Bayou to approach the city from the north, only to find themselves in such trouble that they were only extracted with some difficulty. News in April that David Dixon Porter had received orders directing him to reinforce naval efforts to support Nathaniel Banks's operations south of Vicksburg induced Grant to put his preferred plan into operation. Given the amount of scrutiny he was under, with critics claiming he was incompetent and seeking his removal, the moment had come to see whether he would meet the challenge.

In mid-April Porter's gunboats and transports ran the batteries at Vicksburg under cover of darkness, while lead elements of Grant's army marched southward. Sherman remained opposite Vicksburg to deceive Confederate commander John C. Pemberton as to Grant's intentions. Benjamin Grierson led a column of cavalry through central Mississippi, adding to Pemberton's confusion. At the end of April Grant crossed the Mississippi, defeated a Confederate force at Port Gibson, and entered Grand Gulf. Having not heard from Banks, Grant set aside notions of joining up with him, preferring instead to drive through Mississippi before turning on Vicksburg. Over the next two weeks, he won four more battles, captured the state capital at Jackson, and then trapped Pemberton's army within Vicksburg. Twice Grant tried to take the city by assault; he then settled down to siege operations, thwarting Confederate efforts to relieve Pemberton, all the while receiving reinforcements that secured his force's superiority. On July 4, Vicksburg and its garrison of nearly 30,000 men capitulated. Port Hudson fell to Banks four days later, consolidating Union control of the Mississippi, much to Lincoln's delight: "The Father of Waters again goes unvexed to the sea."

Ironically, although Lincoln came to consider himself something of a self-trained military strategist, he had spent most of his time perusing the war in the East, pressing commanders to act, visiting headquarters, entertaining complaints, and wondering why his generals did not seem up to the task of defeating the foe. His comments on operations in the West were far less frequent and usually more general. When it came to Grant's operations, however, he did admit that when Grant had crossed the Mississippi, he had hoped that the general would link up with Banks. With true grace and humility, the president told Grant, "I now wish to make the personal acknowledgment that you were right, and I was wrong."[5]

The Slavery Problem

As Grant's military accomplishments helped Lincoln achieve his military priorities in the Western theater between 1861 and 1863, so did Grant's position on the larger issue of war aims mirror the evolution of the Lincoln administration's position on the interplay between conducting a war for reunion, the treatment of white civilians in occupied territory, the institution of slavery, and the treatment of enslaved, freed, and free African Americans. Once more, this was more a case of fortuitous coincidence than coordinated policy shifts, although there was certainly interplay between decision-making in Washington and events at the front.

At the outbreak of the conflict, Grant predicted that the friction of war would destroy slavery, but he did not embrace it as a war aim. He went so far as to assert that Union forces would willingly subdue a slave insurrection while instructing his command to leave the peculiar institution alone. While Union policy said nothing about responding to slave insurrections, the Lincoln administration was sensitive to the issue. The president believed that the only way to woo the Confederates back into the Union was to make clear the war was one for reunion, an approach affirmed by a joint resolution from Congress. Generals were not to take these matters into their own hands, as Lincoln made clear when he rescinded John C. Frémont's proclamation freeing those enslaved in Missouri. The president believed that targeting slavery at this early point in the war would destroy his efforts to sway Kentucky from its neutral stance, embitter and intensify Confederate resistance, and undermine efforts to work with southern white unionists.

Yet, as Grant realized, the war had a momentum all its own. What would one do when enslaved people conscripted to work on Confederate fortifications sought refuge within Union lines? Following the model set forth by Benjamin F. Butler in Tidewater Virginia, the same Congress that had passed a joint resolution denying that the object of the war was to destroy slavey weeks later passed legislation declaring that all enslaved workers assisting the Confederate war effort who fell into Union hands were to be treated as contraband of war and thus not subject to return. Further Union offensive operations, especially along the South Carolina coast in November 1861, led to more enslaved people finding refuge in Federal lines, as did advances along the Mississippi, Tennessee, and Cumberland Rivers in 1862. Military commanders, including Grant, sought guidance as to what to do with the enslaved blacks they encountered and whether they should draw distinctions between loyal and disloyal slaveholders in deciding whether to allow such refugees to be returned and thus reenslaved. In March 1862, Congress directed that no escaped slave should be returned to their masters, but military directives and administration policy failed to make this a clear and uniform practice for some time.

Like other commanders, Grant struggled in the absence of policy directives. Slowly, however, an army that was committed to reunion began, however reluctantly, to become an army of liberation as well. The intensity of Confederate civilian resistance did not subside, especially in occupied territory. Nor did the Lincoln administration's rather careful and deliberate course that sought the adoption of a policy of compensated and graduate emancipation followed by the voluntary resettlement (or "colonization") of free and freed African Americans outside the boundaries of the United States gain traction. However, slaveholders were not interested in selling their slaves, while African Americans largely opposed emigration from their true native land, the United States. Much to Lincoln's frustration, southern white Unionists seemed more concerned about protecting slavery than winning the war or restoring the

Union, leaving the president to discount what was once a primary concern of his policy.

By summer 1862, in the wake of McClellan's failure to capture the Confederate capital at Richmond, Virginia, followed by Robert E. Lee's success in driving him away during the Seven Days Battles, Lincoln discerned that to win the war he would have to strike at slavery—or at least threaten to do so to encourage a reconciliationist peace to avoid what all knew would be a measure that would transform the conflict forever. In the west Grant and his fellow generals believed it was time to cease treating Confederate civilians, their property, and the institution of slavery with kid gloves; in passing a second confiscation measure Congress declared the enslaved held by Confederate slaveholders to be free and directed the confiscation of other property held by Confederate supporters.

This escalation, while substantial, was soon outpaced by Lincoln's decision to issue first a preliminary emancipation proclamation in the wake of McClellan's turning back Lee's invasion of Maryland, followed one hundred days later by the Emancipation Proclamation itself, which specified areas where slavery would no longer be recognized while failing to distinguish between loyal and disloyal slaveholders. The preliminary proclamation gave white southerners one last chance to preserve what remained of slavery if they returned to the Union by the end of the year. As with gradual emancipation followed by colonization, which Lincoln pushed for publicly one last time in December 1862, there were few takers. Escalation promised to intensify the conflict; it also opened the way for enlisting African Americans as soldiers, tipping the manpower scales still more.

Grant dutifully complied with such initiatives. As his soldiers liberated enslaved people in western Tennessee and northern Mississippi in 1862, he gathered them in "contraband camps" and looked to use them as laborers. As his operations against Vicksburg evolved, he also embraced black enlistment, despite rumors that circulated in Washington that some of his subordinates did not have their heart in the project. After Vicksburg's fall, he made clear in correspondence with Lincoln that he endorsed the administration's measures concerning black enlistment, a statement that so delighted Lincoln that he shared it as evidence of the success of his policy. At the same time, Grant moved to deprive the Confederates of resources and production capability, while he wrestled with how best to address the pressing need for cotton without becoming entangled in various shady schemes made possible by administration efforts to bring cotton to market (especially for overseas consumption) as soon as possible.

Despite general guidance and advice (but rarely directives) from the authorities in Washington, including Halleck, what is most noticeable about policy and practice toward enemy civilians, the institution of slavery, and the fate of the enslaved between 1861 and 1863 is the degree to which there was no large-scale coordination to implement policy initiatives in explicit ways.

Understandings were shared in private correspondence and through intermediaries, as when Adjutant General Lorenzo Thomas ventured westward from Washington in the spring 1863 to report on Grant's progress in enlisting black soldiers (he was favorably impressed). Halleck offered advice and suggestions, much as he did in overseeing military operations, Although Halleck's support for escalation was clear to Grant, he failed to issue overall statements of policy, and pockets of resistance remained, as in Sherman's hostility to enlisting blacks.

Nor was there centralized strategic planning or coordination, as the efforts to capture Vicksburg demonstrated. David G. Farragut's first 1862 expedition against the city, which fell short because it was poorly supported, was largely undertaken initially at Farragut's initiative; a subsequent effort ordered by the Navy Department did no better. Ironically, the only operation against Vicksburg conceived after consultation with the high command and the sharing of ideas was McClernand's ill-fated effort, in which Lincoln, Stanton, and Halleck were not on the same page, with Halleck working with Grant to thwart McClernand. It was left to Grant to try to figure out how to take Vicksburg during early 1863; his ability to work with David Dixon Porter's Mississippi Squadron obscured the lack of cooperation from Washington authorities, including orders from the Navy Department that directed Porter elsewhere and forced Grant to act quickly if he was to utilize Porter's force to cross the Mississippi below Vicksburg.

Grant defied expectations (but not orders) that he would cooperate with Nathaniel Banks's army once he crossed the Mississippi, in part because Banks, much to Halleck's frustration, engaged in several movements that delayed his movement against Port Hudson, Louisiana, second only to Vicksburg as a Confederate strong point along the Mississippi. William S. Rosecrans rejected Halleck's efforts to have his Army of the Cumberland advance against Braxton Bragg's Army of Tennessee while Grant approached Vicksburg: it was not until the last week of June that Rosecrans embarked on his successful Tullahoma Campaign to clear the Confederates from Middle Tennessee and threaten Chattanooga. Union army commanders acted on their own; Halleck could nudge and advise but failed to order; there was no coordination between land forces; it was left to the commanders on the scene to work out combined arms operations, sometimes under conflicting directives from the Navy Department.

Grant's capture of Vicksburg put an end to one problem that had daunted him for over a year. There would be no more efforts to remove him from command. Recalling these efforts reminds us that the popular tale of Lincoln's unstinting support of Grant requires serious revision. After Fort Donelson Halleck had sought to deprive Grant of field command until Lincoln and Stanton asked him to explain his action; after Shiloh, however, it was Halleck who fended off inquiries from Lincoln and Stanton asking whether the heavy losses suffered were due in part to neglect on Grant's part.

Some thirty years later, a Republican operative and newspaperman Alexander K. McClure would claim that Lincoln sought to shield Grant from public criticism, declaring "I can't spare this man; he fights"; but the remainder of McClure's account of that conversation, including specific descriptions of Lincoln's actions, finds absolutely no support in the documentary record, casting substantial doubt on a tale that all too many people continue to cite. The McClernand project was an implicit admission that Grant could not be trusted to direct operations against Vicksburg, a sentiment expressed repeatedly by McClernand to Lincoln. Nor did it help when Grant issued an ill-considered order expelling Jews from his department in late 1862 due to concerns about their role in cotton transactions. Lincoln rescinded the order, but took no further action against Grant, in part because the latter readily accepted his humiliation.

Rumors of Grant's removal continued throughout the first months of 1863. That Lincoln failed to act in the face of such increasing criticism did not mean that he was not willing to consider it. In February 1863, he contemplated sending Benjamin F. Butler to report on the progress of operations along the Mississippi, while orders were drafted to place him in charge of a department that included Vicksburg. As letters questioning Grant's competency and sobriety continued to arrive at the White House, the president decided that it was time to find out for himself, and he dispatched two representatives to visit Grant's command. Adjutant General Lorenzo Thomas was to check on whether Grant and his commanders were doing all they could to recruit African Americans into military service; newspaperman-turned-troubleshooter Charles A. Dana was to check on Grant under the cover story of inspecting paymaster operations. At the same time Illinois Governor Richard Yates and Congressman Elihu B. Washburne, long Grant's advocate in Washington, journeyed down to Grant's headquarters to survey matters for themselves.

Grant handled the visitors with skill. He impressed Thomas with his commitment to black enlistment; he took Dana into his confidence, and before long the man, sent to spy on him, was sharing and supporting Grant's perspective with his superiors in Washington, including offering critical remarks about McClernand. Washburne regained his confidence, while Yates began to question McClernand's qualifications. Yet Grant waited until after he had cornered the Confederates in Vicksburg to seize upon McClernand's violation of bureaucratic procedure to remove him from command; after Vicksburg fell on July 4, he dispatched Rawlins to Washington to offer an account of the campaign that justified McClernand's removal, while Dana returned to Washington carrying the same message. Finally, in correspondence with Lincoln—the first substantial exchanges between the two men—Grant endorsed administration policy on black enlistment, which the president appreciated.

On July 5, 1863, Lincoln visited Daniel Sickles, wounded at Gettysburg (and all too anxious to raise questions about the performance of his superior, George G. Meade, to anyone who would listen, including the president).

When they met, the news of Vicksburg's surrender had yet to make its way to Washington. What did Lincoln make of Grant? "He doesn't worry and bother me," the president replied. "He isn't shrieking for reinforcements all the time. He takes what troops we can safely give him … and does the best he can with what he has got. And if Grant only does this thing down there—I don't care much how, so long as he does it *right*—why, Grant is my man and I am his the rest of the war!"[6] Two days later, Lincoln received the news. Vicksburg had fallen. Grant had won.

Grant's Rise to Command in the West

The capitulation of the Vicksburg garrison, nearly 30,000 strong, secured Grant's future. Promoted to major general in the regular army—ensuring that he would have a high-ranking place in the postwar military, securing at last his financial future—he no longer had to worry about being replaced. His influence was still not absolute: his proposal to advance against Mobile was set aside in favor of the Lincoln administration's anxiety to secure control of Louisiana in support of that state's establishment of a loyal government and to look westward toward Texas. Much to his relief, administration authorities decided against bringing him east to take over the Army of the Potomac in the wake of Lincoln's disappointment with Meade for failing to conduct what Lincoln believed should have been a more vigorous pursuit of Lee's Army of Northern Virginia after Gettysburg.

In the months after Vicksburg, however, events compelled Lincoln to undertake a reorganization of his command structure to ensure coordination of effort in the Western theater. In September Rosecrans captured Chattanooga, while Ambrose Burnside occupied Knoxville, seeming to secure East Tennessee, long a Lincoln objective. However, Braxton Bragg, reinforced by two divisions from Lee's army, defeated Rosecrans in north Georgia along Chickamauga Creek, drove him back to Chattanooga, and trapped the Yankees by occupying high ground east and south of the city while hampering efforts at resupply.

Lincoln hurried reinforcements to Chattanooga from the Army of the Potomac and Grant's Army of the Tennessee. However, he began to entertain doubts that Rosecrans was equal to the task of holding the city, an impression reinforced by dark and foreboding dispatches from none other than Charles A. Dana, once more acting as Washington's man on the scene. In mid-October, Lincoln decided to do for the entire western theater what Halleck a year before had urged: consolidate the direction of several armies in a theater under a single commander. He picked Grant, who was recovering from a serious riding injury, for the job. The Military Division of the Mississippi united three departments (named after the Mississippi, Cumberland, and Ohio rivers) that together encompassed territory from the Appalachian Mountains to the Mississippi River Valley under Grant's direction: the new commander exercised the option he was given to replace Rosecrans (with whom he did not get along) with George H. Thomas.

Effective unified theater command was a long time coming for the Union war effort. Grant's primary responsibility was to break the Confederate hold on Chattanooga; later he would also have to concern himself with fending off a Confederate advance against Knoxville. Grant did just that: after overseeing the restoration of supply lines and moving his men into place, he drove Bragg away from Chattanooga in a three-day battle, where little went according to plan, and Grant's own role was open to question. Nevertheless, the man in command gets the credit. Grant's interest in pursuing the Confederates into north Georgia and threatening the Confederate heartland gave way when he bowed to Washington's concern about Burnside's fate at Knoxville and sent relief forces that arrived just as the Confederates broke contact.

It had taken thirty months from the fall of Fort Sumter for the Union high command to unify command operations in a major theater. The experiment of a military division that brought departments and armies together was not replicated elsewhere, hampering the realization of strategic objectives through coordinated military operations. Nor was there a structure that realized formal cooperation between land and naval forces: that still depended largely upon how well the commanders on the scene worked together. Absent was an overall plan to implement strategic principles through coordination and cooperation: the shifting of reinforcements in 1863 to Vicksburg and Chattanooga were haphazard responses to circumstances.

As general-in-chief Halleck failed to exercise effective overall command or set forth more than a vague vision of how military operations would meet strategic goals. In that respect, he was no different that McClellan, who could not manage the Western theater while supervising the Army of the Potomac in motion, which led to his displacement as general-in-chief. Halleck's success in unifying operations under his own command in 1862 did not survive his departure for Washington. Unity was finally restored with Grant's installation as head of the Military Division of the Mississippi. Nor was Grant's authority absolute, for Halleck turned down a second proposal to target Mobile in favor of operations west of the Mississippi. Grant had to rest content with directing Sherman to conduct a raid into central Mississippi to shred Confederate logistics in anticipation of spring 1864 operations. By the time Sherman was winding up that campaign, circumstances dictated that there would be a massive overhaul of the US command structure, with both Grant and Sherman destined to play large parts in conducting operations that would do much to determine whether Abraham Lincoln would win reelection in 1864.

A Unified Strategy

At first glance Grant's victory at Chattanooga would have seemed to have cemented his relationship with Lincoln and made him the obvious choice to assume overall command if Lincoln wanted to set aside Halleck. Yet Lincoln hesitated. He argued that it might be best to leave Grant where he was, given his successes; he may also have been disturbed by rumors that Grant had presidential ambitions, given that several papers were now considering the prospect of a Grant candidacy in 1864. It was left to Grant's congressional patron, Elihu B. Washburne, to push for the revival of the rank of lieutenant general: the legislation made it explicit that whoever held the rank would become general-in-chief. As the bill made its way through Congress an amendment made Grant's appointment explicit, although it was later set aside as an unconstitutional infringement on presidential powers.

In contrast to Grant's disinclination to come east in the summer of 1864 to take over the Army of the Potomac, he was willing to consider promotion and elevation to the supreme command, and he did nothing to discourage the discussion. Through intermediaries he made clear to the president his lack of interest in pursuing a political career; only then did Lincoln support Washburne's proposal. Grant took the position upon one condition. He would not be bound to a desk in Washington: army headquarters would be wherever he was, and he would determine that.

In years to come some students of the 1864 campaigns would claim that Lincoln gave Grant a free hand with military operations. This was far from true, and Grant knew it even before he prepared to go to Washington to accept his new rank and command. During the winter Halleck had solicited his ideas about what course to pursue in 1864. Grant reaffirmed his preference for targeting Mobile followed by a strike against Atlanta; in the east he suggested that while the Army of the Potomac held Lee in check, a force of 60,000 men would swing southwest from southeastern Virginia into North Carolina, with the objective of liberating the enslaved, cutting Richmond's rail ties to the south, and encouraging Unionist sentiment among alienated whites. The move would force Lee either to take the offensive in Virginia or come south to North Carolina to counter the invasion in terrain unfamiliar to the Confederate commander.

Such a campaign made no mention of attrition through continuous combat: it struck at the Confederacy's infrastructure, threatened its logistical network, and promised upheaval with both white Unionists and liberated blacks. However, Halleck dismissed the proposal, in part because it did not conform to Lincoln's preferences for an overland approach in Virginia or the president's interest in securing Louisiana and Texas. Whatever plan Grant would develop as general-in-chief would conform to presidential priorities, especially in an election year; moreover, in assigning generals to carry out this pan, Grant would have to heed the perceived political value of several generals, including Benjamin F. Butler, Nathaniel Banks, and Franz Sigel, who were supposed to be influential in securing the support of constituencies essential to Republican fortunes.

Such constraints reveal that Grant never had the total autonomy so often assumed in many accounts. He had his hands tied when it came to certain generals and certain preferences for military operations. He also had to wrestle with the paradox presented by Butler, Banks, and Sigel. Not to place them in suitable commands supposedly would risk losing the support of key notables and constituencies, yet their failure to perform in the field would result in defeats that would demoralize the population and contribute to war weariness just at a time when Lincoln needed military triumphs to secure political success. It would be left to Grant to figure out how to operate under such constraints while securing victory (or the appearance of approaching victory) before voters cast their presidential ballots in November 1864.

Grant's solution was to take elements from his previous suggestions to Halleck, reconcile them with the need to meet Lincoln's concerns, and to embrace coordination and cooperation as keys to the conduct of operations. Setting aside his North Carolina proposal, he envisioned a four-pronged attack in Virginia, with armies clearing out the Shenandoah Valley, severing supply links and destroying resources in southwest Virginia, approaching Richmond from the James River, and opposing Lee in central Virginia. If all went as planned, Lee would find himself in logistical difficulty as he chose whether to save Richmond or confront the Army of the Potomac in a must-win battle. If Lee chose the former, the Army of the Potomac would follow him southward, keeping the pressure on; if Lee gave battle in central Virginia, Richmond might fall. To the west Grant directed Sherman to advance southward from northern Georgia toward the rail junction of Atlanta and the army that defended it, Joseph Johnston's Army of Tennessee. Grant entrusted Sherman to decide how to implement his own campaign: Grant would "simply … lay down the work it is desirable to have done and leave you free to execute in your own way." He would await the conclusion of Banks's efforts to secure Louisiana to Lincoln's satisfaction before drawing on that force to carry out his long-contemplated movement against Mobile. As he explained to Sherman he intended "to work all parts of the Army to-gether … towards a common center."[7]

In contrast to previous generals in chief, Grant took the time to explain his thinking to Lincoln; in turn, the president set aside his tendency to engage in armchair strategy. He was delighted to have a general who could see the whole picture and utilize the forces at his disposal in coordinated offensives. "The particulars of your plans I neither know, or seek to know," he wrote Grant as the time for movement drew near. For his part, Grant was delighted with the support he received and quiet about instances where he complied against his better judgment with some of the president's preferences. Most important, he told Lincoln that he assumed responsibility for whatever came next: "Should my success be less than I desire, and expect, the least I can say is, the fault is not with you."[8]

The spring 1864 campaign did not unfold as planned. Lee chose to fight Grant south of the Rapidan and Rappahannock rivers in a series of bloody battles that featured near-continuous combat followed by Grant's efforts to slide around Lee's right flank to move southward. Lee was able to focus on Grant in what became a struggle of attrition was due to the failure of two of Grant's subordinates to carry out their missions. In each case, the commander owed his command to Lincoln's decision in the early years of the war to commission as generals individuals whose perceived political value supposedly outweighed their deficiencies as army commanders. In the Shenandoah Valley Sigel was checked at New Market by a far inferior force, allowing Lee to draw on that force for reinforcements while dismissing any threat to his army from that quarter. Although Butler moved his newly formed Army of the James along its namesake river to establish a foothold south of Richmond, he failed to threaten either the city or its southward rail links, ending Lee's worries about a quick capture of the Confederate capital. Nor did operations in southwest Virginia make a significant impact.

Grant had commenced the campaign by informing Lincoln that "there would be no turning back;" days later he declared that he was prepared "to fight it out on this line if it takes all summer." Such confidence reassured Lincoln. However, with Butler and Sigel coming up short, Grant decided to force Lee back to Richmond itself. Believing that the Confederates were on the point of disintegration, he ordered a major assault east of Richmond, but the resulting assault at Cold Harbor achieved nothing at great cost: it was a greater disaster in the public eye, however, than on the battlefield. It looked as if Lee had successfully created a stalemate along the lines that he had confronted McClellan in 1862—an image that did not inspire northern voters that their new hero was making satisfactory progress.

This time, however, matters would be somewhat different. Having been deprived of striking at Richmond from the south in his North Carolina plan, Grant had always considered the possibility that if he could not beat Lee north of Richmond, he would move his army across the James and threaten Richmond from the south at Petersburg, eventually cutting it off from the Confederate heartland. Cheered by Grant's resilience, Lincoln wired him: "I begin to see it. You will succeed." It almost worked: Grant eluded Lee, crossed the James in force, and approached Petersburg, only to have the operation sputter out as assault plans went astray.

At the same time, Lee directed Jubal Early to take on Union forces in the Shenandoah Valley; having pushed them aside, Early headed northwards through the valley with Washington as his target in what looked to be a reprise of Stonewall Jackson's campaign. After the high hopes for Union victory in the spring, the notion of Early approaching the outskirts of the capital was enough to raise questions of whether anything had really changed in the last two years. Surely it would be hard for Lincoln to offer a vision of victory in support of his reelection efforts, if Early disrupted Grant's operations or even forced him to relinquish his grip on Petersburg.

Grant set aside Lincoln's suggestion that he come north to confront Early but sent sufficient reinforcements to deter Early from attacking Washington.

However, reinforcements earmarked for operations against Petersburg were diverted to Washington, as Grant contemplated how best to bring the forces around the capital under unified command to protect the capital while removing the Shenandoah Valley once and for all from the Confederate war effort. Meanwhile, he experimented with other ways to secure a breakthrough on the Richmond-Petersburg front, the most notable being support for a plan to explode a mine under Confederate lines outside Petersburg. The explosion on July 30 opened a great opportunity that Union attackers were unable to exploit, and by day's end, Grant understood that the operation was a stupendous failure.

The next day Grant ventured to Hampton Roads to meet with Lincoln. On the agenda was rectifying the confusing command situation in Washington by placing forces under one head. In retrospect, however, the meeting capped six weeks of increasing strain between Lincoln and Grant. The president had paid a visit to Grant in the immediate aftermath of Grant's initial failure to take Petersburg, his first visit to the front since Grant took charge. Although Lincoln left reassured that Grant was determined to succeed, he remarked, "I cannot pretend to advise, but I do hope that all may be accomplished with as little bloodshed as possible." He returned to Washington somewhat disappointed that more had not been done.[9]

Grant was equally disappointed. Yet when he attempted to shift his commanders around in the interest of combat effectiveness, he found that his options were limited. True, the failures of Banks in Louisiana and Sigel in the Valley had afforded him the opportunity to displace them, but it proved far more difficult to shift Butler to a desk job or to quell the infighting among his generals. Politics and appearances deterred him. Fresh from a fight with Congress over Reconstruction policy and having finally accepted the resignation of his troublesome Secretary of the Treasury, Salmon P. Chase, Lincoln knew that his support among Republicans was eroding. Replacing Butler, who had a talent for political mischief, might be too much, and when Grant attempted to do so by seeking Butler's reassignment elsewhere, muddled orders issued by Halleck (and approved by Lincoln) simply created such confusion and friction that Grant kept Butler on and relieved one of his quarrelsome subordinates, William F. Smith, who had fallen into his characteristic habit of criticizing everyone. Meanwhile, Grant sought a new commander for the forces around Washington. He had a weak spot for William B. Franklin, a West Point classmate; perhaps the quarrelsome Meade needed a change of scenery; it was whispered that even George B. McClellan might be persuaded to return to the field, a move that might also sideline Little Mac from consideration as the Democratic party's presidential nominee to oppose Lincoln. The president quickly vetoed Franklin, who had a talent for intrigue; he also declined to shift Meade, arguing that to do so would leave a bad impression; and the talk about McClellan's return fizzled just as quickly as it had once sizzled.

Thus, when Lincoln and Grant met at the end of July 1864, the war was not going well. It was embarrassing enough that Early had threatened Washington in mid-July; as that month came to an end, Confederate forces advanced into Pennsylvania, with Chambersburg being set ablaze when its citizens failed to raise the ransom the Confederates had sought. Coming on the same day as the embarrassing setback at the Crater, it was not an ideal time for Lincoln and Grant to exchange views. The conference's only achievement was an agreement to place Phil Sheridan, the fiery infantryman-turned-cavalryman, in charge of the forces opposite Early. Even that measure faced opposition: Halleck, increasingly difficult and critical, tried to subvert Grant's instructions. Exhausted, Grant momentarily wavered. Watching everything unravel once more, Lincoln intervened. He wired that while he approved of Grant's original directive concerning Sheridan, "please look over the dispatches you have received from here, ever since you made that order, and discover if you can, that there is any idea in the head of anyone here, of 'putting our army *South* of the enemy' or of following him to the *death* in any direction. I repeat to you it will neither be done nor attempted unless you watch it every day, and hour, and force it."[10]

Lincoln's dispatch served as a wake-up call to Grant and a reassurance of the president's support; it also stood as a confession that neither the president nor his commanding general was able to get their way unimpeded. For all the talk about a modern command system in 1864, Halleck's obstructionist behavior and unwillingness to take responsibility, even in a time of crisis, demonstrated that he was, in fact, not even a "first-rate clerk" in Lincoln's words. Grant immediately traveled north to Maryland to see the situation for himself. David Hunter, who carried political clout himself, generously surrendered department command to Sheridan, who was to take no orders unless they came from Grant himself—a sign of just how useless Halleck had become.

At least Grant did not have to worry about Sherman. Between May and July Grant's successor as commander of the Military Division of the Mississippi had played a game of chess with Joseph Johnston, slowly pushing the Confederate back to Atlanta. Frustrated with Johnston's inability to stop Sherman dead in his tracks, Confederate President Jefferson Davis replaced him with John Bell Hood on July 18. Within days Hood twice attacked Sherman, only to suffer heavy losses. By the end of the month siege operations were well underway.

To the unpracticed eye the Union war effort was at a standstill. Secretary of the Navy Gideon Welles, never a fan of Grant, confided to his diary, "A nation's destiny almost has been committed to this man, and if it is an improper committal, where are we?"[11] In fact, however, things were beginning to look up. When Halleck suggested that perhaps it was time to abandon offensive operations against Peterburg to shift troops northward to deal with domestic disgruntlement over the draft, Grant bluntly rejected the idea. Lincoln agreed: "Hold on with a bull dog grip, and chew and choke, as much as possible."

Disgusted with Halleck, Grant went so far as to suggest that perhaps Old Brains could be transferred west to take command of the Department of the Pacific, about as far away as one could be from Washington.[12] At month's end, the Democrats convened in Chicago, nominated McClellan for president, and in their party platform declared the war a failure. They were premature.

On September 2, 1864, Grant opened a telegram from Washington. It contained news that Sherman's forces had entered Atlanta. Finally, the Confederacy had buckled. In truth, Sherman had already effectively nullified Atlanta's importance by systematically severing its rail lines, but the capture of the city played well with a war-weary northern public. Just over two weeks later Sheridan, after meeting with Grant, tore into Early's army at Winchester, followed by a second victory days later at Fisher Hill. Suddenly things were on the move again. This time Lee, pinned in place by Grant, could not reach into his bag of tricks to reverse the course of events. Lincoln's reelection prospects, once so dim that he had predicted defeat, brightened. October contests in Ohio, Indiana, and Pennsylvania proved Republican triumphs; eight days later, when Sheridan turned back Early's last bid to reverse the tide of events at Cedar Creek in dramatic style, prospects shone still more. Grant did all he could to ensure that soldiers were able to vote, confident that the rank-and-file would endorse their commander-in-chief. He became more cautious in his own operations against Lee to preclude another significant battlefield setback that might dampen Northern enthusiasm.

The political calendar shaped the general's thinking in fundamental ways, demonstrating his awareness of Lincoln's political interests. Never was this clearer than in discussions over Sherman's next move. The captor of Atlanta favored striking into the Confederate heartland, destroying resources and demoralizing citizens along the way, before emerging along the coast (exactly where remained unclear at first). Such a march would demonstrate that the Confederacy could not protect its own people: its motive was far more psychological than material. However, he was willing to restrict the actions of his men should Georgia Governor Joseph E. Brown remove Georgia from the Confederacy altogether. When that idea failed to materialize, Sherman, arguing that it was impossible to pin Hood down and that Confederate operations imperiled his supply line back to Chattanooga, renewed his arguments to commence marching through Georgia. "If we can march a well appointed Army right through [Confederate] territory," he wrote Grant, "it is a demonstration to the World, foreign and domestic, that we have a power that Davis cannot resist. This may not be war, but rather Statesmanship"; the march would clinch the case for the inevitability of Union victory.[13]

At first Grant was not overly enthusiastic about Sherman's proposal. He thought it better to remove Hood off the board altogether or advance against Mobile, although David G. Farragut's victory at Mobile Bay in August served to end that city's value as a port. An anxious Lincoln had even less appetite for the plan, fearing that Sherman was placing the fate of his army at risk. Expressing confidence in Sherman's ability to succeed, Grant offered as a concession to Lincoln the assurance that Sherman would not commence his march before Lincoln secured reelection.

On November 8, 1864, a majority of Northern voters cast ballots in favor of Lincoln's reelection. The president's victory was due in large part to the success of his commanding general; in turn, with Lincoln remaining in office, Grant could at last turn to the task of subduing what remained of the Confederacy. In such ways did strategy interweave political goals and military means: the republic was one step closer to the collapse of the Confederacy, the destruction of slavery, and the re-establishment of the Union on a lasting basis. Lincoln's success was Grant's success, and vice versa.

End Game

With Lincoln safely reelected Grant could close out the Confederacy systematically with an eye to postwar concerns. Sherman embarked on his march through Georgia without fear that a setback might have dire political ramifications. By mid-December, his army was approaching the outskirts of Savannah, which capitulated on December 22. At the same time, Thomas turned back John Bell Hood's ill-fated invasion of Tennessee at Nashville, although his deliberate nature caused Grant a great deal of anxiety and dissatisfaction that nearly led to Thomas's displacement. Butler bumbled an attempt to take Fort Fisher, which protected Wilmington, North Carolina, leading to his removal. This time Lincoln offered no opposition, Butler's political value has largely evaporated in the wake of the president's reelection. Several weeks later the fort fell, eliminating the Confederacy's last major port.

The shredding of Confederate logistics continued apace, and Lee's Army of Northern Virginia was helpless to stop it. Grant chose not to undertake any major offensives against Lee or Richmond and Petersburg. Desertion was wearing down enemy numbers through attrition while not risking another bloody battle; so long as Lee remained, however restless, in Richmond, he posed no real threat to Union operations. Lincoln, pleased by the triumphs of Sherman and Thomas, focused on securing the House of Representatives' approval of the Thirteenth Amendment, abolishing slavery throughout the United States.

Complicating that endeavor were signs that Confederate authorities were willing to consider opening the door to a negotiated settlement of the war. Although the Confederacy's prospects seemed dire indeed, Jefferson Davis still held fast to independence. Lincoln had permitted Francis P. Blair, Sr., to visit Richmond with a rather odd proposal that featured an armistice followed by a joint expedition to oust the French from Mexico; Davis responded by allowing three commissioners led by Vice President Alexander H. Stephens to see what

Lincoln was willing to do. The commissioners approached Union lines and met with Grant, who was loathe to send them back without meeting Lincoln. The general cleverly circumvented Lincoln's envoy, Thomas T. Eckert, who informed the president that any proposed meeting was a non-starter because of the commissioners' continued commitment to independence. Lincoln followed Grant's advice, but only after the House had passed the Thirteenth Amendment, and hurried down to Hampton Roads, where he met the Confederate representatives aboard the steamboat *River Queen*.

Nothing came of this encounter, although upon Lincoln's return to Washington, he toyed one final time with a proposal for compensated emancipation, only to have it shot down by members of his cabinet. But the incident may also have raised questions in the president's mind about Grant's acumen in such matters. The Confederate high command, spurred on by a discussion between Confederate general James Longstreet and Butler's replacement as commander of the Army of the James, Edward O. C. Ord, decided to have Lee propose to Grant that the two commanding generals (Lee having been elevated to overall command of Confederate forces in February 1865) met to discuss an array of issues with the hope that such discussions would open the way to an armistice or negotiated settlement.

Grant wired Lincoln asking for instructions: the telegram arrived on the eve of the president's second inauguration. Prodded by Secretary of War Stanton, Lincoln penned a reply sent under Stanton's name that rejected Lee's proposal and reminded Grant of the limited scope of his authority. In handling matters this way, Lincoln (with Stanton's acquiescence) shielded from Grant his own personal reservations, allowing Grant to think that it had been the brusk Stanton who was responsible for the reprimand.

These exchanges revealed that Lincoln and Grant had done little to confer to consider how best to bring the military conflict to an end as so to serve broader policy ends. Grant understood those ends better than Lincoln assumed he did; in turn, Lincoln's willingness to entertain Blair's initial proposal, which had generated these abortive attempts at a negotiated peace, suggested that the president was open to various ways of bringing the war to a close. In turn, Lincoln worried that Grant might be too harsh on the enemy, and he shared such reservations with Secretary of the Navy Gideon Welles. It was left to Grant, however, to take the initiative. Acting upon a comment made by the president's son, Robert T. Lincoln, who had just joined Grant's staff as a captain, Grant invited Lincoln to pay him a visit at headquarters. He decided that it was also time for Sherman to join such a discussion.

The meeting proved valuable as a way for Lincoln to make sure that Grant and Sherman understood his desire for lenient terms of surrender; however, the president committed nothing to paper, trusting to conversation to reveal his position. One speculates whether the generals' reputations had got the better of the chief executive, for both commanders had been thoughtful in dealing with surrenders and capitulations. Perhaps the image of gruff "Unconditional Surrender" Grant and fiery and blunt William T. Sherman was a little too vivid in Lincoln's imagination. In any case, the general understood the gist of Lincoln's message, although a month later Sherman would improvise a peace proposal that went far beyond his authority by claiming that he was simply carrying out Lincoln's wishes, an assertion open to serious question. It would be Grant who understood his boss better. At the same time, the generals impressed upon the president that there was fighting ahead, and it would be up to the Confederate as to how bloody things might get if they decided to make a last stand.

No sooner had these discussions concluded, with Sherman rejoining his command in North Carolina, than the final campaign in Virginia commenced. Union successes forced Lee to evacuate Richmond and Petersburg and head westward: Lincoln visited both cities on the heels of the Confederates' departure. The president shared with Grant his discussions with Confederate representatives who speculated that the Virginia legislature might withdraw the Old Dominion from the Confederacy, adding that such negotiations or rumors thereof would not interfere with military operations. He also carefully monitored his commanders' communications. When Sheridan excitedly concluded his report to Grant about his smashing victory at Sailor's Creek by declaring "If the thing is pressed I think that Lee will surrender," Lincoln telegraphed Grant, "Let the *thing* be pressed."[14]

Lincoln need not have worried. That evening Grant called upon Lee to surrender: two days later Lee did just that, accepting terms that allowed the Confederate to stack arms, disperse, and return home without fear of reprisal so long as they remained law-abiding. It was just the sort of offer that Lincoln desired: as he read the terms, he exclaimed, "Good! ... All right ... Exactly the thing!"[15] Surely he had found the general he had so desperately sought. But their post-Appomattox collaboration proved brief. When the Lincolns ventured to Ford's Theater on the evening of April 14, 1865, observers might have noticed that the officer and his lady who accompanied them were not the Grants. Worried that the First Lady might make a spectacle of herself as she had multiple times over the previous several weeks, the Grants had excused themselves from the theater by claiming that they needed to see their children in New Jersey.

Conclusion

The success of the Lincoln-Grant team is easy to understand. Both men worked together in a unified fashion, sharing the same general strategic vision even as they may have differed over particulars. Over time the communications between the two men improved, especially during Grant's tenure as general in chief. Lincoln was not above nudging his general or in reminding him of what was at stake, and Grant took the hints. Essential to their success was Grant's empathetic awareness of Lincoln's political as well as military concerns and his willingness to accommodate them when possible instead of railing against the restraints thus imposed. If anything, it was his understanding of how to address his superior's concerns that distinguished Grant from his military contemporaries, as well as his own political shrewdness, most evident in dealing with Lincoln's efforts to use intermediaries to investigate him during the Vicksburg campaign and his willingness to express support of administration initiatives, such as black enlistment. Just as Lincoln sometimes played military strategist, Grant played politician, usually with equal (if not greater) skill.

It is well to remember how this relationship evolved over time. It was not always so smooth. Lincoln had reservations and concerns about Grant, fueled by critics who sought Grant's removal. The president, himself prone to inquire about the perspectives of subordinate generals, facilitated such efforts, even if he did not always succumb to them. It was not until the fall of Vicksburg that he became a Grant man; it was not until he reassured himself (with some assistance from Grant) about the general's lack of political ambition that he backed the effort to promoted Grant to lieutenant general and place him in command of the armies of the United States.

Lincoln soon learned that having Grant in charge was a marked improvement over Winfield Scott and especially George McClellan and Henry Halleck, to say nothing of the War Board experiment of 1862. The two men walked together on why to fight the war and how to fight it, eventually accepting emancipation and the destruction of slavery as necessary to the achievement of a meaningful and lasting victory. A shared vision, Lincoln's eventual trust in Grant, and Grant's willingness to accommodate presidential concerns fostered a superior working relationship that saved the republic and crushed the Confederacy.

Notes

1 Horace Porter, *Campaigning with Grant* (New York: Century Company, 1897), 18–19.
2 T. Harry Williams, *Lincoln and His Generals* (New York: Knopf, 1952), 302.
3 John Nicolay and John Hay, *Abraham Lincoln: A History,* 10 vols (New York, The Century Company, 1890), 4:303–4.
4 William T. Sherman to Ellen Ewing Sherman, June 6, 1862, Brooks D. Simpson and Jean V. Berlin, eds., *Sherman's Civil War: Selected Correspondence of William T. Sherman, 1860–65* (Chapel Hill, NC: University of North Carolina Press, 1999), 236; Sherman to Philemon B. Ewing, July 13, 1862, ibid., 253.
5 Simpson, *Ulysses S. Grant,* 215.
6 Simpson, *Ulysses S. Grant,* 215.
7 Ulysses S. Grant to William T. Sherman, April 4, 1864, John Y. Simon, et al., eds., *The Papers of Ulysses S. Grant,* 32 vols. (Carbondale, IL: Southern Illinois University Press, 1967–2012), 10:251–52 (hereafter *PUSG*).
8 Abraham Lincoln to *Ulysses S. Grant,* April 30, 1864, and Grant to Lincoln, May 1, 1864, ibid., 10:380.

9 Simpson, *Ulysses S. Grant*, 341–42.
10 Simpson, *Ulysses S. Grant*, 367–68.
11 Ibid., 369.
12 Ibid., 372–73.
13 William T. Sherman to *Ulysses S. Grant*, November 6, 1864, Simpson and Berlin, *Sherman's Civil War*, 751.
14 Philip H. Sheridan to *Ulysses S. Grant*, April 6, 1865, and Abraham Lincoln to *Ulysses S. Grant*, April 7, 1865, *PUSG*, 14: 358.
15 Brooks D. Simpson, *Let Us Have Peace: Ulysses S. Grant and the Politics of War and Reconstruction, 1861–1868* (Chapel Hill, NC: University of North Carolina Press, 1991), 89.

3

JEFFERSON DAVIS AND ROBERT E. LEE

Steven E. Woodworth

Jefferson Davis and Robert E. Lee enjoyed one of the most successful command relationships in military history. Their collaboration kept Virginia and the southeastern seaboard of the United States in Confederate control through three years of intense Union efforts to subdue the region. When the Confederacy finally tottered to its demise in the spring of 1865, Lee's Virginia was the last remaining militarily viable enclave that national forces overran. Its prolonged, stubborn resistance was partially attributable to the effective collaboration of the Confederate president with his top Virginia general.

The Davis-Lee partnership was not flawless. It could have been better, and it needed to be. The Confederate defeat was not inevitable, nor the unavoidable product of overwhelming Union material and numerical superiority. That the slaveholders' republic finally succumbed may have been partially attributable to the flaws in the command relationship of Lee and Davis and was undoubtedly far more attributable to the far less successful relationships Davis had with his other generals.

The Davis-Lee partnership began on a low-key level, with Davis not yet realizing the asset he had in Lee. Once he discovered Lee's talent, the partnership passed through an exciting but trying phase, as Davis gamely but nervously backed a general whose penchant for risk-taking vastly exceeded his own. This phase reached its crisis in the preparations for the Gettysburg Campaign, which saw Davis continue to support Lee's high-stakes gambling – to a point. Only in this episode did Davis withhold elements of support that had at least some potential to have changed the course of operations. Thereafter, Union opposition-held Lee to the kind of conservative operational decisions Davis was comfortable with, and the partnership ran smoothly and efficiently even as the Confederacy was running down.

DOI: 10.4324/9781003375630-3

Jefferson Davis was born in Kentucky in 1808, the youngest of ten children. His family moved to Wilkinson County, Mississippi, where Davis gained his education in local schools before traveling far from home to study at Transylvania University in Lexington, Kentucky. In 1824, he entered the United States Military Academy and after a West Point career marked by several serious disciplinary infractions, graduated twenty-third among the thirty-three members of the Class of 1828. He served in the 1st Infantry Regiment at frontier posts such as Fort Crawford, in what is now Wisconsin, and resigned in 1835 to take up the life of a Mississippi planter on land south of Vicksburg given him by his older brother.

On the outbreak of the Mexican War, Davis returned to military service, accepting the colonelcy of a volunteer regiment he styled the 1st Mississippi Rifles. At its head, he performed creditably in the Battle of Monterrey, where he suffered a wounded foot, and at Buena Vista, where his performance also drew favorable notice. After the war Davis entered politics, serving in the U.S. House of Representatives, then the Senate, then as secretary of war in the Franklin Pierce administration before returning to the Senate. In February 1861, delegates of the first six seceding states chose him as provisional president of the new government, which they had just formed and christened the Confederate States of America. One year later, while the war was in progress, Davis ran unopposed for election as regular president and, as per the Confederate constitution, won a non-renewable six-year term, which he was unable to complete.

Robert E. Lee was born in 1807 at Stratford Hall Plantation, in Westmoreland County, Virginia. Though the scion of generations of tidewater gentry, Lee was also the son of a father whose many episodes of poor judgment and lack of self-control got him frequently in trouble, sometimes in jail, and head over heels in debt. He died when Robert was eleven years old, leaving the family financially straightened and often dependent on the charity of relatives. Young Robert turned out to be everything his father was not: wise, disciplined, and devoted to duty. Appointed to West Point in 1825, Lee excelled as a cadet, earning not a single demerit during his four-year tenure and graduating second overall among the forty-five members of the class of 1829. As was standard procedure in the army, the top cohort of cadets went to the Corps of Engineers, and there Lee served for most of his career, working on army engineering projects from the waters of the Chesapeake to those of the Mississippi River, while rising to the rank of captain.

The Mexican War revealed an additional dimension of Lee's talents. His assignment was as a member of a group of engineer officers attached to the staff of Winfield Scott during that general's advance from Vera Cruz to Mexico City. Lee was not the ranking engineer officer, but he clearly became the most important, scouting terrain and advising Scott on the best ways to use the maneuver to gain decisive advantages over the defending army of General

Antonio Lopez de Santa Anna. Lee was both brilliant and tireless in guiding Scott's army to victory from Vera Cruz, through Cero Gordo and several other battles, to the storming of Mexico City itself. For his services in Mexico, Lee received three brevet promotions, raising him to the honorary rank of colonel.

When the war ended, Lee went back to duty in his regular rank as captain of engineers, working on forts, harbors, and maps. In 1852, he was tapped for the post of superintendent of the U.S. Military Academy, a job in those days typically reserved for engineer officers. In 1855, Lee received a highly prized promotion and assignment as lieutenant colonel of the newly organized 2nd Cavalry Regiment. Lee served with his new regiment in Texas until 1857 when he took a leave of absence from the army to manage Arlington, the plantation of his late father-in-law George Washington Park Custis, who had named Lee executor of his will and the highly complicated and encumbered estate he left behind. The secession crisis brought Lee promotion to colonel of the 1st Cavalry, which he accepted, and then the offer of a major general's commission and command of United States forces defending the capital, which he declined to take service with the state of Virginia and eventually the Confederacy.

Up to this point in their lives, the interaction between Davis and Lee had remained limited but positive. Though contemporaries for three years at West Point, they seem to have interacted little, if at all, nor in the regular Army during Davis's seven years of service. Contact during the Mexican War was similarly lacking, as Davis served in the army of Zachary Taylor at Monterrey and Buena Vista while Lee served under Winfield Scott in the Mexico City Campaign. When in 1849 Cuban revolutionary Narcisso López approached Davis with an offer of $100,000 and a coffee plantation for taking the military leadership of an expedition to overthrow Spanish rule in Pearl of the Antilles, Davis declined and recommended López try Lee instead. The Virginian also declined. Davis's recommendation probably rested on Lee's reputation, which was widely known in the army. Lee's assignment to the 2nd Cavalry represented a further compliment from Davis, who was then secretary of war.

For all that, the Civil War Davis-Lee relationship almost got off to a rough start. Around the beginning of May 1861, while Lee was commanding general of the Virginia army and Virginia, though having asserted its secession from the United States, was still in an ambiguous relationship with the Confederate States, Davis, still in the original Confederate capital of Montgomery, Alabama, and eager for a thorough briefing on the military situation in the Old Dominion, telegraphed Lee, offering commissions as brigadier general in the Confederate States Army, the highest rank it then possessed, to both Lee and his junior within the Virginia army, Joseph E. Johnston. Davis also suggested in his telegram that it would be nice to meet Lee, or Johnston, or both of them for a conference in Montgomery. Lee responded with telegraphic terseness that Johnston had recently reported himself sick, that he himself was busy organizing the Virginia forces, and that Davis could find out all he wanted to know from Virginia politician Robert M. T. Hunter, then on the way to Montgomery. "My commission in Virginia satisfactory to me," Lee concluded.[1]

Davis did not usually take such rebuffs well, but this time he let it pass. He soon nominated Lee as a Confederate brigadier general anyway, and later that month, once Virginia had begun the process of joining the Confederacy and the Confederacy had moved its capital to Richmond, Davis arrived there and got the conference he wanted with Lee. As the Virginia army was subsumed into the Confederate, Davis retained Lee in nominal overall command of the defense of Virginia, but as would become typical of Davis, the president exercised as least as much command in the state as Lee did. Lee functioned to some degree as Davis's assistant.[2] The role, though a valuable one to Davis and the Confederacy, was not entirely satisfactory to Lee, who wrote his wife that he "should like to retire to private life" but would continue in service for the sake of Virginia.[3]

Late in the first summer of the war, Davis named Lee as one of the Confederacy's first five full generals, outranked only by Adjutant and Inspector General Samuel Cooper, whose appointment was to strictly staff rank, and by Albert Sidney Johnston, both of whom had outranked Lee in the Old Army. Ranking below Lee on the full-general list were Joseph E. Johnston and Pierre G. T. Beauregard, both of whom had stood behind Lee in line rank within the previous service, though the former had briefly jumped ahead of him in a staff position not long before secession. Since both Johnstons, Lee, and Beauregard held line commands in the Confederate service, their relative ranks in that army were, as per the act of the Confederate congress, reflective of their relative line ranks in the U.S. Army.

Shortly thereafter Davis dispatched Lee to try to retrieve the situation in the northwestern counties of Virginia, where Confederate forces had fared badly for a number of reasons, among them, the relatively high quality of the Union opposition, the low quality of the Confederate generals, and the fact that the majority of the local populace did not want to secede from the United States. Davis hoped Lee could help with those sub-standard Confederate generals. Lee, the president imagined, could reinvigorate Confederate command in the region through "his military skill and deserved influence over men."[4] Sending a general to exercise command by means of influence was an idea doomed to failure from the outset. On a mission that made him more of an inspector and advisor than a commander, Lee was tentative in his orders. He did have the military skill, but it was not on display in this campaign, and though he deserved to have influence, he seemed to have none with the several lower-ranking Confederate generals in the region whose incompetence was exceeded only by their determination to gain all available military glory for themselves, even if by means of undercutting and insuring the failure of their rivals wearing the same uniform. As a result, the mid-September Battle of Cheat Mountain, the first Civil War clash more or less under Lee's direct command, was a fiasco. Southern newspapers barbecued Lee.

Lee returned to Richmond in November, and within days Davis dispatched him on another fire-brigade expedition, this time to take command (at least his orders were clear about that this time) of the Confederate Department of South Carolina, Georgia, and Florida, an area in which Union amphibious forces had recently scored some small but disturbing successes. By this time Lee's public reputation in the Confederacy had suffered to the point that Davis felt the need to write a letter to the governor of South Carolina, assuring him of Lee's military ability and devotion to the Confederacy.[5]

The coastal assignment did nothing to raise Lee's standing with the southern public. He had some good ideas, but nothing could change the fact of Union naval supremacy or give the Southern people inspiring victories in the face of it. As the military situation in Virginia steadily grew more threatening over the winter of 1862, Davis began to consider calling Lee back to his duties in Richmond to assist him in the direction of the war from there.[6] He did so on March 2. "If circumstances will, in your judgment, warrant your leaving," Davis telegraphed Lee in Savannah, "I wish to see you here with the least delay."[7] Lee was on the train the following evening and back in Richmond within a few days. On March 13, Davis made Lee's assignment formal in an order issued by the Secretary of War through the Adjutant and Inspector General's office: "General Robert E. Lee is assigned to duty at the seat of government, and, under the direction of the President, is charged with the conduct of military operations in the armies of the Confederacy."[8]

The situation continued to become more alarming that month, as Union shipping began to ply the waters around the Federal enclave at Fort Monroe, portending the waterborne movement of troops and probably a major Union operation somewhere along the coast. On March 21 Lee told Davis he believed North Carolina was the target, and the following day, Davis ordered Lee there. Lee did not like the order, preferring to stay in Richmond and push reinforcements to the threatened coast but dutifully prepared to go.[9]

He need not have feared that Davis would leave him there. No sooner had Lee arrived in the Tarheel State than the president replaced him with Major General Theophilus Hoimes, a native of North Carolina, and brought Lee back to Richmond. He was much needed there as it was becoming increasingly clear the city itself was the target of a major Union advance from Fort Monroe, a movement that would probably proceed up the peninsula between the estuaries of the York and James rivers. Davis used Lee to write dispatches to Joseph Johnston, commander of the Confederacy's main army in Virginia. In the closing days of March, Lee handled the president's correspondence in a hurried exchange regarding the possibility of bringing most of Johnston's army to the peninsula to confront the growing but still partial Union concentration and destroy it. In the end, nothing came of the idea. Confederate peninsula commander John B. Magruder was eager, and Johnston was game, but Davis drew back, unwilling to risk concentrating the force needed for the attack.[10]

Tensions rose in the Confederate high command as George McClellan's Union army proceeded up the peninsula. Ordered by Davis to march his army down from the Rappahannock to block McClellan, Johnston advocated concentrating not only his force and Magruder's but all Confederate troops that could deploy to Richmond within the next few weeks and await the advance of the Union general on the outskirts of the Confederate capital, whose arrival before Richmond at the head of his army would trigger a great showdown battle. The result, Johnston assured Davis in a meeting at the Brockenbrough Mansion in Richmond early on the morning of Monday, April 14, would be a great Confederate victory that would decide not only the campaign but also the war.[11] Davis had great faith in Johnston, but the idea of staking the Confederacy's survival on the outcome of a single battle at the gates of Richmond gave the president pause. He would have to think about this more. Much more. So, he told Johnston to come back at ten o'clock that morning to discuss the question with him, Lee, and Secretary of War George W. Randolph. Johnston asked to bring along his two top lieutenants, major generals Gustavus W. Smith and James Longstreet, and Davis agreed.[12]

The five men arrived at the Brockenbrough Mansion at the appointed hour, were ushered into Davis's office, and began a lengthy discussion. Smith presented a written paper agreeing with Johnston's plan to abandon the peninsula and fight a decisive battle in front of Richmond. Randolph mentioned the importance of holding the peninsula to retain control of the Gosport Navy Yard at Norfolk. Longstreet opined that McClellan would be slow. Thereafter the discussion developed into a debate, at times "very heated," between Johnston and Lee, and it went on all afternoon. After a one-hour recess at 6:00 p.m., the conference resumed with unabated intensity. Lee continued to argue that the peninsula should be held. It was a strong defensive position, he asserted, and by fighting for it the Confederates could buy time, which he thought would allow the recruitment of additional troops. He disparaged the idea of a great battle before Richmond because it would strip the southern coast of its defenders and allow the Federals to approach close to the Confederate capital. Defend, entrench, delay, and maintain the dispersion of Confederate forces. It was in some ways just what might have been expected from a general whom southern newspapers had for months been savaging as "Granny Lee" and "the King of Spades."

Finally, at 1:00 a.m. Davis concluded the conference by announcing that the Confederacy would adopt Lee's program of defending the peninsula.[13] The president believed he had in Johnston a daring commander almost too ready to roll the dice of battle with all staked on the outcome. Yet Davis was, at length, more comfortable with the strategy of the brainy, now desk-bound engineer officer, Lee, a policy that appeared aimed at minimizing risks, buying time, and hoping something would turn up.

Johnston later wrote that he felt somewhat reconciled "to the necessity of obeying the president's order" by his "belief that events on the Peninsula would soon compel the Confederate Government to adopt my method of opposing the Federal army."[14] Indeed, Johnston's own decisions over the six weeks that followed contributed materially to the events that caused that situation. As McClellan's army slowly advanced, Johnston retreated without accepting battle until by late May he had reached the outskirts of Richmond itself, the very ground on which he had, in early April, proposed to fight the decisive battle of the war. Not yet having been reinforced to the degree he thought necessary, Johnston had to be pressured by Davis into giving battle at Seven Pines (Fair Oaks) on May 31. As miscues and poor communication delayed the Confederate attack, Davis and Lee rode out to Johnston's headquarters. Johnston just missed them – some said his departure was a deliberate response to the president's – and rode to the front to survey and possibly rectify the situation. Struck twice in quick succession by a Minie ball and a shell fragment, Johnston was carried to the rear, gravely wounded.

The Confederacy's largest army, which Johnston had recently begun calling "The Army of Northern Virginia," slept on its arms that night, in contact with the enemy and with its own capital in the immediate rear. As Davis and Lee rode the short distance back into Richmond, Davis told the general he was giving him command of the Army of Northern Virginia. There actually was little choice. The army's second-in-command, Gustavus Smith, had been singularly unimpressive and had seemed confused when Davis talked with him on the battlefield shortly after Johnston's wounding. He was not a likely successor. The third-ranking general, James Longstreet, had turned in a singularly bad performance that day, being the chief culprit in the hours-long delay of the attack, and Davis would hardly have thought of giving the army to so junior a commander anyway. No other officer within a day's ride of the army possessed anything like the rank and experience. It was not that Davis did not trust Lee, but that he valued him in his advisory role in Richmond and thought him best suited for that duty. As the president mentioned on more than one occasion, only the extreme necessity of the hour moved him to spare Lee from the valuable tasks he was performing at the capital.

Lee spent the next three and a half weeks getting his army in hand and preparing for a major offensive aimed at driving McClellan away from Richmond and, if possible, trapping and destroying the Army of the Potomac. If Davis had ever thought of Lee as a bookish officer, averse to risks and best suited to the command of a desk, that idea was now dispelled. In mid-June, Colonel Joseph C. Ives of the president's military staff expressed to a fellow officer what was undoubtedly becoming well known to Davis and those around him. While riding the lines outside Richmond, Ives encountered fellow Old

Army Engineer, Edward Porter Alexander, now also in Confederate service. The conversation turned to the Army of Northern Virginia's new commander. Alexander had doubts. "We are here fortifying our lines," he told Ives, "but apparently leaving the enemy all the time he needs to accumulate his superior forces, and then to move on us in the way he thinks best. Has General Lee the audacity that is going to be required for our inferior force to meet the enemy's superior force – to take the aggressive, and to run risks and stand chances?" Ives drew up in the middle of the road. "Alexander," he said, "if there is one man in either army, Confederate or Federal, head and shoulders above every other in audacity, it is General Lee! His name might be Audacity. He will take more desperate chances and take them quicker than any other general in this country, North or South: and you will live to see it, too."[15] What Ives knew and thought, Davis probably did as well.

Davis's altered perception of Lee probably stemmed from what he was learning of the general's plans for the coming offensive. Lee briefed Davis on his plans. He would leave a third of his army on the south bank of the Chickahominy with its back to Richmond and the bulk of McClellan's force directly in front. With the other two-thirds, including Stonewall Jackson's small army hastily brought east from the Shenandoah Valley, Lee would fall on the single Union corps on the north bank of the Chickahominy, where he would overwhelm McClellan's vulnerable northern flank and seize the railroad carrying supplies to the Army of the Potomac from the banks of the Pamunkey River. Then he would trap and destroy the Army of the Potomac.

Davis had his doubts. During the Pierce administration in the 1850s, Davis had been secretary of war and had held a favorable opinion of the rising young officer George McClellan. If "McClellan was the man I took him for," Davis later recalled himself telling Lee, "as soon as he found that the bulk of our army was on the north side of the Chickahominy, he would not stop to try conclusions with it there, but would immediately move upon his objective point, the city of Richmond," overrunning the thin force Lee proposed to place in his path. "If, on the other hand, he should behave like an engineer officer, and deem it his first duty to protect his line of communication," Davis added, the plan "would be a success."[16] McClellan had been an engineer officer in the Old Army. So had Lee. The general replied that he "did not know that engineer officers were more likely than others to make such mistakes," but then added, "If you will hold him as long as you can at the intrenchment, and then fall back on the detached works around the city, I will be upon the enemy's heels before he gets there."[17]

The exchange demonstrates Lee at two of his most valuable traits in working with Davis. These were self-control and an awareness of how to please the president. Davis's remark about the doubtful chances that McClellan would "behave like an engineer officer" was, whether intentionally or not (the latter seems more likely), an insult to Lee. The latter, whose closest staff officers were emphatic in describing him as someone who could have a quick temper, at first responded with a prickly remark of his own. Then, exercising self-control, he stopped and instead said something well-calculated to win Davis's support. The president had originally wanted to be the Confederacy's chief general rather than its chief of state. He considered himself an authority on military matters and liked to be recognized as such. By speaking as if Davis was actually going to be exercising field command over the forces directly in front of Richmond, Lee pleased the president and improved his impression of the plan.

Davis approved Lee's audacious program, but he remained nervous. In a June 21 letter to his wife, the president wrote of the coming offensive, "The stake is too high to permit the pulse to keep its even beat."[18] Lee, it turned out, was more of a risk-taker than Johnston and more than Davis was comfortable with. The president was willing to back Lee's bold plans, though with an elevated pulse rate.

On June 26, Lee put his plan into operation and the results came to be known as the Seven Days' Campaign. It was not the complete success for which Lee had hoped, but it nevertheless accomplished much. McClellan turned out to be anything but the man Secretary of War Davis had taken him to be in the 1850s and instead behaved like Davis's negative stereotype of an engineer officer. Rather than driving directly for Richmond while Lee struck at his flank and supply line, McClellan gave up his offensive, abandoned his supply line to the Pamunkey, and began a twenty-five-mile retreat southeastward to Harrison's Landing on the James River, where he could be supplied by water and enjoy the support of Navy gunboats.

Lee failed to cut off McClellan's retreat and trap the Army of the Potomac. Stonewall Jackson turned in an uncharacteristically sluggish performance. Confederate staff work proved wanting, and the inevitable friction of an army in battle proved more than Lee could overcome. Confederate casualties outnumbered those of the Army of the Potomac. Still, the campaign pushed the Federals back from Richmond and dealt a heavy blow to northern morale while delivering a corresponding boost to the Confederacy. Of equal importance, the campaign greatly increased Davis's confidence in Lee.

Through the week of fighting only a few miles from his office, Davis repeatedly proved unable to resist the temptation to ride out and at least view the Confederate attacks. Lee seemed to suspect the president might indulge his well-known penchant for detail and attempt to take a hand in directing operations. The general displayed a corresponding determination to keep Davis out of any role in direct supervision of the army's operations. Each time he caught the president on the battlefield, Lee lost no time in shooing him off, insisting that any ground potentially within range of the enemy's guns was far too dangerous and no place for the chief executive. Lee avoided any direct clash with the president by making each incident a question of Davis's safety.

The Seven Days' fighting ended on July 1, and the subsequent lull in operations proved short-lived. By July 13 Davis, Lee, Jackson, and several other generals were meeting at the Brockenbrough Mansion to discuss a new Union threat, this one posed by an army under the command of Major General John Pope advancing south through the Virginia Piedmont along the line of the Virginia Central Railroad. While this force drew steadily closer to Richmond, McClellan's Army of the Potomac remained encamped only thirty miles or so downstream from the Confederate capital on the banks of the James. Lee dispatched Jackson with one wing of the army to Gordonville to watch Pope. Over the weeks that followed, it became increasingly clear that McClellan was going to undertake no further offensive action from his base at Harrison's Landing, and on August 15, Lee left with substantial additional forces to join Jackson in confronting the enemy in Piedmont.[19]

On learning a few days later that McClellan had withdrawn his army from the peninsula, Lee wrote Davis a string of dispatches urging, sometimes in almost peremptory terms, the immediate redeployment of nearly all the remaining troops guarding Richmond to join Lee's new offensive aimed not just at repelling Pope but trapping and destroying his army. Again, the general was taking considerable risks in hopes of a major success. Still, Lee was careful to maintain his good relationship with Davis, concluding in one letter, "I beg you will excuse my troubling you with my opinions and especially these details, but your kindness has led you to receive them without objection so often that I know I am tempted to trespass."[20]

Lee's gamble to destroy Pope was not in line with Davis's instincts. In the case of one division that Lee had directly ordered to join him, the general's subsequent dispatch notifying Davis of the move crossed one from the president informing Lee that the division he needed the division to guard Richmond and cover the approach route from Hanover Junction. In response to Lee's repeated calls for troops, Davis wrote to explain that such shifts of manpower left the capital disturbingly exposed. Davis did not like to wager Richmond, but he was willing to bet on Lee. "Confidence in you," he wrote to Lee, "overcomes the view which would otherwise be taken of the exposed condition of Richmond, and the troops retained for the defense of the capital are surrendered to you on a renewed request."[21] Lee thus had all the forces he had requested as he moved against Pope in what became the Second Bull Run Campaign. The result was the dramatic victory culminating on August 30.

After pursuing Pope's defeated army as far as Chantilly, scarcely more than twenty-one miles from the White House, Lee paused and then on September 3 wrote a dispatch to Davis stating, "The present seems to be the most propitious time since the commencement of the war for the Confederate Army to enter Maryland." The Army of Northern Virginia was poorly equipped and much worn down by a spring and summer of hard marching and harder fighting, Lee admitted, and the move was risky, but he believed it just might work and, anyway, the Confederacy could not afford to give up the initiative. So, unless Davis ordered otherwise, Lee would take the army across the Potomac.[22]

Any such order from Davis would have had to have tracked Lee down in Maryland, because leading elements of the Army of Northern Virginia began to cross the Potomac at Leesburg on September 4, and Lee himself crossed two days later.

Davis responded to Lee's letter not by calling off the invasion but rather by expressing his intention to join Lee in person.[23] The president might have been thinking of exercising a moderating influence on Lee's generalship but definitely had a view to conducting peace negotiations with a chastened Lincoln after Lee's army had once again soundly defeated the Army of the Potomac, this time on the north side of the Potomac. Davis immediately started on his proposed journey and had reached as far as the Rapidan River, approximately seventy miles northwest of Richmond before sending Lee a dispatch notifying the general of his approach.

In fact, Lee was thinking along similar lines, at least as concerned the desirability of taking this opportunity of summoning Lincoln to the negotiating table. On September 8, not yet having received Davis's dispatch about coming north, Lee wrote to the president, "The present position of affairs, in my opinion, places it in the power of the Government of the Confederate States to propose with propriety to that of the United States the recognition of our independence." He went on to explain that with his army in Maryland, the Confederacy would be negotiating from a position of strength and that if Lincoln rejected their demands, voters might punish the Republican Party in the elections that fall.[24]

However, Lee was not at all favorable to the idea of Davis joining him and the Army of Northern Virginia in Maryland, and he lost no time in trying to discourage the plan. "I have just received your letter of the 7th instant, from Rapidan," Lee wrote on September 9, "informing me of your intention to come on to Leesburg." Lee said he would "feel the greatest satisfaction in having an interview" with Davis and "consulting upon all subjects of interest," but he believed the route was not safe. He dispatched his aide-de-camp Major Walter H. Taylor to travel back to meet the president, explain to him "the difficulties and dangers of the journey," and, one suspects, see to it that the president did not continue on to Army of Northern Virginia.[25] Lee no doubt did feel genuine concern for the president's safety, but it seems highly likely that he was even more concerned to avoid a situation in which Davis would make the army's operational decisions, or by a two-headed monster composed of Lee with Davis looking over his shoulder and occasionally giving contrary input.

On receipt of Lee's dispatch advising him not to move through the potentially hostile-control countryside between himself and the Army of Northern Virginia, Davis turned around and returned to Richmond.[26] Once again Davis had deferred to Lee in allowing him to keep the Army of Northern in Maryland beyond the first week, when Davis might reasonably have ordered its recall, and in leaving Lee to direct the campaign without presidential interference.

The Maryland Campaign did not turn out as well as the Second Bull Run Campaign. Accepting battle from a defensive position behind Antietam Creek, and with the Potomac at his back barring speedy egress, Lee took an extreme risk but fought the Army of the Potomac, once again commanded by McClellan, to a tactical draw. Yet the battle placed him in a strategic position from which he had no option but to retreat back into Virginia.

A lull in operations followed. The Army of Northern Virginia was worn to a frazzle. The Army of the Potomac was also fatigued, and McClellan, who now had the initiative, pursued a characteristically slow campaign in the Virginia Piedmont, which Lee had no difficulty in checking without bringing on a battle. Thereafter Lincoln replaced McClellan with Major General Ambrose Burnside, who naturally needed time to get his army in hand. During this period, Davis cooperated with Lee in improving the army's officer corps system of officer selection and promotion. Davis could and should have also promoted passage of a bill, introduced that fall in the Confederate congress, to provide for a more adequate number of staff officers for army commanders, but the general showed little interest in developing a larger and more effective staff. In December, Lee easily repulsed Burnside at Fredericksburg. The following month, the Union general put his army in motion toward the Rapidan crossings, putting a brief scare into the Confederate high command, but Burnside's plans were wrecked by a rainy spell that turned the roads to quagmires and put a stop to his offensive before any of his troops had crossed to the Confederate side. Thereafter, Lincoln sacked Burnside in favor of Major General Joseph Hooker.

Through the late winter and early spring of 1863, Davis, while suffering poor health due to facial neuralgia and possibly other complaints, became increasingly concerned about Union threats along the North Carolina coast and in the region west of the Appalachians. His suggestions to Lee that it might be appropriate to transfer a portion of the latter's troops to one or both of the threatened sectors received vigorous counterarguments. It would be better, Lee believed, to keep the Army of Northern Virginia intact and as powerful as possible. He did agree to the temporary transfer of two divisions to North Carolina, where they could assuage Davis's concerns and ease the Army of Northern Virginia's supply problems, but he would want them back first thing in the spring.[27]

In fact, Lee believed the Confederacy's best chance for victory lay in winning victories in major battles fought close to Washington and/or north of the Potomac before the Army of the Potomac could launch its spring offensive. Responding to Davis's renewed pleas to detach troops for service in the West, Lee wrote in mid-April, "I think it all-important that we should assume the aggressive by the 1st of May." If he could do that, Lee suggested, it would allow him to sweep the Federals out of the Shenandoah Valley and force the Army of the Potomac to fall back to the north side of its namesake river.[28] In fact, early in March, Lee had instructed topographical engineer Jedediah Hotchkiss to make a map of the Shenandoah Valley but extend its coverage northward across the Potomac and up the Cumberland Valley to Harrisburg, then eastward across the Susquehanna to Philadelphia. Lee's purpose was obvious. He directed Hotchkiss the project be "kept a profound secret." In fact, he failed to mention the map to Davis.[29] He did, however, continue to reassure the president that the best way to relieve pressure on North Carolina and the Confederacy's western regions would be the Army of Northern Virginia's advance.[30]

Before that could happen, Hooker advanced with the Army of the Potomac. The result was the Battle of Chancellorsville, perhaps Lee's most dramatic and impressive victory, achieved with an army still weakened by the detachment of the two divisions still deployed in North Carolina. It cost him his most intrepid lieutenant general, Stonewall Jackson, a victim of American history's most famous friendly fire incident.

With the battle over, Davis and Lee returned to the pattern that had of late become familiar. Davis, still spending most of his time sick in bed, dictated dispatches to Lee arguing that it would be a good idea to detach troops from the Army of Northern Virginia in hopes of retrieving Confederate fortunes in the West, where Grant was even then marching through the interior of Mississippi to approach Vicksburg from the rear.

Lee again responded that, outnumbered as he was, he needed all the troops he had and then some. Troops should, he argued, be removed from the southern coast and sent to reinforce the Army of Northern Virginia. His troops could not reach Mississippi in time to save it, and the summer sickly season of the Deep South would soon accomplish that on its own. Davis came around to Lee's views.[31] He invited Lee to visit Richmond for further discussions, and the general, though not in the best of health lately, came down to the capital and met with Davis, who himself was still frail and had only just returned to his desk after weeks confined to bed. Their May 14 discussion led to an agreement that Pickett's division, one of the two of Lee's that had spent the winter and early spring in North Carolina, should rejoin the Army of Northern Virginia rather than heading west to Vicksburg. Three of Pickett's five brigades passed through Richmond that day on their way to the camps along the Rapidan.[32]

Later that day, Davis and Lee met with the full cabinet. Lee presented his plan for an invasion of the North, laying special emphasis on the need and opportunity for seizing supplies during the operation. Secretary of State James A. Seddon had previously favored sending a contingent of Lee's troops west, but it was Postmaster General John H. Reagan, of Texas, who championed the cause in this meeting. He suggested Lee feint toward the Potomac and then "detach 25,000 or 30,000 of his army to be sent to reinforce General Pemberton." Someone objected that the Shenandoah Valley would be lost. Reagan said they could still hold Richmond and that was the main thing. Would not victory north of the Potomac force Grant to abandon Vicksburg? No, Reagan insisted, Grant would hold. Yet no one else supported him, so he gave up. The conference continued for a considerable time and finally concluded: "that General Lee should cross the Potomac and put himself in a position to threaten Washington, Baltimore, and Philadelphia."[33]

The next fortnight brought more bad news from the West. By May 26 Pemberton had for a week been besieged inside the Vicksburg defenses, and the outlook was growing worse by the day. On that day a War Department clerk noted that the cabinet was in closed-door session "nearly all day."[34] Probably in response to political pressure, Davis had requested its members to meet "to consider the whole question of the campaign of 1863."[35] Davis defended the previous decision to authorize Lee's foray into the North, arguing that the combined forces of Pemberton and Joseph E. Johnston in Mississippi ought to be enough to deal with the threat there. The result of the day-long conference was a ratification of the cabinet's previous decision. Lee's offensive was still on.[36]

In the weeks leading up to Lee's departure from the Rapidan and Rappahannock, Davis supported the general in the reorganization of the Army of Northern Virginia from two corps to three and made such promotions of generals as Lee requested. He was, he assured Lee, "glad to second your wishes, confiding, as I always do, as well in your judgment as in your information."[37]

But Davis did not support Lee in the matter of reinforcing the Army of Northern Virginia for what Lee envisaged as its supreme operation. Lee wanted four brigades that were presently in North Carolina. Since that state was within Lee's area of command, he sent orders to the local commander, Major General Daniel Harvey Hill, to send the troops. Hill refused, stating that he could not be responsible for defending North Carolina without all four of the brigades, three of which were component units of the Army of Northern Virginia temporarily sent down to North Carolina the previous autumn. When a renewed peremptory order met further defiance, Lee referred the matter to Davis. Rather than force Hill to act as if he were a soldier, obey the order, Davis entered into a time-consuming correspondence with Hill about what strength was truly necessary for the defense of North Carolina. In the end, Lee received none of the four veteran brigades and as compensation received a single brigade of newly recruited Mississippi troops.[38]

The exchange of dispatches, with Lee constantly pleading for the missing troops, continued until it became too late for the lost brigade to catch up with the northward marching Army of Northern Virginia, Lee suggested that General Pierre G. T. Beauregard, commanding in South Carolina and Georgia, be brought up into northern Virginia with such troops as he could spare from his department plus "a part, at least, of the troops in North Carolina," to form a shadow army that would hover in the vicinity of Culpeper Court House, "threatening Washington" and thus distracting Union attention from Lee's advance into Pennsylvania. Throughout the days before Gettysburg cut short his northern foray, Lee continued to insist that "an army, even in effigy, under General Beauregard at Culpeper Court House" would secure Richmond and weaken the Union forces Lee would have to meet north of the Potomac. Davis did not act.[39]

So, Lee and his army marched to Gettysburg and defeat and returned again to Virginia, where the survivors were back in their accustomed positions after scarcely more than a month's absence. Three weeks later, on August 8, Lee wrote to Davis requesting to be relieved as commander of the Army of Northern Virginia. "The general remedy for want of success in a military commander is his removal," Lee wrote. "This is natural, and in many instances proper." If he had lost the "confidence of his troops, disaster must sooner or later come. I have been prompted by these reflections more than once since my return from Pennsylvania to propose to your excellency the propriety of selecting another commander for this army." Neither the troops nor the officers of the army had expressed any lack of confidence in him, but he had "seen and heard of expressions of discontent in public journals" and had to assume those feelings were represented within the ranks as well. "I, therefore, in all sincerity request your excellency to take measures to supply my place." He did not despair of Confederate victory. "Our people," Lee wrote, "have only to be true and united, to bear manfully the misfortunes incident to war, and all will come right in the end."[40]

Davis responded promptly. "I am glad that you concur so entirely with me as to the want of our country in this trying hour," the president wrote. He was confident that "our people will exhibit that fortitude which we agree in believing is alone needful to secure ultimate success." But Davis did not agree that the army had lost confidence in Lee or that he could find a better general. The press was vexing, Davis admitted, but not to be taken seriously. Designing men bent it to the service of their ambition or venality. "But suppose, my dear friend, that I were to admit, with all their implications, the points which you present, where am I to find that new commander who is to possess the great ability which you believe to be required? ... To ask me to substitute you by someone in my judgment more fit to command, or who would possess more of the confidence of the army, or of the reflecting men of the country, is to demand an impossibility."[41]

Lee would stay, and Davis would support him staunchly until the end. Yet this summer marked a change in the nature of their partnership. Davis had always been more comfortable with an approach to the war that emphasized steadfast endurance. He was as eager as any other southerner to strike blows at their enemies, but he did not share Lee's seemingly instinctive urge to take large risks to go for the enemy's throat, even if it meant staking all on the results of a single campaign. If for Lee, the Confederacy could lose the war by not winning, for Davis, it could win the war by not losing. Now the president seemed quietly relieved that Lee had come around to his view that "our people have only to be true and united, to bear manfully the misfortunes incident to war, and all will come right in the end." Davis had always thought so.

Their partnership during the twenty months of war that were yet to come was to be different than it had been during the fourteen months that had passed since Davis had placed Lee in command of the Confederacy's largest army. No longer would a daring Lee be watched anxiously by a nervous but supportive president who would himself not have chosen an audacious strategy but knew that in Lee he had a general with few equals. That being the case, Davis willingly backed Lee's gambles, with clenched teeth perhaps, almost every time the general raised the stakes.

Despite Lee's profession of confidence that the Confederate people could win the war by tenacity alone, Lee was not going to stop being the kind of general he was, a general who looked for opportunities to score a decisive offensive victory. That the last twenty months of the war saw no more daring ventures after the pattern of the Maryland and Gettysburg campaigns was not the result of the losses suffered at Gettysburg but rather of the opposition against which Lee henceforth found himself. Meade was good enough to parry Lee's thrust in the Bristoe Station Campaign in the fall of 1863. Grant was good enough to deny Lee any opportunity of launching a daring foray throughout the rest of the war, apart from the partial one represented by Jubal Early's unsuccessful Maryland raid.

Thus, Lee fought on the defensive during 1864 and 1865, and as he did so, Davis supported him constantly and well. He made sure Lee's army received every replacement soldier the Confederacy could afford, reinforcing the Army of Northern Virginia to the point that by the time of the Battle of Cold Harbor, Lee's heavy losses from the first two battles of the Overland Campaign had largely been made good. Thereafter Davis continued to give Lee everything he asked that was within the Confederacy's resources. When prodded by Lee in January 1865, Davis, who was notoriously loyal to old friends, finally sacked his crony Confederate Commissary General Lucius Northrup and replaced him with a more competent officer. The following month, when Lee recommended it, Davis backed the shocking step of advocating that the Confederacy turn its slaves into soldiers. The bill passed the Confederate Congress, and Davis signed it, but the war ended before the Confederate army issued weapons to the two companies of newly freed slaves it had by then recruited. Throughout the final twenty months of the war, Lee's operations never again gave Davis the disquiet they had in the summers of 1862 and 1863, and the partnership operated smoothly.

Conclusion

The Davis-Lee partnership was one of the most successful in military history, but it was not perfect. Early in the war, it took thirteen months, plus the force of circumstances, to convince Davis that Lee was an excellent army commander. During the next fourteen months, Lee compiled a record of astonishing success that made him a major figure in military history and made the prospect of Confederate victory seem within reach. During that period, Davis struggled to overcome his qualms about the gambles Lee took, but wisely recognizing the enormous asset Lee was. Davis set aside his reservations and usually backed Lee to the hilt. The exception, and perhaps the one great stumble in the partnership, was Davis's failure to reinforce Lee to the greatest extent possible on the eve of the Gettysburg Campaign. The Army of Northern Virginia could and should have marched north with at least four additional brigades of veteran infantry. Whether that would have changed the outcome of the battle can well be doubted – the war much more so – but it was the only significant occasion in the war when Davis failed to make the most of the great general providence had given him.

Notes

1 Lee to Davis, May 7, 1861, in Clifford Dowdey and Louis H. Manarin, eds., *The Wartime Papers of R. E. Lee* (New York, 1961), 21.
2 Jefferson Davis, *The Rise and Fall of the Confederate Government*, 2 vols. (New York, 1881), 1:309.
3 Lee to wife, June 9, 1861, in Dowdy and Manarin, *Wartime Papers*, 46.
4 Davis, *Rise and Fall*, 1:434.
5 Ibid., 1:436.
6 Steven Harvey Newton, *Joseph E. Johnston and the Defense of Richmond* (Ann Arbor, MI, 1991), 79–80, 84–85.
7 Davis to Lee, March 2, 1862, *Official Records (OR)*, 6:400.
8 General Orders No. 14, Adjutant and Inspector General's Office, March 13, 1862, *OR*, 5:1099.
9 Lee to Davis, March 21, 1862, OR 51, pt. 2, p. 512; Lee to his wife, March 22, 1861, in Dowdey and Manarin, *Wartime Papers*, 133–34.
10 Magruder to Lee, March 21, 1862, Lee to Johnston, March 25 and 28, 1862, Johnston to Lee, March 26 and 27, Lee to Johnston, March 27 and 28, *OR*, 11, pt. 3, pp. 389–90, 397, 400–401, 405–6, 408–9.
11 Joseph Eggleston Johnson, Narrative of Military Operations, Directed, During the Late War Between the States (New York: D. Appleton and Company, 1874), pp. 114–15
12 Ibid.
13 Johnston, *Narrative*, 116.
14 Ibid., 116.
15 Edward Porter Alexander, *Military Memoirs of a Confederate* (New York: Charles Scribners's Sons, 1912), 110–11.
16 Davis, *Rise and Fall*, 2:132.
17 Ibid.
18 Jefferson Davis to Varina Davis, June 21, 1862, in Rowland, *Jefferson Davis, Constitutionalist*, 5:283–84.
19 Lee to Davis, August 15, 1862, with Davis endorsement, *OR*, 11, pt. 3, 678.

20 Lee to Davis, August 17, 1862, *OR*, 51, pt. 2, pp. 1075–76; Lee to Davis August 21, 1862, *OR*, 51, pt. 2, p. 609; Lee to Davis, August 25 and 27, 1862, in Freeman and McWhiney, *Lee's Dispatches*, 52, 54.

21 Davis to Lee, August 26, 1862, Rowland, *Jefferson Davis, Constitutionalist*, 5:330.

22 Lee to Davis, September 3, 1862, *OR*, vol. 19, pt. 2, pp. 590–91.

23 Lee to Davis, September 9, 1862, *OR*, vol. 19, pt. 2, pp. 602–3.

24 Lee to Davis, September 8, 1862, *OR*, vol. 19, pt. 2, p. 600.

25 Lee to Davis, September 9, 1862, *OR*, vol. 19, pt. 2, pp. 602–3; Walter H. Taylor, *Four Years with General Lee* (Bloomington, IN: Indiana University Press, 1962), 66.

26 Taylor to Davis, September 20, 1862, *OR*, vol. 51, pt. 2, p. 617.

27 John B. Jones, *A Rebel War Clerk's Diary*, ed. Earl Schenck Miers (New York: Sagamor Press, 1958), 172; Robert Garlick Hill Kean, *Inside the Confederate Government*, ed. Edward Younger (New York: Oxford University Press, 1957), 48; Lee to Davis, January 16, February 18 and 26, March 19, and April 2, 1863, *OR*, vol. 25, pt. 1, pp. 627, 631–32, 642–43, 675, 700–1; Lee to Samuel Cooper, March 28, 1863, with Davis endorsement, *OR*, vol. 25, pt. 1, p. 689; Davis to Lee, March 10 and April 1, 1863, in Rowland, *Jefferson Davis, Constitutionalist*, 5:446, 463.

28 Lee to Seddon, April 9, Lee to Cooper and Davis, April 16, Cooper to Lee April 14, 1863, *OR*, vol. 25, pt. 1, pp. 713–14, 720, 724–26.

29 Edwin B. Coddington, *The Gettysburg Campaign: A Study in Command* (New York: Touchstone, 1968), 8–9; Russell F. Weigley, *The American Way of War: A History of United States Military Strategy and Policy* (New York: Indiana University Press, 1973), 113.

30 Lee to Davis, April 16, 1863, *OR*, 25, pt. 1, pp. 725–26.

31 Jones, *Rebel War Clerk's Diary*, 201–4; Lee to Davis, May 7 and 11, and to Seddon, with Davis endorsement, May 10, 1863, *OR*, vol. 25, pt. 1, pp. 782–83, 790–92.

32 Lee to Davis, May 7, 1863, *OR*, 25, pt. 1, p. 790; R. E. Lee to G. W. C. Lee, May 11, 1863, in Dowdey and Manarin, *Wartime Papers*, 484; Jones, *Rebel War Clerk's Diary*, 209–10.

33 John H. Reagan, *Memoirs*, ed. Walter F. McCaleb (New York: Neale, 1906), 121–22, 150–51.

34 Jones, *Rebel War Clerk's Diary*, 214.

35 Reagan, *Memoirs*, 121, 151.

36 Davis to Lee, May 26, 1863, in Rowland, *Jefferson Davis, Constitutionalist*, 5:496–98.

37 Davis to Lee, May 31, 1863, *OR*, 25, pt. 1, pp. 810–11.

38 Lee to Seddon, May 20 and June 2, Lee to Hill, May 30, Lee to Davis, May 30 and June 2, Davis to Lee, May 31, 1863, *OR*, vol. 25, pt. 1, pp. 811, 832–34, 841–43, 848–49; Lee to Davis, June 8, Lee to Cooper, June 23, Davis to Lee, June 28, Cooper to Lee, June 29, 1863, *OR*, vol. 27, pt. 1, pp. 75–77 and pt. 3, pp. 868–69; Lee to Davis, May 25, 28, and 29, 1863, in Freeman and McWhiney, *Lee's Dispatches*, 91–92, 96–100; Davis to Lee, May 26 and 30, and Lee to Davis, June 7, 1863, Rowland, *Jefferson Davis, Constitutionalist*, 5: 496–98, 500, 506–7; Lee to Davis, June 20, 1863, Library of Congress.

39 Lee to Davis, June 23, Lee to Cooper, June 23, Davis to Lee, June 28, Cooper to Lee, June 29, 1863, *OR*, vol. 27, pt. 1, pp. 75–77; pt. 3, pp. 924–25.

40 Lee to Davis, August 8, 1863, Rowland, *Jefferson Davis, Constitutionalist*, 5:585–87.

41 Davis to Lee, August 11, 1863, *OR*, vol. 29, pt. 2, pp. 639–40.

4

CLEMENCEAU AND FOCH

How Not to Share an Armrest

Michael S. Neiberg

A high-level American political appointee once compared civil-military relations to flying on a cramped commuter flight. If you put your elbow on the armrest too far onto your neighbor's side, you are likely to get glares or maybe even a forceful shove in return. If you keep your arms calmly at your side and mind your own business, your neighbor might take advantage of your docility and take the entire armrest. If both passengers are too afraid of the other's reaction, then the valuable real estate of the armrest sits unused. His point is that civil-military relations is a kind of constant negotiation. While in theory there may be rules and conventions that tell each passenger how to sit and how to behave, in practice, the lines are always blurred and there is a negotiation of sorts between the two "passengers" for control of the "armrest."

Georges Clemenceau and Ferdinand Foch began the negotiation over their shared armrest in 1907, when Clemenceau went against the prevailing political winds and appointed Foch commander of the *École Supérieur de Guerre*. The last few months of the First World War brought these two very different men back together in a powerful, if sometimes strained, relationship to win the war against Imperial Germany. The peacemaking process, however, shattered whatever temporary amity existed between the two, as they quarreled bitterly over the terms of the Treaty of Versailles. Their mutual hatred lasted even beyond their deaths, as the two left behind posthumous memoirs and interviews that contained mutual recriminations and insults that were well beneath their dignity.

It is hard to imagine either man wanting to spend much time seated next to the other, had it not been for their shared desire to prosecute the war against Germany to its fullest. Personally, they could hardly have been more different. Professionally, they each jealously guarded what they saw as their

DOI: 10.4324/9781003375630-4

exclusive role in the civil-military system. Neither showed any reluctance to pushing back when the other's elbow encroached too far across the armrest. In the end, the system held together as well as it did only because in a total war each man came to recognize when it was time to leave the other's sphere alone. It may not have fit the later theories of Samuel Huntington and other political scientists, but in the febrile atmosphere of 1918, the system worked just well enough. Once the war ended, however, the system broke down and produced an outcome that neither believed fully guaranteed the future security of France.[1]

Georges Clemenceau had always made a study of war. He had covered the American Civil War as a journalist (he claimed to have met Ulysses Grant), and he began his own life in politics in the wake of the Franco-Prussian War. From the time he began his political career in the 1870s, Clemenceau built a well-deserved reputation as a tough political infighter, dedicated to the republican principles of the Third Republic. Those principles included an absolute opposition to any institution in France gaining special power or prestige, especially the three traditional power centers of the aristocracy, the church, and the army. "The army is composed of civilians," he had once written, "clothed in a certain fashion and subordinated to a special regime for a certain purpose. Men are neither better nor worse if they wear red pants or gray, a kepi or a bowler."[2]

For this reason, Clemenceau had staunchly defended Alfred Dreyfus, a Jewish officer notoriously framed and prosecuted by the army for an act of treason he had not committed. The scandal tore France apart; Clemenceau placed himself firmly on the side of the Dreyfusards who demanded a fair trial for Captain Dreyfus and punishments for the officers who had suborned justice to serve the army's ends over those of France. Clemenceau had even used one of his newspapers, *L'Aurore* (The Dawn) to give Émile Zola the space to publish his inflammatory article "J'Accuse" in 1898. That article targeted the president of France as a conspirator in the army's coverup and helped to keep the Dreyfus Affair at the center of French politics for another eight agonizing years.

The scandal offered Clemenceau an almost perfect opportunity to target all the threats he saw to French republicanism. The army's crime, in Clemenceau's and Zola's view, was only partly its framing of Dreyfus. More importantly, the army had used its power to try to enlarge its power in France via subterfuge, corruption, and deceit. The army had placed itself above the law and outside the republican values of a modernizing France. Its leaders, Catholic and sometimes royalist, struck Clemenceau as relics of a bygone age and a threat to the democratic, egalitarian France in which he so deeply believed. Any institution, even the army, that claimed to be above the republic was not its protector but a threat to its very existence and therefore had no place in the France that Clemenceau envisioned. That the institution in question was the army only fanned the periodic rumors of coups and counterrevolution.

Ferdinand Foch, then a rising officer in that army and a man, marked for great responsibilities, wisely kept his head down during the Dreyfus Affair. To this day, we do not know what he thought about it because he commented so little about the massive scandal that engulfed France. It is, however, not too difficult to imagine Foch sharing the general view of his uniformed comrades that the fate of a single officer like Dreyfus paled in comparison to the damage the multiple investigations, trials, and civilian interference were inflicting on his beloved army. To have thought otherwise would have placed him well outside the views of his cohort of brother officers, his rural home community, and his wife, whose own correspondence reflected her own dismissive attitude toward the Dreyfusards. We also know that the episode left Foch with a life-long suspicion, if not an outright hatred, of journalists and politicians, whose patriotism he questioned, especially when compared to that of men in uniform like himself who defended France.

Foch, born into a deeply Catholic and conservative community in the Pyrenees, never much cared for the hectic, politicized environment of Paris, where the anticlerical Clemenceau thrived. Foch's first experiences of the city came in the aftermath of the gory Paris Commune of 1871. Some of his first barracks in the city still had blood on the walls. The Third Republic was born out of violence, and, in the view of most conservatives, it was too anti-clerical and too prone to mob rule. Moreover, many of the government's civilian leaders deeply mistrusted the army both for its collapse during the Franco-Prussian War and its willingness to slaughter working-class Parisians during the Commune. While Foch saw it all as a young private who wanted to fight invading Germans, not fellow Frenchmen, Clemenceau was then serving as the mayor of the Montmartre district (*arrondissement*) of Paris, rejecting calls for peace with the Germans and then winning a seat in the new National Assembly.

Foch belonged to a generation of officers who thought the Third Republic, which Clemenceau served, too weak and corrupt to govern France. They nevertheless mostly learned to keep their political views to themselves, if for no other reason than to protect their own careers. Another Pyrenean, Joseph Joffre, rose through the ranks not by showing any particular tactical or operational acumen, but by moving to the left or right of the political spectrum so uneasily that he acquired the nickname "the Crab." The story of Joffre demanding red meat at a Friday dinner during Lent to prove his republican bona fides may be apocryphal, but Joffre had learned, like Foch, to display no outward signs of displeasure with France's republican form of government and not to associate himself too much with any single political party or movement. Given the rapidly shifting political sands in Third Republic France, doing so could easily kill a promising career.[3]

Foch much preferred to avoid the capital's political intrigues and serve in garrison towns in eastern France and his adopted home region of Brittany whenever he could. He did, however, share with Clemenceau a belief that the overseas empire was ultimately a waste of France's men, money, and time. Both men saw Germany, and only Germany, as France's strategic problem. For this reason, Foch wooed key British generals, most notably the future Director of Military Operations, General Sir Henry Wilson.

The Third Republic was no stranger to civil-military scandals, and Clemenceau never seemed to be too far from any of them. The tectonic Dreyfus Affair consumed France from 1894, when Dreyfus was arrested, until his final exoneration in 1906.[4] But there were others. In the late 1880s, General Georges Boulanger, with whom Foch shared a few surface similarities, unified rural Catholics and disaffected workers from the Paris suburbs to form a potent political movement that combined calls for social justice with a vigorous anti-Germanism. For a time, Clemenceau helped him in hopes of coopting Boulanger's populist patriotism to his own Radical Republican movement.[5] Boulanger, however, soon began to appear as an authoritarian threat to republicanism itself, and Boulanger's own role in crushing the Commune called into question his dedication to the people and their rights. The French government feared a coup d'état enough to issue a warrant for Boulanger's arrest, sending the general into exile in Belgium. A French court found him guilty in absentia of treason. The political problems solved themselves when Boulanger's mistress died in his arms, and he committed suicide on her grave in 1891.[6]

The Boulanger scandal left behind bitter suspicions of Catholic and aristocratic plots to replace the Third Republic with a more authoritarian form of government. Catholic generals from rural backgrounds like Foch were especially suspect. To keep an eye on potential plotters, Minister of War General Louis André began to assemble files on the political loyalty of senior French officers. Freemasons like himself wrote reports that recorded how often officers attended Mass or sent their children to Catholic schools. The files, called *fiches* in French, were then used to inform decisions about promotions and assignments. The *Affaire des Fiches* brought down the French government in 1904 when a conservative member of a patriotic league bribed an official to give him some of the incriminating files, which he then published.

In 1907, within this atmosphere of rumors of plots and anti-Catholic counterplots, Clemenceau, then serving his first term as prime minister, had to decide whom to appoint to the critical job of commander of the *École Supérieur de Guerre*, prominently located in a sprawling structure just across the Champ de Mars from the Eiffel Tower. His dislike of Paris notwithstanding, Foch desperately wanted the job, partly for the chance to influence the next generation of officers and partly to avenge André's removal of him from the faculty for being a devout Catholic.[7] Clemenceau, fresh from a term as minister of the interior where he developed a reputation as a ruthless administrator willing to use the army to put down strikes, made reform of the army a top priority. The "Tiger," as Clemenceau was by then widely known, wanted to insure the

French Army would be ready if relations with Germany deteriorated. He also wanted to be sure that it would obey the government.

In their first meeting, Clemenceau told Foch that he would not get the command of the École but refused to tell him why. Foch suspected that the anti-clerical Clemenceau was withholding the job from a Catholic officer either because of his own biases or political pressure from the cabinet or parliament. Foch asked the prime minister if he would read some of Foch's writings before he made his final decision. Clemenceau agreed, although Foch left the meeting assuming that the prime minister would not live up to his end of the bargain. Foch sent Clemenceau copies of his two books, both of which emphasized the need for élan and the importance of the offensive in war. Although they have been caricatured as revealing the single-minded French obsession with the murderous offensive in war, they were in fact much more nuanced. They argued that France had to find ways to compensate for its material shortcomings against the larger and more mobile German Army. Taking the war into Germany would keep the Germans off balance and, subsequently, less able to make their larger numbers and more efficient railway system decisive on the battlefield as they had been in 1870. The books also showed that Foch had made a deep study of German military thought. "Read Clausewitz," Foch liked to exclaim to students, "There was a man for you!"[8]

Clemenceau must have been impressed with Foch's writings or (more likely) his chutzpah, because he sent again for Foch. He showed Foch two files collected during André's ministry. One, written by a former comrade in a garrison town in the Aisne district, called Foch a "doubtful republican," while the other alleged that Foch had given higher grades to Catholic students during his time as an instructor at the École. Those two reports should have been enough to sink Foch, but Clemenceau had been impressed enough by something he saw in the general that he kept a cabinet meeting waiting for almost half an hour while the two men kept talking. Just when Foch had given up hope, Clemenceau told him that he had the job. Foch then told Clemenceau that although he strenuously denied the allegations in the reports, Clemenceau should know that Foch was indeed an observant Catholic and that he had a brother who was a Jesuit. "Je m'en fous" ("I don't give a damn"), Clemenceau replied.

It is certainly possible that Clemenceau had derived from their conversations or Foch's books a respect for Foch's ideas on tactics and operations. It is equally possible that Clemenceau preferred to keep Foch in Paris where officials could keep a close eye on him rather than give him a division or corps command somewhere far from the capital lest he turn out to be the doubtful republican of the Aisne report. Whatever the truth of the matter, the incident over the appointment marked the beginning, without either man yet knowing it, of a history of frankness between them that was sometimes productive and sometimes confrontational. Foch learned, or at least thought he had, that he could tell Clemenceau what was on his mind without the prime minister destroying his career if he failed to like what he heard. Clemenceau learned that he had at least one general in the army whose fighting spirit and determination matched his own. He must also have believed that Foch, unlike Boulanger, had no interest in attaining political power. It would have been easy enough in two interviews to see that Foch was a soldier from head to toe, not a politician in waiting. (After the war Foch refused numerous entreaties to join the French Senate or run for president).

By the time of the outbreak of the war in 1914, Foch had completed his term as commandant of the *École Supérieur de Guerre*. He had taken command of the elite XX Corps and led it into Lorraine southeast of Metz in the war's opening days. He led bravely and courageously, but his XX Corps took enormous casualties, as did most of the rest of the French Army in the war's opening weeks. Critics then and now blamed the French penchant for the offensive that Foch had taught to a generation of officers for much of the bloodshed. Foch paid a huge personal price, losing his son and son-in-law within hours of one another. Still, he had been one of the few French generals who had led with distinction, and he received a promotion to army command in time to help turn the tide at the (First) Battle of the Marne in September. "My center is giving way, my right is in retreat," he famously wrote. "Situation excellent. I attack."

Clemenceau was then out of government and running a newspaper, *L'Homme Libre* (The Free Man). He rejected an invitation to rejoin the cabinet as justice minister, preferring to use his newspaper to criticize the government for not prosecuting the war with sufficient vigor. For his efforts, the government censored and suppressed his newspaper to the extent Clemenceau changed its name to *L'Homme Enchaîné* (*The Man in Chains*). He nevertheless maintained his criticisms as stridently as he could in the face of increasing pressure from the state to remain silent. He, like Foch, was determined to do all he could to help France win the war. Also, like Foch, he knew that he was facing a desperate situation, but he preferred to attack.

The outbreak of war in 1914 led to a strict division of the civil and military spheres in France. Joffre, the army's chief of staff, declared the area near the Western Front a zone of the armies; his staff banned politicians, including President Raymond Poincaré himself, from entering the zone without permission or without their itineraries being approved in advance. Joffre's behavior made him several enemies in the French government. Success on the battlefield might have put the government in a better mood toward his political behavior, but mounting manpower losses in 1915 and his poor handling of the start of the Verdun crisis in early 1916 put him in a vulnerable position.

At Verdun, Joffre found himself trapped in another long line of civil-military tensions. Lt. Colonel Émile Driant, a member of the French Parliament, serving as a battalion commander in the forests northeast of Verdun, had warned his colleagues in the Chamber of Deputies Army Commission (Clemenceau had been a member of that commission at various points) at the end of 1915 that the Germans were preparing a massive offensive in the area. He also accused Joffre of personally ordering artillery moved out of the Verdun region to support futile offensives elsewhere. Driant went outside the army chain of command and asked his colleagues in parliament to conduct an independent investigation. Joffre exploded with anger at his subordinate's behavior, even one who sat in the Chamber of Deputies. Joffre's attitude soon revealed itself as misplaced when the Germans did in fact attack Verdun, killing Driant in the battle's opening hours and turning him into a national martyr. Joffre's relationship with the French government never recovered.

The struggle at Verdun consumed the army, but not Foch. He was instead placed in command of the French end of Joffre's planned Allied offensive on the Somme River, which served as the rough borderline between the French and British sectors of the Western Front. In the plan's initial conception, the Somme was to be mainly a French offensive, with inexperienced British forces in support. Foch had never liked the idea of the offensive, believing that it had little chance of success and that it served no larger strategic purpose. Verdun reinforced his mistrust because it forced the French to reduce their Somme commitment from forty divisions to just eight. Those divisions would now be in support of the British, inverting the campaign's original design. Foch disapproved of the British taking the lead and continued to question the whole point of the offensive. He thought Joffre was making a mistake to continue with the Somme offensive as long as Verdun raged, but he had had no success in talking Joffre into changing his approach.

In May 1916, Clemenceau, then the president of the Senate Army Committee, came to the front lines to see for himself. He did not request permission from Joffre's staff to enter the zone of the armies. It was a desperate time for France, with the battle at Verdun killing French (and, for that matter, German) soldiers at an astonishing rate for no obvious wider purpose. Many French generals had begun to sense that they could win at Verdun, but only in the sense of denying the Germans the attritional victory they sought. What all the killing would mean for ultimate victory – or defeat – few could divine.

Few French commanders had any ideas for how to turn the war around. Joffre had certainly run out of ideas. Despite his pessimism about what the French could achieve on the Somme under such circumstances, Foch remained, in the words of Charles Meunier-Surcouf, a veteran and member of the Chamber of Deputies, the only general "who believed absolutely in a military victory."[9] Whether that belief came from any realistic assessment of the situation in 1916 or the supreme confidence that Foch never lacked no one could say for sure.

But if Foch believed in final victory, he did not think attacking on the Somme would bring France and Britain any closer to it. Foch spoke to Clemenceau with the same frankness he had used almost a decade earlier in their conversations about command of the *École Supérieur de Guerre*. Now, of course, the stakes were higher. Foch told Clemenceau that much of his artillery had been redirected to Verdun; without it, the French armies could only achieve minimal gains to no larger purpose. He may well have asked one of the questions he loved to pose to his staff and colleagues when he had doubts, "De quoi s'agit-il?" ("What is it for?"). Foch urged that the attack be canceled or redirected further north to the Vimy sector where a British offensive might have the effect of forcing the Germans to move units out of Verdun to contain it. The next day, Clemenceau tried, unsuccessfully, to convince British commander General Sir Douglas Haig to consider Foch's advice.

At the same time, Joffre was arguing, contrary to Foch, that the Somme would indeed cause a break in the German lines or force the Germans to ease the pressure on Verdun. He told Prime Minister Aristide Briand and Poincaré that he was even willing to risk Verdun temporarily falling into German hands to give the Somme its best chance of success. Both Clemenceau and an anonymous officer on Foch's staff expressed their displeasure with Joffre's performance at Verdun to members of the government. At a high-level meeting at the end of May called by Poincaré, Foch, and Clemenceau both registered their lack of faith in Joffre's vision. The meeting nevertheless ended with a decision to launch the Somme attack on or about July 1.

The Somme offensive thus went forward and, notwithstanding his doubts about what it might accomplish, Foch remained in command of the French portion south of the river. French forces advanced further than the British north of the river in the first few days. But Foch had been right all along. The Somme offensive did not break German lines or change the momentum of the war. It did, however, convince Clemenceau that if any French general understood the wider strategy of modern war, it was Foch, who argued for a more "scientific" approach. That approach meant an end to soldiers making bloody, heroic charges at enemy machine guns and barbed wire. Instead, heavier and more accurate artillery and aviation would clear the ground, leaving the way clear for soldiers to win battles that did not merely seize small and insignificant plots of ground but achieved major strategic results by threatening enemy lines of communication. The scientific system was surely less heroic, but it promised a better chance of winning the war.

If Clemenceau had read Foch's books, he would have discerned that this approach was far different from the one Foch had advocated back in 1907. Almost uniquely among the French generals of his age, Foch had learned that his prewar beliefs had been wrong; in modern war, élan counted for little. Victory would instead depend on the slow and thorough application of industry and the maintenance of political will to make future sacrifices. As Clemenceau saw first-hand on the Somme, Foch was right and Joffre wrong. The army needed a new approach based on the bloody lessons learned in 1915 and 1916. It also needed better politicians to force the government and industry deeper into a posture of total war. The May visits also convinced Clemenceau that the rumors of Foch's ill health were unfounded, likely spread by people in Joffre's headquarters who wanted to see Foch sidelined as revenge for his campaign against Joffre.[10]

The wartime alliance between Clemenceau and Foch thus took a major step forward because each man saw in the other a useful ally in the twin battles against the Germans and the faults in the French system itself. Clemenceau thought he had found a general who understood modern war and knew how to lead France to victory without killing the youth of France in the process. Foch similarly saw in Clemenceau the one French politician capable of forcing the government not only to see the flaws it did not want to see, but to do what was necessary to correct those flaws. Each saw in the other a fellow patriot whose differences from his own beliefs could surely be forgiven in the mutual quest to win the war. In a revealing remark, Foch (who, as far as we know was monogamous) said admiringly that the notorious womanizer Clemenceau loved France with all his passion, as a man like him could only love a mistress. A Belgian liaison officer who watched the May interactions prophetically wrote in his diary on May 4 that Foch might one day become "Clemenceau's man and become Generalissimo one day if [Clemenceau] managed to get rid of Joffre, for whom he seemed to have little esteem."[11]

The French government did get rid of Joffre, but it did not put Foch in his place. Despite Clemenceau's advocacy of Foch, the job went to Robert Nivelle, who had the advantages of speaking fluent English and promising that he had found the key to winning the war within a few months. Nivelle was just five years younger than Foch but projected an air of youthful vigor that the more cerebral Foch did not. Nivelle promised politicians desperate for answers that the artillery methods he had innovated at Verdun could win the war quickly, if exported on a larger scale. Foch's methods, by contrast, would take time and possibly force major changes in the French political and economic spheres.

Foch's political scheming against Joffre and his staff, moreover, had not gone over well in Paris. Joffre's star may have fallen, but he still had many allies in Paris and was about to be awarded a marshal's baton and then sent to the United States to drum up American support for the French cause. Undermining him would not serve France's interests, even if removing him from command had become a military and political necessity. Joffre told any politician who would listen that Foch was not suited to be his replacement. In the meantime, Poincaré had discovered that Foch had had a hand in the anonymous leaks about shortcomings in the government's prosecution of the war. Some of those leaks went directly to Clemenceau's Senate commission. Poincaré thus had plenty of reasons to grow suspicious of the warmth between Foch and Clemenceau, the latter a man Poincaré had detested and deeply mistrusted for decades.

As a result, Foch ended up in late 1916 and early 1917 with a variety of assignments that were little more than busy work. Those assignments included drawing up a "Plan H" for a French defense of a hypothetical and entirely unlikely German invasion through Switzerland. More productively, Foch worked with the Italians to coordinate British and French assistance to the struggling Italian Army. Still, these assignments were a long way from command of the French Army. Foch had played the political game and, in the short term, had to pay a price. Clemenceau, too, had lost. His behind-the-scenes attempts in December 1916 to bring down the cabinet of Aristide Briand failed. Briand survived a vote of no confidence and reshuffled his cabinet, leaving him in an even stronger position than before. Briand formed his new government on December 13 and sent Foch the telegram notifying him of the reduction in his authority just two days later.

Five days after that, Clemenceau wrote personally to Foch. Whether they had colluded to bring down Joffre and Briand or not, they were both now in eclipse. Clemenceau's note read "Dear friend, in adversity we come closer together. Like you, I am beaten ("frappé"). Yours always, G. Clemenceau."[12] The two men had figured out a way to share the armrest in 1916, only to have the pilot change course. At the beginning of 1917 at least, a few people in the French Army or government complained. They were tired of Foch's criticisms and Clemenceau's machinations.

Joffre's replacement, Robert Nivelle, had not made the same mental adjustments that Foch made. He remained wedded to a belief that the right tactics could still win the big battle that would in turn win a great campaign and then the war itself. Nivelle charmed politicians in France and the British alike by telling them what they most wanted to hear, that he had divined something at Verdun that could lead the Allies to victory. Nivelle's secret was supposedly rooted in his ability to train artillery gunners to fire a carefully choreographed "creeping barrage" that would precede advancing infantry, silence German opposition and return warfare to its natural open form. Once out of their trenches, the French could drive the Germans from their positions on high ground and pursue. Almost all military professionals, including the British and Foch himself, thought his ideas dangerously simplistic and not supported by the endemic fog and friction of the Western Front. In actual combat, Nivelle's careful timing proved almost impossible to execute.

Nivelle knew that he did not have to convince Foch. He only had to convince the politicians, the very men whom Foch and Clemenceau had dismissed as dilettantes. Nivelle therefore decided to take a different approach to his dealings with politicians to separate himself from the now-discredited Joffre. Nivelle opened his headquarters to them and went out of his way to brief politicians in Paris on his plans. Unfortunately, he took his approach too far. He often gave briefings to people who had no need to know and sometimes did so with non-governmental officials in the room. Critics then and now blamed

Nivelle's loose lips for contributing to the disastrous offensive of April 1917 that now nears his name. German airplanes even dropped taunting flyers over French lines that read "When will this offensive of yours begin?"

Nivelle sparked a civil-military crisis of his own, and one that later caused problems for Foch. In order to give his planned offensive on the Chemin des Dames every chance of success, he wanted the British to attack in the Vimy-Arras sector further to his north. Those attacks would in theory draw German reserves away before the French offensive began.

British Prime Minister David Lloyd George, who was having his own civil-military problems with Douglas Haig, saw merit in the idea. He had lost faith in Haig but, lacking the power to remove him, had instead decided on a subterfuge to reduce Haig's power. At a conference in Calais in February 1917, he surprised the British senior generals by effectively ordering them to operate under Nivelle's command. Haig and General William Robertson objected both to the wisdom and legality of the scheme. They decided that they would resign before executing it. Eventually, they worked out a compromise to keep command authority over their soldiers in British hands, while hewing to Nivelle's general strategic vision. But Haig went to bed only after writing in his diary that he was "thoroughly disgusted with our Government and the Politicians."[13]

Haig and Robertson clearly believed Lloyd George had elbowed his way too far across the armrest by asking them to submit to the orders of a foreign general. When Nivelle's offensive failed, as they had predicted, they felt vindicated. The order for fresh attacks near Arras to give the French time to recover from Nivelle's disaster, only served to anger them. Had Lloyd George possessed the sense to listen and respect their expertise, they believed, the Arras battles would not have been necessary. As it was, the British had lost men for no other purpose than to keep the Germans from moving reserves south against the French. This failure of joint command and its attendant problems for civil-military relations cast a long shadow, one that Clemenceau and Foch would have to find a way to handle less than a year later.

Nivelle's replacement, the taciturn and pessimistic Henri-Philippe Pétain, cleaned up the mess, but presented his own problems. We know today how much his authoritarian and anti-republican beliefs would cost France during the crisis of 1940. Even in the First World War, he displayed behaviors that worried some senior politicians. He almost put his own career in jeopardy, when his remark that France was neither governed nor led, made its way back to Poincaré. Pétain cared little for niceties like parliamentary oversight and the laws of France. When at one point, Poincaré challenged Pétain on a point of constitutional procedure, Pétain snapped back "screw the constitution."[14] Pétain may have emerged from the war as a hero, but, like Foch's close aide Maxime Weygand and other French generals, the politicians never fully trusted him. The legacies for the 1930s and 1940s had their seeds planted in the crises of the First World War.

All that still lay in the future. By the time the French government decided to recall Foch to be the chief of staff of the French Army in May 1917, the crisis had only grown. Thousands of soldiers, furious with the way that Nivelle had wasted the lives of their comrades, refused to attack. They remained in their trenches and pledged to defend the soil of France, but they would not, as a popular song went, leave their skins on the heights of Craonne for no purpose.[15] The resulting crisis forced Poincaré to take the unusual step of intervening personally to prevent the army from executing death sentences against some of the men the army accused of treason. As for Nivelle, the government quickly dispatched him to Algeria.

It was not only the military situation that needed reform. The relationship of the generals to France's political leadership lay in tatters. Joffre's approach had been too restrictive, Nivelle's too open, and Pétain's too dismissive of French political sensitivities. At the same time, the cabinet remained a revolving door. From the start of the war to the time Foch assumed command, France passed through six ministers of war, a combination of civilians and politicians that all proved unable to walk the fine line that the job required. Clemenceau continued his drumbeat of criticism of the government and waited for his old nemesis, Poincaré, to call him to form a government.

The new appointments of Foch as chief of staff and Pétain as commander of French field armies did not begin well. Foch and the new war minister, the brilliant mathematician Paul Painlevé, argued and dithered over what, exactly, the government expected Foch to do in his new job. Painlevé envisioned Foch as a "technical adviser" to the government, but such a role could never have suited the energetic Foch. He soon took a firm hand over the army's direction and its relationship with its allies, especially the Americans, who had just entered the war. As to Painlevé, Foch appears to have paid him little attention. There is no mention of Painlevé in Foch's memoirs and just one mention of him in the English translation; that mention comes not from Foch himself but from his American translator.[16]

The legacy of Nivelle and the sensitivities of civil-military tension persisted and continued to cause tensions at the highest levels. In the wake of the Austro-German breakthrough against the Italian Army at Caporetto in October, discussions began about creating a single Allied commander-in-chief to coordinate strategy and allocate resources. Foch, respected (if not liked) by all and the highest-ranking general to have seen the situation in Italy first-hand, seemed an obvious choice. At a hurriedly called conference in Rapallo in November Foch tried to convince the British to create a supreme command, but his allies were not yet ready for such a step. They remembered how poorly Nivelle had treated them, and they recalled with bitterness their attacks around Arras. Instead of a supreme command, therefore, the Allied governments created a Supreme War Council, which met in Versailles and was dominated mostly by civilians.

The crisis in the French government persisted as well, finally forcing Poincaré to call Clemenceau (whom he called this "devil of a man") to form a government. Poincaré knew that as long as Clemenceau was on the outside, he would continue to use his power and influence to destabilize any ministry of which he disapproved, and he was unlikely to approve any ministry he did not lead. Poincaré also knew that Clemenceau's popularity had grown massively among soldiers and civilians alike. He was ruthless, driven, and fully dedicated to winning the war. "I haven't the right," Poincaré said, "to rule him out merely on the basis of his attitude toward me."[17] France needed Clemenceau, if it were to avoid defeat, and Poincaré knew it. The Tiger assumed the job of prime minister and war minister simultaneously in mid-November 1917.

Clemenceau and Foch were now both back in power as 1917 became 1918, although their reunion was not all warmth and joy. It is not clear when Clemenceau first said that war is too important a business to be left to generals, but that the statement reflected a core belief that governed his handling of the war.[18] Strategy, he believed, belonged to the civilians. To make the point as clearly as he could, he told Foch that the Supreme War Council would be led by the prime ministers, with the generals providing only advice. At an early meeting, Foch began to answer a question from Lloyd George, only to have Clemenceau grab his arm and say "Be quiet. I am the representative of France."[19] The prime minister was not interested in sharing the armrest.

Soon thereafter came the real crisis. The collapse of the Russian front meant that the Germans had been able to shift hundreds of thousands of soldiers over the winter and early spring from the east to the west for one last desperate push toward Paris and the Channel. To add to the problem, although the Americans had been technically at war with the Germans for a year, American soldiers were slow to arrive and came to France in a depressingly untrained state. To Clemenceau and others, the obvious answer involved placing American units under sophisticated European higher commands. President Woodrow Wilson and General John Pershing, of course, objected in the strongest terms for the same reason that Haig and Robertson had objected earlier.

Fearful of a German offensive and unsure what he would get from these new Americans, Clemenceau focused on what he could immediately control. He galvanized the French government and people with a stirring speech in which he repeated the four words that would forever be associated with him. "My formula is the same everywhere. Domestic politics? I make war ("Je fais la guerre"). Foreign policy? I make war. Always, I make war."[20] Although then seventy-seven years old, Clemenceau was everywhere, visiting the front lines weekly and giving rousing speeches in the Chamber of Deputies. Consistent with his most famous aphorism, he took a firm hand over the military, reviewing the appointments and promotions of generals, weighing in on tactical debates, and ensuring the civilian government prosecuted the war with energy and efficiency.

The Rapallo discussions about creating a single commander for the Allied armies had continued as one way to coordinate a response to the expected German spring attack. It appears that Clemenceau was willing to consider the idea despite his general fear of putting that much power in the hands of one soldier. Even though he had identified Foch as the most likely general to take over command of Allied armies, he also hinted that he might be amenable to Pétain or even Haig holding such an office. His scheming might have been a ploy to keep Foch from gaining too much confidence or a way to figure out which general would be most obedient. Even if the Allies did create a generalissimo, Clemenceau envisioned himself remaining in charge, using the Supreme War Council to concentrate executive power in his own hands and subordinate the generalissimo to the demands of the civilian governments.

Clemenceau was never shy in interfering in matters down to the tactical level. He insisted on Allied generals building defenses in depth that would contain as many as five layers, with the main combat power in the third. Some Allied generals (Foch and Pétain were not among them) thought defenses in depth a waste of time; if the goal was to chase the Germans from France, they argued, then why expend resources to build defenses? Clemenceau targeted and beleaguered such generals personally, making it a point to visit their sectors and demand that they conform. In doing so, Clemenceau drew no sharp lines between the political and the military sides of the problem. He intended to influence everything directly.

Clemenceau's dominance of the Supreme War Council left Foch with precious little to do, even as signs of an impending German attack mounted. Everyone in Versailles knew that the Germans had no choice but to attack in early spring or risk either the arrival of large numbers of Americans or a Bolshevik-style revolution in Germany. Even if not yet well trained, large numbers of Americans could still defend key points like Paris and the railway junctures upon which Allied logistics depended. The Allied plan of deployment for the Americans appeared designed for such a strategy. French and British liaison officers could meanwhile help these crude soldiers learn the ways of modern war. The Americans would soon be worth far more than their numbers.

A committee like the Supreme War Council might have ameliorated some of the civil-military tensions inherent in winning a war, but it was not well suited to respond to an enemy's next expected move. Foch and his military colleagues from both France and Britain had seen how the politicians tried to use the Supreme War Council to fight a war by committee. They wanted a supreme allied commander instead, one general with the power to direct strategy, move resources, and give orders. That general should also control an independent reserve made up of soldiers from all the Allied armies. Foch and others warned that the politicians were urging deployments around Paris, which was already well defended, for political reasons. The real threat was to unglamorous logistical hubs like Amiens. The professionals intuitively understood that in a way that a committee of politicians based in Versailles never could.

But until the Germans attacked, the chances of the politicians allowing any one person to have that much power remained small. British generals, torched by the experience of Nivelle, remained reluctant to see their soldiers placed under French command. Thus, even though most people recognized that the right single commander could bring coherence and efficiency to Allied strategy, most still saw it as too risky a move. Foch certainly believed that he could be that man, and if Clemenceau was willing to entrust that much power into any man with a gold braided hat, it was increasingly obvious that that man was Foch. But no such plan could win over the Supreme War Council's politicians until a major crisis hit.

That crisis came on March 21 in the form of a massive German attack just north of St. Quentin on the Somme front. German troops passed through the old 1916 battlefield with minimal casualties and opened the long sought-after flanks in enemy lines. The German method of attack utilized new artillery tactics with specially trained soldiers to bypass enemy strong points and disable communications. These attacks worked best where commanders had disobeyed Clemenceau's direct order to put in place a defense in depth that could neutralize much of the new German combat power. For the next few months, the Allies would have to defend as well as they could as the war returned to a mobile state.

The sense of panic soon began to spread, both among politicians and pessimistic generals like Pétain. Some French officials began preparations to move the major organs of the government to Bordeaux. The pessimists argued for retreating and regrouping in the face of repeated German hammer blows. They worried about the safety of key places like Paris and the Channel ports. They also wondered if tired Allied troops, backed now by fresh but raw Americans, could withstand the new German methods. The Americans especially had indoctrinated and trained their troops for an offensively minded "open warfare," which seemed ill-suited to the situation at hand.

The great strategic risk involved the British retreating to the north to cover the ports that were their lifeline to the home islands. If the French simultaneously moved south to cover Paris, the Germans would have a great gap in front of them with few Allied defenses in front of them. Any officer who had even a passing familiarity with the history of the Napoleonic wars could see the danger. Just as Napoleon had done at Jena, Austerlitz, and elsewhere, the Germans could concentrate on one of the two armies, crush it, then turn on the other. They had, in fact, executed just such a maneuver in 1914 against the Russians at Tannenberg and the Masurian Lakes. If they could complete it in 1918, they could win the war.

The best way to stop them from doing so was to return to the proposals Foch had so strenuously advocated at Rapallo: name one man as commander in chief of Allied forces and provide him a multi-national general reserve he could move on his own authority. He would act in the name of the greater coalition, theoretically rising above the politics and inter-alliance squabbling taking place in Versailles. That man would have to be military because only a general could possibly have the necessary knowledge to manage an ever-changing battlefield. He could move troops to plug holes and coordinate movements to ensure that no large gaps appeared in the Allied lines, something a committee run by prime ministers could never achieve.

Foch made his case to Clemenceau personally in the middle of March, as German advances seemed inexorable. At that point, Clemenceau seemed to be leaning in favor of informal arrangements, such as the discussions between Haig and Pétain about where to move the boundary line between British and French units. The farther north the line moved, the more responsibility the French could assume, thus hopefully reducing the British need to retreat to the safety of the Channel ports. Foch thought such plans insufficient because they would rest on compromise rather than command. They therefore increased the risk to Paris and the attendant need to rely on the unproven Americans to make up the falling numbers south of the capital.

It also meant that there would be no general reserve so that when gaps appeared at unexpected places in the line, the entire system would have to change. The bilateral system with no commander in charge worked well enough as long as the front remained predictable, but it proved poorly suited to react to the crisis at hand. It was already showing strains, as the British naturally wanted the line moved farther north, while the French had an interest in keeping it further south. Only a unified command, Foch argued, could successfully rationalize the difference.

Still, to appoint a single commander came with its own risks. If Clemenceau had understood our metaphor, he would have clearly resented the elbow of any military commander pushing into his own comfort zone. Any decision such a general made would inevitably come with political consequences. If, for example, Haig called for reserves to guard the Channel ports and Pétain called for those same reserves to defend Paris, what would a supreme commander do? Foch argued that he could make the right military decision, but Clemenceau worried that it might be the wrong political one. As predicted, the Supreme War Council provided little guidance, failing even to issue preliminary orders as signs of the German offensive multiplied. Haig, moreover, threatened to resign rather than risk a repeat of the Nivelle Offensive planning of the year before. His British troops would remain commanded by British officers, or the King would have to find them a new commanding officer.

By the time of a major strategic conference in the town of Doullens on March 25, tensions were as high as they could be. The front line was within earshot of the participants and moving ever closer. Amid the sounds of distant artillery, the civilian and military leaders met in the town's city hall.

Symbolically, it had temporarily served as Foch's headquarters in 1914. There was now no way to avoid the reality that the Allies were in the desperate straits of March 1918 in no small part because of a lack of a supreme commander. Not only had Foch been the most forceful advocate of such a position, but he was also by far the most positive and most energetic of the attendees. He pledged that he could stop the Germans from getting anywhere near Paris (a sentiment he later repeated to his wife, who was then living in the capital), cover the critical rail juncture of Amiens, and make sure that the British had what they needed to keep the Channel ports from falling.

Clemenceau once more became Foch's greatest supporter, especially after Pétain stunned the attendees with a pessimistic speech that predicted a German victory. Seeing Foch as offering the best chance for the Allies to win and swept up in Foch's energy, Clemenceau gave Foch "strategic coordination" of the Allied armies and control over a strategic reserve. Foch convinced his British colleagues by exclaiming, "My plan is not complicated. I would fight without a break. I would fight in front of Amiens. I would fight in Amiens. I would fight behind Amiens. I would fight all the time and by force of hitting, I would finish by shaking up the Boche. He is neither cleverer nor stronger than we are."[21] Unlike Pétain, he had figured out that the Germans were not trying for Paris. Like Foch, the Germans knew that rail junctures like Amiens held the key.

With Haig and the British on board, the Allies finally had their strategic commander and the right man in the job. Still, Foch would only really have the power to set general guidelines and move reserves. Haig would still issue orders to the British Army and Pétain would issue them to the French Army. The arrangement fell far short of what Foch thought the situation required, but even Foch himself knew that troops would fight best if their orders came from their national commander. Still, Foch now had more power than any Allied coalition commander had had thus far in the war, perhaps more than any coalition commander had had in any war. But Clemenceau was misguided if he thought Foch satisfied. "Well, you've got it at last, your high command," Clemenceau told him before leaving Doullens. Foch replied, "It's a fine present you made me. You give me a lost battle and tell me to win it."[22]

Winning would require working more closely than any French politician and general had done to this point. Those close to Foch had faith in his energy and his understanding of what the Germans were trying to do. He knew that the ground the Germans had gained was militarily useless, most of it, land that they themselves had devastated the year before when they retreated to a prepared set of defenses known as the Hindenburg Line to conserve manpower. In most places, the Allies had held on to key places like the rail juncture of Amiens and the high ground around Arras. These successes suggested to Foch the German method only worked where the Allies had poor defenses in place. Where commanders had installed the defense-in-depth system, the German attacks faired poorly. The Germans, moreover, would find it impossible to supply their forces forward through devastated ground; their attacks would force their heavily trained special infantry to pay a devastatingly high price in casualties, leaving poorly trained second-line troops in their place. In other words, the situation was not nearly as bad as the maps made it seem.

Sooner or later, Foch knew, the advancing Germans would hit what Clausewitz called the culminating point. They would face insurmountable logistical problems, and their uneven advances would create salient ripe for Allied counterattacks. The power of German attacks would at some point decline to the point where they produced rapidly diminishing returns. Moreover, Foch knew that even if the Americans lacked staff officers, modern equipment, and experience, they were arriving in large enough numbers to make sure that the Allies could shift manpower around the Western Front using the new authority that the Doullens meeting bestowed upon him. He, thus. moved inexperienced American units to relatively quiet sectors south of Verdun, freeing experienced French ones to come north. If no one in London or Paris panicked, Foch knew, the German attacks would slow, then stop. At that moment, the Allies needed to be to counterattack and drive the Germans back to the Rhine.

It was Clemenceau's job to prevent panic and stamp out defeatism. He vastly increased the power of the state to crack down on defeatists and targeted politicians, like Joseph Caillaux, who publicly advocated a negotiated peace with Germany. His harsh treatment of Caillaux sent a clear signal to the French establishment that Clemenceau would tolerate no criticism and weakness, an ironic position for him to take given the French government's own censorship of Clemenceau in the war's early months. To increase the speed of decision-making, Clemenceau created a small war cabinet filled with men loyal to him. Their decisions were then presented to the full cabinet for a rubber stamp in meetings that rarely lasted more than an hour.

But the lines on the map kept moving west with each German success, and even some of Clemenceau's supporters demanded to know how much longer the prime minister would keep Foch in office. After his success at Verdun and his calming of the army after the Chemin des Dames crisis, Pétain's popularity had risen to celestial heights. Those who knew him seemed to understand that he would make a poor replacement for the more cerebral and strategic-minded Foch, but with each step backward calls grew for Foch's replacement. Throughout May and June, Clemenceau repeatedly urged Foch to take the offensive and use the Americans in larger and larger numbers. Foch calmly explained that the time had not yet come for a major counterattack and Clemenceau listened, giving a fiery speech in favor of Foch to a frightened Chamber of Deputies on May 30. He also told influential members of the Senate that he would resign if they continued their pressure to replace Foch with Pétain. The system seemed to be working and each man seemed to have success in finding a way not to encroach on the other man's side of the armrest.

The culminating point Foch had been waiting for finally came in mid-July on the Marne River. Allied intelligence gave Foch a clear picture of German intentions to cross the river near the town of Dormans. Allied staff officers worked feverishly to move French, British, and American divisions from the general reserve and other sectors of the western front to the Marne. While some of the units blunted the German crossing at Dormans, others assembled behind a forest west of the Marne valley ready to counterattack as soon as the Germans overextended themselves and created flanks they could not defend. Foch's move changed the entire war. Although no one could have known it at the time, the Allies were on their way to victory. They did not lose another battle.[23] A British attack two weeks later cleared the Amiens sector and, like the Second Battle of the Marne, produced thousands of prisoners, an indication German morale and will were fading.

Defeating the German Army on the Marne and at Amiens did not require any shoving over the armrest; figuring out how to convert battlefield success into the end of the war, however, did. Clemenceau pushed Foch to make political decisions, including a demand that Foch appeal directly to Wilson to relieve American Expeditionary Forces commander Pershing over what Clemenceau saw as Pershing's unwillingness to let the Americans assume the full burden of combat. Foch not only ignored the demand, but he also extended Pershing's area of responsibility. The incident appears to have sparked the premier's paranoia. Clemenceau soon began to fear that Foch might be getting ideas about parlaying his military glory into political power and maybe becoming a new Boulanger. In that, he was clearly wrong. Foch did not want Clemenceau's job. He merely wanted the prime minister to keep out of what he saw as his own job.

Foch's eyes were squarely on the Rhine River in front of him, not the political machinations of Paris behind him. By summer's end, Foch sensed the Allies could reach the river and win the war in 1918, not in 1919 as Clemenceau guessed or even 1920 as Pétain and others feared. But deciding what that peace might look like would cause intense elbowing because it involved so many essentially political questions. As victory came into view, Foch repeatedly asked Clemenceau for information about both the discussions inside the French government itself and any discussions the government might be having with foreign governments.

Clemenceau and British Lloyd George both blanched at that idea. The British Prime Minister, as suspicious of soldiers as Clemenceau, said "If Foch decides, the governments are suppressed." Foreign Minister Stephen Pichon rejected Foch's request merely to be put in touch with a senior government official who could act as his liaison to the cabinet. "Each man to his own profession," Pichon warned Foch. Only that way, he argued, could France avoid "any confusion of powers."[24]

For Foch, the sharp distinction that Lloyd George and Clemenceau tried to draw made no sense. The German government was then trying to reach out to Wilson through Prince Max of Baden to obtain an armistice based on the ideas in Fourteen Points. Clemenceau had already expressed a healthy skepticism of Wilson (upon seeing the Fourteen Points, Clemenceau is said to have remarked that God Himself had been content with just Ten), and he was furious with Wilson for talking to Prince Max without informing the other Allies. Foch believed, not without reason, that Max was trying to lay a trap for the Allied governments by splitting them at the political level since, thanks to the appointment of Foch as supreme commander, they could no longer hope to split them at the military level.

Foch also took it as axiomatic that the commander-in-chief of the armies had an obligation to know what was happening on the political side. How else could he craft a military strategy, in true Clausewitzian fashion, to pursue a political aim? Recalling a tense discussion he had with French government officials in mid-October 1918, Foch later wrote: "As for the notion so vociferously proclaimed by [Foreign Minister Stephen] Pichon and Georges Clemenceau, that a general works on one side of a barrier and the politicians and diplomats on the other, there is nothing more false, or, one can even say, absurd. War is not a dual object, but a unity; so for that matter is peace.... The two aspects are clearly and inseparably linked."[25]

Clemenceau, Lloyd George, and Pichon may have had good reason to be suspicious. Foch had already begun to think of peace terms, and some of those peace terms clearly crossed the line into politics. In particular, he sought to encourage separatists in the Rhineland either to form a separate Rhenish state between France and Germany or, in the wild-eyed fantasies of the most virulent French nationalists, to attach the Rhineland to France as a kind of payback for the loss of Alsace and Lorraine in the 1870s. Both Clemenceau and Lloyd George vigorously opposed such schemes, which Lloyd George called an "Alsace-Lorraine in reverse" that would cause more friction in the postwar years.

Lacking guidance from the politicians, and no doubt worried that they might throw away the victory he had so recently assured, Foch drove forward. He waved away the objections of senior officials of the French government like Clemenceau and Pichon, later writing "I had no need of such a pedantic lecture on constitutional law and the limitation of power – especially pedantic on the part of the Quai d'Orsay (the Foreign Ministry). I had simply taken my stand on the level ground of reason and common sense. Peace is the logical finish of a war."[26]

Despite his later claims that he had envisioned war and peace as a "dual object," he chose to draw a barrier when it came to finalizing terms for the armistice. Deciding that an armistice was an agreement between soldiers, and not being given the opportunity to discuss matters with the government, he drew up a list of three primary and six secondary conditions that he felt were necessary preconditions for peace. The terms made no reference to Wilson's Fourteen Points and did not acknowledge the so-called "peace notes" from

Prince Max of Baden. Foch transmitted the terms to Clemenceau's office as a courtesy, but he received no authorization and no acknowledgment in return. The primary conditions were: German evacuation of Belgium, Luxembourg, and France (understood to include Alsace and Lorraine); punitive reparations; and three allied bridgeheads across the Rhine River. The secondary conditions demanded German troops leave military equipment, railroad rolling stock, industrial resources, and other materiel in place rather than take them with them as they retreated.

Obviously, these conditions crossed the line from the military and into the political. Clemenceau, Lloyd George, and others grew suspicious, but did not object or try to rein Foch in, as victory was coming into view. They may not have wanted to interfere while the war entered its final stage (everyone on the Allied side desperately wanted Foch to deliver victory in 1918 to avoid a 1919 campaign) or they may have assumed that they could later modify whatever terms Foch imposed in an armistice. Still, the lines were being drawn. In a late October memorandum, Foch quoted Helmuth von Moltke the Elder who had written that to control Germany, France only needed to control Coblenz, Mainz, and Cologne. Foch thus proposed those cities as the center points of his bridgeheads, each to be 18 miles deep and controlled by one of the victorious Allied powers.

At about the same time, Wilson, in a remark obviously aimed at Foch, announced that "frontiers have nothing to do with soldiers."[27] Armistices, of course, did have to do with soldiers, and Foch went ahead without any civilian representative. When he met the Germans in a railway clearing in the forest of Compiègne he was appalled to find among them two civilians. One of them, Matthias Erzberger, seemed to be in charge.

In fact, Prince Max, who headed the German government after the Kaiser's abdication, hoped that Erzberger, a prominent member of the Catholic Center party, might prove more amenable to Foch than Prussian military officers. Max was wrong. Foch imposed harsh conditions on the Germans, proved deaf to their demands for leniency (*"Krieg ist Krieg,"* he responded, using the words Bismarck had used in response to French pleas for leniency in 1870), and repeatedly reminded them an armistice was a military agreement only. The bridgeheads and the naval blockade would continue until the Germans agreed to final peace terms.

Years ago, in the French military archives at Vincennes, I happened by accident upon the documents that showed Clemenceau's first response to the communiqué from Foch confirming that the Germans had signed the armistice in Compiègne. Clemenceau wrote a message to the national representatives to the Supreme War Council meeting in Versailles sharing the good news but indicating he did not yet know the terms. "Dès que je sache les détailles," he wrote, he would share them. It struck me then and it strikes me now as remarkable that he used the subjunctive voice (roughly translated "As soon as I shall know the details"), indicating clearly that he did not know what Foch had negotiated. He may later have complained that "I fear the marshal is mixing policy with strategy," but by not keeping Foch informed about policy he had given him little choice but to act within his own discretion.[28]

According to the legends (which might well be true), Foch did not want to take the risk of telegraphing or telephoning Clemenceau the details of the armistice lest some journalist anxious for a scoop get a hold of them and leak them. Instead, he personally took the signed documents to Clemenceau's office in Paris, placed them on the prime minister's desk and said, "My work is finished. Yours begins."[29] But if the anecdote is true, Foch was either misguided or carried away by the emotions of the moment. His sharp elbows at the time of the armistice would soon force a strong response from his seatmate, who was more determined than ever to take full control of the armrest.

None of the so-called Big Three (Clemenceau, Lloyd George, and Wilson) wanted their soldiers to play an active role in the peace conference. In much the same way that the Supreme War Council had functioned, civilian politicians would run the show. They would call on the military men only if they needed what they called "technical advice." Otherwise, the soldiers were to remain silent and keep their armies as prepared as possible in case the Germans refused to sign and an invasion of Germany became necessary.

Sidelining Foch was not enough for Clemenceau. Each of the major powers authorized five plenipotentiaries to the conference; Clemenceau put Foch's name sixth on the list. Foch did not miss the insult. More importantly, he quickly grew disenchanted with Clemenceau's plans to ensure French security in the long term. Foch knew that Clemenceau's hopes for a permanent Anglo-French-American alliance were a pipe dream, as was the prime minister's hope that he could use the League of Nations as a permanent anti-German coalition. With Imperial Russia now the Soviet Union, Foch also knew that France could no longer count on an alliance with a major power to Germany's east. Geopolitically, France's position was already significantly worse than it had been in 1914.

As Clemenceau's schemes for alliances fell apart, he turned to reparations and statutory limits on the size of the German armed forces. Foch dismissed these ideas out of hand, correctly predicting that absent an Allied occupation of Germany (which he did not think the demobilizing Allied armies could enforce) there was no way to monitor German activity or punish the Germans for minor violations of the treaty terms. Foch grew more and more frustrated with Clemenceau's handling of the conference. In March, he heard Clemenceau had agreed to abandon the idea of Rhenish separatism in exchange for a pledge from Britain and the United States to come to France's defense against future German aggression. Foch though the pledge worthless, especially given the time it took the Anglo-Saxon powers to mobilize and join the fight in the war just ended. Clemenceau had also agreed to firm deadlines on the bridgeheads, with the one at Cologne to close in five years.

Foch therefore continued to meddle in the politics of Rhenish separatism. Only by splitting the Rhineland from Prussia, he believed, could France have a reasonable chance of safety. Foch assigned officers to the French occupation bridgehead who shared his views. They reached out to like-minded German politicians, one of whom was the young mayor of Cologne, Konrad Adenauer.[30] While Foch saw Rhenish separatism as the only way to save France from Clemenceau's incompetence (or maybe, Foch feared, even his senility), Clemenceau worried that separating the Rhineland from Germany would discredit France's claims to have fought the war for moral and just reasons and leave France diplomatically alone in the postwar world. France, he believed, needed allies more than a separate Rhineland acting as a buffer between it and Germany.

By early April there was no room between the two for compromise. Foch thought that Clemenceau was throwing away a victory won through the sacrifice of the French Army, leaving France weaker not stronger. Clemenceau openly worried about Foch leading a coup in the Rhineland, if not in France itself. Rather than open a channel for communication, Clemenceau sidelined Foch even more and at one point told the War Ministry to prepare to replace Foch with Pétain. Foch replied with increasingly intemperate newspaper interviews, including one in April with the *Daily Mail* (so the French government could not censor it) in which he alleged Clemenceau was making it likely the women who gave their husbands for France would soon have to give their sons as well.[31]

Soon thereafter Clemenceau summoned Foch to the peace conference to advise on the state of the Allied armies if the Germans refused to sign the punitive treaty the politicians were then in the process of completing. Foch warned that demobilization and the end of wartime funding levels had reduced the capability of the Allies to march into Germany. He doubted that they had enough men or weapons to achieve anything worthwhile. He proposed instead that the victors exempt Bavaria and the Rhineland from reparations in exchange for their help in compelling Prussia to sign the treaty. He never spoke before the Big Three again.

In the end, Foch refused to attend the signing ceremony in Versailles the symbolism of which Clemenceau so carefully orchestrated. Foch famously said that the treaty was not peace, but an armistice for twenty years. He was off by just three months. While the disagreements between the two men are, of course, not solely responsible for the disaster, Foch was undoubtedly correct that France, despite victory, was weaker in 1919 than in 1914. Perhaps, if he and Clemenceau had figured out a way to share the armrest, the Paris Peace Conference might have produced a better outcome for France and Europe.

Notes

1 Samuel Huntington, *The Soldier and the State* (Cambridge, MA: Harvard University Press, 1957).
2 David Newhall, *Clemenceau: A Life at War* (Lewiston, ME: Edwin Mellen Press, 1991), 195.

3 A few French generals, notably Maurice Sarrail, did attach themselves to politicians and learned to play the political game well.

4 A recent English-language treatment is Piers Paul Read, *The Dreyfus Affair: The Scandal that Tore France in Two* (London: Bloomberg Publishing, 2012).

5 They were not as radical as the term suggests. They stood for a "radical" form of republicanism that rejected political alliances with non-republican communists, monarchists, and Bonapartists. They drew a great deal of their support from the middle and lower-middle classes. Claiming the mantle of 1791, they stood for anti-clericalism, opposition to secret ballots, and resistance to dictatorship.

6 A memorial in Boulanger's honor is one of the few original structures in the small town of Nantillois to survive the destruction of the region during the Meuse-Argonne campaign of 1918.

7 Today, on the other side of the Eiffel Tower and the Trocadéro, a statue of Foch keeps watch over the École.

8 Sir George Aston, *Biography of the Late Marshal Foch* (New York: Macmillan, 929), 90.

9 Elizabeth Grenhalgh, *Foch in Command: The Forging of a First World War General* (Cambridge: Cambridge University Press, 2011), 154.

10 In fact, Foch did have health problems, possibly related to his prostate, liver, or gall bladder.

11 Major Ferdinand de Posch quoted in Greenhalgh, *Foch in Command*, 198–99.

12 Clemenceau to Foch, December 18, 1916, Fonds Foch, Archives Nationales, Paris, 414/AP/3.

13 Gary Sheffield and John Bourne, eds. *Douglas Haig: War Diaries and Letters, 1914–1918* (London: Weidenfeld & Nicolson, 2005), 272, diary entry for February 26, 1917.

14 Elizabeth Greenhalgh, *The French Army and the First World War* (Cambridge: Cambridge University Press, 2014), 170.

15 https://encyclopedia.1914-1918-online.net/article/the_song_of_craonne.

16 Ferdinand Foch, *The Memoirs of Marshal Foch*, translated by T. Bentley Mott (Garden City, NY: Doubleday, 1931), 222.

17 J. F. V. Keiger, *Raymond Poincaré* (Cambridge: Cambridge University Press 1997), 233.

18 He also said, "It takes more than a hat with gold braid to turn an imbecile into an intelligent man." Jean-Baptiste Duroselle, *Clemenceau* (Paris: Fayard, 1988), 596.

19 B. H. Liddell Hart, *Foch: The Man of Orleans* (London: Penguin Books, 1932), 258.

20 Jean Jules Henri Mordacq, *Le Ministère Clemenceau: Journal d'un Témoin*, volume 2 (Paris: *Librairie Plon*, 1930), 54.

21 B.H. Liddell Hart, *Foch, The Man of Orleans* (London: Penguin Books, 1932), 275.

22 Ibid., 278.

23 Michael S. Neiberg, *The Second Battle of the Marne* (Bloomington, IN: Indiana University Press, 2008).

24 Liddell Hart, *Foch*, 395 and 391.

25 Ibid., 391.

26 Ibid., 391.

27 George Aston, *The Biography of the Late Marshal Foch* (New York: Macmillan, 1932), 423.

28 Eliot A. Cohen, *Supreme Command: Soldiers, Statesmen, and Leadership in Wartime* (New York: Free Press, 2002), 86.

29 Liddell Hart, *Foch*, 405.

30 The classic study of this controversy is Jere Clemens King, *Foch Versus Clemenceau: France and German Dismemberment, 1918–1919* (Cambridge, MA: Cambridge University Press, 1960).

31 Greenhalgh, *Foch in Command*, 505.

5

LLOYD GEORGE, HAIG AND THE SUPREME COMMAND, 1917–1918

John Gooch

> [A]lthough in this war there is much to be done in regard to policy or diplomacy or whatever it may be called, at the same time whatever is done must be in harmony with strategy.
>
> General Sir William Robertson, 31 October 1916[1]

In October 1916, as the Somme campaign ground to a conclusion, David Lloyd George, then secretary of state for war, told the prime minister, Herbert Asquith, that he was "very disgusted at the heavy losses involved in the offensive on the Somme as contrasted with the relatively small success achieved." Two years earlier, Asquith had been "profoundly dissatisfied" at the prospect of what now lay ahead – "an enormous waste of life & money day after day with no appreciable progress."[2] In May 1915, in the wake of a crisis in which both the Secretary of State for War, Field Marshal Kitchener, and the First Sea Lord, Admiral "Jacky" Fisher, threatened to resign, Asquith had found himself forced to form a coalition, allowing the Conservatives under their leader Andrew Bonar Law to join his Liberal government as minority members. Now, living with an increasingly shaky political truce, Asquith's eight-year premiership was nearing its end.

Asquith chose to direct the war by what were essentially ordinary peacetime administrative methods, reflecting his Liberal preference for "business as usual." The full Cabinet remained the deciding authority with ad hoc bodies were bolted onto the machinery of the government as the need arose, ministries and departments spawning commissions and committees – on sugar supplies, on fair wages and reserved occupations, on requisitioning, on ship licensing. Improvisation – which was what this was – had serious drawbacks. The full cabinet could not give the fighting the attention it demanded; for one

DOI: 10.4324/9781003375630-5

thing, most of its members had their hands full with departmental business. So, to start with the pre-war Committee of Imperial Defence determined major decisions. That morphed into a War Council and then, when the idea of "finding a flank" took hold, into the Dardanelles Committee. Finally, when the promise of victory at the Dardanelles ended in the bonfires of defeat, that body was replaced in its turn by a War Committee. Awkwardly constructed and inadequate, Asquith's war committee was, in the words of one of its most astute historians, "[a] system of strategic direction [that] could only respond in a series of jerks to fast moving events."[3] When Lloyd George came to power the "supreme command" was in a state of considerable organisational and personal disarray.

Under Asquith's distant leadership, strategic failures piled up. "Classic" strategy failed on the Western Front, where Sir John French's attacks at Festubert (9 May 1915) and Loos (25 September 1915) achieved nothing. The "Easterners" experimental strategy failed at the Dardanelles (25 April 1915–6 January 1916). And traditional imperial strategy, in the form of a classic punitive expedition writ large, came spectacularly to grief in Mesopotamia.

There, despite warnings from the Army Council, Kitchener and Lord Curzon, a former viceroy, the majority of the cabinet decided to back the Indian government's plan to take Baghdad. The viceroy, Lord Hardinge, entrusted the expedition to General Sir John Nixon, "a fiery little man" who would brook no interference from anybody. The resulting double disaster – defeat at the battle of Ctesiphon (22–24 November 1915), then the siege and finally the surrender of Kut (29 April 1916) – played to the advantage of Haig and Robertson. India lost control of military operations to London, strengthening Sir William Robertson's hand as Chief of the Imperial General Staff, and the report of the commission of enquiry, published on 20 June 1917, lambasted everybody directly involved in the catastrophe. The politicians in London were accused of subordinating military conditions to political considerations in the shape of prestige and imperial expansion. Mesopotamia helped put the ball firmly in the army's court. Haig and Robertson determined to keep it there.

By December 1916, the Conservatives had had enough of Asquith, and so had some of his own Liberal party. Militarily, a lot had gone wrong during the previous two years and not much had gone right. Asquith was, in the words of the American ambassador, "a spent force, at once nimble and weary." It was obvious that his "grip" on the war was simply too weak, and on 5 December, after a week of intense political machinations, he resigned. Two days later, David Lloyd George became prime minister. Next day, Robertson handed him a note. The prime minister must not expect the war suddenly to come to an end. "It is much too big for that. Germany is fighting for her life."[4] Carefully crafted, it was a warning: the British Army was now engaged in an existential struggle on a Darwinian scale.

Prime minister at 53, eleven years younger than the man he was replacing, Lloyd George came into office with a wealth of experience. First in peace and then in war, he had served successively as chancellor of the exchequer, minister of munitions and secretary of state for war. A Welshman (he spoke English as his second language) and a Nonconformist, he was also very much an outsider in a world of politicians and soldiers who came mostly from the public schools and the older universities. Energetic, unconventional in his approach to the business of government, his mind awash with ideas ranging from the inspired to the foolhardy, Lloyd George came into office determined to "make the weather."

The soldiers, with whom he now had to deal, had a clear and exact vision of what they were doing and how they were going to do it. Their objective, set down by Robertson in November 1915, was the complete and decisive defeat of the Central Powers. They had a strategy, forged by Robertson and Joffre at the first Chantilly Conference in December 1915. The Western Front would be the principal theatre of operations. The Allies would defeat Germany through simultaneous co-ordinated offensives by all four allies which would produce "a strategic rupture." And Haig had the requisite operational method: attacks on a wide front, "wearing down" the enemy, and then sending in the reserves. He had arrived at it, he said, by "applying old principles to present conditions." "Wearing out" – or attrition – was for him an article of faith, and he believed in it to the end. After the war, a frustrated and furious Lloyd George accused the high commands and the chiefs of staffs of the Western Powers of having concluded that this was to be a war of attrition, and having "so contrived matters that their strategical notion should be the only one left on the board."[5]

Despite going their separate ways, the Central Powers turned out to be strong enough to contain the Chantilly strategy. Verdun bled the French Army, and the Somme did the same to the British army. In November 1916, shored up by Haig's belief (shared by Robertson) that the Somme offensive, which cost the British army an estimated 582,919 casualties, was a definite stage on the road to victory, an inter-allied conference agreed to continue the Chantilly strategy in the coming year, though this time they had to accept that their respective offensives would not and could not be simultaneous.

The Western Front was still the main theatre. Asquith endorsed Joffre's and Haig's plan to renew the Somme offensive the following February and told Haig that he was "very pleased with our success." "Lloyd George thought otherwise. Believing, like the cabinet secretary, lieutenant-colonel Sir Maurice Hankey, that the 'Red-Hatted staff' was bleeding Britain to death, he came into office determined to bring about fundamental changes in both British and Allied strategy" Times were changing, Robertson warned Haig, and likely not to their advantage. "There is," he told Haig two weeks into the new regime, "a very dangerous tendency becoming apparent for the War Cabinet to direct military operations."[6]

Before he could begin to exercise "supreme command," Lloyd George had to create the instruments through which to act. At the helm of a new five-man war cabinet, intended to sharpen decision-making and therefore largely free of departmental responsibilities, he had to keep a pair of its members, the powerful and independently minded Conservative imperial pro-consuls, Lords Milner and Curzon, on his side. He subcontracted much of the detailed work to a web of committees and sub-committees. Two secretariats serviced the new organisation; the cabinet secretariat run by Hankey, who once described himself as "Lloyd George's valet" (like another British civil servant much later, he was being somewhat economical with the truth), and the premier's "garden suburb," a small private office whose five members went wherever Lloyd George wanted them to go across government, probing as they went. Their job was to stir things up.

In London, the new Liberal prime minister was dependent for power on the support of a Conservative opposition whom by inclination strongly backed the generals. For the better part of two years, Lloyd George would strain every political sinew to impose his view of where, and therefore how the war should be fought on men, described Hankey as "the most conservative class in the world, forming the most powerful trade union in the world." In France and Belgium, Douglas Haig was fighting three separate but inter-related campaigns, one against the Germans, a second part competition and part co-operation with and against the French, and a third defending his strategic autonomy against the politicians in London. There, Robertson unwaveringly supported him. "There is only one way of ending this war satisfactorily," he declared in February 1915, "and that is by putting our troops where they can kill the most Germans and by trusting to ourselves and not to other people." To do that, the soldiers must be left alone to get on with the war. As he told Geoffrey Dawson, editor of *The Times*, on the eve of the Somme campaign, anything that could be done to keep politics and politicians out of the War Office would be "for the good of the country."

Asquith had set out Britain's war aims – the restoration of Belgium, French security against aggression, adequate guarantees of the independence of small states, and the destruction of Prussian militarism. Lloyd George, too, believed that no negotiated peace or lasting settlement was possible with Germany until "German Militarism" had been crushed. "We have accepted this war for an object, and a worthy object," he told the House of Commons in his first speech as prime minister, "and the war will end when that object is attained." The destruction of Prussian militarism would require a complete and decisive military victory. On this, the new premier and the generals, on whom he depended to fight the war, thought as one. But it was also where they parted company. Where and how that all-encompassing victory was to be achieved were as much questions of grand strategy as of strategy. The soldiers thought they owned the answers. On the evidence of past performance, Lloyd George was sure they did not. Resolving the issue meant dissolving the frontier between policy and strategy which Haig and Robertson regarded as fixed.

To win the war, Britain had to mobilise and efficiently deploy national resources of wealth, manpower and industrial capacity fully. For Lloyd George, these were complex policy issues. For Haig and Robertson, the matter was simple. "We must fully spend all we have," Haig had noted in his dairy as the Somme campaign entered its third week, "energy, life, money, everything in fact, without counting the cost."[7] Lloyd George had to count the cost. More than that, he had to apportion the nation's resources, human, material and psychological, to secure Britain's war aims before the country ran out of any or all of them. In a word, Lloyd George had to shape a grand strategy and then implement it.

Apportioning effort meant rather more than devoting the lion's share of British manpower and resources to the Western Front, as Haig and Robertson demanded. Ottoman Turkey was a threat to Britain's imperial interests across the Middle East from the Suez Canal and the Straits to India, with its substantial Muslim population. Townshend's surrender at Kut had been a blow to British imperial prestige which Britain could not allow to go unpunished, and a subsequent Russian advance towards Teheran seemed to presage Russian possession of Baghdad. General Sir Stanley Maude received sufficient strength to put matters right, which he did by first overwhelming a Turkish army at Kut and then by capturing Baghdad in March 1917. In Palestine, where the Turks were entrenching themselves along a line north of the Sinai, the war cabinet unleashed General Sir Edmund Allenby in August 1917 with instructions from Robertson to "give the Turks in front of you a sound beating" but not, for the time being at least, to follow that up with an advance into northern and central Palestine. Tellingly, the two arguments advanced by Robertson for not extending the campaign were his doubts about "whether we can, having regard to all the circumstances of the war, maintain ourselves after going forward *and to a useful purpose*."[8] Allenby duly obliged, smashing the Turkish forces at the Third Battle of Gaza (31 October–7 November 1917) and capturing Jerusalem.

The Politics of War

The character and personality of the political leader are always key factors in the strategy-making process. A politician to his finger-tips, Lloyd George readily admitted to being a "past-master" at craftiness. What many, particularly among the upper ranks of the army, regarded as evidence of shiftiness and unreliability was for a prime minister who carried only half of his own Liberal Party with him, and who was shored up by Conservative politicians and a largely Conservative press, an essential weapon in his political armoury. "For political ascendancy," as one of his biographers has remarked, "he had to depend ... very largely on his own adroitness and personal prestige."[9] Doing so came naturally to "the Welsh wizard." Passionately self-absorbed in his own role in running the war, according to one observer "he acted all his rivals off the stage."

The new prime minister valued imagination and flair. "Bring me a list of persons with ideas," he is supposed to have said when manning one of his many committees. Haig, "a painstaking professional soldier with a sound intelligence of secondary quality," did not fit the bill. Settling old scores in his Memoirs, Lloyd George said later that he had "never met any man in a high position who seemed to him so utterly devoid of imagination."[10] This was less than fair to Haig. Like other European commanders, Haig was learning by experience how to lead, administer and direct a mass citizen army. And with Robertson's help, he soon proved adept at walling his armies – and his command – off from intervention by the civilian administration in Whitehall.

But Lloyd George had a point. Haig believed that the righteousness of the cause must ultimately bring victory. His singleness of purpose was both a strength and a weakness. It was a strength because he was sure that his decisions, once reached, were the right ones. "I have been in the field now for 3 years & know what I am writing about," he told Robertson in August 1917. It was a weakness because it closed his mind off to strategic alternatives, both on the Western Front and beyond. And behind a determined exterior, there lurked a personalised sensitivity, evident in Haig's readiness to identify all disputes as undermining his authority and thereby weakening the spirit of the army, which he depicted in his official and semi-official correspondence as "a delicate plant." When the Supreme War Council was unveiled in November 1917, Haig believed that it was intended to vindicate Lloyd George's conduct of the war in the eyes of the public, and in so doing "put the people against the soldiers."[11]

Generals liked to present themselves – and be depicted – as blunt warriors devoted to their profession and above political scheming. This was a convenient fiction. Haig had seen at first-hand how Lord Roberts had cultivated the press during the South African War. The first commander of the BEF, Sir John French, had used the press to stir up trouble for Kitchener over the "shell scandal" and to evade criticism of his handling of the Loos offensive. Haig knew the power of the press, and he knew exactly what the press was for: to prevent the abandonment of what he regarded as "sound military principles … owing to the pressure of ill-informed public opinion."[12] He also knew how to use it. Press barons were regularly entertained at his Headquarters; half-a-dozen tame war correspondents were embedded at GHQ, making no criticism of it or of the success or failure of its strategy; and Haig even invited two pressmen (Gibbs of the *Daily Chronicle* and Beach Thomas of the *Daily Mail*) to compose his own weekly commander-in-chief's reports on the war.

The press played ball. At the front, the war correspondents disguised the unpleasant realities of war behind a tissue of patriotic fiction. As one of them admitted, lies were necessary in wartime because "a crusading cause" created its own moral conditions which obtained until peace was restored. So, the reputations of commanders were defended against political attacks in London and shielded from public scrutiny at the front. Behind the front, the press barons played their part. As the Somme campaign ground to its end, Lord Northcliffe, proprietor of *The Times* and the *Daily Mail,* ran a "hands off the army" campaign, declaring in the *Mail* on 13 October 1916 that "Ministerial meddling means military muddling."

If Lloyd George could not wrench the land war out of the hands of Haig and Robertson, he would try to redirect it away from the Western Front. A month into office, and armed by the Italian general staff with a promising picture of a "decisive result" that could be achieved on the Isonzo front against the Austrians, Lloyd George called a conference in Rome (5–7 January 1917). There, he argued that concentrating British and French artillery on the Isonzo would allow the allies to make "a great and sudden stroke" against a weaker enemy. The scheme foundered immediately. Seduced by the promise of a short, sharp offensive modelled on his successes in the later stages of the battles at Verdun, the War Cabinet decided on 16 January to back Nivelle's forthcoming offensive. That decision, Robertson told them, ruled out sending any British troops or guns to Italy, either now or in the summer, given the uncertainty of the situation. There would, for the time being, be no British support for an attack on the Italian theatre. Nor was there any question of sending reinforcements to Italy, even if she was attacked: "[To] move troops about from one front to another for *defensive* purposes" was, Robertson pronounced, "unsound in many ways, and to be strongly deprecated."[13]

As far as concerned the soldiers, Italy was never a key plank in Allied strategy, but Russia was. Within months it gave way. At the end of December 1916, the Russian general staff withdrew its commitment to "swift and decisive" blows against Germany's eastern and western fronts that had been a core part of an allied strategy. Sporadic mutinies were already occurring in Russian units. On 23 February 1917 (8 March New Style) strikes and street demonstrations erupted in St. Petersburg, and the first Russian Revolution began. Three weeks later, General Alexeev told London that the loss of morale and discipline in the Russian Army made it unlikely that there could be any large-scale operations before June or July. That, for Robertson, was more or less that as far as Russia was concerned. She holds enemy divisions on her own front, but beyond that, he did not anticipate military assistance from Russia that year.[14]

Always ready to believe that the French Army was more efficient at killing Germans than his own army and won over by General Robert Nivelle's accommodating personality and excellent command of English, Lloyd George forced a reluctant Haig to accept local and temporary subordination to the French. The two generals had agreed on a co-ordinated three-phase operation: simultaneous attacks by both armies to "draw in and use up the enemy's reserves;" a "very short" and "decisive" attack by the French, in tandem with continuing operations by the British; and then the exploitation of successes gained, provided that they promised complete victory, or at least would force the enemy to abandon the Belgian coast. The corollary was that Haig should take over fifteen miles of the French line, which he was reluctant to do.

Called to London to discuss the arrangements, Haig and Robertson found themselves embroiled in what Lloyd George regarded as a "trial of strength" with the generals. Wanting to make the attack as successful as possible, the war cabinet told Haig that he must extend his line. All was not yet done, however. Having put their names to an agreement that Haig would "conform to the orders of the Commander-in-Chief of the French Army in all matters relating to the conduct of the operations." Haig and Robertson then objected. Robertson detected the thin end of a dangerous wedge. Agreement on a temporary subordination was finally reached, but only after Hankey had smoothed over some rough edges to gain Haig's acquiescence.

Nivelle's offensive began on 25 April 1917, and within twenty-four hours it was obviously in trouble. Instead of stopping it, as he had said he would, Nivelle pressed on. It was the end of the Frenchman's career. Would it also be the end of Haig's? Two weeks into the battle, Lloyd George asked Hankey whether the British commander-in-chief should be replaced. Hankey started from the first principles. The commanders-in-chief of the British and French armies must have confidence in one another, and secondly, the prime minister and the war cabinet must have confidence in the British commander-in-chief. Unfortunately, neither of these principles applied to Haig. Nivelle appeared to have little confidence in Haig and did not work well with him. Nor did Lloyd George have much confidence in him – misgivings that Hankey thought were based "partly perhaps on instinct, but more on his excessive optimism, and on the fact that the results of his previous operations have never come anywhere near his own anticipations." On the other hand, the war cabinet had confidence in Haig, and – more to the point perhaps – there was no obvious successor.[15]

Unable to remove Haig and by-pass Robertson, Lloyd George could not risk a direct confrontation. Their strategy, afterwards summed up by Robertson as keeping up the pressure at the decisive point and resisting the temptation to divert power to what both he and Haig regarded as side-shows, was all the more difficult to dislodge because it was now backed by the Navy. Unable to find a solution to the growing problem of submarine warfare, the Admiralty advocating capturing U-Boat bases in Flanders as the solution to their problem.

Nivelle's fall made it more difficult for Lloyd George to back the French against the British, as he liked to do. It also changed the strategic balance. Haig's attacks at Arras, originally intended as a subsidiary operation, now continued with the French in the supporting role. More broadly, the disappearance of Tsarist Russia made Italy appear even more of a liability. At the Paris Conference on 4 May 1917, Britain and France agreed that it was essential to continue offensive operations on the Western Front so as not to give the enemy the opportunity to attack Russia – or Italy. Russia's obviously failing strength reverberated across multiple theatres. Robertson had to strike out any possibility of withdrawing troops from Mesopotamia "if and when Russia drops out," and hopes of active Russian support operations in northern Mesopotamia were now a will-o'-the-wisp.

The "defection" (as Milner described it) of Russia and the appearance in the lists of the United States raised major questions about the future shape and conduct of the war. Milner for one was less than happy about how decisions were currently being made. The country was drifting. Strategic cases needed examination by a small committee which would look into the military, naval and political aspects "not separately but in combination with one another." The next day, the war cabinet requested Lieutenant-general Sir Henry Wilson, then head of the British mission to the French Army, to provide his personal view on the prospect of "a considerable military victory." He could see none anywhere except possibly Flanders, "where he understood that Field Marshal Sir Douglas Haig was hopeful." The war cabinet was persuaded of the need, as Churchill put it, for "a fresh stocktaking of the whole war situation."[16] That same day – 8 June – Lloyd George created the five-man War Policy Committee. It met sixteen times in little over a month (11 June–18 July 1917), tasked with weighing the pros and cons of Haig's forthcoming Flanders campaign.

Haig planned a two-phase battle: first exhausting the enemy's reserves in Flanders and then a decisive sweep across north Belgium. Securing the Belgian north coast would, he argued, meet the Admiralty's demand that the army must take that area by the winter if the U-boat threat were to be overcome; it would deprive Germany of a launching pad for future air raids (the first Gotha raid hit London on 13 June 1917); and it would bring the key Roulers-Thourout railway within gun-range. In two meetings, on 19 and 20 June, the War Policy Committee explored the thinking behind the plan and tested Haig's reasoning. They were among the most important discussions of the war.

At the first meeting Haig cited his successes at Messines and Vimy Ridge, suggested that his campaign would be "the beginning of a very great strategical operation," and pointed out that if he did not attack in the current year, then the enemy would attack him, likely losing his army "the same number of men and guns without any advantage." Ending the meeting early (his daughter was getting married that day), Lloyd George asked the generals to consider all the difficulties. Personally, he wanted to reserve British strength until 1918, when the French army had been "resuscitated by the intervention of America."

Overnight he set out his case. Could the French Army, which according to Wilson's report was suffering from "unrest," pull its full weight? Even if it did, the Allies had no more than a bare numerical superiority on the Western

Front. Did Robertson anticipate anything better than Vimy and Messines? He doubted that. Then he floated his two preferred alternatives – overthrowing Turkey and knocking Austria out of the war by giving the Italians the guns and ammunition with which to capture Trieste.

He had inadvertently handed the generals the arguments with which to defeat him. With Russia now inactive in the theatre, a trilateral attack on Turkey from Armenia, Mesopotamia and Palestine was out of the question. Giving the Italians seventy-five batteries of guns would force Haig's armies onto the defensive and would do nothing to diminish the danger of German submarines operating from the Belgian coast. The next day Haig assured the committee that he intended to proceed step by step and that he had no intention of entering into "a tremendous offensive involving heavy losses." His plan "was aggressive without committing us too far." Backed up by the First Sea Lord, Haig carried the day.[17]

Were Robertson and Haig ever likely to reverse course and abandon carefully developed plans founded on their core professional judgements? No, they were not. Was Lloyd George's case well made? No, it was not. Accusing the military of having a "narrow and unimaginative" conception of military strategy was not language likely to win them over to his point of view. In committee, Lloyd George acted like an advocate presenting a case to a judge and jury. There was no judge to direct the jury (or at least, Lloyd George could not reasonably claim to act as both advocate and judge) – but there was a jury: the War Policy Committee.

If the first half of his case was potentially persuasive, the second was not. Lloyd George's core argument – "If success was achieved on the Italian Front … victory in the War was assured" – was nothing more than an assertion. Unable to carry the committee with him, and therefore unable to over-rule the chief military adviser to the cabinet and the commander-in-chief of the British Armies in France, the prime minister had no option but to leave responsibility for the decision to them. Conscious that France was now in the grip of strikes, and fearing that she might go the same way as Russia and empower a new premier to look for a separate peace, the committee formally endorsed the Flanders offensive on 16 July. There are two provisos: that Haig would keep to his promise of a step-by-step advance, and that he would not allow it to degenerate into a "Somme-type battle."

Haig had his battle. Now Robertson had to kill the alternative lest the war cabinet swerve away from Haig and the Western Front and towards Allenby and Palestine. It was up to them, he told them, to judge whether the political advantages that would come from the occupation of Jerusalem and southern Palestine were sufficient to justify "a new and great campaign" at this stage of the war. The "purely military" advantages were insufficient to justify the expenditure of force that would be required and the risks that would be incurred. [18]

Third Ypres, or Passchendaele, began on 31 July 1917. In his first attack, General Sir Hubert Gough piled up 27,000 casualties to take eighteen square miles of enemy-held territory. In the next big attack, on 20 September, General Sir Herbert Plumer added 21,000 casualties to the tally for a "gain" of 5.5 square miles. Haig was able to marshal an array of reasons for carrying on with the battle, but doubts were beginning to arise. In August the Director of Military Intelligence, Sir George Macdonogh, found it difficult to imagine that the Allies could fight their way into Germany and dictate peace terms unless "some miracle" happened on the Eastern Front.

In late September Robertson confessed to Haig that he stuck to their plan "more because I see nothing better, and because my instinct prompts me to stick to it, than because of any good argument by which I can support it." Terrible words, Churchill thought, "when used to sustain the sacrifices of nearly four hundred thousand men." Leading figures in both parties were starting to lose faith in the generals. Churchill, whom Haig regarded as a dangerous meddler in "the larger questions of strategy and tactics." doubted whether the Allies could defeat the Germans on the Western Front, while Milner and Bonar Law were rapidly losing patience with the current strategy of "Hammer, Hammer, Hammer."

The War Policy Committee went into recess for the whole of August and the first three weeks of September. It did, though, issue a report on 10 August. It had "grave misgivings" about Haig's plan. Did he have "sufficient superiority of force" to justify the attacks? Could the French be relied upon to do their share? And if Haig's attacks failed would that not produce "a disastrous loss of confidence" everywhere and depression at home? But after weighing the pros and cons, it decided that Haig was to be given his chance – which he had already taken. The full War Cabinet, which rarely discussed military operations at all, never discussed the course of the Flanders campaign. This was perhaps Lloyd George's most signal failure at the helm of the supreme command.

Instead of monitoring the campaign and subjecting it to ongoing critical scrutiny, he spent much of August and September trying to breathe new life into his Turkish and Italian gambits. At a meeting of the War Policy Committee in late September, after criticising Plumer's gains as unlikely to bring much benefit to a war-weary country, he proposed reinforcing Allenby in Palestine "to make sure of one offensive being successful." Then, early in October, after advancing the claim that Nivelle's offensive had produced "the biggest result this year," he recommended the War Cabinet decide on "definite action … which would inflict such a defeat on the Turkish Army as would force the Turkish Government to consider peace." In quasi-legalistic terms, he was arguing that Haig's and Robertson's plea had failed. The case should now be decided in his favour, not theirs.

Robertson counter-attacked. No country had ever had "or probably ever will have" the resources to seek a decision in two theatres at the same time. So, if it were "eventually" decided to get Turkey out of the war, Turkish territory would become the decisive theatre "for an indefinite period." Counting on anything less than a decisive defeat to get the Turks to the table represented a gamble, "and a gamble at this stage of the war would be more dangerous than usual." Time and distance played to Germany's advantage: she could get troops to that front faster than Britain could, and there was no guarantee that British troops sent out from France could get back in time to participate in next summer's fighting in Flanders and France. Weakening the Western Front would be unwise, not least because of the French situation. And in any case "events have shewn [sic] that we can beat the Germans every time we fight them and inflict heavier losses than we ourselves suffer."[19]

The battle of Cambrai, which began on 20 November 1917, was in many ways a typical Haig-Robertson product. In London, building on an argument by Macdonogh that if pressure on Germany were relaxed she might then defeat Italy, exhaust France, and force peace on her own terms, Robertson pressed the importance of an offensive strategy to beat Germany, which would otherwise try to defeat Britain and France before the Americans got into action. At the front, Haig expanded an already grandiose plan, which had been to break the enemy's front by a surprise attack with the aid of tanks, use cavalry to seize Cambrai and then push northeast. Now the cavalry received the task of only "masking" Cambrai and Haig shifted the direction of the drive west, apparently intending to roll up a lengthy stretch of the German front. Five days before the battle began, he assured Robertson that the operation could be stopped at once if it appeared likely to entail "greater losses than I can afford."

Haig justified the action with what was, as Paul Harris has pointed out, contradictory logic: the Germans were strong enough to launch an offensive of their own if he did not attack first, while simultaneously being weak enough to succumb to his attack if and when he did.[20] London was kept entirely in the dark, so the news that the first day had seen an advance of some four miles and the capture of 4,000 German prisoners and 100 German guns, seemed to promise great things. Across England, church bells were rung to celebrate victory. But within twenty-four hours the attack had run completely out of steam, and after a week it was halted. On 30 November the Germans counter-attacked and within five days the British troops were back more or less where they had started. The battle cost Haig another 40,000 casualties.

Cambrai raised big questions, and the war cabinet demanded answers. Why had there been such a surprise if British superiority was as complete as had been alleged, and defensive arrangements were properly organised? And how did Haig explain the discrepancy between the nature of the Germans' success and "the reports that have been consistently received from official sources in regard to the weakness and the deterioration of the[ir] moral[e]?" Haig's response – in which he acknowledged that the German attack had not been a surprise but also that "guns and troops behind the front line were taken unawares" – went down badly.[21] Cambrai finally disillusioned Northcliffe, who had trusted Haig and Robertson "implicitly and explicitly," and had been an enthusiastic backer of the Somme campaign. On 12 December 1917, *The Times* ran a leader headlined "A Case for Inquiry." A press campaign to boost Haig's popularity, possibly orchestrated by Robertson, quickly back-fired, and by the beginning of January 1918 only two newspapers – *The Morning Post* and *Daily Globe* – remained in his corner.

Haig was on the back-foot. Grilled by the war cabinet on the German success, his answer was that the situation had been "somewhat unique in character" because the officers had suddenly had to deploy defensive tactics when hitherto their minds had been wholly on offensive ones. Lloyd George told the cabinet – that is, he told Haig, for the cabinet already knew – that effective defensive measures were vital because the country was reaching the end of its manpower resources. Sir Edward Carson put the point more bluntly: if the war was to go on, then it was "essential that we save men." Pressed on whether it would pay the Germans to attempt "a smashing offensive" and accept the losses that might incur, Haig gave a hostage to fortune. It seemed to him that an expensive offensive would not pay the Germans: "If they failed, they were so much the worse off, while the present position gave them little hope of substantial success." But he was taking no chances. Preparations were in hand to meet the anticipated enemy offensive.

Given a copy of the draft minutes, Haig clearly realised he had been too hasty in brushing off the problem of a major German attack. He adjusted his position. He expected to be "seriously attacked," pushed back in places, and lose ground and guns. But he was confident that he could hold his front "provided the Divisions were maintained at proper strength."[22] It was a clever ploy: if he was wrong, and if the front gave way, it would be the war cabinet's fault for not giving him the men he needed.

Haig was still too powerful to be removed, but deputy heads could roll – and did. Haig's *côterie* at GHQ had been over-subservient to their master and guilty, consciously or unconsciously, of aiding and abetting him. Haig's director of intelligence, brigadier-general John Charteris, whom the secretary of state for war, Lord Derby, thought had taken a "quite unjustifiable view of the fighting value of the enemy" (with which Robertson concurred) and his chief of general staff, lieutenant-general Sir Launcelot Kiggell, were both replaced, as was Haig's quartermaster-general, Sir Ronald Maxwell. If these machinations were intended to undermine Haig, then they had an entirely unintended consequence. The new management team at GHQ was much better than the old one and served Haig well over the next eleven months.

If Haig could not be removed, neither could Robertson. But he could be manoeuvred out of power. The lever that Lloyd George would apply to prise the CIGS out of his seat came to hand when Foch proposed creating an Allied staff. Haig thought the idea "quite unsound" but others – chief among them Henry Wilson – did not, and by early September the idea of what Lloyd George described as "an Allied Council and General Staff in Paris to direct the war" was in circulation. From the prime minister's standpoint, the Supreme War Council, as it would come to be known, had everything to recommend it. It would side-line Robertson and the general staff in London; it would break the hold of the Chantilly agreements and allow for the creation and adoption of a new strategy; and because all parties would reach a consensus, it would enable a fully coordinated war effort. As an added bonus, it would also correct an adverse tendency in British military culture, modifying the national particularism that was especially strong at Haig's GHQ.

First, Lloyd George set out to recruit Woodrow Wilson to the cause. "I believe," he told the President, "that we are suffering to-day from the grooves and traditions which have grown up during the War, and from the inevitable national prejudices and aspirations which consciously or unconsciously influence the judgment of all the nations of Europe." What was needed were "independent minds, bringing fresh views." [23] Then he set Henry Wilson and field marshal Sir John French to "clip Robertson's wings."

At a meeting of the war cabinet on 11 October French and Wilson, who had both dined with the prime minister the previous evening, did the job they were put up to do. French, determined to break down the Haig-Robertson ring, comprehensively undermined Haig's strategy and Robertson's justifications of it, and backed the setting up of a "Superior Council of the Allies." Henry Wilson made a carefully calibrated contribution. The West was "the decisive front" – but it was no use throwing "decisive numbers at the decisive time at the decisive place" (as Haig had argued in a paper which Lloyd George afterwards described as "optimistic slosh") if "the decisive numbers do not exist, if the decisive hour has not yet struck and if the decisive place is ill chosen."[24]

No doubt delighted, Lloyd George read this as meaning that the Western Front was not yet the decisive front, and perhaps never would be. National predilections, and a war front that was split into three more or less independent segments, meant that no-one was taking "the long view." The Allies held all the cards – "men, munitions, guns, aeroplanes, food, money *and* the High Seas" – in their hands. A Superior Direction, or Supreme War Cabinet, as he called it, could best decide how and when, and also presumably where to play them. The Cabinet agreed to the proposal for a Supreme Inter-Allied Council, and a Permanent Inter-Allied General Staff, and on 2 November, Lloyd George told Henry Wilson that he was to be Britain's military representative on the advisory staff.

The genesis of the Supreme War Council signalled the arrival of Lieutenant General Sir Henry Wilson in the inner circle of power. Greatly disliked and distrusted in some military quarters for his (mis-) behaviour during the Curragh mutiny in 1914, Wilson was also suspect because of his brief flirtation with a nascent "National Party" in the summer of 1917, which suggested that he was not without political ambitions of his own. His political and military judgement was far from faultless. Reporting in March 1917 on a visit to Russia, he had not thought that there would be "any deadly internal upheavals during the war." A fortnight later the Tsar abdicated. His record of predicting German moves, on which he spent a great deal of time, has been described as "abysmal."[25] And his abiding conviction that conscription should be enforced in Ireland – the lobster-pot on the sea-bed of war-time British politics – was equally awry. But for Lloyd George, Wilson's greatest claim to admittance into the inner circle was that he was *not* Sir William Robertson. Long a believer in the idea of a small, powerful body to co-ordinate Franco-British policy making, and with a uniquely intimate and sympathetic knowledge of the French Army, Henry Wilson was a man whose hour had come.

When Lloyd George put the idea of what would some to be known as the Supreme War Council to the Allies at Rapallo on 7 November 1917, the wind was in his sails. Militarily, Haig's doings on the Western Front were outshone by Allenby's taking of Gaza that same day. Geo-strategically, the Bolshevik revolution in Russia on 6–7 November changed the configurations of the war yet again. New circumstances called for new measures – and new machinery.

When the plan for a Supreme Allied Council with its accompanying staff was tabled, Robertson immediately got up and left the meeting, asking Hankey to record his action in the minutes. That he got away with such a spectacular display of bloody-mindedness speaks volumes: despite the bloodletting over which they had presided, Haig and Robertson were both still too firmly stuck to their seats for Lloyd George to decant them. After Robertson left, Lloyd George outmanoeuvred a suggestion by the French war minister, Paul Painlevé, that Foch, the French chief of staff, should also be the French representative on the new Allied general staff – which would have put Robertson there was well.

The French bought into the idea of a Supreme War council partly because they saw it as a way to get the British to take over more of the front line in France. Extension of the British line had been agreed in principle in September 1917, the details left to Haig and Pétain. After some complex wheeling and dealing, during which Clemenceau threatened to resign unless the British took over more line and the new permanent military representatives muddied the waters by suggesting a compromise that neither general wanted, Haig agreed to their proposal – but then ignored it. In the end, he added twenty-eight miles of French line to his current ninety-seven. This seemingly minor episode suddenly took on a high profile when the manpower question exploded in May.

In late January 1918, the permanent military representatives at Versailles issued two Joint Notes. The first stated that there was no likelihood of either side securing a decision "in the main theatres" in 1918, and proposed instead "a decisive offensive against Turkey," where a "decisive result" might be possible. The second proposed the creation of a general allied reserve. That carried in its train some highly contentious issues. Who would provide the necessary troops? Should it be under a single general direction – an allied *generalissimo*? And if so, who?

Lloyd George went to Versailles for the discussion of the two papers, and after what Wilson described as a "great fight" over the first he had to settle for a compromise. Clemenceau accepted his proposal to knock out the Turks in 1918 – against the opposition of Foch, Petain, Haig and Robertson – but only in return for a promise that there would be no reduction of effort on the Western Front. No British soldiers would go from France to Palestine. Lloyd George was ready to make Joffre the *generalissimo*, but Haig drew the line at that, and so did Henry Wilson. Wilson produced the solution: the creation of an executive war board to oversee the general reserve, chaired by Foch. Robertson and Lord Derby, the secretary of state for war, at once appealed to Haig to back them in opposing what they saw as unconstitutional command arrangements. Outside Versailles, wily national commanders-in-chief guarded their independence. Haig flatly refused to release any of his divisions in France to an independent general reserve, and he and Petain evaded the SWC's plan to create one under Foch simply by arranging to give one another mutual support in the event of a German offensive. When the SWC met in London on 14–15 March, the reserve was abandoned.

The smouldering conflict over war-time civil-military relations was about to burst briefly into flame. The military correspondent of the *Morning Post*, lieutenant-colonel Charles à Court Repington (himself something of a military outcast) lit the fuse. On 8 February 1918, the paper carried his demand that a parliamentary committee should examine the proposed arrangements for the control of the general reserve while taking into account "the opinions of our General Staff and of our Commanders in the field." Three days later he gave away the whole scheme, including the strategic intentions for 1918, and invited the Army Council to make "a firm and united stand" against the Versailles arrangements "in the interests of the rest of the Army."

For Milner, perhaps the most powerful member of the war cabinet and certainly one of the most forceful, enough was enough. "I think the sooner we make a move the better," he told Lloyd George. "This kind of thing cannot be allowed to go on." He doubted that Haig would "make common cause with only W[ar] O[ffice] people against the Government" but if he did "stick his toes in the ground" over the general reserve, which for Milner was crucial, then "it would be better to lose both Haig and Robertson than to continue at the mercy of both or either of them."[26] Lloyd George wanted to charge Repington and the *Morning Post* with high treason but the lawyers advised otherwise. On 13 February Repington and his editor, H. A. Gwynne, were convicted of breaching the Defence of the Realm Acts and fined £100.

Over the next week Lloyd George, now more convinced than ever that he was being thwarted by the machinations of a military clique, carried out what Churchill afterwards described as "a series of laborious and extremely mystifying manoeuvres," Haig was interviewed and told that the prime minister intended to send Robertson to Versailles as a military representative and make Henry Wilson CIGS in his stead. After warning Lloyd George about "the distrust in which Henry Wilson is held by the Army," Haig judiciously stepped back, telling Robertson that it was his duty to go where the government wished and urging King George V to insist that he go to Versailles. Eventually, Robertson was given a choice: CIGS with reduced powers or Versailles and declined them both. On 18 February 1918, Henry Wilson was appointed CIGS, and the military removal van took Robertson off to Eastern Command. Lloyd George had his man. Would the Supreme War Council now give him the war he wanted?

News that the Bolsheviks had signed the Peace of Brest-Litovsk on 3 March 1918 momentarily focused all eyes on the Turko-German threat to the Middle East. Alarmists detected a pan-Turanian project to link all Turkish-speaking peoples under German guidance. Three days later, Allenby received the go-ahead in Palestine. At first, things did not go well: two attempts to take Amman, in March and May, were both repulsed. The Turks were checking Allied forces in Palestine and Mesopotamia, the Hashemite revolt in the Hejaz was momentarily faltering, and the complete collapse of the Russian military presence in the Caucasus conjured up the spectre of a joint German-Turkish offensive in Persia, threatening Afghanistan and ultimately India. Allenby was ordered to resume his offensive, and on 19 September 1918, his forces smashed the remnants of three Turkish armies at the battle of Megiddo. But by then the main issue was being decided elsewhere.

The German assault on the Western Front on 21 March came as no surprise to GHQ in France. Germany's "offensive intentions" there had been noted since early January, confirmed by estimates of the build-up of enemy troops, and the likely targets (Third Army and the northern portion of Gough's Fifth Army) identified. Four days before the attack, Haig's chief of Intelligence told him that although an attack was not "imminent," he should be ready for one "at short notice." Haig was expecting "a very strong attack on a fifty mile front," but was completely confident that his men could withstand what he expected to be a lengthy "wearing down" fight.[27] In London, Henry Wilson played his part in confecting an air of confidence. By his estimation, Haig had a clear numerical superiority over the enemy who, in any case, would only "threaten" France before attacking in Italy.

Gough's Fifth Army collapsed with shocking speed, and Hindenburg's offensive did what all Lloyd George's machinations had been unable to do. At Doullens on 26 March Haig did an about turn and Foch received powers to "co-ordinate" the Allied armies on the Western Front. This quickly proved insufficient, and on 3 April at Beauvais Foch was entrusted with co-ordinating the actions of the British, French, and American armies on the Western Front and with the strategic direction of military operations. Eleven days later he was made Général-en-Chef of the Allied armies in France. Foch would prove more than up to the task, and Haig co-operated fully in the fighting that followed.

Haig's explanation for the breakthrough, which could have cost him his job, was that it was a matter of numbers. He had had to extend his line by twenty per cent; he had 100,000 fewer men that a year before; and the Germans had three times as many men on the British front as they had had a year ago. Manpower, always a cause of conflict between the soldiers and the politicians, now took centre stage. The army's needs were rapidly becoming unsustainable: in 1917 it had received 800,000 class A recruits, and in 1918 it was set to get another 700,000. In 1919, the minister for national service, Sir Auckland Geddes, would only be able to find at most 300,000 men, of whom at least 130,000 would have to go to the navy and the air force.

An excoriating report by the parliamentary exemptions committee exposed the army's recruiting practices It described "extraordinary abuses of medical examinations, systematic misclassification and general incompetence" and painted an overall picture of "bungling malevolence." Its attitude towards the conscripts with which it stocked and re-stocked its ranks was revealed when the parliamentary select committee on public expenditure, which had been appointed to enquire among other things into the War Office's use of manpower, published its first report. Receiving the report on 11 December 1917, the War Office flatly dismissed the notion that Britain should take the resource costs into account when planning military operations. Haig, looking at war-time domestic politics through the wrong end of a trench periscope, thought simply that the government was afraid to introduce conscription into Ireland – an act which would be "not only in order to get men but for the good of Ireland" – and force the trade unions to disgorge more men. In fact, Lloyd George was willing to transfer men from the munitions factories, the mines and the dockyards, but not to replace Haig's losses ad infinitum. And he knew all too well that Irish conscription was political dynamite.

Robertson was gone and Haig and his army were now fighting for their lives. Was Lloyd George as much, or more, to blame for that as Hindenburg and Ludendorff? The question hit the front pages on 7 May 1918, when the former director of military operations, major-general Sir Frederick Maurice, published an incendiary letter in four major London newspapers accusing Lloyd George of having misled parliament in a speech a month earlier about the numbers of men on the Western Front in January 1918 compared with January 1917. Two days later Lloyd George faced what was in effect a parliamentary vote of no confidence. Selecting his statistics carefully, and using his very considerable debating skills, he saw off the challenge.

Maurice's own figures, supplied by the War Office in April, showed that British combat strength on the Western Front had been greater in January 1918 than a year previously. In fact, the War Office had miscounted. A corrected return, which Lloyd George knew about before the debate, showed that at 969,283 men Haig's fighting strength in January 1918 was down 100,548. A wily premier chose his facts skilfully, winning the debate by 293 votes to 106, but (as ever) statistics could be made to say whatever either side wanted them to say. So, the War Office figures included tank drivers and machine gunners in "ration strength" (which had increased by 45,000 men over the twelve months), but excluded them from "fighting strength." After the war, Lloyd George decided that Maurice had been "the fizzling cracker that was chosen to blow up the Government." Robertson had certainly encouraged Maurice to publish, but beyond that there seems to have been no "military conspiracy."[28]

The Maurice debate taught Lloyd George a lesson – or perhaps it confirmed an intention already forming in his mind. To prevent any more bamboozling by the military, and to boost his authority, he needed to know with much more exactitude what was going on. On 15 May he convened a new four-man "X" committee. Milner, now secretary of state for war, and Henry Wilson the CIGS sat alongside him, along with the ubiquitous Hankey. The cabinet secretary disliked this "new and tiresome method of doing business," but clearly it served Lloyd George's needs during a tense period of exceptional military pressure. Official War Office statements could be unpacked, Wilson and Macdonogh grilled, and arguments rehearsed before the premier tried them out in the war cabinet.

Over the next three-and-a-half months, telling the committee that "our whole organisation was wasteful and unsatisfactory," Lloyd George used it to probe War Office numbers and estimates of enemy reserves, demanding assurances that "less efficient" corps and divisional commanders were being weeded out, and sending envoys to the front to see that labour was being properly applied. He was ready, he told the others, to take on "the unpleasant business" of running Haig's army in detail, but when he tried indirectly to unseat Haig, Milner calmly dismissed any such idea. The question of changing the commander-in-chief had been discussed repeatedly "but he was not yet clearly convinced that a better substitute could be found."[29]

In June, the Dominion premiers arrived in town for the second Imperial War Conference (the first had taken place the previous spring). Sir Robert Borden lost no time in making his and Canada's views felt. He was convinced that "our want of military success had been largely due to lack of foresight and preparation, and to defects in the organisation and leadership of our forces." Speaking on behalf of South Africa, General Smuts first assured everyone that "we had superior resources in every form of war-power," and then, obliquely criticising the entire military machine, added that "all we needed was improved organisation, training and leadership." "Seizing on these remarks,

Lloyd George announced that the issues raised by the Dominion representatives "could not be left where they were."[30] Hedging his bets, Henry Wilson told the conference that no decision in the West could give a decision in the East, so it was necessary to get a decision in both. Curzon told it that the Germans were advancing east along two axes towards India, their real objective. Picking up on this, Wilson pointed out that the collapse of Russia offered Germany and Turkey the opportunity to force their way into the Caucasus and Central Asia, threatening British positions in Mesopotamia, Persia and even India. The British presence in the area must be reinforced, but not by reducing the number of British troops in the West. That was where the war could and must be won. There, Wilson argued for holding the line in the West and building up an arsenal of machine guns, tanks, aircraft and artillery in preparation for an offensive in summer 1919.[31]

Milner was sceptical. The Western Front was "a candle that burned all the moths that entered it." Would we have the necessary three-to-two superiority to force a decision there? He thought not. His preference was for the French and the Americans to provide the bulk of the forces on the Western Front, freeing ten or fifteen British divisions to operate "in other parts of the world," where they should be able "to achieve a great deal." Billy Hughes, the Australian premier, made the obvious counterargument: the powers that had the largest forces on the Western Front at the end of the war would probably exercise the greatest influence on the peace terms. Lloyd George demurred: he thought that the power that was obtaining a decision elsewhere might carry the most weight. Of one thing he was sure – the enemy's weak points were not on the German front. Smuts did not think the Allies could force a decision on the Western Front in 1919 and believed instead that they should concentrate their military effort against Austria, Bulgaria and Turkey. Discussions went on for days.[32]

Finally, in mid-August, the conference reached some conclusions. The government was "ultimately responsible" for directing war policy, and "immediately responsible" for providing the means to carry it out. That included manpower, the husbanding of which was now "a consideration on which the whole future of our Empire depends." Therefore, while not interfering with minor operations, the government had "a right to insist that the general lines of major operations involving the possibility of a heavy casualty list are submitted for their approval."

On strategy, the committee agreed that the Western Front was "the decisive Front" but questioned whether, unless the Eastern Front were recreated, the Allies would possess the necessary superiority to ensure success there in 1919. The whole situation would have to be "most carefully reviewed" early in the new year before a final decision to attack was taken. Meanwhile, no opportunity should be lost to "embarrass" the enemy on the Eastern Front, and British and American divisions should be sent to Italy "o take advantage of any opportunity offered for an offensive blow at Austria."[33]

No more Passchendaeles, then, and a half-open door for Lloyd George and the "neo-Easterners." But the Imperial Conference was already behind the times. If Foch's attack on the Marne between Soissons and Château-Thierry on 18 July was not the beginning of the end, then Haig's attack at Amiens on 8 August certainly was. Together, they signalled the start of the violent campaign that decided Germany's fate. French pressure helped ensure that the strategic focus stayed where Haig and Robertson had always wanted – France and Flanders. So did the threat that Britain's influence at the peace conference for which the politicians were now preparing would decline in proportion to any decline in the number of its troops in Flanders. Old ideas died hard though. Lloyd George never entirely gave up on finding a successor to Haig. And Haig continued to regard politicians as for the most part a lower species of life. In early September 1918, Henry Wilson warned him that the metropolitan police strike and other "cognate matters" were making the cabinet sensitive to heavy losses. "How ignorant these people are of war," was Haig's reaction.

Conclusion

If there is one single war-time episode that bedevils Lloyd George's reputation as a war-time premier, it is surely Passchendaele. For some historians, the responsibility for the bloody debacle lies not with Haig, who dreamed it up and carried it out, but with Lloyd George. Haig was allowed to embark on Third Ypres because "the civilian rulers of Britain gave their consent." This, in turn, was because the War Policy Committee's decisions were "nebulous and did not clearly favour any one task."[34]

Lloyd George had his own answer to that charge. The government could have stopped the Western Front attacks, he told the Dominion premiers in August 1918, if it had had the moral courage to do so. However, if it had done so, "the Military Authorities would have insisted that they had been on the point of breaking through, that the enemy was demoralised, and at the last moment they had been stopped by civilian politicians." True perhaps, but also a tacit admission of weakness. Stopping Haig in his tracks, which would probably have meant firing him, would have required a measure of undisputed authority that Lloyd George never had, and would have used up much and perhaps all the political capital he possessed.

As a wartime prime minister, Lloyd George was in many respects a success. His advocacy and application of business methods revolutionised the way the state managed its business and did its work. His conduct of that business, focusing decision-making within a narrow circle of politicians and statesmen supported by a co-ordinating secretariat, marked a way-stage in the evolution of cabinet government. As well as handling generals, imperial proconsuls, dominion premiers and party politicians, he had also to survive in what Churchill called "the smithy of public life" – and he did. If his wartime premiership was, as has been suggested, "a unique exercise in instant leadership" then by and large it worked in all dimensions save one. Despite eventually ridding himself of Robertson and replacing him with the more pliant Henry Wilson (who proved such a disappointment that he later described him as giving "the impression of unreliability"), Lloyd George failed to overturn Haig's and Robertson's conception of the strategy-policy relationship. After the war, more than one general poured scorn in his memoirs on "the perils of amateur strategy." But in the long run, the pair of them did the job for him – or more precisely, for his friend, ally and successor, Winston Churchill.

Notes

1 Lord Milner to Arthur Steel-Maitland, 2 December 1916: P. A. Lockwood, "Milner's entry into the War Cabinet, December 1916," *Historical Journal* vol. 7 no. 1, 1964, 129.
2 Asquith to Venetia Stanley, 30 December [1914]: *H. H. Asquith Letters to Venetia Stanley*, selected and edited by Michael and Eleanor Brock (Oxford: Oxford University Press, 1985), 346; Hankey Diary, 28 October 1916: Stephen Roskill, *Hankey. Man of Secrets* I: *1877–1918* (London: Collins, 1970), 311–12.
3 John Ehrman, *Cabinet Government and War* (Cambridge: Cambridge University Press, 1958), 60.
4 Liddell Hart Centre for Military Archives [LHCMA]. Unheaded memorandum, 8 December 1916: WRR I/19/9.
5 David Lloyd George, *War Memoirs of David Lloyd George*, III (London: Odhams Press, 1932–1936), 1,084.
6 Robertson to Haig, 24 December 1916: David R. Woodward, ed., *The Military Correspondence of Field Marshal Robertson Chief of the Imperial General Staff, December 1915-February 1918* (London: Bodley Head, 1989), 131–32.
7 *Marshal Sir William Robertson Chief of the Imperial General Staff December 1915-February 1918* (London: Bodley Head: d Haig Diary, 16 July 1916): Keith Grieves, "Haig and the Government, 1916–1918," in Brian Bond and Nigel Cave, eds., *Haig: A Reappraisal 70 Years On* (Yorkshire: Barnsley, 1999), 112. This entry does not appear in either the Blake or the Sheffield/Bourne editions of the diary.
8 David R. Woodward (ed.), *The Military Correspondence of Field Marshal Sir William Robertson* (London: The Bodley Head), 210.
9 John Grigg, *Lloyd George War Leader 1916–1918* (London: Faber & Faber, 2011), 8.
10 Lloyd George, *War Memoirs* IV, 2266, 2267.
11 Haig Diary 4 November 1917: Robert Blake, ed., *The Private Papers of Douglas Haig 1914–1919* (Ann Arbor: University of Michigan, 1952), 263.
12 "Memorandum on Policy for the Press": Stephen Badsey, "Haig and the Press," in Bond and Cave, *Haig*, 183.
13 The National Archives [TNA] Note on a proposal for combined operations on the Italian Front, 29 January 1917, and attachment: W.O. 106/1511; Robertson to Nivelle, 16 March 1917 (original emphasis): W.O. 106/765.
14 TNA. C.I.G.S. to Delmé-Radcliffe, 23 April 1917: W.O. 106/765.
15 TNA. Memorandum for the Prime Minister, 8 May 1917, para. 7: CAB 63/19.
16 TNA. War Cabinet #159a, 8 June 1917: CAB 23/16.
17 Grigg, 164–67; Lloyd George, *War Memoirs*, IV, 2163–75.

18 LHCMA. "Palestine," 19 July 1917: Robertson Papers WRR I/16/6.
19 LHCMA. "Future Military Policy," 9 October 1917: Robertson Papers WRR I/16/7/2.
20 J. P. Harris, *Douglas Haig and the First World War* (Cambridge: Cambridge University Press, 2008), 388–94.
21 TNA War Cabinet #229, 5 December 1917: CAB 23/4: Haig to Robertson, 18 December 1917: CAB 24/36/G.T. 3039.
22 TNA. War Cabinet 316, 7 January 1918, pp. 5, 8, 9, with handwritten amendments by Haig: CAB 23/44b.
23 Lloyd George to Woodrow Wilson, 3 September 1917: Lloyd George, *War Memoirs* IV, 2354.
24 TNA. "The present state of the War and the future prospects and future action to be taken," 20 October 1917: CAB 27/8/61; Lloyd George, *War Memoirs* IV, 2360, 2380.
25 Keith Jeffery, *Field Marshal Sir Henry Wilson. A Political Soldier* (Oxford, 2006), 101, 186; David Woodward, *Lloyd George and the Generals* (Newark, DE: Oxford University Press, 1983), 282.
26 Milner to Lloyd George, 8 February 1918: Lloyd George, *War Memoirs* V, 2790–91.
27 Jim Beach, *Haig's Intelligence: GHQ and the German Army, 1916–1918* (Cambridge: Cambridge University Press, 2013), 274–88.
28 David R. Woodward, "Did Lloyd George Starve the British Army of Men prior to the German Offensive of 21 March," *Historical Journal* vol. 27 no. 1, March 1987, 241–52.
29 TNA. X-2, 16 May 1918; X-21, 16 July 1918: CAB 23/17.
30 TNA. Imperial War Cabinet #17, 14 June 1918: CAB 23/41.
31 TNA. British Military Policy, 1918–1919, 25 July 1918: CAB 27/8/WP 70.
32 TNA. Imperial War Cabinet #27a, 31 July and 1 August 1918: CAB 23/44a.
33 TNA. Report of the Committee of Prime Ministers, 14 August 1918, Pt. I, pp. 7–8; Pt. IV, pp. 2–5. CAB 23/44a.
34 Robin Prior and Trevor Wilson, *Passchendaele: The Untold Story* (New Haven, CT: Yale University Press, 1996), 38, 41.

6

IMPERIAL GERMANY'S SUPREME COMMAND DURING THE FIRST WORLD WAR

Holger Afflerbach

Both World Wars had a tendency to radicalize their intensity and embrace entire societies. They came close to what Clausewitz had called "absolute" war.[1] Clemenceau, Ludendorff, and Goebbels all spoke about "total wars" or "*guerre integrale*."[2] Strategic planning in such a conflict was a massive task; it had to integrate societies, to co-ordinate the war efforts and to develop war aims which were widely supported by the own population.

As far as the First World War, no European state entered the war, as Hew Strachan convincingly argues, with a clear strategy; the upmost of what they had was a plan for operations.[3] But the strategy is more all-encompassing than that; it has to include the aim of the war and a plan for how it can be achieved. According to definitions given by the doyens of military history, strategy is the plan for how a state can achieve its political aims by war, and how it needs to coordinate its political, economic, and especially military efforts.

Thus, the strategy must represent the integration of internal and external politics, military, and psychological planning and the conduct of war and of economics and armaments by the leadership of a state to realize an ideological and political aim.[4] Michael Howard phrased it in the following terms: "Grand strategy in the first half of the twentieth century consisted basically in the mobilisation and deployment of national resources of wealth, manpower and industrial capacity, together with the enlistment of those of allied and, when feasible, of neutral powers, for the purpose of achieving the goals of national policy in wartime."[5]

German War Aims and Strategic Leadership

Before addressing Germany's strategic leadership, one needs to address several basic questions. The first is what the German people wanted to achieve during the Great War, and what Imperial Germany's strategic aim was. The answer to

DOI: 10.4324/9781003375630-6

the question could be short: this author claims that Imperial Germany had no strategy in 1914 and no aim except the idea of national self-defence. Moreover, it was incapable of developing a coherent strategy at any time later.

Not all historians would agree. Some would argue the German leadership had a massive responsibility for the outbreak of war, but more because of major mistakes, carelessness, and mishandling than of an active desire to bring about a continental war, especially not in the form it took in August 1914, which included Britain. The German approach was not a deliberate attempt to unleash the war, but a playing with options, and its main purpose was to stabilize its ally, Austria-Hungary, and end the internal undermining waged by nationalists supported by Serbia. Preserving the potential collapse of the most important German alliance partner was the main political objective during the July Crisis and considered to be a strategic life-or-death question. These historians find themselves divided as to whether the German leadership expected their promise to help the Austrians against Serbia (Blanc cheque) might trigger an escalation into a European War.

A fundamentally different opinion follows the research of Fritz Fischer, who argued in his major studies *Germany's War Aims* (1961) and *War of Illusion* (1966) that Imperial Germany wanted the war and even prepared for it beforehand. His key evidence is the so-called September Programme 1914 which aimed at European hegemony and, according to Fischer, represented a blueprint for all German designs of conquest during the First World War.[6] The divergence in these opinions leads to a completely different evaluation of German strategic leadership during the First World War. Fischer and his followers argued that Imperial Germany pursued a plan of conquest. Therefore, in this view, Imperial Germany had a clear war aim and a clear strategy, even if it failed in the end.

The first group of historians (and also this chapter as well) interpret the German conduct of war differently, namely as a muddling through, a constant search to find a good or at least acceptable way out of the war, and a permanent struggle between differing concepts by competing centres of power. A major scholarly achievement was Gerhard Ritter's *Sceptre and Sword*, in which he interpreted Germany's leadership as the struggle between a moderate political leadership, Bethmann Hollweg, and the military who tried to dominate and militarize and radicalize German warfare to pursue their plans of conquest. In Ritter's view, Ludendorff, in particular, was the key figure of German "militarism."[7]

How Strategic Decisions Were Made, and by Whom

The historical debate comes down to the question of who was controlling Imperial Germany in 1914, a society with 65 million citizens. Who was responsible for formulating war aims and the strategy to achieve them? And did German society support them? Thus, the question boils down to the real nature of the political and constitutional structure of Germany during the war. In examining this question, on discovers that Imperial Germany was not a rigid hierarchical structure where a top-down approach can explain wartime politics and strategy, but a cumbersome political machine where dissenting "power centres" (*Herrschaftszentren*) had to bargain constantly to find common ground for central strategic decisions.[8]

This was different from what most contemporaries believed and how they interpreted Imperial Germany at home and abroad. The views of the time were closer to Fischer's idea of a nearly monolithic structure, of Germany being a rigid monarchy under the semi-absolutist leadership of Wilhelm II and aiming for European hegemony. The reality was a "polycratic chaos" where competing power centres rivalled each other for influence in the decision-making process. This was and is probably true for many societies, but Imperial Germany represents an extreme case. Too many individuals and institutions were able to exercise a veto on one another, mutually blocking each other's suggestions. The mechanisms underpinning German leadership were utterly chaotic. This is an image that seems to confirm the view of the British Minister of War, Haldane, that in the well-organized German nation, there was not simply confusion but outright chaos at the highest ranks of leadership.[9]

Not surprisingly, Imperial Germany had no proper strategy, except the widely accepted goal of national self-defence. Thus, it was unable to develop a coherent plan, because the various political factors could not agree on one and vetoed those proposed by others. Moreover, the Reich possessed no strong wartime political leader, like Lloyd George or Clemenceau, or somebody like Bismarck. Bethmann himself admitted that he was "no Bismarck."[10] The Iron Chancellor, the founder of the Empire, had dominated Prussian and German strategy during the wars of Unification even though the circumstances and internal structures were even more confusing than during the First World War. It was not the result of a faulty constitution or political structures alone that resulted in Germany's defeat; individuals mattered as well. The Empire's structures were complicated and required a skilful and determined leader to function properly. During the First World War, the Reich lacked such a figure.

The Power Centres

The Kaiser and His Entourage, Especially the Military, Naval, and Civil Cabinet

The Kaiser was, according to the constitution, the wartime leader of the armed forces of Imperial Germany, and responsible for the coordination of military and civilian efforts of warfare. It was up to him to develop a coherent strategy. Wilhelm II was incapable of performing that task. Historians have examined his personality and intentions, among them his plan to make Germany a global power, in great detail.[11] But what matters here was that the Kaiser was a volatile, undisciplined individual, who failed to live up to his constitutional task to coordinate German strategy. Probably even Bismarck would have struggled to control the military and political conduct of this war; but the Kaiser was particularly inept. The head of his military cabinet, General von Lyncker, who part of the emperor's daily entourage, observed in May 1917 that: "He is not equal to this great challenge, having neither the nerve nor the intellect to tackle it."[12] That left a crucial void in the making of German strategy that Wilhelm II refused to allow anyone else to fill. Yet, it was impossible to ignore him. In spite of his erratic personality, he remained a dominant personality who refused to allow others to push him aside. He was therefore half an obstacle and irritant, and half a coordinator of German strategy. In some cases, he participated in the decision-making process with reasonable, but in many other cases his decisions were truly terrible.

The Kaiser blustered in peacetime that he would be, if needed, his own chief of staff; but he was unable to lead. He was self-aware enough to realize his shortcomings as a leader, which often kept him from event trying to grab the reins. This restraint was wise but surely frustrating. During the war, he was with the army command in GHQ and was briefed daily by the chief of staff, but not in a way which offered or allowed him active involvement. The Kaiser often complained that he was not even being kept up to date. On 6 November 1914, he made a semi-ironic comment to the chief of the naval cabinet, Admiral von Mueller, that has cemented the image of Wilhelm as a powerless commander-in-chief: "The general staff tells me nothing and does not even consult me. If people in Germany imagine that I command the army, they are much mistaken. I drink tea and chop wood and like to go for walks, and from time to time I find out what has been done, just as it pleases the gentlemen."[13] His complaints were a permanent feature: he was often bad-tempered and argued "that he is being completely side-lined by the chief of staff and that he does not find out anything. He complains that he is expected just to say 'yes' to everything and says he could do that just as well from Berlin!"[14]

The Kaiser's opportunities to influence operational decisions remained limited, and this becomes striking when one compares his authority with the manner Hitler controlled the movements of the biggest and smallest units of the German Army. But leading and ruling by himself, or meddling into the details, had never been the real source of Wilhelm's power; appointments and dismissals were. During his entire reign, his power did not rest on his ruling the Reich, despite countless attempts and public declarations. His direct interventions tended to fail miserably; but choosing who ruled on his behalf was a more powerful political approach.

The Imperial constitution gave Wilhelm the right to appoint and dismiss the chancellor, the chiefs of staff, and many other high-ranking personnel in the army, navy, and higher administration. The Kaiser made history by using this lever of personal politics during his thirty years of ruling Germany. Three prominent examples underline this point: the dismissal of Bismarck in 1890; the appointment of Tirpitz in 1897, which started the German battlefleet building program; and the appointment of the architect of *Weltpolitik*, Bernhard von Bülow, as chancellor in 1900, as well as his dismissal in 1909, after Bülow failed the Kaiser during the *Daily Telegraph* affair.

Being Imperial Germany's Head of Human Resources was much less than the Kaiser wanted and pretended to be but offered him considerable power which did not stop in August 1914. During the war, the Kaiser continued to influence events by choosing, rejecting, and dismissing high-ranking decision makers, or by hanging on to individuals and supporting them against opposition. A prominent example is his second chief of staff, Erich von Falkenhayn, whom he nominated in September 1914 and kept in the office until late August 1916 against strong opposition which included Bethmann Hollweg, Hindenburg, Moltke, large parts of the army leadership, and even his own wife.

Leading and ruling himself, or meddling in the details of military planning, was not the real source of Wilhelm's power; appointments and dismissals were. The three chiefs of his cabinets aided him in this task. General Moritz von Lyncker, Head of the Military Cabinet, determined Prussian Army promotions; Admiral Georg Alexander von Müller, Head of the Naval Cabinet, did the same for the Imperial Navy, and Rudolf von Valentini for civilian posts, including the position of Chancellor.

It was up to Valentini to look, if needed, for candidates for the chancellorship, and he had to do that twice during the war. Events later proved that his searches – during an ongoing world war – for the highest political leader of Germany were astonishingly incompetent.[15] Still, being responsible for such appointments represented a major task, and the three men were, thanks to the Kaiser's constitutional powers, potentially powerful individuals and key advisors. All three cabinet chiefs were, in principle, a moderating force, conservative, but reasonable and moderate. They tried to keep the unstable emperor in line. With the lever of personal politics in their hand, the Kaiser and his advisors did not lead themselves, but they operated a control over the people who acted on the emperor's behalf.

However, neither the Kaiser nor his key advisors had a proper and powerful strategic vision. Nevertheless, Wilhelm II had to appear more than once in the centre of strategic decision-making, namely in all cases when the civilians and military leaders could not agree on major decisions with political and military implications. Examples include the question of East or West in 1914, of employing new reserves on the Eastern Front against Russia or on the Western Front against France and Britain; this decision led to a serious leadership crisis, and Wilhelm solved it somehow in January 1915. The Kaiser also chaired several important meetings in which the leaders of the army, navy and civilian leaders discussed the strategic implications of unlimited submarine warfare from 1915 to 1917. The Kaiser had to decide, or to bring about a decision, when military, naval, and civilian leaders disagreed; then they appealed to the emperor, for example in questions of war aims. Wilhelm II was uncomfortable with chairing these meetings when he had to try to reconcile hostile opponents; he tried to avoid doing so wherever possible, but in some cases his intervention was essential and unavoidable.

The Chancellor

Wilhelm II could have been a powerful war leader but was not. Another who might have provided leadership and who was responsible for strategic leadership was the Imperial chancellor. There were four chancellors during the war. The most important of them, Theobald von Bethmann Hollweg, served in office from 1909 until July 1917. Imperial chancellors only needed the approval of the Kaiser for their nomination and did not require a supporting parliamentary majority in the Reichstag, something Bethmann never had. On the contrary, in December 1913, nine months before the outbreak of war, he lost a vote of no confidence (during the Zabern affair) by 293 votes to 54, with four abstentions, an event that would have collapsed a British government. But he could ignore the vote because he still had the Kaiser's backing, which he enjoyed until his resignation in July 1917. Nevertheless, he also needed the Reichstag to approve the imperial budget. In wartime, this budget approval was required to maintain *Burgfrieden* (truce) – the consent of the German people, to avoid strikes. It was this that preserved political consensus and public support for the war. If the budget failed to pass, the internal stability of Germany would falter.

Authoritarian governments may be weaker than democratic ones because of the permanent problem of legitimacy and lack or uncertainty of public backing. This was surely a central weakness of Bethmann's position. Not having full public support represented a major problem for a wartime leader. How could he coordinate German strategy, or formulate war aims, if he did not know whether the German people backed him? The truth was that they did not. The maximum he could manage was to keep the parties and the Reichstag in line for a war of national defence and keep in check strong groups and associations who were demanding large annexations in the first two years of the war.

The lack of public support was a serious, but not Bethmann's only problem; another one was his personality. He was a highly intelligent and honourable man but tortured by self-doubts and certainly not possessing the material to be a great wartime leader. Among his biggest flaws, besides his sense of responsibility for the outbreak of war, was the fact he let himself be repeatedly overruled by others who were less insightful but more determined. His instincts were more often than not perceptive, but he lacked the will to drive them through. The most striking example was the declaration of unlimited submarine warfare which he opposed but allowed the military to overrule his judgment.

Army Leadership, General Staff, Prussian Ministry of War, and Senior Commanders

Military leaders filled partially filled the void at the top of the German strategic leadership created by Wilhelm II and Bethmann. At the top of the German armies – the plural is necessary because there were four separate army organizations (the Prussian, Bavarian, Wurttembergian, and Saxonian armies) – was the chief of the general staff, who acted on behalf of the emperor. The chief of staff was originally not a supreme commander, but only responsible for military operations. There were three chiefs of staff during the First World War, the younger Moltke from the outbreak of war until September 1914, then Erich v. Falkenhayn until August 1916 and finally Hindenburg and Ludendorff until October 1918, when Groener replaced Ludendorff, while Hindenburg remained.

Moltke the Younger succeeded Schlieffen as chief of staff in 1906. He was considered a good organizer but had a frail health. During the July Crisis, he displayed on several occasions outbursts of hysterical nervousness, so that the chief of the military cabinet, Lyncker, was already looking for a replacement in case of his breakdown. That moment came quickly: When the offensive in the West collapsed in September 1914 and German armies had to retreat after the Marne battle, the Prussian Minister of War, Erich von Falkenhayn replaced Moltke. The military cabinet had already asked the latter in August 1914 to replace Moltke if necessary.

Falkenhayn was the candidate of the Kaiser and the military cabinet, but not of the army. This proved to be a major problem for the entire duration of his tenure and a serious limitation on his position. The top echelons of the army did not trust Falkenhayn who had an unusual career; he had served for several years as a military advisor in China instead of being under Schlieffen in the general staff. Falkenhayn failed to win over his critics, a task made much more difficult when his resumption of the Western offensive after the Marne battle ended in November 1914 in First Ypres and a second costly defeat.

Against strong opposition, Wilhelm II and the military cabinet, kept Falkenhayn in office. His successes in 1915 stabilized his position, even if he never became popular. His reputation suffered again in 1916: the battle of Verdun, which was his brainchild, was a complete failure, and the Allied coordinated offensives brought about a massive crisis for the Central Powers. In late August 1916, the Kaiser dismissed Falkenhayn for not having foreseen the Romanian intervention, an event which seemed to be, in the strategically overstretched situation of August 1916, the death knell for the Central Powers.

His replacement was Hindenburg and Ludendorff, who had plotted for some time against him, helped by the chancellor and high military leaders, such as Crown Prince Rupprecht.

Hindenburg and Ludendorff were popular.[16] The chancellor trusted them, but his high initial opinion of the two changed quickly. Ludendorff was an excellent staff officer, while Hindenburg enjoyed immense popularity after having won the battle of Tannenberg in August 1914 and having saved Eastern Prussia from a Russian invasion. Hindenburg and Ludendorff matched a number of criteria needed to be effective wartime leaders: they enjoyed significant public support and had the confidence of the German people and the army. Once in office, they started large programs to increase German military capabilities. They radicalized German warfare by the Hindenburg program, a large armament program; they tried to use Belgian and Polish-enforced labour for German war production; they overhauled German tactics, for example by giving up terrain on the Western Front: and they created in army and society a feeling of reckless energy and dynamism.

The Hindenburg myth filled the void at the top, but only to a certain extent. Hindenburg was physically and mentally slow, and without Ludendorff he would not have been more than a paternal figurehead. Ludendorff, the brains of the duo, lacked the talents of a politician. Still, he intervened in politics whenever he saw a military necessity for it, and the list of his interventions steadily increased. But when he was confronted with the idea of being or becoming a dictator in Germany, he energetically refused.

Despite his own view that the German political establishment lacked a leader capable of making real decisions, Ludendorff had no desire to take on the political leadership himself. This is confirmed by many, among them Walther Rathenau, who in 1917 placed his hopes in Ludendorff as a leader and on several occasions attempted to persuade him that he was "unconsciously enforcing a dictatorship, and that if he had confidence in his own power he would find himself supported not only by the parliaments, but also by public opinion, no matter which authority he was facing."[17] Rathenau practically begged Ludendorff to grab ultimate power: "he does not recognise his own power, [...] he has almost as much control as a dictator, and this brings with it a certain responsibility: he is capable of making history." Ludendorff disagreed and "countered that I [Rathenau] was still overestimating him, that his power did not have access to the Kaiser, and that he faced obstructions on all sides. I answered by drawing his attention to the muddled, shifting nature of our power structures: the under-secretaries of state can do nothing because the Chancellor stands in their way; the Chancellor can do nothing because he does not have the backing of Main Headquarters; at Main Headquarters, Ludendorff is restricted by Hindenburg; and Hindenburg for his part steps back into line as soon as the Kaiser taps him on the shoulder. The Kaiser, in his turn, feels hampered by the constitution, and thus the circle is complete."[18]

Rathenau was referring to the complex decision-making structures of Wilhelmine Germany, earlier described as "polycratic chaos." The result was not a Ludendorff dictatorship, but rather a vacuum that made Crown Prince Rupprecht feel "as though I am in a rudderless boat, being pulled irresistibly by a riptide towards the cliffs."[19] Moreover, powerful and popular army leaders could not fill the void at the top; Hindenburg and Ludendorff lacked political understanding and a strategic agenda which could have been the basis for a proper wartime program. Their concern was always a narrow military one; this became especially obvious when they insisted on future annexations.

The general staff was only one of the top echelons of the German armies. Another one was the Prussian Ministry of War, mainly responsible for manpower and equipment. It had a largely subordinate role; its chief was first Falkenhayn, then Adolf Wild von Hohenborn, Hermann von Stein, and Heinrich Scheuch. However, their say remained limited, and the ministry was more a provider of men and material than a strategic decision maker. Wild von Hohenborn felt treated poorly by the general staff, like a "soldier 2nd class," and complained that his ministry was treated like a "Cinderella."[20]

Alongside the general staff and ministry of war, the army commanders – the top echelon of the army – represented a military power centre. During Moltke's and Falkenhayn's tenure many of the army commanders were in open opposition to the chief of staff. There were a considerable number of intrigues undermining the authority of the second chief of staff. The Bavarian Crown Prince Rupprecht, a major commander on the Western Front, hated Falkenhayn and considered him dishonest and incompetent; he plotted against him as did Hindenburg and Ludendorff who were also in open and hostile disagreement with the chief of staff. Their differences rested not just on military, but also on personal matters. This went so far that Ludendorff refused to take the same train as Falkenhayn, when invited to do so.[21] Still, these intrigues had only a limited influence on strategy; Falkenhayn could push through his decisions, even if there were constant fights, mainly over reserves needed for any offensive. But it eroded his authority and did not help to provide efficient and coherent leadership.

The military, taken as a block – chief of staff, War Ministry, army commanders, and the general commanders who had taken over political control inside Germany – was powerful in wartime Germany, but failed to exercise strategic leadership in the proper sense of the term. Instead, it was the war itself, and its necessities, that took control. The war was, in the view of Vice Chancellor Karl Helfferich, a "violent and tyrannical tool."[22] Nevertheless, the military was an ever-present spectre, often in the form of *OHL*, sustained on the one hand by the feeling that there was no political way out of the war and on the other by the popular belief in their nation's own military superiority, an idea that seduced the whole of German society with few exceptions until September 1918. Indeed, confidence in Germany's military strength was one of the few issues, the various centres of power in Imperial Germany could agree on throughout the conflict. Almost until the end, many Germans, conservatives, liberals, and even social democrats, believed the only way out of the war was by military means, and that Germany could pull a victory off. Therefore, the term military dictatorship is misleading, and it is equally misleading to think that the general staff provided something like proper strategic leadership.

The Navy Leadership – Admiral Staff and the Imperial Naval Office

Independent of the armies was the Imperial Navy. The chief of the admiralty staff, responsible for operations, reported to the emperor. The various chiefs – the Admirals von Pohl, Bachmann, von Holtzendorff, and Scheer – were nowhere near as influential as their army colleagues; even more so because the secretary of state of the Imperial Naval Office – the naval minister – was the powerful figure Admiral Alfred von Tirpitz, who did not leave much space for others. In the case of the navy, the naval minister was more influential than the chief of staff, it was exactly the other way around than in the army. The naval command was furthermore split between the chief of the admiral staff and the commanders of the High Seas Fleet.

Regarding strategy, the army and navy staffs planned independently from each other, and thus cooperation failed to develop as it should and could have. The army entered the war with the Schlieffen plan, while the navy had prepared for a scenario which was not realistic: a close British blockade of German harbours. This would have provided the navy options to challenge and destroy sufficient British blockading ships so that the High Seas Fleet could, at some point, risk a decisive battle. But this was the reason why the Royal Navy decided to blockade the entire North Sea instead and to remain far away in Scapa Flow. By doing so, it rendered the German battlefleet helpless, as the navy's leadership did not want to risk a battle against the Royal Navy's Grand Fleet far from German ports.

Instead, the navy turned to the submarine weapon. The first big success, the sinking of the British cruisers *Aboukir, Cressy,* and *Hogue* in September 1914 by U 9 (Otto Weddigen), raised hopes that Germany had an effective weapon against Britain, and the leaders of the Imperial Navy laid more and more their focus on submarine warfare, which had not played a dominant role in their planning before 1914. In a newspaper interview given to the American journalist Karly Henry von Wiegand in December 1914, von Tirpitz complained about the lack of an American intervention against the British blockade of the North Sea. He added that Germany could hit back with a U-boat campaign against all enemy merchant shipping heading for Britain. "We have the resources to torpedo every English or Allied ship approaching a British port."[23] This gave voice to a focus on the U-boat which inspired considerable hope among German leaders that they now had a weapon that could inflict serious damage on their "major enemy" and force the British to compromise.[24]

State Governments

The long list of competing power centres in strategic decision-making in Imperial Germany would be incomplete without mentioning the Reich's federal structure. The Bundesrat, the Federal Chamber, was still influential, and the princes and governments of the various German states had their say. In terms of strategy, the interference from this side remained limited, largely because of the centralizing tendency in Imperial Germany, which had made so much progress by 1914 that the federal government clearly dominated the member states, who did not challenge the empire's central authority.[25]

Still, they were potentially powerful, and a factor that one should not overlook. Some of the German member states even had war aims of their own; Bavaria, for example, had interests in annexing parts of Belgium, and German princes aspired for crowns in Eastern Europe in 1918.[26] Furthermore, the state governments were also centres of opposition, for example, against the chief of staff, and on several occasions, they even asked when the government intended to make peace moves. Still, one can ignore the factor of the member states and the Bundesrat in our search for strategic leadership because although they occasionally intervened in wartime Germany they were not a powerful and central player.

The Reichstag and the Parties

The weakness of the state governments was not replicated in the central body of German politics, the Reichstag. While Imperial Germany had a constitutional, not a parliamentary government, the Reichstag gained significant influence during the war. It could not nominate the chancellor but was responsible for the budget and therefore also for financing the war. Therefore, it had powerful political tools of control. Every vote over new war bonds represented a political fight for the government, and again and again it had to convince the parties to cooperate.

The Reichstag was important for the entire duration of the war, starting in August 1914 when the government did everything it could to portray Russia to the Reichstag and the German public as the aggressor. Bethmann used the early Russian mobilization to win over the Social Democrats (who, since 1912, had been the biggest party in the Reichstag) whose support for the war effort was initially uncertain, but considered essential. Another crucial problem for the government was to find common ground among the parties in the Reichstag, because any dissent among its members threatened to be catastrophic for the Reich's internal unity. This was difficult because the parties were notoriously divided over nearly every question, especially the Social Democrats and left-wing liberals on the one hand and the Conservatives and National Liberals on the other. There were also insurmountable obstacles that made it impossible to define a clear line of strategy. The SPD cooperated to fight a war of national defence, but not of conquest. While the conservatives favoured annexations; the SPD insisted on internal reforms as remuneration for the war efforts of the German people, reforms which the National Liberals and Conservatives rejected, fearing the erosion of their political power. The other parties wavered, on the question of annexations, depending on the military situation. A program of conquest did not have a majority in the Reichstag, even if there was in the first few months of the war a broad annexationist mood, best summarized in the belief that if Germany won quickly, annexations would have found support even among the left.

There was consensus only around one issue: that Germany was fighting a war of national self-defence against the attack of the enemies, especially Russia; and Germany was not willing to give up even an inch of its national territory. This blocked any possibility for a political deal, such as ceding Alsace-Lorraine to win over the French and to broker peace in the West, while the desire for making gains in the East – schemes which some politicians discussed in 1917 – made it difficult to make a separate peace with Russia. This kind of annexationist policy, a cabinet policy of the old style, had no backing in parliament. The German Reichstag stuck to Wilhelm II's statement from August 1914: "We are not driven by lust of conquest," as it was the only way to continue SPD support and finance for the war. Still, the wartime politics proved too divisive for the SBD, and it split during the war, the more left-wing and anti-war members founding the USPD. The support of the left was also crucial to preserve inner unity and to prevent strikes. This worked well until 1916, but in the last two years of the war internal unrest increasingly became a major problem.

The Reichstag was also unable to develop a proper political strategy to end the war, something similar to what Lenin or Wilson did later. Possibilities that might have been attractive to other people, not only to the Germans, did not come up. Closest to this came Friedrich Naumann's book on *Mitteleuropa*, published in 1915, which outlined the idea of a great economic bloc under German leadership. The idea was popular in Germany, but nowhere else, not even in Austria.

Pressure Groups

Last but not least, we have to mention briefly pressure groups which could influence strategic decisions. In August and September 1914, individual politicians and nationalistic-minded associations handed over petitions and memoranda asking for annexations; this continued well into 1915 and never ceased entirely during the war. The government was not immune to such public pressure, even more so because it keenly felt the lack of a solid base of public support. This was also the reason for the September Programme of 1914, written by Kurt Riezler for Bethmann. This chapter was a preparation for eventual peace negotiations and tried to synthesize annexationist demands. Most of these memoranda remained a paper exercise but were not unimportant, because public pressure hindered the government from pursuing a clear anti-annexationist policy to work towards a peace of understanding.

Strategic Decision-Making

These factors did not describe strategic leadership but offer some structural reasons for the lack of it. The power centres which were responsible for developing a German strategy failed to do so or blocked each other while trying to do so. Without a clear consensus, except the basic idea of national self-defence, it was impossible to develop a coherent strategy, and it was not by chance that many contemporaries complained about a strategy of "muddling through (*durchwurschteln*)," hanging on without a plan and hoping something would turn up.

However, the lack of consensus and strategic leadership did not mean that strategic decisions did not occur. They were taken, but often in an incoherent and occasionally chaotic manner. Some deserve our attention to see how they came about, who was involved, and if and how the various power centres cooperated and consented to them or were overruled and left out. Seven strategic decisions will get a short description and analysis, namely the Schlieffen plan of 1914; Falkenhayn's separate peace strategy in 1914; the strategy of 1915 and the decision of focusing on the East or West; the war plan for 1916 and the battle of Verdun; the decision to open unlimited submarine warfare in 1917; the decision to start the Western offensive 1918; and finally the Armistice 1918.

The Schlieffen Plan 1914

In 1914 Imperial Germany had no coherent strategy, no proper positive political goal, but an elaborate military plan. Most (but not all) historians refer to it as the Schlieffen Plan.[27] His conception was to win by concentrating Germany's major forces on one theatre of war; his recipe for modern warfare was a combination of good leadership, superior numbers on the battlefield, the use of inner lines in a two-front war, and especially by flanking manoeuvres to avoid frontal attacks. Schlieffen had some sound insights, among them his belief that a long, protracted war would prove detrimental and dangerous to the interconnected European economies. Therefore, he preferred to keep the war as short as possible. Schlieffen left office and the younger Moltke took over as chief of the general staff in 1906. He modified the plan, but the conception remained the same.[28] The Reich's civilian leaders failed to object to the plan, despite the fact it violated Belgian neutrality. The French had made a different, and wiser, decision in 1912 in forbidding their army from invading Belgium in case of war.[29]

There was a major political big problem, which the Germans of the time were incapable of understanding. The belief they were acting in national self-defence made little sense in the eyes of the Reich's enemies and the neutrals. The massive Western offensive of 1914 reached the outskirts of Paris, after German troops had conquered Luxembourg, as well as large portions of Belgium and Northern France. In the eyes of all non-Germans, this did not look like a defensive strategy but rather an attempt to gain military control on the European continent. Indeed, this was the goal of the plan, and it is plausible to assume that if the Schlieffen plan had worked, political and economic demands would have followed; Moltke's suggestions and the September Programme, compiled by Riezler for Bethmann for the case of victory in the West, are the best proof of that reality.

Falkenhayn's Suggestion of a Separate Peace, 1914

The Schlieffen plan failed in September 1914, even if the Germans tried until November 1914 to envelop the British and French by enlarging the attacks farther West and to enforce a decision. These attacks failed, and in mid-November the fighting came to a standstill, the result of mutual exhaustion and lack of ammunition. At that moment, Falkenhayn, who had replaced Moltke the Younger, suggested a new strategic approach.[30] Meeting Bethmann, he warned that the army could not achieve victory. The result was going to be a war of attrition and that if the Allied powers possessed time to mobilize their superior resources, Germany was in danger in the long run of being overwhelmed by superior forces.

Therefore, Falkenhayn suggested a new strategy: The war had to end by political compromise. He favoured a separate peace with the continental enemies – Russia and France – and added that Germany keeps political or territorial demands to a minimum to make this peace possible. His mantra was: If we do not lose the war, we have won it, even without having made any gains, because it would prove Germany could withstand the strongest potential enemy coalition.[31] Bethmann was far from enthusiastic. He understood the difficulties of finding political solutions with the enemy powers that had agreed not to conclude any separate peace deals; he was also afraid of making peace without bringing some gains to the home front which he could present as compensation and justification for the enormous losses. The British historian David Stevenson has called this the "war trap:" it seemed to wartime governments politically impossible to conclude the war without gains which justified the sacrifices.[32]

Bethmann also questioned whether Falkenhayn, who continued to press for negotiations on a nearly daily basis, was the right man for the position as chief of the general staff. He considered asking the Kaiser to replace the chief of the general staff with Hindenburg, who in August 1914 had won the battle of Tannenberg in East Prussia. However, Falkenhayn had the backing of the Kaiser. Nevertheless, Bethmann tried, in cooperation with Hindenburg, Ludendorff, and Moltke, to get Falkenhayn sacked, but this plan failed in January 1915.[33]

Muddling Through: Eastern or Western Front

The German leadership had a dilemma, but no strategy: The military leader, Falkenhayn, believed German armies could not bring victory and suggested political solutions which the political leader, Bethmann, considered impossible to achieve and unattractive; he hoped instead for military victory which a new chief of the general staff could achieve. The result was a strategic "muddling through"; there was no chance to "win" the war, to bring it by own actions to a satisfactory conclusion – even if there were heated debates.

From 1914 to 1916, there were two schools of thought in the army leadership: Falkenhayn believed Germany lacked sufficient strength to force a military decision, but others, including the Bavarian Crown Prince Rupprecht, commander of the Sixth Army, and Hindenburg and Ludendorff, commanders of German armies in the East (*OberOst*), thought Germany could win, if well led (this meant not by Falkenhayn) in the West or in the East. Hindenburg and Ludendorff argued vociferously that they could beat the Russians decisively if Falkenhayn provided more troops. However, Falkenhayn was aware of Napoleon's disaster; moreover, he lacked the reserves needed for *OberOst* to pursue a wide-ranging invasion of Russia. He also pointed out that the Russians could always retreat deep into their interior, while the Germans lacked the manpower, time, and resources to "run after them indefinitely."[34]

One of Falkenhayn's major problems was that he lacked the confidence of the army and civilian leaders. He had alienated both by a sarcastic and biting sense of humour and a certain arrogance. Bethmann heard him expressing deep satisfaction over the outbreak of war in Europe in August 1914: "Even if we may perish, it was wonderful."[35] Crown Prince Rupprecht despised Falkenhayn also; one of the issues between them was that Falkenhayn was a much better debater, and the prince could not hold his ground. Furthermore, the Bavarian prince and his chief of Staff, Krafft von Dellmensingen, had a strong aversion to Prussia. The most important military opponents were Hindenburg and Ludendorff who insisted on a decisive offensive on the Eastern Front. The debates about striking in the East or West, the deployment of reserves, and the question of whether Germany could achieve a complete military victory extended from late 1914 until Falkenhayn's dismissal in August 1916, driven by a mixture of differing strategic views, personal animosities, and a mutual lack of trust.

Falkenhayn remained in power against strong opposition due to the support of Wilhelm who agreed with Falkenhayn's main strategic ideas. Lacking a better approach, the task was to keep the ship above water for the time being and hope Germany's enemies would compromise at some point.

Not without reason Thomas Mann's essay on "Frederic and the Great Coalition," published in 1915, was a great success: It compared the situation of Prussia during the Seven Years War with the Reich's situation in the present conflict. Nevertheless, the strategy of "muddling through" was unappealing. The German public did not understand the full severity of the situation, as the government forbade public discussion of war aims. Nevertheless, early in the war many politicians and associations nurtured ideas of annexation. Many were so convinced of German military superiority that they expected the German army to deliver a decisive blow and to end the war with military victory.

The War Plan for 1916

Despite these problems, 1915 was probably the most successful year of the war militarily for the Central Powers. Falkenhayn's strategy of limited offensives worked well. German armies won victories not only against the Russians, but they conquered, together with the Austrians and Bulgarians, the entirety of Serbia in the autumn of 1915 and cleared the Balkans, while an Allied expeditionary force remained trapped in Salonika. At the end of 1915, the Central Powers' situation looked militarily solid. All attacks of the Entente in the West had failed, and their own position appeared secured. The Central Powers controlled vast conquered territories. Furthermore, the German general staff had accumulated a substantial reserve of twenty-five divisions which while considered insufficient for a major breakthrough in the West, was still a significant force.

In autumn 1915, the question of a new strategic approach came up. The waiting game seemed a dangerous proposition, because the Reich's enemies still had the opportunity to mobilize their worldwide resources and overwhelm the Central Powers in the long run. Furthermore, the internal situation was not sufficiently stable to believe popular support would remain strong enough to continue the fight. Here we have to take into consideration that each day of the war killed, on average, more than 9,000 people, soldiers and civilians alike.[36] By the end of 1915, there was a clear national mood for bringing about the decision in the war by attacking the West. The Russians seemed to be immobilized, even if not entirely beaten. Moreover, the Balkans were under control, while the Italians were not threatening. Therefore, action in the West seemed the best alternative to bring the war to a conclusion.

The general staff, Falkenhayn, the Kaiser and his entourage, as well as influential individuals like Walter Rathenau, were in favour of a major operation in the West. Still, the concrete plan for 1916 was top secret and the work of Falkenhayn alone. He believed that Germany did not possess the strength to attempt a breakthrough and thought that such an attempt would only cause enormous casualties. Instead, he wanted to use the considerable advantages the defender possessed in trench warfare. To do so, he decided to attack Verdun for a number of reasons, among them a quick but limited infantry attack on the hills in front of the city and the posting of heavy artillery there. That, he believed would force the French to surrender the city or to try to reconquer the hills, an attempt which Falkenhayn thought would cost them dearly. He also hoped the British would start a hasty and ill-prepared attack to assist the French and preserved a significant part of his reserves to counter that attack.

The aim was to place the French under enormous pressure and hopefully, after having already immobilized Russia, France would abandon the war. Falkenhayn also wanted to attack the British by using unlimited submarine warfare, a measure used in 1915 to counter the British blockade, but which the Germans had abandoned after the sinking of the *Lusitania* and American protests. Now Falkenhayn wanted to resume unlimited submarine warfare.

To start with the second argument: Submarine warfare was a naval matter and had strong political implications because of the probable reaction of the neutrals, particularly the United States. Therefore, the chancellor intervened, while the chief of the admiralty Staff, Holtzendorff, wavered. Bethmann argued strongly against unlimited submarine warfare. In this case, two of the competing power centres in Germany disagreed sharply, the third one did not make a strong case and the fourth one, the Kaiser, had to decide, which he did in favour of Bethmann. Thus, unlimited submarine warfare was off the table in 1916.

While the second part of Falkenhayn's concept was not executed, he could commence the first part which was in his own domain. The attack on Verdun started on 18 February 1916. It was a fatal half-success: The Germans took a significant portion of the hills in front of the city, including the major fortress Douaumont, but not all of them; then they decided to seize the remainder of the hills to the West as well, accepting slow progress and high losses. The battle soon became a synonym for useless slaughter.

Thus, the German strategy for 1916 was therefore a far-reaching failure. The plan for the land attack failed, while the chancellor had prevented the plan for a naval operation, which would have been an enormous mistake with fatal political consequences. That was bad enough, but there was more. In 1915, the Central Powers had been successful because they coordinated their military efforts against Russia and then against Serbia. Planning for 1916, Falkenhayn and his Austro-Hungarian counterpart, Conrad von Hötzendorf, had been unable to agree on a common strategy: Falkenhayn wanted to attack on the Western Front and Conrad in Italy.

In the end, both decided to operate separately. Falkenhayn's offensive at Verdun got stuck, while Conrad's attack in Italy failed disastrously. To support the attack against Italy and compensate for the lack of German assistance, Conrad had decided to weaken his other fronts. This explains how an extended Russian attack, undertaken in June 1916 and led by Alexej Brussilov, became a major success. The Russians destroyed several Austro-Hungarian armies, and only German help prevented a complete breakdown of the Austrian Eastern Front. The Brussilov offensive, originally planned as a subsidiary operation became the first of a combined all-front attack on all fronts.

Allied leaders had agreed at Chantilly in late 1915 that they would attack at the same time to prevent the Central Powers from transferring reserves from one front to another. While German troops stabilized the lines on the Eastern Front, a major offensive in the West began, the British-French contribution to Chantilly's strategy. The Somme Battle began in late June with a one-week bombardment of German lines and continued with an infantry attack on 1 July 1916, the costliest day in British military history. The battle raged on until November but was an Allied failure because it realized none of its objectives. Nevertheless, the German armies suffered heavy casualties, which the nation could not afford.

The Allied all-front offensives, and especially the artillery bombardments on the Somme had demonstrated the Western Powers' material superiority and raised serious doubts for the Reich's future prospects. These developments led to the dismissal of Falkenhayn. Bethmann, Hindenburg, Ludendorff, Crown Prince Rupprecht, and others were finally able to convince the Kaiser and the military cabinet to change the chief of staff who had not foreseen Romania's declaration of war, this being the immediate reason. Hindenburg and Ludendorff took over and the period of the "Third *OHL*" began.

Peace Offers and Submarine Warfare 1915–1917

Autumn 1916 saw the culmination of the war in several ways. On hand, the Central Powers had defeated the Allied offensives. This great employment of military force was not sufficient to beat the Central Powers. While this represented a success, on the other hand, the military leaders of the third *OHL*, were worried about not being able to keep up with the Western allies on the Western Front. They initiated a massive program to raise German armament and ammunition production, called the Hindenburg program; the program represented a general failure. The industry could not simply be ordered to produce more weapons and ammunition. A second, step was to use the inhabitants of occupied territories for forced labour in German factories. A third step was the retreat on the Western Front to carefully prepared new fortified positions, the so-called Hindenburg or Siegfried line.

At the same time, an even greater problem for the strategic leadership appeared. Bethmann and the government initiated a peace initiative in the autumn 1916, which resulted in the peace offer of the Central Powers in December

1916. The Entente Powers immediately rejected it. At the same moment, the American president, Woodrow Wilson, attempted to mediate a peace; his intervention appeared to offer a serious chance to end the war, but failed because of the German decision to resume unlimited submarine warfare.[37]

The *OHL* had agreed to the peace offer but did not believe in its success and were pushing for a resumption of the unlimited submarine warfare in case the Entente Powers rejected the offer. The internal debates over these steps were a crucial moment in German strategic decision-making and a moment where serious inter-service and inter-departmental cooperation was necessary. The decisions taken had crucial consequences not only for Germany, but for the entire twentieth century.

Opinions about resuming submarine warfare remained divided, and it was not an easy decision to make. On the one hand, the harvest of 1916 had been catastrophically bad. Despite food rationing, there were insufficient stocks to provide for the population. Calories per day dropped during the so-called turnip winter 1916/1916 to only 880 calories per person. The general mood was one of sheer despair: The solid military situation was of no use, if the German population was starving to death. The second argument was the harsh reply of the Entente to the peace offer. It seemed obvious the enemy was not ready to negotiate, and therefore all available military means had to be used to force them to compromise.

The navy believed it could offer a way to force to the enemy to sue for peace. A number of new submarines were ready for service. Thus, the navy could employ more U-boats against the British Isles. The Chief of the Admiral Staff, Admiral von Holtzendorff, found his subordinates enthusiastic about launching reckless submarine warfare against Britain. They believed there was a unique opportunity to turn the tide of the war: The world harvest of 1916 had been poor, and Britain's merchant navy would find it difficult to import grains from countries distant to the British Isles. It seemed possible to reduce British shipping capacities following a few months of submarine warfare to a level Britain would have to ask for peace.

In the debate over this most important strategic decision of the war, the following players had a say: First, the navy, with von Holtzendorff in the lead, with support from a body of civilian specialists, grain traders, shipping experts, bankers, and economists. They had collected data and supporting materials which seemed to prove that unrestricted submarine warfare could reduce the British merchant navy in a few months in half a year to a point that Britain would have to sue for peace. They also claimed that the window of opportunity caused by poor harvests was unique and limited in time. The army leadership, Hindenburg and Ludendorff, did not have a proper grip on the material and left the details to the navy. The army's position was nearly exclusively driven by the desire to avoid a second Somme Battle. They worried about the Western Front and wanted to reduce American supplies.

Second, the Chancellor was against unlimited submarine warfare which he considered dangerous, particularly because he did not want to bring the United States into the war. He was supported here by Vice Chancellor Karl Helfferich, an experienced economist who highlighted numerous mistakes in the memoranda, but the chancellor found himself incapable of preventing the decision in favour of a resumption of unrestricted submarine warfare from happening.

Third, much of public opinion and of the Reichstag were in favour of submarine warfare.[38] They believed the catastrophic internal situation in Germany required a quick decision, otherwise, the war would be lost anyway. In retrospect it is clear why so many leaders and individuals in Germany supported the decision: they believed the navy's claim that unlimited submarine warfare could decide the outcome of the conflict. This was a powerful argument in Germany, where civilian society was barely surviving under the war's strain. However, even some proponents of the idea had doubts. General von Lyncker in January 1917 noted: "The U-boats will probably come, but will this be a decisive success? Who knows? It is a leap in the dark. But the risk must be taken and so it will be."[39]

Fourth, the Kaiser and his advisors, in this case, the chief of the naval cabinet, Admiral von Müller, a former voice of moderation, supported submarine warfare as well. They based their opinions mainly on the Allied rejection of the German peace offer which offered, in their eyes, no other option other than the use of any available means to force the main enemy, Britain, to compromise.

The final discussion of the issue came on 9 January 1917 in German headquarters at Pless, Belgium. Bethmann was the only participant against unrestricted submarine warfare, but he defended his cause poorly. He felt he was arguing for a lost cause, because the army and navy leaders cooperated closely, public opinion and Reichstag were backing them, and the Kaiser was now in favour of unrestricted submarine warfare. He had practically surrendered before discussions began. Hindenburg, Ludendorff, Holtzendorff, and the Kaiser all demanded a declaration of unlimited submarine warfare and Bethmann surrendered. He considered resigning, but decided to remain in office, not wanting to display internal disunity.

The fatal decision to declare unlimited submarine warfare brought the United States into the war and decided its outcome. It was the result of a broad discussion among the military and civilian German leaders and supported by a significant portion of German public opinion. Still, it was a catastrophic decision. Max Weber, an opponent of unlimited submarine warfare, records that this was the first time he started to fear that Germany might lose the war.[40] Indeed, Germany's defeat was sealed at the moment when its leaders declared unlimited submarine war. Had this not happened, the first Russian revolution in March 1917 would have offered an excellent chance to avoid defeat and to get out of the war with at least a draw: the impending breakdown of the biggest of the enemy powers had started.

Strategic Decision 1917 and Brest-Litovsk 1918

In terms of strategy, 1917 saw the declaration of unlimited submarine warfare with the American declaration of war in April 1917. This did not have an immediate military impact. At first, the navy reported sinkings that exceeded expectations, but the Royal Navy was able to counter the submarine threat. The central objective of the U-boat campaign, to force Britain out of the war, failed completely. Throughout the year, Germany remained on the defensive in the West, waiting for the success of the submarine warfare. The German retreat on the Western Front and defensive battles, like Passchendaele, represented successes for the Reich's defensive strategy. On the Eastern Front, there were long periods of reduced fighting and local armistices. The "November revolution" brought Lenin to power, who immediately started peace negotiations with the Central Powers. There was no longer an Eastern Front.

In summer 1917, the Reichstag, under leadership of the Centre party deputy Matthias Erzberger, issued a new peace offer. It rested on the Kaiser's statement of August 1914 that Germany did not want conquests. Nevertheless, the initiative did not bring peace, but it had one remarkable result: German politicians felt that they could not go back from this declaration and reject annexations. This belief dominated German attitudes at the start of peace negotiations with the Soviets at Brest Litovsk in December 1917. Germany did not ask for annexations but attempted to create an informal empire with new states in Eastern Europe which would be dependent on the Reich. In fact, Brest was a nightmare of German hypocrisy and lack of clarity, divided between the desire for peace in large parts of the Reichstag and German population and annexationist designs in the *OHL* and nationalistic associations like the *Vaterlandspartei* which were angry with politicians who sought a "meagre" peace. The contestants could not hide the conflict in Brest where the Foreign Minister, Kühlmann, and the representative of the *OHL*, General Max Hoffmann, openly clashed, to the amazement of the Bolsheviks.

The Western Offensive 1918

The peace in the East offered the chance to establish a numerical superiority on the Western Front, for the first time since summer 1914. The way out of the war seemed clear: military victory. There was unity in Germany, as political leaders, like Chancellor Hertling, the military, and German public opinion had lost hope a negotiated peace was possible. Furthermore, the Bolsheviks in Moscow had opened their archives and started to publish the secret treaties of the Allies, proving vast expansionist aims at the expense of the Central Powers. It seemed obvious the enemy was waging a war of conquest. Therefore, only a military victory could bring peace. Furthermore, Russia's collapse had immensely boosted German confidence.

In this situation the *OHL*, Hindenburg and Ludendorff, as well as the Kaiser and the chancellor, agreed on the necessity of military victory. Ludendorff was probably correct when he wrote in February 1918 that a Western "offensive [...] would be not the 'offensive of the German General Staff' but rather the offensive of the German army and therefore also of the German people,"[41] despite, or because, Germany's population was by now extremely war-weary. Victory in the West seemed the fastest path to ending the war.

The question was, how to plan this operation. The German public took it nearly for granted that a breakthrough in the West was now possible. The general staff was more sceptical. But still, there was no opposition to Ludendorff's idea of a major offensive in the West, which was, from the beginning, designed as a multi-stage offensive operation. The first attack began on 21 March 1918. It had initial success, but as it was badly planned and ineptly led, tactical success failed to lead to operational or strategic gains, while German casualties were heavy. Four additional major German offensives followed; all of them failing with heavy casualties while extending German lines. Major Allied counterattacks followed which turned the tide. On 8 August 1918, the British offensive at Amiens proved the darkest day for the German army and made it obvious that the situation was desperate. The spring offensives had overstretched the resilience of the German army, which suffered nearly one million casualties.

The army had been ready in winter 1917/1918 to attempt a final assault, but it had failed. Now confronted with the prospect of millions of Americans arriving in France, German morale broke. From then onwards, German armies in the West were in retreat and increasingly outnumbered, while on other fronts the Italians, the Armee d'Orient in Saloniki and Allenby's troops in Syria attacked.

Armistice 1918

The decision to terminate the war, surely a strategic decision of first importance, was initiated by Ludendorff, who at the end of September 1918 arrived at the conclusion the war was lost with a military catastrophe looming. The German leadership made the decision for peace when German forces on the Hindenburg Line on the Western Front collapsed; at the same time Bulgaria surrendered, forcing Ludendorff to recognize that it was time to ask for an armistice. As always, his approach had a narrow military perspective. Still, his pressure for an armistice led to a change of government; Hertling resigned, and Max von Baden became the new, and last, Imperial Chancellor. The final strategy, an appeal to Wilson to broker a deal on the basis of his Fourteen Points, was the work of Admiral von Hintze, Secretary of State of the Foreign Office. During the month of October, Hindenburg's and Ludendorff's power evaporated with the latter dismissed on 26 October. Two weeks later the Kaiser had to abdicate as well. The end of the war resulted in a revolutionary situation beyond the control of the military and civilian authorities.

Conclusion

In May 1919, Falkenhayn noted about strategic leadership: "I quite agree with the view that the highest political and military leadership in a war such as we have had must be in one hand, but not with the view that the man who conducts the political business should be subordinate to the man who supervises the military business. In the second part of the war, we practically had such an arrangement, and we now know where it has led us. The right thing to do is to have supreme authority over warfare and politics, whether his name be Emperor, President or Prime Minister (Lloyd George). It has only to be the right man."[42] Falkenhayn was, not surprisingly, highly critical of his successor Ludendorff and criticized his interferences in the political field. His comment was also a clear admission of the lack of wartime leadership in Germany. In his eyes, Lloyd George was a model of how to successfully lead a country in wartime.

Falkenhayn's comment highlighted one of the reasons why Germany had no proper strategic leadership during the war. But his was a remark in a private letter, not a proper and comprehensive analysis. As explained above, there was not a single problem; there were many which hindered the development of a realistic and coherent German strategy, among which were a cumbersome bureaucratic structure, the wrong people at the helm, a lack of ideas, contradictions in Germany's military and political actions and unclear and contested war aims. Imperial Germany had risked a World War for reasons which got immediately disappeared once the war had begun; Austria-Hungary and the Serbian problems became secondary.

Most Germans believed they were fighting a defensive war but failed to see that their own aggressive military strategy appeared to prove the opposite, namely they were fighting for European domination. The civilian leadership was unable to formulate a strategy which did not rely on military success, but the army could not provide it. The military tried hard and being the only possible provider of victory and peace, they were the decisive and dominant factor in German strategy. There was considerable influence "from below": the public mood in wartime Germany was an intangible factor which is difficult to quantify, but annexationism at the outbreak of war, and public unrest and fear for the home front in its second half created political pressures which led to strategic mistakes.

The war was lost as well because the public refused to stomach a strategy of simply waiting and holding out, which might have guaranteed a tolerable outcome. The decisive mistake was not made, differently as the stab in the back legend claims, in autumn 1918, but during the turnip winter 1916/1917.

The decision to start unlimited submarine warfare was a catastrophic mistake which one can explain not only by looking at individuals like Holtzendorff, the Kaiser, and Ludendorff, but also at the public mood.

Strategic leadership is a complex problem, and its analysis has to include not only politicians and military leaders, but the entire framework of the society. Imperial Germany was not doomed to lose the First World War. The outcome was on a knife edge. Germany had a chance to end the war with a draw; even more: a stalemate was the main strategic feature of this war, over most of its duration. A draw was also, its most likely outcome.[43] Imperial Germany and its alliances were the weaker contestants, but its deficiencies in strategic leadership, caused by a combination of structural and individual failures, made the difference and were mainly responsible for the catastrophic outcome.

Notes

1 Carl von Clausewitz, *On War*, Book 8, Chap. 2.
2 Daniel Marc Segesser, "Controversy: Total War," in: 1914–1918-online. *International Encyclopedia of the First World War*, ed. by Ute Daniel, Peter Gatrell, Oliver Janz, Heather Jones, Jennifer Keene, Alan Kramer, and Bill Nasson, issued by Freie Universität Berlin, Berlin, 8 October 2014. DOI: 10.15463/ie1418.10315.
3 Hew Strachan, "Military Operations and National Policies 1914–1918," in Holger Afflerbach, ed., *The Purpose of the First World War. War Aims and Military Strategies* (Berlin: De Gruyter, 2015), 7–25.
4 Andreas Hillgruber, "Der Faktor Amerika in Hitlers Strategie 1938–1941," Wolfgang Michalka (ed.) *Nationalsozialistische Außenpolitik* (Darmstadt, 1978), 493–525, 493, defines strategy as "die Integration von Innen- und Außenpolitik, von militärischer und psychologischer Kriegsplanung und Kriegführung, von Wehrwirtschaft und -rüstung durch die Führungsspitze eines Staates zur Verwirklichung einer ideologisch-politischen Gesamtkonzeption." See also Wilhelm Deist, "Strategy and unlimited Warfare in Germany: Moltke, Falkenhayn, and Ludendorff," in Roger Chickering and Stig Forster, eds., *Great War, Total War. Combat and Mobilization on the Western Front, 1914–1918* (Cambridge: Cambridge University Press, 2000), 263–81.
5 Michael Howard, *Grand Strategy*, vol. 4, *August 1942–September 1943* (London: Her Majesty's Stationery Office, 1972), 1.
6 Fritz Fischer, *Griff nach der Weltmacht. Die Kriegszielpolitik des kaiserlichen Deutschland 1914–1918* (Düsseldorf: Droste, 1961); idem: *Krieg der Illusionen. Die deutsche Politik 1911–1914*, 2. ed. (Düsseldorf: Droste, 1969).
7 Gerhard Ritter, *Staatskunst und Kriegshandwerk. Das Problem des 'Militarismus' in Deutschland*, 4 vols. (München: R. Oldenburg, 1954–1968).
8 Hans-Ulrich Wehler, *Deutsche Gesellschaftsgeschichte*, vol. 3, *Von der 'Deutschen Doppelrevolution'bis zum Beginn des Ersten Weltkrieges 1849–1914* (München: Verlag nicht ermittelbar, 1995), 849–89.
9 Quoted in Holger Afflerbach, *Falkenhayn. Politisches Denken und handeln im Kaiserreich* (Munich: Oldenbourg, 1994), 233.
10 Karl-Heinz Janßen, *Der Kanzler und der General. Die Führungskrise um Bethmann Hollweg und Falkenhayn, 1914–1916* (Göttingen: Musterschmidt, 1967), 22.
11 John C. G. Röhl, *Wilhelm II.: Die Jugend des Kaisers 1859–1888* (München, 1993); *Wilhelm II.: Der Aufbau der personlichen Monarchie 1888–1900* (München, 2001); *Wilhelm II.: Der Weg in den Abgrund 1900–1941* (München: C.H. Beck, 2008); on

the role of Wilhelm II during the First World War, see Holger Afflerbach, "Wilhelm II as Supreme Warlord in the First World War," *War in History 1998 5 (4)*, 427–49; Holger Afflerbach, ed., *Kaiser Wilhelm II. als Oberster Kriegsherr während des Ersten Weltkrieges – Quellen aus der militärischen Umgebung des Kaisers 1914–1918* (München: R. Oldenbourg, 2005).

12 Lyncker to his wife, 19 May 1917, quoted in ibid., Nr. L 605.

13 Müller, diary entry for 6 November 1914, in: Georg Alexander von Müller: *Regierte der Kaiser? Kriegstagebucher, Aufzeichnungen und Briefe des Chefs des Marine-Kabinetts Admiral Georg Alexander von Müller 1914–1918*, Walter Görlitz, ed. (Göttingen: Musterschmidt-Verlag, 1959).

14 Plessen, diary entry for 23 November 1914. Afflerbach, *Kaiser Wilhelm II, Nr.*, 108.

15 On Lyncker: Afflerbach, *Kaiser Wilhelm II.*, 65–124; see p. 30 f. for the grotesque search for a replacement for Bethmann Hollweg in July 1917.

16 Wolfram Pyta: *Hindenburg. Herrschaft zwischen Hohenzollern und Hitler* (München: Pantheon, 2007); Manfred Nebelin, *Ludendorff. Diktator im Ersten Weltkrieg* (München: Siedler Verlag, 2010).

17 Rathenau's notes of a conversation with Ludendorff of 16 February 1917, in: Moscow Special Archive, Rathenau papers, 634–1,286.

18 Ibid., 10 July 1917.

19 Dieter J. Weis: *Kronprinz Rupprecht von Bayern. Eine politische Biografie* (Regensburg, Friedrich Pustet Verlag 2007), 144.

20 Wild v. Hohenborn to his wife, 5 July 1915, in Adolf Wild von Hohenborn: *Briefe und Tagebuchaufzeichnungen des preussischen Generals als Kriegsminister und Truppenführer im Ersten Weltkrieg*, Helmut Reichold and Gerhard Granier, eds. (Boppard a.Rh., 1986), Nr. 43, 77.

21 Afflerbach, *Falkenhayn*, 225.

22 Karl Helfferich: *Der Weltkrieg* (Karlsruhe, Verlegt bei Ullstein & Co in Berlin, 1925), vol. 2, 391.

23 Arthur S. Link: *Wilson*, vol. 3, *The Struggle for Neutrality 1914–1915* (Princeton: Princeton University Press, 1960), p. 315; Joachim Schröder: *Die U-Boote des Kaisers. Die Geschichte des deutschen U-Boot-Krieges gegen Grossbritannien im Ersten Weltkrieg* (Bonn: 2003), 85f.

24 Link, *Wilson*, vol. 3, 315.

25 Frank-Lorenz Mueller, "Symptomatisch für den Niedergang des Bismarck-Reiches? Die leise Entkrönung der kleineren deutschen Königreiche im November 1918," in Holger Afflerbach and Ulrich Lappenküper, eds., *1918 Das Ende des Bismarck-Reiches* (Paderborn, Ferdinand Schöningh, 2021).

26 Karl-Heinz Jansen, *Macht und Verblendung. Kriegszielpolitik der deutschen Bundesstaaten 1914/18* (Göttingen, Wissenschaftliche Reihe, 1963).

27 Hans Ehlert, Michael Epkenhans, and Gerhard Gros, eds., *Der Schlieffenplan. Analysen und Dokumente* (Paderborn, 2006); Terence Zuber, *Inventing the Schlieffen Plan: German War Planning, 1871–1914* (Oxford: Oxford University Press, 2002).

28 Annika Mombauer, "Der Moltkeplan: Eine Modifikation des Schlieffenplans bei gleichen Zielen?," in Ehlert, Epkenhans and Groß, *Schlieffenplan*.

29 Georges-Henri Soutou, "French War Aims and Strategy," in Afflerbach, ed., *Purpose*, 30.

30 Afflerbach, *Falkenhayn*, 198–210.

31 Ibid., 198.

32 David Stevenson, *1917. War, Peace and Revolution* (Oxford: Oxford University Press, 2017), 9.

33 Ekkehard P. Guth, "Der Gegensatz zwischen dem Oberbefehlshaber Ost und dem Chef des Generalstabes des Feldheeres 1914/15. Die Rolle des Majors von Haeften im Spannungsfeld zwischen Hindenburg, Ludendorff und Falkenhayn," in *Militärgeschichtliche Mitteilungen* 35 (1984).

34 Afflerbach, *Falkenhayn*, 294–312.

35 Ibid., 147.

36 Afflerbach, *Purpose of War*, 3.

37 Philip Zelikow, *The Road Less Traveled. The Secret Battle to End the Great War, 1916–1917* (New York: Public Affairs, 2021).

38 The Reichstag had voted on 6 April 1916 on the submarine warfare, the majority basically supporting it, as long as the rights of the neutrals were respected. Ritter, *Staatskunst*, vol. 3, 208; Wild, *Briefe*, 146.

39 Lyncker to his wife, 26 January 1917, in *Kaiser Wilhelm II as Supreme Warlord*, L 550.

40 Holger Afflerbach, *Auf Messers Schneide. Wie das Deutsche Reich den Ersten Weltkrieg verlor* (Munich, C. H. Beck, 2018), 269.

41 Ludendorff to Friedrich Naumann, 22 February 1918, in Herbert Michaelis und Ernst Schraepel, eds., *Ursachen und Folgen. Vom deutschen Zusammenbruch 1918 und 1945 bis zur staatlichen Neuordnung Deutschlands in der Gegenwart. Eine Urkunden- und Dokumentensammlung zur Zeitgeschichte*, 26 vols. (Berlin, 1958–1980), vol. 2, No. 329 a, 250.

42 Falkenhayn an Tappen, 25 May 1919, quoted in: Afflerbach, *Falkenhayn*, p. 501 ("Der Ansicht, dass die hoechste politische und militarische Fuehrung in einem Kriege, wie wir ihn hatten, in einer Hand liegen muesse, pflichte ich durchaus bei, dagegen nicht der, dass der Mann, der das politische Geschaeft ausfuehend besorgt, dem der das Militaerische ausfuehrend vbersieht, untergeordnet sein soll. Im zweiten teil des Krietges haben wir ja praktisch eine solche Regelung gehabt, und wohin sie uns gefuehrt hat, wissen wir jetzt. Das Richtige ist schon, dass ein Hoechster ueber Kriegfuehrung und Politik steht, mag er nun Kaiser, Preasident oder Ministerpaesident (Lloyd George) heissen. Es muss nur der richtige Mann sein.")

43 Afflerbach, *Auf Messers Schneide*, passim.

7

STALIN AND THE STAVKA

Formulating Soviet Strategy During the Great Patriotic War

Alexander Hill

Introduction and Overview

Georgii Zhukov might have liked this article to have been all about him and his role as 'architect' of Soviet victory. His boss, Iosif Stalin would certainly have expected it to be all about him. After Stalin's fall from grace under Nikita Khrushchev's premiership of the Soviet Union, Zhukov usurped Stalin as the key military decision maker in the developing Soviet folklore of the war – the man behind the key decisions on the road to Soviet victory. Although Stalin to a limited extent crept back into the frame under Leonid Brezhnev, his status suffered further damage under Mikhail Gorbachev and Boris Yeltsin. Despite a degree of revival for Stalin under Vladimir Putin, in contemporary Russia Zhukov remains the government's poster figure for Soviet victory in the Great Patriotic War – 'the architect of the Red Army's key victories over the Nazis' in a government-sponsored site intended for Western consumption.[1]

Stalin and Zhukov were both central to Soviet military decision-making prior to and during the war. It would however be a mistake for this piece to be an essay about the decision-making relationship between Stalin and Zhukov along the lines of Andrew Roberts's *Masters and Commanders* and other similar works on the British and the US strategic decision-making processes.[2] Soviet military decision-making during what for the Soviet Union was the Great Patriotic War was significantly different from decision-making for the Western Allies. Not only did Stalin hold civilian and military authority in his hands, but he clearly relied on greater regular face-to-face input from a wider range of military leaders than in the cases of leaders in Britain and the United States. Stalin consulted widely – often face-to-face – despite the fact that as principal decision maker he had far greater authority to decide as he

DOI: 10.4324/9781003375630-7

pleased than either Franklin Roosevelt or Winston Churchill. To some extent, face-to-face interaction was facilitated by the relatively close proximity of the fighting to the heart of the Soviet government – Soviet military leaders could be invited back from their front and other commands to meet with Stalin far more easily than a US commander could be invited back from Europe or the Pacific theatre to meet with Roosevelt. Unlike Adolf Hitler – who himself had consolidated civilian and military decision-making in his own person – as the war progressed and Soviet fortunes improved Stalin was increasingly willing to listen to the advice of others – and not just to Zhukov. Towards the end of the war, Stalin would even give his commanders a degree of freedom in fine-tuning operational decision-making that would have been unthinkable earlier in the war.

Prior to the war Stalin had already defined Soviet grand strategy – and could reasonably claim to be following a line set by Vladimir Lenin. Whilst Soviet military power was in the first instance to be geared towards the defence of the revolution, in the longer term it was widely understood within the Soviet leadership that the best defence for the revolution in the Soviet Union was international revolution – something that could be brought about with the help of the Red Army should the 'international circumstances' be conducive.[3] We have far less clarity on the formulation of Soviet pre-war strategy than that during wartime – in part because neither Soviet nor contemporary Russian governments have any interest in undermining the notion that the Soviet Union had purely defensive intentions on the eve of Barbarossa. We can however be confident that it was Stalin who pushed for and ultimately took the key decisions that set the Soviet Union on a long-term trajectory towards future war. The collectivization and industrialization that began in earnest in the late 1920s were to a meaningful extent geared from the outset towards the development of increased Soviet military power that could be used on both the defensive and offensive.[4]

Although one might argue that the Red Army was the strongest army in Europe by 1936, the Great Purges – themselves born out of fear of future a future war – were one factor that seems to have convinced Stalin that the Soviet Union was not ready for war in the late 1930s. The Red Army was also not seen as ready for war at this time given the perceived need to introduce a new generation of weapons systems in an army that had started to rearm in earnest before the others, and where disagreements on how best to use these weapons many have further reduced Stalin's confidence in the Red Army during the period 1937–1941.[5] Nonetheless, by 1941 the Soviet Union had a clear mobilization plan for the Red Army to be ready for offensive operations by 1942, even if this plan was behind in early 1941. In the meantime, territory acquired under the auspices of the Nazi-Soviet Pact would provide a buffer in the event of enemy attack, and ultimately a springboard for the Red Army when it was ready to go over to the offensive.[6]

Had Germany not attacked the Soviet Union in June 1941 then it is quite possible that later in 1942 the Red Army would have attacked Germany – at a point at which Soviet mobilization plans had been completed. However, the Soviet Union was clearly neither ready to do so in June 1941 nor indeed in May 1941 when plans for a pre-emptive strike against German forces massing on the Soviet frontier were put before Stalin.[7] Stalin's personal unwillingness to accept that Hitler might beat him to pulling the trigger played a large part in leaving the Red Army in a precarious position in June 1941 when German-led forces attacked the Soviet Union. Soviet military dispositions in June 1941 were clearly neither suited to the defence nor offense, with the best explanation for them probably being that Stalin was both slowly overseeing Red Army preparations for an offensive war at some time in the future, and at the same time offering a limited display of strength along the border to dissuade any German attack or provocation in the meantime.[8] The extent to which Soviet military leaders such as Chief of Staff Zhukov or Defence Minister Semen Timoshenko voiced opposition to this stance is unclear, although one might take the fact that contingency plans for a pre-emptive strike against German forces were put to Stalin in mid-May speak for themselves.

Stalin undoubtedly dominated Soviet military decision-making at the beginning of the Great Patriotic War – despite the fact that he had little understanding of modern war having only really started to show interest in operational matters after the debacle in Finland in late 1939. During the early war period, it seems that the extent to which senior Soviet military commanders – including the much-vaunted Zhukov – were able to influence Stalin's hold ground and counterattack at the first available opportunity policy of the first weeks of the war was limited. However, we can certainly be confident in suggesting that by the mid-war period, Stalin had grown to trust those military commanders that made up the inner circle of military decision-making, with Georgii Zhukov certainly being *primus inter pares*. Those personally closest to Stalin who had arguably been the principal military leaders at the beginning of the war – and in particular Kliment Voroshilov and Semen Budennii – had for slightly different reasons proven not to be up to the job, and Boris Shaposhnikov's ill health meant that his role as Chief of Staff was cut short. Replacements for such figures – slightly younger men who had not been associates of Stalin back during the Civil War, such as Zhukov, Aleksandr Vasilevskii, Aleksei Antonov, and Sergei Shtemenko – lacked the personal connection to Stalin borne out of the struggles of the Civil War period to allow any of them to become too central to decision-making. Stalin's apparent fear of being usurped by Zhukov as the figurehead for military success probably kept the latter from dominating decision-making as the war progressed when that might otherwise have threatened.

Not making this a paper about Zhukov and Stalin doesn't mean that Zhukov isn't a key figure in it. In his biography of Zhukov, Geoffrey Roberts is certainly correct to highlight Zhukov's importance in Soviet military decision-making.[9] Through much of the war Stalin not only frequently met with Zhukov when the latter was in Moscow but communicated with him frequently when Zhukov was off on one of his many postings to key front commands or serving as a coordinator between fronts for the Stavka. However, other key figures in decision-making also had Stalin's ear – and are clearly in strong evidence in the documentary record. As first deputy – and then Chief of Staff for much of the war – and a trusted lieutenant at the front – the more self-effacing Vasilevskii was often as significant a figure and certainly warrants deeper biographical treatment, as indeed does his successor Antonov who would be the face of the General Staff for much of the late war period. The importance of the Chief of Staff – or his deputy acting in a *de facto* role as Chief of Staff in the case of Antonov for much of the mid-war period – is perhaps best illustrated with some indication of the tasks that Antonov carried out during a particular day. In Antonov's Soviet-era biography as part of the Soviet Warlords [*polkovodtsi*] and Military Leaders series Antonov's day on 7 September 1943 is reported in some detail. It is clear that even without consideration of his role in advising Stalin the cumulative impact of such actions as 'establishing new boundaries between fronts, reallocating armies between them and carrying out partial re-groupings of forces' could ultimately have a meaningful impact on operational and operational-strategic outcomes.[10]

In his memoirs – despite numerous distortions of what actually took place to bolster his significance – Zhukov was willing to acknowledge the importance of both Vasilevskii and Antonov in the military decision-making process. On Vasilevskii, Zhukov noted:

> Stalin showed the greatest respect towards A.M. Vasilevskii. Alexandr Mikhailovich did not fail to accurately assess the operational-strategic situation. … In those situations where I.V. Stalin did not agree with Aleksandr Mikhailovich's opinion, Vasilevskii was able with dignity and through weight of argument convince the Supreme Commander that in the given situation there wasn't an alternative to the decision that he was putting forward.

Zhukov went on to point out that:

> The Supreme Commander always listened intently to the opinions of A.I. Antonov, even when he wasn't a member of the Stavka and was only temporarily carrying out the role of Chief of the General Staff. Aleksandr Innokent'evich's signature often followed that of Stalin on Stavka directives.[11]

Nonetheless, despite the input of all of these figures into command decisions, as Evan Mawdsley has succinctly pointed out 'Stalin selected effective subordinates…, but he made his own decisions.'[12] Even Zhukov came to accept that by the second half of the war Stalin himself had learned much about military strategy, even if he lacked a level of understanding of operational matters and below that might have reduced Soviet losses. Zhukov's unexpurgated memoirs note that after Stalin had thrown so many recently mobilized and poorly equipped units into battle during the early war period – leading to 'unnecessary casualties' – subsequently:

> Stalin did grasp the basic principles of the organisation of front-level operations and those of groups of fronts, and directed them with appropriate knowledge and understanding. Stalin's capabilities as Supreme Commander were in particular revealed starting with the battle for Stalingrad.[13]

Even well after Stalin's death, in a 1966 speech Zhukov is reported as having suggested that:

> And as far as the third period of the war is concerned ... I must say to you – and here Zhukov's voice took on a special tone – here was a real military commander [*polkovodets*] of modern world war on a large scale. And coming to a general conclusion, said Zhukov, in this war we had a worthy Supreme Commander-in-Chief.[14]

Nonetheless, even later in the war when his knowledge and experience of Soviet offensive operations was at its peak, Stalin was more than willing to continue to push the Red Army forward with what by Western or even German standards was reckless abandon, even after he had come to realize that frontline soldiers were a finite resource. At the end of the war, it seems to have been Stalin himself who made sure that Red Army operations were not just focused on defeating Germany and her allies, but on mopping up as much territory and leverage for the Soviet domination of Eastern Europe as possible for the post-war world. The likes of Zhukov, Vasilevskii, and even the supposedly more humane Konstantin Rokossovskii were more than willing to do their master's bidding – they were after all part of a cohort of senior Soviet military leaders who had willingly put aside their scruples regarding losses to a considerable degree in order to further their careers. Stalin's bidding was increasingly feasible as the war progressed thanks to the fact that their advice had informed what he saw as viable and he himself had a better idea of what would be successful in the sense of achieving objectives in what he saw as a timely manner, even if the human cost was very high.

The Sources

Before discussing the nature of and changes and continuities in Soviet wartime higher-level decision-making in greater depth, it is perhaps useful to make a note of some crucial differences in the sources available for the study of upper-level military decision-making in the Soviet Union compared to for the Western Allies or even Germany. In the Soviet case, not only did Stalin not leave memoirs (as Hitler didn't), but nor did he hold the sort of documented military conferences held by Hitler or the Western Allies. Stalin preferred to divide and rule over his subordinates, meaning that meetings to discuss military affairs were typically kept small, with meeting participants entering and leaving a discussion as it progressed, with the key constant being Stalin. Frequently, given the absence of memoirs by Stalin, official meeting transcripts, and the sort of personal diaries that might have got Soviet military leaders into trouble, we are left with only the retrospective testimonies of a number of military leaders to shed light on what took place in a particular meeting. Those testimonies were produced – and in some cases published in truncated form – by and large during a period in the Soviet historiography when candour was at best only possible in coded form. Even during the Khrushchev 'thaw,' when for example Vasilii Chiukov produced his what by Soviet standards were explosive memoirs on the late war period, there were limits to which memoirs could rock the boat and present discord amongst Soviet military leaders, even if Stalin's role could for a time be played down.[15]

Particularly important in this piece both directly and indirectly is an analysis of one of the most useful single sources we have on Stalin's wartime activity, his Kremlin appointment book. This material gives us dates, times, and durations for meetings held by Stalin in his Kremlin office over the course of the war (and indeed before it and beyond it), and has been widely used by historians since it first emerged in the early 1990s.[16] Although Stalin did on occasion meet key figures elsewhere, his Kremlin office was the hub of the Soviet war effort. Together with a number of key memoirs, and documents produced by the Stavka and GKO, Stalin's Kremlin appointments diary is a crucial source for building up a picture of Soviet operational and strategic decision-making during the Great Patriotic War.

The Great Patriotic War

As already made plain in the introductory material to this piece, from the very beginning of the war Stalin was central to Soviet military decision-making. Stalin was a key decision maker from the outbreak of war both in a *de jure* and a *de facto* sense, and was the ultimate arbiter of strategy throughout the war. In a *de jure* sense, when the first iteration of the Stavka – the military headquarters for the war – was established on 23 June 1941, Stalin was however initially just a member. The first Stavka was to be chaired by Semen Timoshenko as People's Commissar for Defence, with Zhukov in his then role as Chief of Staff joined by Stalin's close associates Viacheslav Molotov as foreign minister, Kliment Voroshilov, and Semen Budennii as army representatives and People's Commissar for the Navy Nikolai Kuznetsov.[17]

Voroshilov was the sole military member of the initial State Defence Committee – the Soviet equivalent of a war cabinet established on 30 June 1941 and discussed further below. He had at least been Commissar for Defence until the spring of 1940, but lost that position and some of his prominence in military decision-making to Timoshenko after the debacle in Finland required that he be seen to take responsibility for what initially at least had been something of a debacle. Formally though, Voroshilov remained a deputy minister for defence in the leadup to the Great Patriotic War. That he had got to the point of being Marshal of the Soviet Union without having any formal military education highlights not only his close relationship with Stalin, but also the continued store that Stalin put on Civil War-era experience in the credentials of military leaders prior to and at the beginning of the Great Patriotic War.

The formation of a State Defence Committee on 30 June 1941 formally put Stalin – as its chairman – at the apex of decision-making on all matters relating to the conduct of the war. The State Defence Committee was the supreme decision-making body for the Soviet war effort and is perhaps best seen as a sort of inner cabinet combined with elements of the military leadership. On this committee, Stalin and Voroshilov were initially joined as part of a very select group by Viacheslav Molotov (foreign affairs), Lavrentii Beria (internal security), and Georgii Malenkov (a trusted Party functionary). As of 30 June Stalin was also still head of the Party apparatus as General Secretary of the Communist Party – a role he had held continuously since before Lenin's death. On 19 July Stalin also made himself Commissar for Defence within the Soviet government structure – relegating Timoshenko to future roles as a front commander and later Stavka representative at the front, and making it plain that he was going to take a central role in military decision-making.[18]

Although Stalin made himself minister for defence after the formation of the State Defence Committee, both formally and informally the State Defence Committee had already brought together the Party and state apparatus in a single decision-making body with the scope for taking decisions within all spheres of the Soviet war effort. The only one of the initial members of the GKO having a formal position in both the Party and state structures was Stalin – who then added the post of Minister for Defence to ram home his leadership position. By 8 August 1941 Stalin had promoted himself to Supreme High Commander of the armed forces and head of a headquarters given the title Headquarters of the Supreme High Command to further highlight that he was in charge of all aspects of the Soviet war effort. Changes in a formal title for the Soviet military headquarters did not mean that its short-form title changed – throughout the war, it was known as the Stavka – and with Stalin at the helm, it took the key strategic, operational-strategic and often operational decisions.[19]

It is clear from the very beginning that Stalin intended to take a very much hands-on approach to military decision-making in all its forms and monopolize the strategic direction being taken by the Soviet war effort. All the way through from the production of weapons and equipment and the mobilization of reserves – to which the GKO paid considerable attention – to their use at the strategic and operational-strategic levels – that was very much within the remit of the Stavka – Stalin was at the helm. Stalin could not of course run the war effort by himself, and even if he was going to take the key decisions, he not only needed others to execute them but increasingly would acknowledge that he needed the advice of specialists in particular spheres – including the military one.

As already suggested, the initial membership of the State Defence Committee offered little military expertise, where at that point Voroshilov's lack of ability and understanding of military matters had apparently not been made plain enough to Stalin despite the debacle of the opening phase of the war against Finland in late 1939. That Timoshenko was not a member of the State Defence Committee, despite being chair of the Stavka at the beginning of the war, may suggest that Stalin was already considering taking over that role himself by the end of June.

At the beginning of the war the Chief of the General Staff – responsible for informing and carrying out the decisions of the Stavka – was Zhukov. The Soviet General Staff that he led was a relatively new development – only having come into being in 1935 in place of a Headquarters of the RKKA – the former having far wider competencies and responsibilities than the latter. Given that Stalin had not encountered a General Staff during the Civil War, it is quite possible that the fact that the organization was relatively new in 1941 was a factor limiting its significance for the development of Soviet strategy at the beginning of the Great Patriotic War.[20] That the work of the General Staff was not necessarily seen as being of the greatest importance during the first year of the war is suggested by Vasilevskii, who in his memoirs noted Stalin's tendency to routinely send capable members of the General Staff to the front earlier in the war, and questioned Vasilevskii's request to have Vatutin return from the front in the spring of 1942 for work as head of operations for the General Staff with the remark 'but isn't he needed at the front?'[21]

At the beginning of the war it seems that Head of the People's Commissariat for Internal Affairs (the NKVD), Lavrentii Beria – a member of the State Defence Committee – sought to expand the role of the NKVD in military affairs. He quite possibly hoped that the NKVD might end up with a military wing not dissimilar to the Waffen SS in Germany, giving him considerable input into military affairs. Certainly, at the beginning of the war, Beria had Stalin's ear – being one of the most consistent visitors to Stalin in his Kremlin office during 1941.[22] Stalin however, compared to Hitler, was more careful to limit the powers that subordinates could accrue who might ultimately threaten his position, and throughout the war, Stalin was careful to keep a lid on the military role of the NKVD. A good example of this was the fact that when the organization for the Soviet partisan movement was refined in the spring of 1942, it was the Party and Red Army that were the principal players in developing and co-ordinating the movement, and not the NKVD.[23] Beria had the opportunity to influence military matters in the Caucasus during the late summer and autumn of 1942 after he was sent there to help stabilize the military position – to the point that the commander of the Trans-Caucasian Front, Ivan Tiulenev claims to have offered Beria command, which the latter declined.[24] Beria's role in the Caucasus of course had Stalin's sanction – and is consistent with Stalin's appointment of politically reliable figures to key positions with influence over local military decision-making during early war periods of crisis. However, once the crisis was over, Beria's direct input into military affairs ceased. As the war progressed, NKVD military units – lacking the armour and artillery of their Waffen SS counterparts – were increasingly assigned to line-of-communication duties rather than having a frontline combat role. Consequently, Beria's involvement in military decision-making was kept to a minimum, and particularly once counter-intelligence within Red Army units was nominally transferred from the NKVD's Special Sections to the Ministry of Defence as SMERSH during 1943.[25]

Whilst the membership of the above institutions – initially the State Defence Committee and Stavka in particular – was important, it was however more an indicator of the perceived importance of individuals at the time they were named to them than a guarantee that someone would be consulted on military decision-making as time went on. Stalin did not tend to convene meetings of the State Defence Committee or Stavka in a formal sense – but to consult with their members and others as required – either alone or in very small groups. It is certainly telling that towards the end of the war – in February 1945 – when Vasilevskii was to take over command of the 3rd Belorussian Front after the death of rising star Ivan Cherniakovskii (instead of co-ordinating the activities of 1st Pribaltic and 3rd Belorussian Front as planned) he was provided with a document from the Stavka that in amending a GKO decree of 10 July 1941 on the membership of the Stavka, he was only then being made a permanent member of that body as a deputy minister for defence![26] This was simply a formal acknowledgement of what had been the case for some time – that Vasilevskii was central to high-level Soviet military decision-making. At the same time, Voroshilov didn't lose his nominal membership of the GKO until 21 November 1944, even though it is quite clear that his influence over key war-related decisions had been limited for some time despite the fact that Stalin kept giving his 'friend' chances to redeem himself with new military and quasi-military appointments.[27]

At the beginning of the war the formal membership of the GKO was soon very quickly increased through positions as permanent advisers, and key members of the GKO were given responsibilities for carrying out its decision and reporting back on aspects of the Soviet war effort as plenipotentiaries of the committee. The GKO may not have issued operational orders, but it was more directly involved in military decision-making with strategic significance than for example the British cabinet. For example, the State Defence Committee often micromanaged the distribution of military equipment, as in the case for example of all of the military equipment that arrived with Allied convoy PQ-12 to the Soviet Union in the spring of 1942.[28] Nonetheless, the Soviet situation was in some senses similar to other wartime examples in the sense that Stalin would carry through decisions from what was clearly within the GKO's remit into his role as Supreme High Commander, much as Churchill or Hitler did after meeting Beaverbrook or Speer respectively and then moving onto more clearly military matters.

In many ways the operational model for the GKO was followed in the solely military sphere, where the plenipotentiaries of the GKO were similar in function to the strategic direction commanders or Stavka representatives at the front later in the war. After the aborted use of multi-front or 'strategic direction' commanders in the autumn of 1941 this role of multi-front co-ordination on behalf of the Stavka was carried out by Stavka representatives that were part of a machinery that both informed Stalin about what was going on at the front and ensured that what had been decided upon centrally was indeed being carried out. This apparatus relied not only on the big-name Stavka representatives to fronts or groups of fronts – with Zhukov frequently leaving Moscow to carry out such a role – but also lesser representatives of the General Staff – the so-called Officers of the General Staff posted down as low as divisional level as required.[29] Until mid-1944 even when Zhukov and Vasilevskii were Stavka representatives at the front they did not have the authority to change plans decided upon back at the Stavka without consulting Stalin first – to the extent that according to Vasilevskii that even the transfer of a single division from one front to another required the approval of Stalin.[30]

Within this what in practice was a loose framework, at the beginning of the war those military personnel central to Soviet military decision-making were relatively few in number. The narrow circle of decision makers nominally formulating Soviet strategy at the beginning of the war seem to have had little impact on Stalin's initial decisions, that seem to have been more about hiding the strategic failure to be ready on almost any level to meet the Axis invasion than providing a well thought out defensive strategy that suited the actual circumstances. The order to counterattack on the borders in the immediate aftermath of the German-led invasion more deeply condemned those forces in the border regions to encirclement and destruction than need have been the case, although it was Dmitrii Pavlov and his colleagues in command of the Western Front, and not Stalin, who would be blamed for the subsequent slew of defeats and encirclements. The order for the execution of Pavlov and his associates on 28 July 1941 contained a warning to others where 'cowards and panic-mongers' who gave ground to the enemy 'on their own and without a fight' would be 'mercilessly punished.'[31] The extent to which key military figures at the time such as Chief of Staff Zhukov opposed the blind counterattack approach is unclear, but they had certainly played a significant role in setting up the disasters on the ground. Soviet strategic deployment at the time that was neither suited to the defence nor the offense given the fact that so many forward-deployed formations lacked the basic resources for anything other than short-term defence in extremely exposed positions.[32]

Stalin's state of mind in the spring to late summer of 1941 was probably not one that was conducive to Zhukov et al. having a meaningful impact on Stalin's iron will. On the positive side, the holding of ground and counterattacking where possible strategy to some extent inevitably screened attempts to build up strong defensive positions on key German axes of advance, as for example the Mozhaisk line before Moscow or the Luga line before Leningrad. However, without strong forces to counterattack against German breakthroughs of these positions or circumvention of them, this strategy was doomed to failure. Stalin's closest associates at the time – and in particular Voroshilov and Budennii – proved either to have the insufficient military ability as was primarily the case for Voroshilov, or were insufficiently aggressive as in the case of Budennii, to both seize even local initiative from the Axis and satisfy Stalin's desire for successful counterattacks – no matter how fleeting their success. Nonetheless, both continued to be frequent visitors to Stalin's Kremlin office and were evidently consulted on military matters long after both were no longer seen as suitable for front or multi-front command positions.[33]

Zhukov's El'nia counterattack of early September 1941 against the German Army Group Centre was trumpeted as a major success, but was exacted both at a high cost and against an enemy temporarily on the defensive on that sector of the front and stripped of its armoured formations. Militarily the El'nia counterattack had a little longer-term impact, where that taking place further north near Staraia Russa that summer – whether intentionally or not – probably had longer-term ramifications given that it struck in the no-man's land between principle German thrusts even if it too was costly in terms of lives lost.[34] The role of Stalin's generals in all of this beyond their sometimes instigating and commanding local counterattacks is difficult to ascertain, but it is highly likely that all were less than willing to stand up to Stalin's one-sided approach to resistance given the potential consequences – and particularly given what had recently happened to Pavlov et al. There certainly wasn't clear direction for trying to screen a withdrawal in order to concentrate forces around and to counterattack near planned defensive lines, where the intentional giving of ground was simply unacceptable to Stalin. The same fate as befell Pavlov for the failures of the Western Front during the first days of the war would no doubt have been suffered by Mikhail Kirponos in the south in the aftermath of the Kiev debacle in September had he not been killed in action, and even Budennii was removed from his command role in the region primarily for having the temerity to ask for permission to withdraw.[35] In the case of the

Kiev debacle, Stalin seems to have been willing to buy into commander of the Briansk Front Andrei Eremenko's claims that counterattacks by his forces could transform the situation in the region – something that both Zhukov and Shaposhnikov apparently questioned to no avail.[36] Eremenko's star may have waned for a time in the aftermath of this failure, but Stalin had the tendency even during the early war period to forgive those commanders who showed the right combination of sufficient ability with considerable drive and ruthlessness – and Eremenko's star would bob back up before the war's end.

The use of commanders for strategic directions during this early period of the war – that is in command of a combination of Soviet fronts that resulted in formations akin to German Army Groups – was a short-lived phenomenon and restricted to the autumn of 1941. Why these strategic directions did not last is not fully clear, although at this time the Red Army was suffering from a horrendous shortage of competent staff officers, and adding another formal layer to the Soviet chain of command would have further exacerbated this problem.[37] The 'Direction' command seems to have been replaced with the dispatch from the centre of trusted commanders to key front commands or as Stavka representatives on them. An example of the former would be the dispatch of Zhukov to command the Leningrad Front in early September 1941 after his fleeting success at El'nia and just after Leningrad had been encircled. Soon Zhukov would be sent as a Stavka representative to the Reserve Front near Moscow. Just what Zhukov had achieved in Leningrad is unclear – as was whether the fact that Leningrad did not fall owed anything to Zhukov's intervention at all. Certainly, the Khrushchev-era accounts by some of Zhukov's subordinates there of him barking orders without necessarily having a coherent plan are plausible, and his intervention did not lead to the siege of Leningrad being lifted as intended.[38]

Despite Voroshilov's removal as head of a North-Western Direction command defending Leningrad in the late summer of 1941 (prior to Zhukov's intervention), the second half of 1941 and early 1942 would still see a sustained and prominent role for what I have termed the 'politicals' in the Soviet military leadership – i.e. those who were there more for their political reliability than military abilities or credentials. A good example of the rise of such a figure – with some input into strategic and operational-strategic decisions – was Lev Mekhlis. Mekhlis fitted in well with the narrative that Stalin seemed to adhere to at the time that the debacles at the front were the product of a lack of political will and reliability amongst Red Army commanders and indeed the whole army – circumstances that required the reintroduction of the dual command of the Civil War era between commissars and military commanders that ran all the way up to front level.[39] Dual command was supposed to prevent unauthorized withdrawals and limit the impact of the lack of will that was – in Stalin's mind at least – a key factor in the defeats of 1941 and 1942.[40]

At this time Lev Mekhlis was the head of the Main Political Administration of the Red Army, and as such might be seen as chief commissar. His attempts to reinforce the idea with Stalin that defeat was all too often a product a lack of political will with the Red Army's leaders fell on the fertile ground during the summer of 1941, and gave Mekhlis an opportunity to become involved in military decision-making – despite his lack of a military education and experience. Mekhlis's participation in the debacle of the Kerch' landings that would end in abject failure in May 1942 ultimately sealed his fate as someone who would be closely involved in operational decision-making, and this event was certainly a stepping stone towards Stalin's greater reliance on those with military education as the war progressed.[41]

Although the role of the 'politicals' in military decision-making certainly declined during 1942, political appointees continued to have a role in assessing the suitability of commanders for their front-level commands through the military soviets of fronts – essentially the highest level of the political-military apparatus for the Soviet armed forces, on which both the military leadership of the front and political appointees were represented. It is worth mentioning that political appointees could contribute to damage to the reputations of military leaders through reports to Stalin, as for example in the case of Ivan Konev – whose performance as commander of the Western Front in early 1943 came in for blistering criticism from member of the military soviet for the front Nikolai Bulganin. Konev was subsequently removed from the command for 'failing to cope with the task of managing the front,' being placed 'at the disposal' of the Supreme High Command.[42] However, as the direct role of the 'politicals' in military decision-making further declined their indirect influence seems to have done so as well – and Konev in the longer term of course weathered the storm and ended up being a key participant in the battle for Berlin. His replacement on the Western Front in February 1943 was a Vasilii Sokolovskii, whose capable staff work didn't necessarily mean he would be a successful front commander – a distinction that Stalin would appreciate more as the war progressed.[43]

Back in the summer of 1941 Zhukov had been replaced as Chief of Staff by the older Boris Shaposhnikov, someone who clearly commanded Stalin's respect and had played a significant role in getting a Soviet general staff created during the mid-1930s. In fact, Shaposhnikov was exceptional in the sense that he had experience of staff work during the First World War. Why Zhukov left the position of Chief of Staff is still a matter of some debate. It does however seem that Zhukov was probably not best suited to straight-up staff work – something that he at least seems to have been aware of at the time. Boris Shaposhnikov's role as Chief of Staff probably went some way to strengthening the position of the General Staff in Stalin's mind, where Stalin showed an unusual respect for the ailing Shaposhnikov, to the extent of referring to him using the formal first name patronymic combination rather than simply using his family name.[44]

With the German advance having slowed by early November 1941 – and with that advance petering out in the face of local Soviet counterattacks that would culminate in a wider offensive near Moscow during the weekend of 5–7 December 1941 – Stalin's attitude towards the General Staff and his generals more broadly certainly seems to have softened. Whilst key military figures such as Zhukov were clearly instrumental in the initial Soviet counteroffensive near Moscow, their role in turning that offensive into one that would take place across most of the frontline is unclear. It does seem likely that Zhukov and Shaposhnikov spoke against it, but the extent to which they were forceful in doing so is not apparent.[45] Initial successes seemed to vindicate Stalin's position, but soon the Red Army was bogged down across the length of the frontline as it became clear that the shift in the resource balance in Soviet favour was far from dramatic enough at this point to justify a wholescale offensive. Any assessment of how much Stalin learned from the experience contains a strong element of speculation, but his acceptance of the half-baked Khar'kov offensive of May 1942 as the first Soviet offensive of the new campaigning season suggests that his overconfidence in his own unadulterated judgement was still considerable. A lack of obvious scapegoats for the operation's failure certainly suggests, as Geoffrey Roberts points out, that Stalin was willing to see it as a collective failure – tacitly acknowledging his own role in the debacle.[46]

The failure to predict the German summer offensive in the south in 1942 seems perhaps to have shaken Stalin more than the failure of the wholescale winter offensive of 1941–1942 to achieve more. Whilst railing against 'commanders, commissars, political workers, units and formations which on their own initiative give up fighting positions' in his infamous 'Not a Step Back!' order of July 1942, once again Stalin did not blame individual generals in the same way as he had done during the summer and early autumn of 1941.[47] In May 1942 Shaposhnikov was still alive and serving in the role of Chief of the General Staff, and it is quite possible that Shaposhnikov's poor health in combination with Stalin long-term respect for him shielded him from Stalin's wrath – where there were other softer targets. One such softer target was the aforementioned Lev Mekhlis – whose failure at Kerch' put him in the crosshairs during this period – a period during which the 'politicals' would fall significantly from Stalin's grace. As already pointed out, neither Voroshilov nor Mekhlis – both of whose status in the decision-making process were highlighted by their positions as deputy commissars for defence – had any formal military education, as was the case for another early war favourite who fell rapidly from grace, Grigorii Kulik. Kulik was stripped not only of his rank of Marshal of the Soviet Union, but also both his position as a deputy Commissar for Defence and his Party membership in a Politburo decree of 19 February 1942 – also as a result of the debacle of the Kerch' landings in the Crimea in early 1942.[48] The 'politicals' were clearly on their way out in terms of having a role in higher-level operational and operational-strategic decision-making.

The declining influence of the 'politicals' and the rise of the General Staff during 1942 coincided with an improvement in the resource situation in the

Soviet Union. By the late summer of 1942 as the battle for the city of Stalingrad raged and German forces were being held off in the Caucasus, it was certainly apparent to Stalin and Soviet military leaders than the resource crisis of late 1941 had eased, and that the Soviet side had the opportunity to amass resources for successful regional offensive operations against an enemy that was increasingly overextended. Resources built up around Moscow to guard against a German offensive against the capital were in part committed to the Red Army's own offensive operations in the region, but could also be sent southwards for a counterstrike against the dangerously overextended Axis forces in and around Stalingrad. On 26 August 1942, Stalin appointed Zhukov as Deputy Supreme Commander. Zhukov's appointment as Stalin's deputy commander was followed the next day by his appointment as first deputy Commissar for Defence – clearly marking Zhukov out in the hierarchy as Stalin's number 2 on military matters. It would not be long before he would be promoted, in some ways belatedly, to Marshal of the Soviet Union on 18 January 1943.[49]

As Stalin's deputy, it stood to reason that Zhukov would take much of the responsibility for the most significant Red Army operations being planned at that time – and in particular further operations against Germany's Army Group Centre. Operation 'Mars' was to take place later that year, and hopefully not only rip the heart out of the German Army Group Centre, but also remove the ongoing German threat to the Soviet capital. This operation was on the back of piecemeal offensive operations against German forces in the Rzhev salient that had been ongoing since the spring and for the failure of which the new favourite Zhukov has to take some responsibility. He was also certainly involved in the planning of the Stalingrad operation – Operation 'Uranus,' but where former Deputy Chief of Staff Vasilevskii – who took over as Chief of the General Staff from the ailing Shaposhnikov in June 1942 – was clearly also central to it. According to Vasilevskii, the broad conception for the counteroffensive was established 'in the middle of September after an exchange of opinions between I.V. Stalin, G.K. Zhukov and myself.' Zhukov was subsequently dispatched to Stalingrad Front, and Vasilevskii to the South-Eastern Front as part of the development process for the offensive.[50] Zhukov's self-serving account in his memoirs that suggests that Operation 'Mars' against the Rzhev salient was of secondary importance to 'Uranus' near Stalingrad – with the purpose of the former being to prevent the transfer of German reserves to the latter – is at best misleading. David Glantz has certainly convincingly argued that 'Mars' was considered to be as, if not more important than 'Uranus' at the time.[51]

At the time of Operations 'Mars' and 'Uranus' it is quite likely that for Stalin there was something of a leap in trust in the new wave of military leaders at the top of the Red Army's command structure – and not just Zhukov and Vasilevskii. Zhukov may at this time have been *primus inter pares*, but Vasilevskii and a number of front commanders such as Konev and

Rokossovskii had clearly moved into a distinct category of the trusted as advisers. Russian historian Iurii Gor'kov's tally of audiences that front commanders had with Stalin during the war using his appointment diary suggests that on only 8 occasions during 1941 did Stalin meet with commanders of specific fronts, whereas during 1942 he met with front commanders on 43 occasions – including a total of 13 meetings with Konev.[52] In fact, Stalin's growing trust in the Red Army officers corps (where down the whole chain of command they were by now being allowed to call themselves officers rather than the designation of commander that had been the norm since the revolution) is certainly evident by late 1942. Perhaps the strongest indication of this is Stalin's decision to abolish dual command in the Red Army, whereby since July 1941 political commissars and their subordinates had equal authority with military commanders on tactical and operational matters. Although much relating to operational matters still remained indirectly within the remit of political officers after the abolition of dual commander on 9 October 1942, this move sent out a clear signal of Stalin's growing confidence in the Red Army officer corps.[53]

Although the resource balance was clearly shifting in Soviet favour in mid-late 1942, that Stalin would sanction two major counteroffensive operations against German forces in both the centre and south in late 1942 is highly consistent with Stalin's tendency to want to do too much rather than too little in terms of offensive operations. In this case the evidence does tend to suggest that with counteroffensive operations already in the offing against Army Group Centre in the Rzhev region, the Stalingrad encirclement operation – Operation 'Uranus' – was added on as an operation to take advantage of an opportunity. Zhukov was clearly keen to preserve the Rzhev salient operation – Operation 'Mars' – as an operation of sufficient importance for him to continue to focus on it at a time when he was increasingly in favour with Stalin and could probably have opted to take the lead on either 'Mars' or 'Uranus.'

The success of 'Uranus' clearly boosted the reputations of those senior Red Army leaders involved. That Zhukov's 'Mars' Operation ended in abject failure does not seem to have damaged his reputation with Stalin, suggesting that as Zhukov claimed he did play a significant role in the planning of 'Uranus' as well. Although the subsequent 'Little Saturn' did not lead to the destruction of German forces in the southern part of the Soviet Union, it did nonetheless cause significant damage to German and allied Axis forces in the region and force the evacuation of Army Group A from the Caucasus. In the aftermath of 'Little Saturn' Germany's Italian and Hungarian allies were spent forces on the Eastern Front, and only Romania would soldier on as a significant contributor to the fighting in the south. That operations to cut off the German Army Group A in the Caucasus – Operation 'Saturn' – were downgraded to 'Little Saturn' in the light of Hoth's German counterattack to try to break through to the Stalingrad pocket is certainly indicative of Stalin's increasing willingness to accept advice to trim down expectations for offensive operations in the light of actual circumstances. Quite possibly Stalin had learned something from the dissipation of strength leading to a string of only partial but costly successes during the winter of 1941–1942 across the whole of the frontline.

For all his personality failings, Stalin was clearly able to learn something from past mistakes and grow to value the advice of senior military leaders who showed the necessary loyalty and drive to push home attacks even as casualties mounted. On Stalin's willingness to take advice from and even defer to his military commanders later in the war Aleksandr Vasilevskii would record a frank conversation he had with Kliment Voroshilov in March 1944, in which Voroshilov suggested that:

> Earlier on Stalin wasn't like that. In all likelihood the war has taught him a lot. He apparently understood that he can be wrong and that his decisions need not always be the best, and that the knowledge and experience of others might also be useful. The passing years have also had an impact him – before the war he was younger and more self-confident...[54]

Vasilevskii goes on to note how in a speech on 24 May 1945 – admittedly with victory over Nazi Germany safely in the bag – Stalin would not that during the early phases of the war 'our government made a significant number of mistakes [*ne malo oshibok*]' – in a statement that clearly included himself.[55]

As well as becoming capable of at least a hint of self-criticism and to value the advice of others, Stalin's own abilities increased as the war progressed. Not only Zhukov would acknowledge Stalin's growing abilities as a supreme commander, but also his colleagues, such as Vasilevskii. In his memoirs, Vasilevskii would point out that in general Stalin's demands on his subordinates regarding operational achievement later in the war would be 'reasonable, even if harsh.' Like Hitler, Stalin apparently had a phenomenal memory for detail – something that became an asset where he was more willing to listen to advice and contribute to discussion rather than impose his will upon it as a default approach.[56] Even before the war Stalin had been willing to encourage learning from the debacle in Finland as long as any blame for what had happened was not pointed in his direction. Stalin's interventions in operational matters in the early period of the Great Patriotic War may have been largely negative – and include his pushing for numerous offensive operations to relieve Leningrad and destroy sizeable German forces that were beyond the Red Army's capabilities at the time – but even during this period not all of his interventions in military affairs were similarly detrimental. Stalin was the final arbiter in all military matters of significance, and prior to the war had backed the right horses in terms of the development of Soviet tanks and indeed other weapons, such as mortars, rocket mortars, and in the early war period the PPSh sub-machine gun. These may not have been strategic decisions, but had strategic significance. By the mid-war period, Stalin was adding informed strategic and operational-strategic decision-making to his list of competencies.

By the time of Stalin's Order of the Day of 1 May 1943 it is clear that Stalin felt considerable satisfaction with the progress of the war at that point – a state that can only have encouraged him to further listen to advice rather than lash out blindly at both the enemy and his commanders as he had done in the summer of 1941.[57] Only a year after the Khar'kov debacle, during the spring of 1943, Stalin was willing to listen to Zhukov and Vasilevskii when they suggested that given intelligence of German intentions to attack the Kursk salient, it would be better for the Red Army to allow Germany to strike first before counterattacking. Whilst both Zhukov and Vasilevskii note that Stalin's resolve on this matter was shaky after the German Operation 'Citadel' did not begin in May as expected – helped by the prompting of the Voronezh Front's commander Vatutin for immediate Soviet action – they were nonetheless apparently able to persuade Stalin of the wisdom of continuing to wait for Germany to strike the first blow against well-established Soviet defences.[58] The subsequent Soviet counterstrikes would take the Red Army to the Dnepr River and beyond by the end of the year were a considerable success, at which point it was clearly looking like a case of when rather than whether Germany and her allies would be defeated.

During the latter part of the war the Red Army enjoyed a position of overwhelming strength over the German armed forces and the vestiges of the alliance that had invaded the Soviet Union back in June 1941. The Red Army could comfortably launch overlapping offensive operations thanks to the material superiority it now enjoyed – even if manpower levels, and particularly in the infantry – were difficult to maintain. During the planning process for major operations, Stalin consulted widely not only with members of the Stavka and General Staff, but also with an increasingly wide group of front commanders. During 1944, Stalin met with specific front commanders on 61 occasions – compared to only 8 for the second half of 1941. Nine of those 1944 meetings were with young rising star Ivan Cherniakhovskii, who had met Stalin once in 1942 and four times in 1943, but other names include Fedor Tolbukhin (whom Stalin met on eight occasions in 1944), long-time front commander Leonid Govorov (who met Stalin on five occasions in 1944 – compared to three in 1943 and one each in 1941 and 1942), as well as a rehabilitated Kirill Meretskov (whom Stalin met on six occasions in 1944, compared to only one in 1943 and five in 1942) and Ivan Konev (meeting on six occasions in 1944 – compared to only three in 1943, 13 in 1942 and one in 1941).[59] Certainly, during 1944 there were a large number of operations on which front commanders could be consulted. What came to be known as the 'Ten Stalinist Blows' of 1944 were akin to a series of punches from a boxer who was threatening to overwhelm his opponent. Operation 'Bagration' stands out as the most significant of these offensives, and it is worth focusing on elements of the planning and execution of this operation as an illustration of the manner in which operational-strategic decisions were being taken by this point in the war.

Not only did Stalin clearly consult widely on Operation 'Bagration' – that would involve the co-ordination of multiple fronts – but it is clear that this consultation had a meaningful impact on planning. The extent to which Stalin was willing to listen to and seriously consider the suggestions of his generals by this point of the war is well illustrated by the following vignette at the time during which Operation 'Bagration' was being planned. Certainly, not only did Stalin frequently meet with those many front commanders involved in the operation, but he was also willing to change his mind on their advice. Stalin's apparent acceptance during discussions to finalize the 'Bagration' plan on 22–23 May 1944 of Konstantin Rokossovskii's insistence that his forces on the right wing of the offensive strike with two equally important thrusts with a view to encircling German forces on his sector rather than with a single principal blow as initially supported by Stalin and 'certain members of the Stavka,' is a case in point. Others present during the discussions – namely GKO members Foreign Minister Molotov and Malenkov – were apparently concerned that Rokossovskii's stubborn insistence on two blows would land him in hot water with Stalin – where Rokossovskii claims to have offered to resign his post as commander of 1st Belorussian Front if Stalin and the Stavka were to insist on a single blow. That Stalin ultimately acquiesced – purportedly suggesting that 'the stubbornness of the front commander proves that the organisation of the front's attack has been through. That is a reliable guarantee of success. We confirm his plan' – would have been unlikely to have been the case back in 1941, and certainly where Rokossovskii's career seems not to have been damaged as a result.[60]

According to Vasilevskii, both he and Zhukov were frequently recalled from trips to the front at various locations associated with the planning of future operations in the leadup to 'Bagration' in order to consult with Stalin – and would frequently consult with Stalin on specific details by telephone. Rokossovskii's frequent involvement is also noted by Vasilevskii in developing a plan that was finalized on 30 May 1944.[61] The success of 'Bagration' brought the close of the war significantly closer, and particularly as it coincided with the Western Allies cementing their foothold on the continent.

The initial successes of 'Bagration' also seems to have given Stalin the confidence to allow his most prominent military leaders – and in particular Zhukov and Vasilevskii – to take at least some decisions as representatives of the Stavka at the front without always having to seek his approval. According to Vasilevskii's memoirs it was during July 1944 that 'during the period of the Belorussian operation, when the Stavka instructed G.K. Zhukov not only to co-ordinate the activities of 2nd and 1st Belorussian Fronts alongside 1st Ukrainian Front, but to direct them, and I at the same time was instructed to do the same regarding 3rd Belorussian Front along with 2nd and 1st Pribaltic Fronts.' As such, as Vasilevskii goes on to note, they were being given considerably greater responsibility for operational-strategic decisions being made when operations were in progress than before.[62] One might associate their greater autonomy with the decreasing likelihood that the Soviet Union would be defeated, but that need not completely diminish the significance of this change.

There can be little doubt that by the late winter and early spring of 1945 the Soviet Union could have finished off Nazi Germany and brought the war in Europe to a close significantly earlier than May 1945. That it didn't was also most probably a conscious decision by Stalin – backed up by Zhukov and others – to delay the inevitable and extract the maximum in terms of concessions for the post-war world from the Western Allies at key conferences, namely in this instance Yalta in February 1945. The delay not only kept the war going, but allowed the Red Army to liberate – or seize depending on your perspective – territory with a view to gaining influence over it in the post-war world. Certainly events surrounding the launching of the Berlin Operation highlight this and the significance of political factors in Soviet strategy at this point in the war.[63]

The Berlin Operation was undoubtedly launched in something of a hurry in response to Allied successes in the West, and it is reasonable to speculate that Stalin had probably thought it likely that the Red Army would have had more time in order to conclude operations elsewhere before delivering what was probably going to be the *coup de grâce* for Nazi Germany by capturing Berlin.[64] There can also be little doubt that the final plans for the Berlin Operation – with Zhukov serving as commander of the principle 1st Belorussian Front, and Konev of the 1st Ukrainian Front – saw Stalin attempt to put Zhukov in his place as a subordinate to the overall wisdom of the Supreme Commander, Stalin. By this point – as of mid-February 1945 – Vasilevskii had chosen to give up his position as Chief of Staff, where he would subsequently claim in his memoirs that 'I was spending most of the time directly at the front carrying out the tasks of the Stavka, and was only in Moscow when summoned,' and where Antonov had practically been serving as Chief of Staff for some time. Vasilevskii would subsequently be Stavka co-ordinator for the 1st Pribaltic and 3rd Belorussian Fronts in East Prussia – before being dispatched to the Far East for the war against Japan.[65] Zhukov too was committed at the front, and by being given command of 1st Belorussian Front Zhukov had been given the most prestigious front command at the time (having displaced Rokossovskii as the commander of the front) that was supposed to take the lead in taking Berlin. That Stalin built into the plan the possibility that Konev's 1st Ukrainian Front might race Zhukov's forces for control of the German capital was hardly a decision taken at this stage of the war out of any sort of military necessity. In fact, Stalin's decision to allow Konev's forces to head northwards after the dividing line between the fronts was cut short at Lübben might even have increased the cost of the operation for the Red Army in terms of increasing the frequency of 'friendly fire' incidents within Berlin and wider losses given the urgency with which both front commanders pushed their troops forward. The end result was probably the capture of the city more quickly than would have been the case had it been a solely 1st Belorussian Front operation – but with the benefit for Stalin that Zhukov could not take all the credit for its fall. [66]

Concluding Remarks

By the end of the war Stalin was appearing in an increasing number of propaganda posters as leading the Soviet Union to victory – having been notably absent when things had not been going anything like as well back in 1941–1942. Stalin's generals – even collectively – were not given the same honour, despite what they had contributed to Stalin's victory. Nonetheless, a significant number of them had played a meaningful part in developing Soviet strategy and carrying out or co-ordinating Soviet operations – both in executing plans issued in the name of the Supreme High Commander, but also increasingly in shaping them. In my *The Red Army and the Second World War*, I reproduce a photograph from the end of the war that I have captioned 'The winning team.'[67] Zhukov is prominently place in the middle of the front row – the *primus inter pares*, but with Vasilevskii on Zhukov's right leaning in towards the centre of the photo. To Zhukov's left is Rokossovskii followed by Meretskov, while on Vasilevskii's right sits Konev. Behind them are Tolbukhin, Rodion Malinovskii, Govorov, Eremenko and Ivan Bagramian. Alongside those whose rise during the war was significant – such as Rokossovskii (and to whom we would be adding Ivan Cherniakovskii had he not been killed in early 1945) – are those such as Eremenko who were already prominent front commanders in 1941 but whose fortunes had risen, fallen, and risen again (with Vatutin missing, having been killed by Ukrainian nationalist partisans in 1944). Notably absent from the photograph and decision-making are those who were at the top of the military hierarchy in June 1941 – Shaposhnikov through his death, but also Timoshenko, Kulik, Voroshilov, and Budennii because they had fallen out of favour having been seen as falling short as military commanders. All of those in the photograph had met Stalin in person in 1944 on more than one occasion – and indeed only Eremenko and Bagramian are not recorded as having met Stalin in person in 1945 – during which period he only met front commanders on 12 occasions compared to 61 the previous year. Although Stalin is missing from this photograph, it in many ways is a good encapsulation of the 'team' – 'captained' by Zhukov, and 'managed' by Stalin – that would shape Soviet strategic, operational-strategic, and operational decision-making that would ultimately bring the Soviet Union victory.

If anyone should bear the mantle of architect of victory (and of the initial defeats suffered by the Soviet Union) it would have to be Stalin – but a Stalin who increasingly drew on the advice of trusted military advisers around him. Stalin could take much of the glory for having backed success, but even during the latter half of the war, he has to take much of the responsibility for the human cost of operations that were pushed forward beyond by him and his willing accomplices the point at which most commanders and political leaders would have balked at the cost. As the war progressed his accomplices quite probably ameliorated those costs both through their advice at the planning stages and capabilities in execution. Had they not been willing to do so, then Stalin would have found others who might have been more or less capable leading to greater or lower losses, but who would have had to have been willing to show the necessary ruthlessness in getting things done the way the boss wanted – and in the timeframe he expected.

Notes

1 The BEST Soviet military commander of World War II – Russia Beyond, https://rbth.com [accessed 2 September 2021].
2 Andrew Roberts, *Masters and Commanders: How four titans won the war in the West, 1941–1945* (London: Allen Lane, 2008).
3 See Alexander Hill (ed.), *The Great Patriotic War of the Soviet Union, 1941–1945: a documentary reader* (Abingdon, Oxon: Routledge, 2009), Chapters 1 and 2, and within those chapters particularly Documents 6, 12, and 14.
4 Ibid., chapter 1, and in particular Documents 2, 3, and 5.
5 For a detailed analysis of the development of the Red Army in the leadup to the Great Patriotic War, see Alexander Hill, *The Red Army and the Second World War* (Cambridge: Cambridge University Press, 2017), chapters 2–9.
6 Ibid., chapter 9, and particularly pp. 192–95.
7 This plan for a pre-emptive strike is provided in English translation as Document 15 in Chapter 2 of Alexander Hill (ed.), *The Great Patriotic War...: a documentary reader...*, pp. 29–34.
8 See also Alexander Hill, "Offense, Defence or the Worst of Both Worlds? Soviet Strategy in May-June 1941," in *The Journal of Military and Strategic Studies*, Volume 13, Number 1 (Fall 2010), pp. 61–74. Available online without charge at https://jmss.org/article/download/57937/43601/157596 [accessed 19 October 2021]. For a detailed examination of the state of the Red Army on the eve of Barbarossa, see David Glantz, *Stumbling Colossus: The Red Army on the Eve of World War II* (Lawrence, KA: University Press of Kansas, 2011).
9 Geoffrey Roberts, *Stalin's General: The life of Georgy Zhukov* (New York: Random House, 2012).
10 I.I. Gaglov, *General armii A.I. Antonov.* 2-e izd., dop. (Moscow: Voenizdat, 1987), pp. 104–5.
11 G.K. Zhukov, *Vospominaniia i razmishleniia. V 3-x tomakh. T.2. 12-e izdanie* (Moscow: "Izdatel'stvo 'Novosti,'" 1995), p. 117.
12 Evan Mawdsley, "Stalin: Victors are not Judged," in *The Journal of Slavic Military Studies*, Volume 19, Number 4 (2006), p. 719.
13 Alexander Hill, *The Red Army and the Second World War*, p. 374.
14 Evan Mawdsley, "Stalin: Victors are not Judged," p. 719.
15 Chuikov would claim that Berlin could have been captured well before May 1945. See Alexander Hill, *The Red Army and the Second World War*, pp. 543–44.

16 See A.A. Chernobaev (gen.ed.), *Na prieme u Stalina. Tetradi (zhurnali) zapisei lits, priniatikh I.V. Stalinim (1924–1953). Spravochnik* (Moscow: Novii khronograf, 2010).

17 'Permanent advisers' to the Stavka were Marshals of the Soviet Union Grigorii Kulik and Boris Shaposhnikov, along with Nikolai Vatutin, heads of the air force (VVS) and air defence forces (PVO) Pavel Zhigarev and Nikolai Voronov respectively, head of the Political Administration of the Red Army Lev Mekhlis and non-military members Anastas Mikoian, Lazar Kaganovich, Lavrentii Beria, Nikolai Voznesenskii, Andrei Zhdanov and Georgii Malenkov. See On the joint decree of the SNK SSSR and TsK VKP(b) on the creation of a Headquarters of the High Command, 23.6.1941, in Alexander Hill (ed.), *The Great Patriotic War...: a documentary reader...*, p.44. The latter non-military members would soon have their attentions shifted to the State Defence Committee, leaving the Stavka as a more obviously military body.

18 Prior to Stalin becoming Minister for Defence the beginnings of a precedent that Ministers for Defence were to be military men – that would continue after Stalin's death – were being established, and where both Voroshilov and his successor Timoshenko served as Minister for Defence as such.

19 Alexander Hill, *The Great Patriotic War...: a documentary reader...*, pp. 44–45; *The Red Army and the Second World War*, p. 221.

20 Alexander Hill, *The Red Army and the Second World War*, p. 49.

21 A.M. Vasilevskii, *Delo vsei zhizni. ... 2*, p. 228. In Vatutin's case he was probably better employed at the front.

22 According to Vladimir Kisilev's tally of visitors to Stalin's Kremlin office during the second half of 1941, Beria was in fact the only military or quasi-military leader to meet Stalin on a number of occasions every month from May through to October 1941, frequently spending more time with Stalin per month than military leaders. See Vladimir Kisilev, *Vstrechi Stalina. V kabinete u Verkhovnogo* (Moscow: Kontseptual, 2019), pp. 58–59.

23 See Alexander Hill, *The War Behind the Eastern Front: The Soviet Partisan Movement in North-West Russia, 1941–1944* (Abingdon, Oxon: Frank Cass, 2005), chapter 9.

24 Alexander Hill, *The Red Army and the Second World War*, p. 361.

25 As in the James Bond movies, the acronym SMERSH stood for *Smert' spionam!*, although the activities of the real-life SMERSH were typically somewhat more domestic and often more prosaic than their movie counterpart.

26 A.M. Vasilevskii, *Delo vsei zhizni. Kniga vtoraia. Izdanie shestoe* (Moscow: Politizdat, 1989), p. 185.

27 Postanovlenie Politburo TsK VKP(b) "Ob osvobozhdenii Voroshilova K.E. ot obiazannostei chelna Gosudarstvennogo Komiteta Oboroni i vvedenii Bulganina N.A. v sostav Gosudarstvennogo Komiteta Oboroni," 21 noiabria 1944 g., in L.P. Kosheleva et al., *Sovetskoe voenno-politicheskoe rukovodstvo v godi Velikoi Otechestvennoi voini* (Moscow: Kuchkovo pole Muzeon, 2020), p. 69.

28 See Alexander Hill (ed.), *The Great Patriotic War...: a documentary reader...*, pp. 177–79.

29 See Alexander Hill, *The Red Army and the Second World War*, pp. 379–80.

30 A.M. Vasilevskii, *Delo vsei zhizni. Kniga pervaia. Izdanie shestoe* (Moscow: Politizdat, 1989), p. 211.

31 Alexander Hill, *The Red Army and the Second World War*, p. 222.

32 See David Glantz, *Stumbling Colossus....*

33 In the case of Voroshilov, according to Kisilev's analysis of Stalin's Kremlin appointment diary, with the exception of August 1941 when he was away in Leningrad, Voroshilov would meet Stalin every month between May and October 1941.

During June and July 1941 he was the fourth most frequent visitor to Stalin's office in terms of time spent there (with Molotov, Beria and Malenkov – all members of the State Defence Committee – all also being frequent visitors), although for September and October Voroshilov's position had dropped to tenth and seventh respectively. See Vladimir Kisilev, *Vstrech Stalina. V kabinete u Verkhovnogo*, pp. 58–59.

34 See Alexander Hill, *The Red Army and the Second World War*, pp. 233–37.

35 Ibid., pp. 244–47.

36 Ibid., p. 373.

37 On shortages of competent staff officers in the Red Army, see ibid., pp. 49, 176, 376, 444, 569, 579.

38 See Geoffrey Roberts, *Stalin's General: The life of Georgy Zhukov*, pp. 128–35.

39 On the re-introduction of dual command in July 1941, see Alexander Hill, *The Great Patriotic War...: a documentary reader*, Document 30, p.53, and on its dissolution in October 1942, Document 84, p. 114.

40 See in particular the infamous Orders Number 270 of the Headquarters of the Supreme High Command of 16 August 1941 and Number 227 of the People's Commissar for Defence of 28 July 1942, in ibid., pp. 55–56 and 100–102, respectively.

41 On Mekhlis's rise and fall as a military commander, see Alexander Hill, *The Red Army and the Second World War*, pp. 363–65.

42 Dokladnaia zapiska chlena Voennogo soveta Zapadnogo fronta N.A. Bulganina I.V. Stalinu o komandovanii fronta, 26 fevralia 1943 g., in L.P. Kosheleva et al. (eds.), *Sovetskoe voenno-politicheskoe rukovodstvo v godi Velikoi Otechestvennoi voini*, pp. 323–25.

43 It is worth noting that Bulganin's career also progressed successfully, where for example he formally replaced Kliment Voroshilov on the State Defence Committee in November 1944.

44 Alexander Hill, *The Red Army and the Second World War*, p. 268.

45 Ibid., pp. 341–42.

46 Geoffrey Roberts, *Stalin's General: The life of Georgy Zhukov*, pp. 151–52.

47 Much of this order is provided in English translation in Alexander Hill (ed.), *The Great Patriotic War...: a documentary reader*, pp. 100–102.

48 Postanovlenie Politburo TsK VKP(b) o marshale G.I. Kulike, 19 fevralia 1942 g., in L.P. Kosheleva et al., *Sovetskoe voenno-politicheskoe rukovodstvo v godi Velikoi Otechestvennoi voini*, p. 315.

49 Geoffrey Roberts, *Stalin's General: The life of Georgy Zhukov*, pp. 164, 175.

50 A.M. Vasilevskii, *Delo vsei zhizni. ... 2*, p. 242.

51 The section in Zhukov's memoirs on this matter is provided in English translation in Alexander Hill (ed.), *The Great Patriotic War...: a documentary reader*, p. 106. See also David Glantz, *Zhukov's Greatest Defeat: The Red Army's Epic Disaster in Operation Mars, 1942* (Lawrence, KA: University Press of Kansas, 1998).

52 Iurii Gor'kov, *Kreml'. Stavka. Genshtab.* (Tver': ANTEK, 1995), p. 302.

53 See On the establishment of full unitary command..., 9 October 1942, in Alexander Hill (ed.), *The Great Patriotic War...: a documentary reader*, p. 114.

54 A.M. Vasilevskii, *Delo vsei zhizni. ... 2*, p. 235.

55 Ibid., p. 236.

56 As noted by Vasilevskii in Ibid., p. 233.

57 See Alexander Hill (ed.), *The Great Patriotic War...: a documentary reader*, p.123 for extracts from this order.

58 See for example Vasilevskii's recounting of the situation in A.M. Vasilevskii, *Delo vsei zhizni. ... 2*, p.24.

59 Iurii Gor'kov, *Kreml'. Stavka. Genshtab.*, p.302.

60 See Konstantin Rokossovskii, "Dva glavnikh udar," in *Voenno-istoricheskikh zhurnal*, Number 6 (1964), pp. 14–15, and Iurii Gor'kov, *Kreml'. Stavka. Genshtab.*, p. 117.

61 A.M. Vasilevskii, *Delo vsei zhizni. … 2*, pp. 120–22.
62 Ibid., pp. 211–12.
63 See Alexander Hill, *The Red Army and the Second World War*, pp. 542–44 and David Glantz, "Stalin's Strategic Intentions, 1941–1945: Soviet Military Operations as Indicators of Stalin's Postwar Territorial Ambitions," *The Journal of Slavic Military Studies*, Volume 27, Number 4 (2014), pp. 676–720.
64 Alexander Hill, *The Red Army and the Second World War*, chapter 23.
65 A.M. Vasilevskii, *Delo vsei zhizni. … 2*, p. 183.
66 See the extract from Zhukov's memoirs regarding planning for the Berlin offensive in Alexander Hill (ed.), *The Great Patriotic War…: a documentary reader*, p. 265.
67 See Alexander Hill, *The Red Army and the Second World War*, p. 571.

8

THE GERMAN HIGH COMMAND

Williamson Murray

The nature of the German high command in the Second World War reaches some seventy years back to the formation of the Second Reich in the period 1866–1870.[1] To understand the bizarre nature of how the Germans ran the war in the 1940s, one needs to understand the historical background of their military culture as well as the factors that influenced their approach to the war in the period before Adolf Hitler became the Reich's Chancellor on 30 January 1933. Thus, this essay begins with historical background before examining Hitler's reign, which we will divide into two distinct periods, prewar and war-time. Above all, this essay stresses that the nature of the German high command in no fashion resembled how the Anglo-American powers organized themselves and conducted the two great world wars.

Before Hitler

The formative period of the German approach to the organization of the nation's high command lies very much in the period of Otto von Bismarck's control of German strategy and the wars of German unification. The "Iron Chancellor" assumed his position in control Prussia's internal and foreign policies after an extended confrontation between the king and the parliament. The latter quite simply refused to provide the king the financial support, i.e., taxes, required to support the army. Bismarck solved the problem by simply refusing to pay any attention to the constitution and proceeded to collect the necessary funds to support the army.

Whatever the consequences of the quarrels between Bismarck and the parliamentarians, he proved one of the great statesmen in history.[2] By isolating Austria and then creating a situation in which the Austrians appeared to be the

DOI: 10.4324/9781003375630-8

aggressors, Bismarck created a strategic framework where the Prussian Army could destroy the Austrian Army in the Battle of Königgrätz. He then insured Austria would not become a permanent enemy by arranging a truce and then a peace, which cost the Austrians no territorial losses. Nevertheless, the generals were furious to be denied the opportunity to complete the destruction of the Austrian Army and hold a victory parade in Vienna. Similarly, in 1870 Bismarck set the strategic stage so that the Prusso-German armies could crush the French without interference by the other major powers.

Yet when the dust settled Graf Helmuth von Moltke and the demi-gods of the general staff received most of the credit for the unification of Germany. As Holger Herwig has pointed out: Otto von Bismarck's skillful diplomacy, which had allowed Prussia to tackle each adversary one by one, was blithely ignored. So was the Iron Chancellor's sagacious policy of constantly reassessing the war as it escalated beyond the initial clash of forces. The General Staff's writers instead attributed victory solely to the regular army – its discipline, drill, and weaponry – and particularly to its staff officers....[3]

The result in the army was an almost total focus on tactics and operations and a contempt for strategic issues and politics. General Geyer von Schweppenburg wrote to Liddell Hart after the Second World War: "[y]ou will be horrified to hear that I have never read Clausewitz or Delbrück or Haushofer. The opinion on Clausewitz in our general staff was that [he was] a theoretician to be read by professors."[4] Instead, the Reich's military leaders emphasized what they termed "military necessity."[5] Their argument was that the nation's leaders must place military necessity above all other concerns, especially political or strategic concerns. Obviously, the heavy focus on tactics and operations led the Germans to minimize the study of strategic issues, while logistics and intelligence received short shrift in the *Kriegsakamie* both before and after the war.

Not surprisingly, while the Germans performed more than adequately in the First World at the tactical level, but their political and strategic conduct was appalling.[6] When the war was over, the general staff focused on what it had done well, namely tactics that had seen the army make major strides toward the invention of combined arms warfare.[7] As for the strategic and political causes of defeat, the officer corps believed that the army had stood unbeaten and unbroken in the field. Only the fact that the Jews and Communists had stabbed it in the back had prevented the Germans from winning the war.[8] That myth led many in the officer corps to argue that in the next war, the army would need strong political leadership at home to support fully those in the field.

Whatever the myths, in 1919 the German military confronted the reality that the Reich was a beaten nation, and it would have to live by the strictures the Treaty of Versailles imposed on its structure, organization, and size. The Weimar Republic, replacement of the army's beloved monarchy, possessed a Ministry of Defense, which allowed the military free reign. Versailles limited the *Kriegsmarine* to a few light cruisers, destroyers, and pre-*Dreadnought* battleships. The limits imposed on the *Reichswehr*, the army's new title, were 100,000 long-serving soldiers with an officer corps of approximately 4,000. It also forbade the *Reichswehr* to possess tanks and aircraft and demanded an end to the general staff. The Germans quickly got around the latter prohibition by calling the general staff the *Truppenamt.*

Although the defense minister was responsible for both services, since the army and navy had failed to cooperate during the last war, they saw no reason to cooperate in the period after the war. In terms of how the army saw itself, General Hans von Seeckt, the father of the postwar army, termed the *Reichswehr* as "a state within a state." Whatever its pretensions, the German military was in no position to defend the Republic from outside invaders, while it had little interest in defending it against internal enemies. Unlike Britain, there was no means to coordinating national defense in Germany. Before 1914 the British had created the Committee of Imperial Defense (CID) to examine the empire's strategic issues. As a result of the war, they then created the Chiefs of Staff Subcommittee in 1923 to advise the CID and the Cabinet.[9] There would be no similar system of coordination in Germany until the creations of the *Bundesrepublik* in the 1950s.

The Nazi Regime and Rearmament, 1933–1939

The collapse of the world economy in 1929 hit Germany particularly hard. Moreover, the ancient field marshal, Paul von Hindenburg, had been elected president of the Weimar Republic in 1925. Never the brightest light in the closet, Hindenburg provided neither leadership nor wisdom to the Republic, threatened as it was by radical movements on both the right (the Nazis) and left (the Communists). On 30 January 1933, Hindenburg appointed Adolf Hitler as Chancellor of the Reich. The conservatives around the president believed they had appointed a cabinet that would be able to control the new chancellor. They could not have been more mistaken. Among the crucial appointments to the cabinet was General Werner von Blomberg as the Minister of Defense. The general had been serving at the disarmament conference in Geneva.

Five days after his appointment, Hitler met with Germany's senior military leaders. To their delight, he made clear he was providing them with a blank check to begin massive rearmament. He also made clear that he intended not just to overthrow Versailles and make minor adjustments to Europe's territorial borders, but rather to acquire for Germany the *Lebensraum* (living space) to allow the Reich its proper place in the world.[10] Considering the weaknesses of their forces, the military undoubtedly took Hitler's long-term goals with a grain of salt. But they were delighted to have *carte blanche* to begin major rearmament programs. Within a matter of months, the *Heer* (army) and *Kriegsmarine* would have an additional service at the table, namely the *Luftwaffe*.

As Minister of Defense and then War Minister, Blomberg attempted to bring a joint framework to Germany's defense policies. He had little success. Herman Göring, head of the *Luftwaffe* was one of the most powerful leaders of the Nazi Party Hitler and was not about to allow Blomberg any say over the air force's armament efforts. Not surprisingly, the chiefs of the army and navy were no more willing to cooperate in creating some form of a joint-service high command. Thus, German rearmament forged ahead with no strategic framework except to spend money and resources as fast as they became available. Here lay a considerable problem because throughout the 1930s Germany verged on the brink of financial bankruptcy. The foreign exchange was simply not available to purchase the bulk of the raw materials the massive rearmament effort required.[11]

In the desperate effort to produce the armaments Hitler demanded, there was a considerable waste, exacerbated by the lack of a strategic framework. The leading economic figure in the *Wehrmacht* argued that there existed "in economic affairs a complete absence of leadership, and an indescribable duplication of effort and working at cross purposes; for Hitler shut his eyes to the need for fixed, long-range planning, Göring knew nothing about economics, and the responsible professionals had no executive powers."[12] Underlining German economic problems was the fact that between September 1937 and February 1939, industry met only 58.6 percent of contracted orders for the *Wehrmacht* because of a lack of raw materials and industrial capacity.[13]

However, Blomberg and his thoroughly Nazi assistant, General Walter von Reichenau, had more success in tightening the links between the services and Hitler. When Hindenburg died early in August 1934, they ordered the members of the military to swear a direct oath to Adolf Hitler, rather than to the nation or constitution.[14] The navy and the newly forming *Luftwaffe* had no difficulty in swearing an oath of fealty to Hitler. There were a few doubters among the army generals, but in the end, they too came around. Shortly thereafter the military had sworn that oath, and the title of the Ministry of Defense was altered to War Ministry. Blomberg also succeeded in having those of Jewish ancestry removed from the services. For the next four years, the military got on with the business of massive rearmament, while the strategic and economic consequences appeared only occasionally.

The first and most important debate over German strategy occurred in November 1937. By that point, economic difficulties had already had a significant impact on the rearmament effort. Hitler called the meeting because he believed that he needed to speed up the pace of German pressure internationally. There were two meetings, the first dealing with strategic issues, and the second with economic matters. We only have the minutes of the first meeting, and it indicates much about the course of the succeeding four months. Hitler began by arguing that German rearmament would soon tip the scales in the Reich's favor. His arguments were such that, as one historian has noted: "even if [the meeting] were not a timetable for aggression, it was a ticket for the journey and the first stops Prague and Vienna were clearly marked."[15]

The discussion did not go as the *Führer* had planned. Instead of meeting approval, he met considerable pushback from his diplomatic and military advisers. For one of the few times in the history of the Third Reich, Hitler found his basic strategic assumptions questioned by his senior advisers. Blomberg, the army's chief of staff, General Werner von Fritsch, and to a lesser extent, the foreign minister, Konstantin von Neurath, objected that Germany was not prepared to face a war with England and France, while the Italians could offer little help. Moreover, Blomberg had the temerity to warn that Czech fortifications would present significant difficulties to the *Wehrmacht*'s military operations.[16]

The meeting clearly upset Hitler. Nevertheless, he bided his time. Three months later he moved. A number of Germany's leaders found themselves on the outside looking in. He also altered the high command's structure. The occasion that allowed the *Führer* to act came as the result of a scandal involving Blomberg, who had married a secretary with a checkered career, including posing for pornographic pictures. Once the scandal broke, Hitler acted with dispatch. Blomberg went; von Neurath went; and utilizing a falsified dossier manufactured by the Gestapo, Hitler fired von Fritsch. The latter case caused an uproar among the army generals because the Gestapo had fabricated an entirely false case. Nevertheless, Hitler defused the troubles by instigating a crisis in Austria, which allowed him to occupy that country to shouts of delight from its inhabitants.

The most important result of the crisis lay in Hitler's reorganization of the government and his appointment of senior officers to replace those fired. First, Hitler replaced Blomberg with himself. He then changed the name of the War Ministry to that of the *Oberkommando der Wehrmacht* (*OKW*, high command of the armed forces). As his immediate subordinate in the *OKW*, he appointed Wilhelm Keitel, a particularly obsequious, pro-Nazi general, who would slavishly do Hitler's bidding to war's end. From its creation, the *OKW* was little more than an office of clerks to allow Hitler to pass his orders and intentions along to the service chiefs and their staffs. To replace Fritsch, Hitler chose another pro-Nazi general, Walther von Brauchitsch. He provided that general with a substantial donative so that he could divorce his wife and marry a second time. Brauchitsch proved a perfect choice because he proved incapable of standing up to Hitler.

It is here that one must note from this point on there was no joint high command, each service still maintains considerable autonomy. Thus, there was little coordinated planning, *Weserübung*, the invasion of Norway the one notable example. For the most part, historians have focused their studies of the German high command on the squabbles between the *OKW* and the *OKH*. That is a mistake because over the course of the last three years of the war over 60 percent of German resources went to supporting the *Luftwaffe* in its efforts to defend the Reich against the Combined Bomber Offensive (CBO).[17] Thus, the relations between Hitler and particularly the airmen are instructive for understanding the failures in German strategy at the level of both grand and military strategy.

Matters did not settle down in the aftermath of the Anschluss. With the aid of his malicious propaganda minister Joseph Goebbels, Hitler began stoking a crisis with Czechoslovakia, the borderlands of which contained a significant number of German speakers, ripe for manipulation by the Nazis. Claiming they wanted to join their racial brothers in Germany, the Sudetenlanders came up with the slogan, *Heim in Reich* (home to the Reich).[18] By August, the diplomatic crisis was heading toward a war between Germany and Czechoslovakia, one that would involve the Western Powers, since the Czechs were allied to the French.[19] As the crisis increased, British and French diplomats scrambled to surrender the Czechs to the tender mercies of Nazi Germany.

At the same time, a crisis broke out between a number of senior army generals and Hitler, who appeared determined on launching a war. While most senior officers displayed little interest in the strategic issues, the chief of the general staff, General Ludwig Beck, raised substantive, strategic points about the dangers of Hitler's course. Over the summer of 1938, Beck composed a series of memoranda, making clear his objections to Hitler's strategic policies.[20] The most impressive of those was one dated 5 May 1938. In it, Beck examined three elements of the strategic situation Germany confronted: the international balance, the military situation of the West, and the Reich's military situation.[21] Beck recognized the advantages of Britain as a world power and saw little possibility that either Italy or Japan would cooperate with Germany in a major war. He believed the British understood the Reich's economy was in serious difficulty and German rearmament was incomplete. He recognized that France did not desire war, but there were significant limits beyond which the French would not go. Moreover, Beck believed the French army was still the best in Europe and Czechoslovakia represented a point of honor for France. If the *Wehrmacht* attacked Czechoslovakia the French would come to her aid followed by the British.

As for the strategic approach of the Western Powers, Beck believed they would pursue a limited strategy. The crucial point was that as with Serbia in World War I, Czechoslovakia's fate would not determine the conflict's outcome. The Reich possessed neither the economic nor military base to conduct a major war, much less world war. In sum, Beck believed that if Germany attempted to force a solution against Britain's will, the Reich would face a coalition of overwhelming strength – France, Britain, and Russia. The Americans would certainly support those powers economically and financially. Moreover, once Britain had turned against the Reich, the smaller European powers would follow. The result would be a war Germany would lose.[22]

Over the following months, Beck wrote a series of memoranda that would state similar views about Germany's strategic and military weaknesses, should she risk launching a major war against Czechoslovakia. What Beck discovered was that few of the army generals and even fewer *Luftwaffe* and *Kriegsmarine* senior officers had any interest in addressing the strategic issues a major war would raise. In mid-July, Beck wrote his last memorandum, which again summed up the dangerous political and strategic consequences of an attack on Czechoslovakia.

In August, a letter from General Erich von Manstein to Beck sums up the attitude of most of the army's senior generals. The future field marshal, whom Beck had mentored, argued that the issues whether the Western Powers might intervene, should Germany attack Czechoslovakia, were solely Hitler's responsibility. What mattered was that "Hitler has so far always estimated the political situation correctly." Manstein then spent most of his letter worrying about the possibility the *OKW* under Keitel might assume the army's traditional position as the government's chief strategic advisor.[23] The pedantic advice of a general who supposedly possessed the greatest operational mind in Germany suggests much about the strategic wisdom, or lack thereof, in the German military.

In the largest sense, Manstein represented the weaknesses of the German officer corps (all three services): brilliant in tactics and simple operations that did not involve strategy, logistics or intelligence. Blind to the larger framework of the war, the field marshal would win tactical victories of increasing insignificance during the war that could not solve the larger strategic and economic issues confronting the Reich. The title of his memoirs, *Lost Victories*, misses the fact that, as Gerhard Weinberg has pointed out, had he won a series of victories that lengthened the conflict, Germany instead of Japan would have had the first atomic bomb dropped on her.

In August, Beck resigned as chief of the general staff. His replacement was General Franz Halder, who would claim after the war that he had remained an opponent of the Nazi regime throughout the war. In fact, he was nothing of the kind, but his actions suggest much about the dysfunction characterizing high command in the Third Reich. In 1938, Brauchitsch and Halder barely escaped a war that the *Wehrmacht* was unprepared to fight. The surrender by Neville Chamberlain and Eduoard Daladier of Czechoslovakia at the end of September 1938 at the Munich Conference destroyed Czechoslovakia and turned her industry and armaments over to the Reich. By occupying the remainder of the Czech state in March 1939; the Germans gained Czech armaments, raw materials, and financial resources, a windfall, and a major aid to continued rearmament.[24]

As for the *Wehrmacht*'s continued buildup in 1939, there was only the wildest setting of future goals that bore no reality to Germany's strained economy and financial position. Not surprisingly, given that Keitel was already a fanatical devotee of the *Führer*, the *OKW* played no role in bringing sense to service planning. In Hitler's view, the generals were there not to provide advice, but to carry out orders.[25]

In fact, spurred on by Hitler's response to Britain's stronger foreign policy line, the *Luftwaffe*'s chief of staff, General Hans Jeschonnek announced to his astonished staff that the *Führer* now wanted a quintupling of the air force. When one of the officers objected that such a force represented an impossible goal (it would have required 85 percent of the global production of aviation fuel), Jeshonnek's reply was "[g]entlemen, in my view, it is our duty to support the *Führer* and not work against him."[26]

At the same time, Admiral Erich Raeder and his naval staff were creating a plan equally out of touch, the so-called Z Plan that would allow Germany to challenge the Royal Navy. The navy's commander, Admiral Erich Raeder, and his staff were planning for a massive navy of heavy battleships and cruisers by 1948, the former with tonnages equal in size to the Japanese battleship Yamato. But nowhere was there any coordinated effort among any of the services to place their plans within a military policy or strategy that reflected Germany's economic and financial realities.

The Second World War

In 1939, unlike the year before, the army generals were delighted to have the opportunity to smash the hated Polish state, while Hitler interfered minimally in the planning and conduct of operations. There was one blip, and that occurred shortly after the *Wehrmacht* had completed the conquest. The commander of occupied Poland, General Johannes Blaskowitz issued an official complaint about atrocities committed by the SS and political authorities.[27] He was immediately removed from his position, although he served loyally until the war's end.

Victory over Poland almost immediately brought Hitler and the *OKH* (*Oberkommando des Heeres*, army high command) into immediate conflict. Confronting serious economic and raw material difficulties, Hitler demanded an immediate offensive against France and the Low Countries. His rational appears to have been that the seizure of air bases in Belgium and Holland would so threaten the Chamberlain government in Britain that the British would quit the war. After all, as Hitler had commented in the spring, "he had seen his enemies at Munich and they were worms."[28]

However, after examining the performance of its units in the Poland campaign, the *OKH* mounted objections that it needed time to repair serious tactical deficiencies that had appeared during the campaign. The result was a serious row, in which Hitler exploded at Brauchitsch at what he regarded as the generals' pusillanimity and demanded the army launch its forces in a major offensive against the West.[29] Unfortunately, atrocious weather intervened to prevent such an offensive, which had little chance to obtain a significant victory.

Before the French campaign, the Germans invaded Norway in Operation *Weserübung* in early April 1940. The invasion represents one of the few times the Germans launched a successful joint operation. Over the winter of 1939–1940, the *Kriegsmarine* and Raeder had persuaded Hitler the invasion was both doable and necessary. The army provided the necessary second-line troops for *Weserübung*, while the *Luftwaffe* cooperated with aircraft. In the end, the operation succeeded because the invasion caught the Norwegians completely by surprise, the Royal Navy's performance was less than impressive, and the British Army showed itself completely unprepared.[30] In fact, a careful analysis of what had happened should have alarmed the Germans. Had Norwegian commanders reacted as effectively as the colonel in charge of the Oslo Fiord, the Germans would have failed in their attempts to capture most of the ports.[31] Moreover, the losses the *Kriegsmarine* suffered took the navy out of any possibility it might support a cross-Channel invasion of the British Isles that coming summer.

There is one interesting footnote to *Weserübung* that sheds considerable light on the inability of the navy to think in strategic terms. In a discussion between Hitler and Raeder during the French campaign, as the Dunkirk battle was beginning, the former commented that it might be necessary to invade the British Isles. Nevertheless, shortly thereafter Raeder ordered the two most powerful ships remaining undamaged from the Norwegian campaign, the battle cruisers *Scarnhorst* and *Gneisenau* to sortie off the North Cape to gain a major success in order to influence "postwar budget debates."[32] Both battlecruisers were damaged during the sortie and were thus unavailable during the planning and use for Operation Sea Lion, the potential invasion of the British Isles.

Over the winter and early spring of 1940, the army repaired the deficiencies that had appeared in Poland. Meanwhile, senior army generals worked out a far more imaginative campaign plan. Significantly, Hitler participated in the planning far more than had been the case during the Polish campaign.[33] Yet, in the end, the plan was that of the *OKH*, the framework of which allowed the panzer generals to take advantage of appallingly bad Allied leadership.[34] Once the panzers broke out into the open, Hitler and the *OKW* did attempt to intervene, largely through fears that somehow the French were about to make an astonishing recovery, as they had on the Marne in 1914.

The larger operational problem was that none of the senior leaders had any idea of what they might do if the panzer divisions reached the English Channel. In the last week of May considerable muddle at the highest level prevented the Germans from reaping full advantage of their entrapment of the Allied left wing against the Channel. Part of the problem lay in a general disorganization at the highest levels, which allowed Göring to step in and claim the *Luftwaffe* could destroy Allied efforts to escape from Dunkirk. Stymied by cloud cover and resistance from Spitfires and Hurricanes, the *Luftwaffe* failed to make good on the Göring's promise.[35]

But there were other problems. After the war, a number of German generals claimed Hitler was responsible for the so-called "stop order" preventing the panzer divisions from finishing off Dunkirk. Admittedly the *OKW* did issue the stop order, but senior generals including Gerd von Rundstedt, Ewald von Kleist, and Heinz Guderian all urged a halt to allow the panzer divisions to rest and refit. Moreover, as late as 27 May, no less than two army groups, four armies, and sixteen corps commands were controlling operations around Dunkirk, far too much structure to allow reasonable command and control.[36] Finally, from the German perspective, military operations ended on the shores of the English Channel, while to the British, the Channel represented a broad highway to the open seas.

The fall of France ushered in a month-long period, during which Hitler went on vacation, while the leadership awaited him to make the decisions as what to do next. The entire German leadership was astonished by the British refusal to surrender. One cannot talk about serious joint planning over the summer. The *Kriegsmarine* had already forfeited its opportunity to protect *Operation Sealion*, the proposed landing on the British Isles, by its heavy losses suffered in *Weserübung*. None of the three services had thought seriously about the possibility of launching a major amphibious operation. Keitel referred to an amphibious assault on the British Isles as a mere river crossing.[37] The navy drew up plans that involved landing the ground forces on a span of beaches less the ten miles. The *OKH* for its part suggested the navy launch its troops on a beach front of ninety miles. Both services clearly were not interested in serious joint planning and hoped the *Luftwaffe* would settle matters by destroying the RAF and forcing the British to surrender.

Not surprisingly, the *OKW* chimed in with its assessment. Keitel's assistant, General Alfred Jodl, suggested there were two potential strategic approaches to the British Isles: the first, an attack on Britain's positions in the Mediterranean and Middle East; and second attacks on the British Isles, 1) air-sea attacks aimed at shipping, 2) terror attacks against major population centers, and 3) an amphibious landing on the British Isles. Jodl did suggest defeat of the RAF was essential but believed that victory in the air war did not pose much of a problem. Summing up his estimate of the situation, Jodl noted that "the final victory of Germany over England is only a question of time."[38]

The *Luftwaffe's* leadership was as optimistic as the other portions of the German high command. Their confidence reflected a flawed intelligence organization, the estimates of which miscalculated every element of the upcoming battle. The incompetence of *Luftwaffe* intelligence was only one indication of how generally the Germans undervalued assessing and analyzing the enemy.[39] The initial estimate for how long it would take to defeat the RAF was four days to defeat Fighter Command and destroy its bases in southern England; then over the next four weeks, German long-range fighters and bombers would mop up the remainder of the RAF and destroy Britain's aircraft industry.[40]

Specifically, German intelligence underestimated the effectiveness of British radar, missed entirely the fact that the British utilized a systemic approach to air defense, and mistakenly calculated that the Bf 110 was superior not only to the Hurricane but also to the Spitfire.[41] Perhaps the most egregious misestimate lay in belief German industry was out producing the British in aircraft. In fact, the Germans were well behind in aircraft design. Moreover, in the last half of 1940, British industry produced 491 fighters per month; on the other hand, German factories turned out only 156.[42]

German production remained at the same low levels throughout 1941, a harbinger of what was to come in the air war over Europe in the war's last three years. But blithely ignorant of how far they were behind in the armaments race, the *Luftwaffe*'s leadership assumed that its production numbers would receive prompt attention once the invasion of the Soviet Union had succeeded. Once the Battle of Britain had resulted in a German defeat, Göring took less and less interest in the day-to-day management of his service, while Hitler assumed that *der Dicke* (the fat one) knew what he was doing. The production side of the house was under the command of the former fighter pilot and cartoonist, Ernst Udet, who knew how to fly but not much else. The services' chief of staff Jeschonnek summed up his attitude – and that of most *Luftwaffe* officers – when he commented about the coming invasion of the Soviet Union, "at last a proper war."

The Battle of Britain proved a learning experience for the British. That was not the case with the Germans. In particular, the *OKW* might have displayed some interest in forcing the *Luftwaffe* and the *Kriegsmarine* to coordinate in the war against Britain's commerce. It did not. During the night-time *Blitz* from September 1940 through May 1941, the *Luftwaffe* focused only one third of its bombing on Britain's ports, while the remainder of its attacks raided London and industrial cities of the Midlands. Thus, the British were able to keep their ports generally operating at full capacity despite damaging air attacks. Moreover, Göring resolutely refused to make any significant effort to help the U-boats in the Atlantic, whereby the spring of 1941 the lack of intelligence on convoy movements was already causing difficulties.

Hitler displayed little interest in the war against the British from the beginning. Thus, the air offensive against the British Isles was the only major campaign during the course of the war where he interfered not at all. Instead, by July 1941, his interest was already turning to Russia. Not surprisingly, so was that of the army. Two weeks after signing the armistice with France, Brauchitsch ordered Halder to initiate planning for an invasion of Russia. Part of the reason lay in a desire to compete with the *Kriegsmarine* and *Luftwaffe* for resources. On 22 July the two senior army leaders met with Hitler and Raeder to discuss future German strategy. After the admiral had left, the *Führer* got down to business; he believed the British had remained in the war only because they hoped "for change in America... [and] hope in Russia."

For Halder, it was not clear what a Russian operation would entail. He noted "What operational objective could be obtained? What strength have we available? Timing and Area of Assembly?"[43]

Serious planning for the invasion began almost immediately. At Halder's direction, General Erich Marcks worked out an initial design that he delivered on 5 August 1940, even as Halder formed his own conceptions. Major operations targeted against Moscow would force "Russian concentrations in Ukraine and at the Black Sea to accept battle with an inverted front."[44] Marcks' conception was similar to that of his boss. It posited the main drive occurring north of the Pripyat Marshes with the aim of capturing Moscow, while northern and southern advances would protect the flanks. Marcks believed that the opening weeks would prove decisive with the *Wehrmacht* destroying the bulk of Soviet armies along the frontier. German troops would then mop up what was left, as it reached the Archangel-Gorky-Rostov line. Marcks argued it would take between nine and seventeen weeks for the *Wehrmacht* to achieve its goals.

An *OKW* study appeared in September 1940, and while it agreed it would not take long for the Germans to overthrow the Red Army, it had a different focus. It argued the major emphasis should be on the flanks with the Ukraine and Leningrad as special targets. Hitler was obviously behind the *OKW* focus. In a conversation with Halder and Brauchitsch in early December, he commented that "what matters most is to prevent the enemy from falling back before the onslaught... Aim of the campaign crushing of Russian manpower; no group capable of recuperation must be allowed to escape." But Hitler also made clear his fundamental difference with the conceptions *OKH* leaders held. Protecting the Baltic with its iron ore trade from Sweden was crucial, while "Moscow [is] of no importance."[45]

Thus, even before Operation Barbarossa began, there was a fundamental division between the *OKH*'s conception and that of Hitler and his minions at the *OKW*. Nevertheless, whatever their differences, both firmly believed, in the *Führer*'s words that the Soviet Union would collapse "like a house of cards." There were warning signs. The geographic section of the *OKH* warned that the Soviets had made major investments in building up the industrial infrastructure east of Gorki and even beyond the Urals.[46] Equally important should have been the fact that logistical war games indicated that once German spearheads reached Smolensk, two-thirds of the way to Leningrad, and Kiev in the Ukraine, they would run into significant logistic difficulties. Neither one of these crucial pieces of intelligence raised the slightest worry. After all, if the Germans had destroyed the Red Army by that point, which was a certainty, such factors were of little importance.

What is astonishing is that the planners in both the *OKW* and *OKH* assumed that the initial surge would destroy the Red Army and that Soviet reserve formations would play little role. Crucially, intelligence on Soviet industrial potential was non-existent and would remain so though summer

1942. Thus, in July and August, *Luftwaffe* intelligence entirely missed that hundreds of train-loads were relocating factories from western portions of the Soviet Union to east of Moscow and the Urals.[47] Over 1942, the Soviets would outproduce the Germans by a four-to-one margin in tanks and a three-to-one margin in artillery in spite of the damage inflicted in 1941.[48] The fact that German intelligence across the board underestimated Soviet productive capabilities by an order of magnitude must be counted as one of the greatest intelligence failures of the Second World War.

To avoid Hitler's interference, Halder took the disastrous expedient of limiting planning to only the first stage of Barbarossa, leaving substantive issues to be decided after the Germans had completed the campaign's first stages.[49] Such was the level of distrust between *OKH* and *OKW* that even army group commanders were unsure of how to fit their operations into Barbarossa's larger framework. In the invasion's opening days, neither Field Marshal Ritter von Leeb, commanding Army Group North, nor *Generaloberst* Erich Hoepner, commander of Fourth Panzer Group, knew whether their mission was to drive north on Leningrad or east to cover Army Group Center's advance on Moscow.[50]

Within the first weeks, a significant argument broke out between the *OKW*, fronting for Hitler, and Brauchitsch and Halder. The former, noting that large numbers of Soviet soldiers were escaping from encirclements formed by the mechanized advance, argued the panzers should make tighter encirclements, which would have tied up the mechanized forces and prevented them from driving deeper into Soviet rear areas. The real problem reflected that within the first week the infantry divisions, which made up over 80 percent of the invasion were falling farther and farther behind and were proving incapable of closing the encirclements.

By the time the Germans reached Smolensk, they discovered they had made two terrible miscalculations.[51] First, their logistic system proved incapable of keeping up with the advance of mechanized forces, so that the latter found themselves reduced to relying on emergency supplies of fuel and ammunition.[52] Second, the Red Army proved more resilient and deeper in reserves, as a series of fierce Soviet counterattacks hit German spearheads in the Smolensk area.[53]

The so-called August pause did not reflect the inability of the German leaders to make up their minds, but rather that, short of supplies and with the infantry divisions only beginning to catch up, the Germans had no possibility to advance farther. Halder's diary caught the extent of the surprise: "the whole situation shows more and more clearly that we have underestimated the colossus of Russia… We have already identified 360 [infantry divisions]. The divisions are admittedly not armed and equipped in our sense and tactically they are badly led. But there they are; and when we destroy a dozen the Russians simply establish another."[54]

After a furious quarrel between Hitler on one side and the *OKH* and the Eastern Front commanders on the other, the *Führer* decided that Guderian's Second Panzer Group would drive south to meet up with Ewald von Kleist's First Panzer Group to entrap Soviet armies in the Ukraine. Thanks to Stalin's stubbornness in refusing to yield any territory, the Germans succeeded beyond their expectations. The resulting Kiev pocket ripped a gigantic hole in Soviet lines and yielded over 600,000 prisoners, most of whom would be dead before the next spring.[55] Hitler was so delighted that he allowed Guderian's Second Panzer Group to return to Army Group Center, while Hoeppner's Fourth Panzer Group would also participate in the advance on Moscow.

Operation Typhoon caught the Red Army by surprise. For the second time in a month the *Wehrmacht* broke a monstrous hole in Soviet lines, this time opening the road to Moscow. By the time Typhoon's spearheads had mopped up the wreckage of the Bryansk and Vyazma encirclements, the Germans had added another 600,000 Soviet prisoners to their total. For once Hitler and the *OKH* were in full agreement that the advance should continue on to Moscow. So was Field Marshal Fedor von Bock. However, the realities of Russian weather now intervened, as the *rasputitsa* and its rain turned Russian roads into a morass of mud and the German advance slowed to a crawl.

Halder continued to hope for the best. In a meeting with the army chiefs of staff in mid-November, he pontificated that cold weather would allow the advance to resume at its previous hectic pace, while it might not snow for another six weeks. Guderian's chief of staff replied more realistically that Second Panzer Army was "neither in the month of May nor in France."[56] Bock remained optimistic as did other senior army leaders, many of whom remembered the myth that, if the army had only pushed on in 1914, it would have taken Paris and won the war. Relying on the usual bad intelligence, reporting that recent defeats had exhausted the Red Army, Bock commented that the *Wehrmacht* "could now afford to take risks."[57]

Of senior generals, only Günther von Kluge sensed the danger. His war diary noted operations had reached a turning point, "since the troops on one hand with no winter clothing and on the other facing impossible and tenacious opponents defending the roads found the advance extraordinarily difficult."[58] After the war, a number of German generals laid the defeat in front of Moscow as due to Hitler's mistakes. In fact, the smash-up was as much the fault of the army's senior leadership as of Hitler's.

Not surprisingly, the *Führer* refused to take any of the blame, and so most of the army's senior leaders had to go. Rundstedt was the first senior general fired after ordering a retreat from Rostov at the end of November. Brauchitsch, and the other two army group commanders, Bock and Leeb, also found themselves removed from office. Two of the panzer group commanders, Guderian and Hoepner found themselves on the outside looking in, with the latter stripped of rank. Hitler now appointed himself as the commander in chief of the army, although he was willing to keep Halder on as chief of the general staff.

During this period of reorganization and replacement of senior army generals, Hitler made the disastrous decision to declare war on the United States. Astonishingly that decision received hardly any notice among the senior generals and admirals. Moreover, in the summer 1941, Raeder and Admiral Karl Dönitz had met with Hitler to argue that Germany should declare war on the United States to make it easier for the U-boats to strike at commerce supporting the British Isles.[59] Hitler had put them off with the argument the decision should wait for the completion of Barbarossa. The army generals appear to have made no mention of the addition of the United States to the list of the Reich's enemies.

As for the *Luftwaffe*, only Field Marshal Erhard Milch, who had spent a considerable amount of time visiting the United States in the interwar period voiced some worries. The reaction of the *OKW* staff, which applauded the news of the declaration of war on the United States, suggests how far removed from strategic reality the military leadership was. When Hitler asked his military staff where Pearl Harbor was not a single one knew.[60]

1942–1943

For the army, the question was what should follow the disaster of the defeat in front of Moscow. In fact, the Germans were lucky to escape a collapse of the entire Eastern Front. Only by the slimiest of margins did the Germans avoid the destruction of several of the major armies, if not the entire Army Group Center over the winter from 1941 to 1942.[61] For the Germans, the question was what next? In the middle of the disastrous winter, Hitler began to think seriously about the possibility of a summer campaign to regain the initiative and perhaps to address the problem of the *Reich*'s shortages of raw materials, particularly in terms of petroleum.[62] The result was a bifurcated strategy that aimed at capturing Stalingrad to prevent the movement up the Volga of petroleum from the oilfields in Baku to supply the Red Army.

The other portion of Operation *Blau* (Blue) was to drive deep into the Caucasus to capture the Maikop and Grozny oilfields. The aim of capturing Stalingrad and cutting off the Volga represented a real possibility, but the attempt to drive into the Caucasus to capture the Grozny and Baku oilfields represented logistic insanity. Not only did the Germans lack the logistical support for such a drive, but also the Soviets had already indicated that should the Germans capture those oil fields, none would remain in working order. Moreover, even if the Germans captured them in working order, there was no way to move the petroleum back to the Reich.

Almost immediately, Operation *Blau* went off the rails. Furious at the handling of the advance on Voronezh, on 16 July 1941 Hitler fired Field Marshal

Bock, who had returned briefly to command Army Group South. With Bock's firing, Hitler assumed command for Army Group South, with Army Group A advancing into the Caucasus and with Army Group B in charge of the northern flank of the advance, including Sixth's Army' push to Stalingrad. On 9 September Hitler fired Field Marshal Wilhelm List, commander of Army Group A, the southern wing of Army Group South. The *Führer* would remain in command of that army group until 22 November. Thus, in terms of the German high command, Hitler was now in command of the *OKW*, the *OKH*, Army Group South, and Army Group A.

Adding to German troubles, the Soviets finally began trading space for time; there would be no more large encirclements of large Russian formations. Six days after Bock's firing Hitler reoriented *Blau*'s focus from the Caucasus to Stalingrad. The result was order, counterorder, order, counterorder. In late summer Jodl returned from a visit to Army Group South with warning about emerging difficulties. For his troubles he almost got the sack with Paulus as a potential replacement. Halder did receive the sack, to be replaced by General Kurt Zeitzler with little to recommend him except enthusiasm and loyalty to Hitler.

Adult supervision virtually departed from the German high command. With Hitler now in charge of the *OKH* and Army Group South, there was no sensible leadership in charge of the fighting in the east. The battle for Stalingrad soon disintegrated into a street-by-street fight in which both sides suffered heavy casualties, but the Germans achieved nothing except rubble.[63] Meanwhile, Sixth Army situation grew ever more precarious as massive Soviet armies built up on both the flanks of the army, largely missed by German intelligence and certainly ignored by Hitler.

Beginning at the end of October 1942, troubles mounted, as from Egypt to western North Africa, to Stalingrad, Allied forces assumed the offensive. Their successes underlined that Hitler's assumption of all responsibility had created an impossible situation for the defense of the Reich. The first blow came in late October in North Africa, when the British, under the future Field Marshal Bernard Law Montgomery, struck the *Afrika Korp* at El Alamein. Rommel was on medical leave in Germany but hurried back to the battle. By then it had already been lost. Rommel put up a desperate defense, but after recognizing that the *Afrika Korps* was in a hopeless position, he ordered a retreat, only to be countered by the *Führer*'s demand that he hold his army in place. Eventually, Hitler relented, but the band of trust between the two men had been broken. Rommel would add further to the distrust in Hitler's mind, when he suggested that, given Allied material, naval, and air superiority, North Africa was not worth holding.[64]

Further events quickly underlined the strategic and operational consequences of Hitler assuming that he would make all the important decisions. No sooner had the Axis position at El Alamein crumbled, than major amphibious landings, launched by Anglo-American forces hit the beaches of Vichy French-controlled Morocco and Algeria in early November 1942. At the time Hitler was in his rail car, traveling from East Prussia to Munich, to deliver his annual beer-hall diatribe celebrating the 1923 attempted putsch. There were hurried consultations by teletype from Thuringia, and the *OKW* staff that had remained in East Prussia strongly recommended against a major commitment of forces to North Africa. However, as one staff officer noted their assessment "passed unnoticed in the general jumble of vague political and strategic ideas based primarily on consideration of prestige."[65]

Clearly, there was no serious strategic or operational discussion of what the Germans should do about the rapidly evolving situation in North Africa. The result was that Hitler determined to ship paratroopers over to Tunisia, followed up by armored and infantry units to ensure Axis forces could hold Tunisia. In effect, Hitler created a gigantic pocket in Tunisia of German and Italian forces that were in an impossible strategic situation. By March 1943 Allied air and naval forces had completed the task of cutting the German and Italian forces off from resupply from Italy. By early May it was over, and the Germans had suffered a defeat close to that suffered at Stalingrad.

Much the same response at the highest levels came with the news on 19 November 1942, that the Red Army had launched major drives against the flanks north and south of the Stalingrad Battle. Initially, Hitler assumed that XLVIII Panzer Corps could patch the breakthrough in the north, but the Soviets had already destroyed the corps. As the situation deteriorated further, Hitler decided to return to his headquarters in East Prussia. Once again there were hurried discussions by teletype, but for most of the 21st and 22nd, while Hitler traveled, no one in the *OKH* was willing to make substantive decisions that might at least have saved a portion of the Sixth Army.[66] Once again, Göring managed to muddy waters by claiming the *Luftwaffe* could supply Stalingrad by airlift, but the responsibility for the Stalingrad disaster was Hitler's and the disastrous high command he had established. In February 1943, the beleaguered Stalingrad encirclement surrendered, the worst defeat, thus far, in German military history.

The Naval and Air Wars

From December 1941, the German High Command was set. Hitler was directly in command of *OKW, n*ow responsible for operations in the Mediterranean and Western Europe. It had no responsibility for either the *Kriegsmarine* or *Luftwaffe*, which responded directly to Hitler. For those two services, the *Führer* did not make the day-to-day decisions, but rather occasionally interfered to influence procurement and operational decisions. But there was no doubt he was in command and would demand obedience to whatever his decisions might be. In effect, the German high command ran directly from the *Führer* to the services and increasingly to field commanders.

The *Kriegsmarine* for its part had had a dismal war. With those few ships not sunk during *Weserübung*, moldering in German ports, while the RAF shot the *Luftwaffe* out of the skies in the Battle of Britain, only the U-boats had inflicted serious damage on British shipping. But there were far too few of them; only in the long term would they represent an existential threat. Moreover, with Barbarossa about to begin U-boat construction would remain at minimal levels well into 1941. Meanwhile, the surface navy continued its unabashed record of failure. The *Bismarck* did manage to sink the *Hood* but was in turn almost immediately sunk.

Thanks to the fact that the German Navy managed to get its cyphers broken for a second straight war, the last half of 1941 saw U-boat sinkings of Allied merchant tonnage drastically fall. The German history of the war estimates that the breaking of the Enigma codes over the last half of 1941 saved well over a million tons of Allied shipping. Only the abysmal performance of the US Navy in the first half of 1942 allowed the U-boats to again achieve a major success, what they called a second "happy time." But it could have been far worse. At the end of 1941, Hitler ordered Dönitz to transfer significant numbers of U-boats to the defense of Norway against a potential British invasion and another group into the Mediterranean to harass Royal Navy attacks on Rommel's supply lines to North Africa. The former was a complete waste, while the latter's successes represented small potatoes to what might have been achieved against the American SLOCs.

But the writing was on the wall. As the production of, long-range aircraft, particularly the B-24, increased, the gap in air cover between Newfoundland and Iceland steadily shrunk. Moreover, despite heavy losses, Allied surface anti-submarine technological capabilities were increasing. The turn would come with drastic suddenness in May 1943 when Allied anti-submarine forces would sink forty-one U-boats, and Dönitz would pull his boats out of the Battle of the Atlantic.

The final dénouement between Hitler and Raeder came at the turn of the year between 1942 and 1943. On 31 December, the heavy cruiser *Admiral Hipper*, and the pocket battleship *Lützow* attacked a British convoy, protected initially by destroyers and then by light cruisers, in the Barents Sea. The attack was a complete failure; so outraged was Hitler that he fired Raeder, appointed Dönitz as his replacement, and ordered that all the navy's surface ships be paid off. As a good navy man, Dönitz avoided doing that, but the British, at no cost to themselves, sank the surviving battleships, the *Scharnhorst* and *Tirpitz* with somewhere over 3,000 German sailors dying. As a fanatical Nazi devoted to his *Führer*, he continued to push his obsolete U-boats out into the Atlantic where the Allies sunk them in ever larger numbers. In 1944, the Germans lost 111 U-boats, while sinking only thirty-one merchant vessels. The totals for

1945 were even worse seventy-one U-boats lost for only nineteen merchant vessels sunk.

The air war was in the end as crucial as the war in the east. One recent estimate has the Germans devoting well over 50 percent of its airpower to defending the skies over the Reich during the last three years of the war. In May 1942, the British launched a thousand-bomber raid against the ancient city of Cologne. The damage was extensive, and a furious Hitler told Jeschonnek that the British were attempting to open a second front. But he indicated that the German response should not be an emphasis on air defense, but rather on replying in kind. Despite Bomber Command's success at Cologne, British attacks over the remainder of the year were not nearly as successful. Following Hitler's inclinations, the *Luftwaffe*'s chief of staff continued to emphasize the production of bombers over fighters.

Over 1942, there was no consistent focus to the German air effort. The high command dispersed major portions of the *Luftwaffe*'s forces to the war in the Mediterranean, to support of operation *Blau* in Russia, and even off the North Cape against Allied convoys to Russia. Production runs remained far behind those of the British and Americans, although no one except Air Marshal Erhard Milch, who had had extensive experience in the United States before the war, was particularly worried.

But beginning in the spring 1943, the roof over the Reich fell in. After almost three years of dismal failures, RAF's Bomber Command had reached the point where it could and did began to have a significant impact on the Third Reich's war economy. A series of heavy attacks on the Ruhr beginning in March 1943 brought the upward swing in German weapons production to an abrupt halt. We will not cover the vicissitudes of the air war, but rather point to the major influence that Hitler exercised over the conduct of the air war against the CBO and how he determined the German response.

By 1943, Göring's position had gone into eclipse and his influence at this point was limited to his willingness to echo Hitler's opinions. It is worth noting that there were a significant number of air force officers and party officials who supported him not merely because of slavish opportunism, but because of the belief in the *Führer*'s wisdom. The first major argument had come between those in the *Luftwaffe* who argued on the basis of statistics that anti-aircraft fire was cost ineffective and the heavy emphasis that it was receiving should be scaled back in favor of fighter production, which was proving a combat enhancer against the British night bombing offensive. Hitler came down firmly on the side of those arguing in favor of increased production of flak. He indicated his firm belief that the firing of large numbers of guns at night was beneficial for the morale of the German people, whereas they did not care how many bombers the *Luftwaffe* shot down.

The second major argument was between those who possessed what we might term a Douhetian approach to air war: that the proper response to enemy air attacks was the same in kind. The other side, namely the German fighter community, argued that the proper response to Allied CBO was one that emphasized air defense to destroy enemy bombers. As had been the case with the *Luftwaffe* in the Battle of Britain, the Allies would have to call off their bomber offensive. Not surprisingly, Hitler came down forcefully in favor of the former.

Thus, through the end of 1943 the Germans were placing as much effort building bombers as they were on fighters to meet the CBO. Even more to the point, the Germans made a massive effort to design, test, and then produce the V-2 (*Vergeltungswaffe* – revenge weapon), the world's first ballistic missile rocket. The US Strategic Bombing Survey estimated that the V-2 program cost the equivalent of 24,000 fighter aircraft for a weapon that had a CEP of London. Thus, until the spring of 1944 when the US Eighth Air Force mounted a massive air offensive against German fighters and their production, German fighter production remained relatively low on the *Luftwaffe*'s priority list. This was a direct result of Hitler's interference; nevertheless, it represented an interference that had considerable support within the air force and senior policy makers.

To the End of the War

By 1943, the framework for the German high command had become settled. The *OKW*, led by Keitel and Jodl was now responsible for passing along Hitler's orders to the theater commanders in the Mediterranean and northern France. The *OKH*, under Zeitzler and after 20 July 1944 Heinz Guderian, was responsible for the Eastern Front. There was virtually no cooperation between the two headquarters and a good deal of competition for resources. Everything ran through Hitler. In effect, there was no German high command, although Hitler continued to fire and replace generals and admirals.

The *Luftwaffe*'s high command's role in the making of major decisions was by 1943 minimal. Göring was out of the loop except to echo the *Führer's* disastrous orders. And those decisions in almost every case worked to the advantage of the Allies. Among them were the orders that in 1939 forbade any long-term research and development programs; that ordered the production of bombers at the expense of fighters; the emphasis on anti-aircraft gun production at the expense of fighters; and the enthusiastic support for the V-2 Rocket program, which proved to be the most cost ineffective weapon of the war. The *Kriegsmarine* had even less of a role except to get young Germans killed.

Conclusion

When the war was over in 1945, innumerable German generals began a chorus that blamed Hitler entirely for the German defeat. In fact, they were just as culpable. The army's leadership had waged a stolid effort to prevent the establishment of anything resembling a joint staff. Throughout the war, there was minimal cooperation among the services. In December 1941, Major Klaus von Stauffenberg, a future leader of the attempt to overthrow Hitler, commented that: "Our high command organization in the... war is more idiotic than the most idiotic General Staff officer could invent, if he received the task to create the most senseless wartime high command structure he could."[67] One can argue that was certainly what Hitler wanted, but it was also what the services wanted.

Notes

1 The foremost study of the German high command in English is Geoffrey P. Megargee, *Inside Hitler's High Command* (Lawrence, KS: Kansas University Press, 2000). However, Megargee's study focuses almost entirely on the army and ground operations with hardly a mention of the Luftwaffe and the Kriegsmarine.

2 For Bismarck's career as a statesman, see A. J. Taylor, *The Man and the Statesman* (New York: Ashgate, 1967); Marcus Jones, "Strategy as Character," in Williamson Murray, Richard Hart Sinnreich, and James Lacey, eds., *The Shaping of Grand Strategy, Policy, Diplomacy, and War* (Cambridge: Cambridge University Press, 2011); and Marcus Jones, "Bismarckian Strategic Policy, 1870–1890," in Williamson Murray and William Hart Sinnreich, eds., *Successful Strategies: Triumphing in War and Peace from Antiquity to the Present* (Cambridge: Cambridge University Press, 2014).

3 Holger Herwig, "The Immorality of Expediency, The German Military from Ludendorff to Hitler," in *Civilians in the Path of War*, ed. by Mark Grimsley, and Clifford J Rogers (Lincoln, NB: University of Nebraska Press, 2002).

4 Geyer von Schweppenburg attended the Kriegsakademie immediately before the outbreak of the First World War. Letter from Geyer von Schweppenburg to Basil Liddell Hart, 1948, BHLH Archives, King's College Archives, London, 9/24/61, 32.

5 On this, see particularly Isabel Hull, *Absolute Destruction, Military Culture, and the Practices of War in Imperial Germany* (Ithaca, NY: Cornell University Press, 2004).

6 Hull's *Absolute Destruction* is particularly good on this. See also Holger H. Herwig, *The First World War, Germany and Austria Hungary, 1914–1918* (London: Bloomsbury Publishing,2014).

7 For the army's efforts to study and learn from its experiences, see James Corum, *The Roots of Blitzkrieg, Hans von Seeckt and German Military Reform* (Lawrence, KS: Kansas University Press, 1992).

8 Along with the myth of the "stab-in-the-back" legend went the fact that the German government waged a massive effort to distort and hide Germany's responsibility for the Great War. See particularly Holger H. Herwig, "Clio Deceived, Patriotic Self-censorship in Germany after the Great War," *International Security*, 12, no. 2 (Fall 1987).

9 For the British structure of government in the 1930s, see Williamson Murray, *The Change in the European Balance of Power, 1938–1939, The Path to Ruin* (Princeton, NJ: Princeton University Press, 1984), pp. 55–57.

10 "Aufzeichnung Liebmann," *Vierteljahrshefte für Zeitgeschichte*, 2, no. 4 (October 1954).

11 For the difficulties the German rearmament ran into in terms of finance and lack of resources, see Adam Tooze, *The Wages of Destruction, The Making and Breaking of the Nazi War Economy* (London: Viking Press, 2006); and Murray, *The Change in the European Balance of Power*, chap. 1.

12 Quoted in Berenice Carroll, *Design for Total War* (The Hague: De Gruyter, 1968), p. 73.

13 Gerhard Förster, *Totaler Krieg und Blitzkrieg* (Berlin: Deutscher Militarverlag, 1967), p. 101.

14 For relations between the party and the army, see John Wheeler Bennett, *The Nemesis of Power, The German Army in Politics, 1918–1945* (London: Macmillan, 1964).

15 Gordon Brook-Shepherd, *The Anschluss* (Philadelphia: Lippincott, 1963), pp. 11–12.

16 *Akten zur deutschen auswärtigen Politik*, Series D, 1, Doc. 19, "Niederschrift über die Besprechung in der Reichskanzlei am 5." November 1937 von 16, 15–20, 30 Uhr, 10.11.37.

17 See Philips O'Brien, *How the War Was Won, Air and Sea Power and Allied Victory in World War II* (Cambridge: Cambridge University Press, 2015), p. 484.

18 The irony of the slogan came in the period after the Second World War when the returning Czech government kicked the Sudeten Germans out of Czechoslovakia and sent them off to live in Germany.

19 For the course the Western Powers would pursue over summer and fall 1938, see Murray, *The Change in The European Balance of Power*, chaps. 5 and 6.

20 The contrast between Beck's memoranda – and they are memoranda – and the carefully worded and analyzed strategic surveys that the British Chiefs of Staff produced are worth noting. The second has very much an amateurish element, while the latter were clearly written by professional strategists.

21 Bundes/Archiv, Militärarchiv, N 28/3, Beck Nachlass, "Betrachtung zur gegenwärtigen mil. Politischen Lage, 5.5.38."

22 Ibid.

23 Telford Taylor, *Munich: The Price of Peace* (New York: Doubleday, 1979), p. 695.

24 Murray, *The Change in the European Balance of Power*, pp. 291–292.

25 Wilhelm Deist, Manfred Messerscmidt, Hans-Erich Volkmann, Wolfram Wette, *Das Deutsche Reich und der Zweite Weltkrieg*, vol. 1, *Ursachen und Voraussetzung der deutschen Kriegspolitik* (Stuttgart: Deutsche Verlags-Anstalt, 1979), p. 645.

26 Edward L. Homze, *Arming the Luftwaffe, the Reich Air Ministry and the German Aircraft Industry, 1919–1939* (Lincoln, NB: University of Nebraska Press, 1971), pp. 223–224.

27 Williamson Murray and Allan R. Millett, *A War to Be Won, Fighting the Second World War* (Cambridge, MA: Cambridge University Press, 2000), pp. 50–51.

28 For a further discussion of this, see Murray, *The Change in the European Balance of Power*, pp. 336–338.

29 Murray and Millett, *A War to Be Won*, p. 55.

30 For the dismal performance by the British at all levels in the campaign, see Lieutenant General John Kiszely, *Anatomy of a Campaign, The British Fiasco in Norway, 1940* (Cambridge: Cambridge University Press, 2019).

31 The commander of the Oslo Fiord with obsolete cannons and torpedoes at his disposal and with no orders from above, ordered his men to open fire and their fire sank the brand-new heavy cruiser Blücher and killed over a thousand Germans.

32 Klaus A. Maier, Horst Rohde, Bernd Stegemann, and Hans Umbreit, *Das Deutsche Reich und der Zweite Weltkrieg*, vol. 2, *Die Errictung der Hegemonie auf dem europäischen Kontinent* (Stuttgart: Deutsche Verlags-Anstalt, 1979), pp. 378–379.

33 There are a number of excellent accounts of the 1940 French campaign. Among them are Robert A. Doughty, *The Breaking Point, Sedan and the Fall of France, 1940* (Hamden, CT: Stackpole, 1990); and most recently, Karl-Heinz Frieser, *The Blitzkrieg Legend* (Annapolis, MD: United States Naval Institute Press, 2013). See also Williamson Murray, "May 1940, Contingency and Fragility in the German RMA," in MacGregor Knox and Williamson Murray, eds., *The Dynamics of Military Revolution, 1300–2050* (Cambridge: Cambridge University Press, 2001).

34 The German historian Karl-Heinz Frieser makes a compelling case for Rommel's breakthrough as providing the crucial advantage to the panzer drive.

35 It was the first time that German fighter pilots ran into Spitfires, and it was a nasty surprise. The Luftwaffe suffered heavy losses during the aerial combat over the British beaches.

36 Murray and Millett, *A War to Be Won*, p. 80.

37 Ibid., p. 84.

38 Chef WFA, 30.6.40, "Die Weiterführung des Krieges gegen England," International Military Tribunal, *Trial Major War Criminals*, vol. XXVII, pp. 301–303.

39 For an estimation of the weakness of German intelligence, see particularly Williamson Murray, "Net Assessment in Nazi Germany in the 1930s, in Williamson Murray and Allan R. Millett, *Calculations: New Assessment and the Coming of World War II* (New York: Free Press, 1992).

40 Basil Collier, *The Defense of the United Kingdom* (London: H.M. Stationery Office, 1957), p. 160.

41 For the weaknesses of German intelligence during the Battle of Britain, see Williamson Murray, *Military Adaptation in War, For Fear of Change* (Cambridge: Cambridge University Press, 2011), chap. 5.

42 Murray, *Luftwaffe*, Table XXII, p. 104.

43 Franz Halder, *The Halder War Diary, 1939–1942*, ed. by Charles Burdick and Hans-Adolph Jacobsen (Novato, CA: Presidio Press, 1988), p. 232.

44 Ibid., p. 233.

45 Ibid., pp. 293–294.

46 Megargee, *Inside Hitler's High Command*, pp. 114–115.

47 Fred Kagan, "The Evacuation of Soviet Industry in the Wake of 'Barbarossa': A Key to Soviet Victory," *Journal of Slavic Military Studies*, vol. 8, no. 2, June 1955.

48 Tooze, *Wages of Destruction*, p. 588.

49 The most outstanding recent studies of Operation Barbarossa are by David Stahel: *Operation Barbarossa and Hitler's Defeat in the East* (Cambridge: Cambridge University Press, 2011); *Kiev, 1941, Hitler's Battle for Supremacy in the East* (Cambridge, 2013); *Operation Typhoon, Hitler's March on Moscow, October 1941* (Cambridge: Cambridge University Press, 2015); *The Battle for Moscow* (Cambridge: Cambridge University Press, 2017).

50 Murray and Millett, *A War to Be Won*, p. 121.

51 Both of these should have been avoidable or at least recognizable in what was knowable before the war.

52 For the German logistical problems and Barbarossa, see Martin van Creveld, *Supplying War, Logistics from Wallenstein to Patton* (Cambridge: Cambridge University Press, 2004), chap. 5.

53 For the German difficulties in July, see Stahel, *Operation Barbarossa and Hitler's Defeat in the East*.

54 Halder, *Halder War Diary*, p. 506.

55 For the Kiev battle, see Stahel, *Kiev, 1941*.

56 Klaus Reinhardt, *Die Wende vor Moskau: Die Scheitern der Strategie Hitlers im Winter 1941/1942* (Stuttgart: Deutsche Verlags-Anstalt, 1972), pp. 139–140.

57 Ibid., p. 71.

58 Ibid., p. 77.

59 Murray and Millett, *A War to Be Won*, p. 259.

60 I must thank Dr. Horst Booze, senior research at the Militärgeschichtliche Forschungsamt, for this information.

61 For how close the Germans came to a catastrophic Campaign after the defeat in front of Moscow in December 1941, see David Stahel, *Retreat for Moscow, A New History of Germany's Winter Campaigns, 1941–1942* (Cambridge: Cambridge University Press, 2019).

62 How short the Germans were is suggested by the fact that in summer 1942 the Luftwaffe found itself forced to shut down its training program for pilots, while the navy was forced to halt all training activities with major fleet units in northern Norway.

63 David Glantz's masterful studies of the Battle of Stalingrad sets the standard for the scholarship on the battle: David Glantz with Jonathan House, *To the Gates of Stalingrad: Soviet German Combat Operations, April-August 1942* (Lawrence, KS: Kansas University Press, 2009); *Armageddon at Stalingrad, September-November 1942* (Lawrence, KS: Kansas University Press, 2009; and *Endgame at Stalingrad, November 1942–February 1943* (Lawrence, KS: Kansas University Press, 2014).

64 After the War, a number of German generals suggested that Rommel had no real sense of either logistics or strategy, and that he was a mere tactician. The evidence suggests that such criticism could not have been more wrong.

65 Warlimont, *Inside Hitler's Headquarters,* p. 272.

66 Murray and Millett, *A War to Be Won,* p. 287.

67 Quoted in Megargee, *The German High Command,* p. xiii.

9

ROOSEVELT AND MARSHALL

The Road to Overlord

James Lacey

The Men

First Meeting

In mid-November 1938, President Roosevelt met with his prewar military teams, including among others: current Army Chief of Staff General Malin Craig, General Hap Arnold, and Deputy Army Chief of Staff General George C. Marshall. The topic was plans to purchase thousands of new aircraft. With the President was Secretary of the Treasury Henry Morgenthau, and presidential advisor Harry Hopkins. Roosevelt started the meeting with a bang by announcing his disappointment with the Army's current plans to expand the Air Force. Commanding the room as only Roosevelt could do, the President laid out a vision for 20,000 new aircraft, a multiple of what Congress had declared it was prepared to pay for. Completing his grant rhetorical exercise FDR polled the audience for comments, pleased to find that everyone was in agreement. That was until he came to Marshall. In this, possibly their first official meeting, Marshall replied to the President's smile, with coldness "I am sorry, Mr. President, but I don't agree with that at all." Startled, Roosevelt ended the conference, without asking Marshall to explain the reasons for his statement. Marshall later remembered that as they exited the White House everyone at the meeting bade him farewell, believing his time in Washington had just come to and sudden end.[1]

Marshall, who was still mostly unknown to Roosevelt was probably closer to removal from the center of power at that moment then even he realized. For, Roosevelt was never reluctant to fire anyone he believed was an obstacle to his achieving his ends, with the exception of those who had entered his

DOI: 10.4324/9781003375630-9

inner circle or had served him loyally for long periods. He was particularly vindictive to those who had crossed, betrayed, or purposely disobeyed him. But firing people loyal to him was a different matter. Eleanor Roosevelt once observed that FDR "had a great sympathy for people and a great understanding, and he couldn't bear to be disagreeable to someone he liked.... And he just couldn't bring himself to really do the unkind thing that had to be done unless he got angry."[2] But for those who had crossed him Roosevelt could inflict punishment with merciless cruelty. Eleanor, also noted, that when FDR was pushed beyond a certain point, he could icily detach himself from anyone, no matter how close the relationship.[3] Still, for most of his professional life he maintained a gentle touch with those who remained loyal and done his bidding. When those persons failed him, Roosevelt turned into a softie, and sent someone else to fire them, or move them to a position where they could do no further damage.

The explanation for Marshall's survival is likely found in more in his connections then competence, the latter was still a mostly unknown quantity to the president. Marshall, after World War I, Marshall was the de facto Army chief of staff, as General Pershing spent over half his tenure in that position in France. Here he made life-long friendship with many of the most powerful financiers and politicians in the United States. In fact, he made it a habit to cultivate powerful politicians in every position he was assigned. Some of them were men now in positions that made them impossible for FDR to ignore. Among them was Senator Jimmy Byrnes, who was Roosevelt counted on to drive forward his agenda on Capitol Hill, and Bernard Baruch, who personally funded the campaigns of dozens of Democratic congressmen and Senators. Most crucially, Marshall, because he was a strong supporter of New Deal programs, had come to the attention of Harry Hopkins, who was FDR's closest adviser. Throughout the war, Marshall would continually employ Byrnes and Hopkins both as sounding boards and to influence Roosevelt's decisions.

Just as crucially, Roosevelt did not mind criticism based on professional knowledge and which he did not perceive as a personal attack. In this case, it was left to Hopkins and Byrnes to convince Roosevelt that Marshall was the right man for the job and he would remain loyal to the administration. Roosevelt would rapidly come to appreciate Marshall's abilities, but he also saw something else in Marshall that FDR very much appreciated. Unlike his dealings with previous Army Chief of Staff General Douglas MacArthur, Roosevelt never detected any political ambition within Marshall. Even more valued, in the political circus that was Roosevelt's daily existence, Marshall never fought his battles through leaks to the press. Rather, he would give Roosevelt his best military advice and then do his best to carry out the President's decisions. While FDR warmed to future leading military adviser, Marshall's continued survival near the pinnacle of power rested upon Hopkin's influence.

Still, Marshall's relationship with FDR was never close. Marshall had seen first-hand how Roosevelt employed his bountiful political gifts to co-opt those around him, and move them toward his position on particular issues. Thus, Marshall made a conscious decision to never humor the president or to allow himself to be drawn into FDR's web, where he would be influenced by FDR's undeniable charm and personal charisma. While Chief of Staff he took this resolution to extremes, even refusing to smile at the President's jokes. After the war he said, that he never went to Hyde Park or Warm Springs for private talks, as he had discovered that "informal conversations with the President would get you into trouble."[4] Some, like Harry Hopkins, took the other route and entered fully into the presidential orbit and use that position to impact FDR's agenda and decisions. It is impossible to know which was the most effective approach. But then, of course Marshall hedged his bets by always maintaining close professional and sometimes personal relations ship to FDR's intimates.

Roosevelt took note of Marshall's attitude right from the start, and like early on, and like the master politician he was, he accommodated himself to it. In fact, this first meeting was the first and last time Roosevelt ever referred to Marshall as George. Marshall, for his part, also learned to read his man, once advising a subordinate, who was preparing to meet with FDR not to press the president so as to make a point or hand him lengthy papers. Instead, Marshall advised" "A little sketch … is the most effective method, as he is quickly bored by papers, by lengthy discussions, and anything short of a few pungent sentences of description. *You have to intrigue his interest, and then it knows no limit.*"[5]

Soon after his meeting with Roosevelt, Marshall visited Hopkins, who was now the Secretary of Commerce, at his office in the Commerce Building. Unlike FDR, Hopkins lived for detail and minutiae, and it was this encyclopedic knowledge of ongoing military affairs and problems that made him so valuable to FDR in the early years of the war. Marshall, took this opportunity to detail the state of the army and air force in such stark terms that a shocked Hopkins begged him to go directly to FDR's personal residence at to Hyde Park and inform the president of the true facts. Marshall, not yet Army Chief of Staff, demurred. But he had accomplished his goal, Hopkins was now sympathetic to the army's needs and he had been moved closer into Marshall's corner. Hopkins could now be counted upon for two things: to continually build up Marshall in the president's eyes, and to employ his relationship to ensure Roosevelt paid more attention to army requirements.

Marshall's Rise

Almost from the start of his military career, Marshall was viewed by both his contemporaries and superiors as different. Even as a relatively young captain, the graduate of the Virginia Military Institute, was considered the most competent officer in the service. One early example may suffice to cover the whole. In 1914, Marshall, although only a lieutenant, was acting adjutant for the "White Force" in a major field training exercise. Despite his junior rank, he threw himself into the planning for the operation. When the White Force Commander, a senior colonel, arrived drunk on the exercise's first day, the general leading the exercise ordered him to check with Marshall before making any decision.[6] The next day, Marshall, the youngest officer present, was officially put in charge of a brigade size force, usually commanded by an officer four ranks senior with two decades more experience.

An even more junior Lieutenant, involved with the exercise, wrote his wife: "Marshall still holds the job of main guy for this detachment and tells colonels where to take their regiments and what to do with them. However, everyone agrees he has the ability to handle the situation, so there is no hard feeling."[7] A few days later, that officer – Lieutenant "Hap" Arnold, the future Chief of Staff of the Air Force – informed his wife: "That man [Marshall] will one day be the Army Chief of Staff."

Marshall's chance to truly shine came during World War I. In early October, 1917, Pershing visited the 1st Division to witness Major Theodore Roosevelt Jr. the son of the former President, demonstrate a new method for taking a fortified position. When Pershing asked General Sibert, the division commander, to critique the unit's performance Sibert flubbed it. Pershing reacted with hot fury, but when he turned to leave, Marshall reached out and grabbed him: "General Pershing, there's something to be said here and I think I am the one to say it," Marshall then went on at some length about the division's difficulties and the lack of support from Pershing's headquarters. Similar to his later experience in the White House, observers stood mute convinced that Marshall's temper had cost him a promising career. When it was over, and Pershing had departed, the Division's officers bid Marshall farewell, certain he was about to be fired. Instead, Pershing, as he stood up First Army headquarters, remembered the brash, but highly competent Captain Marshall, and pulled him up to his staff.

Marshall's first proved his metal in planning the Saint Mihiel offensive, which was a spectacular success for the fledgling American army. At its conclusion, a French sent a team to study how the Americans had moved so quickly concluded that was because the Americans had long legs and large feet, making it easier to step on and over barbed wire.[8] Not a word was said about Marshall's meticulous planning that brought together 550,000 American and 110,000 French soldiers, 3,000 artillery pieces, 40,000 tons of ammunition, 267 light tanks (commanded by Colonel George S. Patton), and 1,400 aircraft (commanded by Colonel Billy Mitchell) together into a single powerful punch.

Marshall was just getting started, as Pershing, even as the St Mihiel fighting continued, agreed to move the bulk of the American Army into position for a great offensive in the Meuse-Argonne, set to start even before the Saint Mihiel Offensive had begun. Following Marshall's plan fifteen American divisions moved into the line, using only three roads. Moreover, when the Saint Mihiel Offensive concluded, Marshall planned and directed the movement of all of these divisions into the Meuse-Argonne battle. In all, Marshall planned for the movement of over a million troops, the construction of eighty massive supply dumps, building forty-four hospitals, extending multiple rail lines, emplacing 3,000 artillery pieces, and transporting 900,000 tons of supplies and ammunition.[9] When it was done, Marshall had earned the nickname "The Wizard."

After the Armistice, Pershing retained Marshall as his aide. He was still in that position in 1921, when Pershing became Army Chief of Staff. It was during this time that Marshall became accustomed to dealing with Congress and the White House. More crucially, as was mentioned above he enlarged his circle of influential friends well beyond the military sphere. One of those new friends as Pershing's best-friend and current Director of the Budget, Charles Dawes. During many long conversations with Dawes, Marshall developed a firm grasp of government finance, as well as how to make the budgeting system work to the army's benefit. Another was financer and World War I production czar Bernard Baruch, a man who was to wield great influence during the next war. Marshall always enjoyed his time with Baruch, considering him one of the most fascinating men in Washington.[10]

After tours in China and at the War College, Marshall was assigned to Fort Benning as assistant commandant of the Infantry School. Fort Benning, then and now, was where the army sent captains to learn the business of war. Over the next year Marshall revolutionized the course curriculum, emphasizing, uncertainty, innovation, simplicity, and speed. What became known as the "Benning Spirit" spread to remake the training foundation of the entire United Stars Army. Of the officers who trained or acted as instructors at Benning during his tenure 200 eventually put on generals' stars.[11] After departing Fort Benning, Marshall took a series of assignments in Screven Georgia, Columbia South Carolina, Chicago Illinois, and Vancouver Washington. The most important facets of these assignments were that Marshall made it known that he strongly supported several major New Deal initiatives, Thus, vastly expanding his civilian political contacts across the country. Foremost among these was the close relationship he developed with powerful South Carolina Senator James Byrnes, who became a hunting partner while Marshall was assigned to duties in the Senator's home state.[12] His total support for the Civilian Conversation Corps (CCC) did not go unnoticed. At a time when many army officers were hostile to the administration and the New Deal, Democratic politicians took note of those who got behind the New Deal programs.

In 1938, Marshall now finally a brigadier general had his tour of duty at Vancouver Washington cut short by Chief of Staff Malin Craig, who wanted him to head the War Plans Division (WPD) in Washington. Marshall did not remain in the job long. Marshall, was not to head WPD for long. Assistant Secretary of War Louis Johnson was looking for a way to stope General Hugh A Drum – Marshall's direct superior in World War I – from becoming Chief of Staff, and was impressed by what he saw in Marshall. Taking advantage of an extended absence of his superior Johnson forced General Craig to appoint Marshall as his deputy.[13] Marshall was now poised to replace Craig as the next army chief of staff. His promotion was less than a year off, as was the German invasion of Poland and the start of World War II.

Roosevelt at War

When Marshall moved into the army chief of staff's office, Europe was at war and Roosevelt was in the midst of an unprecedented run for a third term. Roosevelt's second term had been difficult and only in its last year did he start to recover from two self-inflicted wounds – a scheme to pack the Supreme Court and an attempted purge of his own party – and find his political footing. America, also was finally coming around to the idea that it could not ignore the brewing global war. While most Americans hoped they could stay out of the fighting – offering all aid short of war – polls showed that large majorities supported sending U.S. aid to the Allies. Roosevelt, had already recognized that the United States would, at some point, have to enter the war as a belligerent, but the politics of the time forced him to move gingerly. American was still home to a large and vocal isolationist movement. Moreover, Roosevelt understood that support for the war was very shallow and would rapidly reverse when the effort met its first setback. During the war, Roosevelt' son, James, asked him about his lack of action, and why, during the elections, he lied to the American people about the likelihood of America's entry into the war, Roosevelt answered: "I could not come out and say a war was coming, because the people would have panicked and turned from me. I had to educate the people to the inevitable, gradually, step-by-step, laying the groundwork for the programs which would allow us to prepare for the war that was drawing us into it."[14] He could have added that he had to educate Congress and in many cases the civilians and military officers in the War Department. It took the rapid fall of France in May–June 1940 to wake up Congress to the Looming threat and Pearl Harbor, over eighteen months later, to galvanize the American people for war.

In the meantime, Roosevelt and Marshall were taking each other's measure. From the start, Marshall found himself frustrated by FDR's style of leadership. Roosevelt possessed a tremendous love of secrecy – he was never happier than when he could surprise his staff – which Marshall found infuriating. For instance, in August 1940, Roosevelt ordered Marshall, and the other Chiefs to join him on the USS Augusta, without giving them a reason. Only when they were at sea did the Chiefs learn they were going to meet Churchill and their

British counterparts, without being given even a moment to prepare for their first-ever meeting.

Throughout the war Roosevelt would send cables, discussing future military strategy, to Churchill without informing the Joint Chiefs. It was only because Churchill always shared these correspondences with his senior military commanders that Marshall had any idea what was being discussed and decided by the war's political leaders. These cables only made their way to the American chiefs through the good graces of former Chief of the Imperial Staff Field Marshall Sir John Dill, who was acting as the British liaison to the Joint Chiefs. Marshall, fully aware the Roosevelt took great glee in keeping his Chiefs in the dark as much as possible, never told Roosevelt that Dill was providing copies of his message traffic with Churchill for fear Roosevelt would find a way to cut off the information flow. As one further example of how far Roosevelt would go to keep the Joint Chief in the dark, when he sent any message out of the White House he would have one Service encode outgoing messages, while another decoded incoming messages. FDR's hope was that this would keep any one Service chief from being able to piece together his entire conversation. It was one of Roosevelt's many personality quirks that drove Marshall to distraction.

More concerning was the fact that, throughout his first year as Army Chief of Staff Marshall doubted that Roosevelt was up to the task of being a war leader. His opinion only changed during the dark days immediately after the attack on Pearl Harbor. The immediate catalyst for the change was dealing with General MacArthur who was trapped with his army in the Philippines. On February 8, 1942, Manuel L. Quezon, president of the Philippines, was with MacArthur on the fortress island of Corregidor. Discouraged by seeing his country overrun and by America's failure to launch a relief expedition, Quezon sent a message to Washington, asking for immediate independence and the withdrawal of all American troops from the Philippines. He then planned to disarm his own forces and declare Philippine neutrality, in the naive belief that the Japanese would depart soon thereafter. Such a flight from reality might be excused from an old and sickly man, but what shocked Marshall was MacArthur's supporting cable, stating: "... the plan of President Quezon might offer the best possible solution of what is about to be a disastrous debacle."[15]

A dismayed Marshall had expected more from MacArthur. Considering the combined messages "ghastly in their responsibility and significance" Marshall went to work on a reply.[16] With the War Department's official reply in hand, Marshall and Secretary of War Stimson went to the White House. Both Marshall and Stimson were apprehensive. For more than a year they had worked with a President who in their judgment had shied away from making the hard decisions, as he was unwilling to get ahead of public opinion. Neither yet realized how the war had liberated Roosevelt. Prior to Pearl Harbor,

Roosevelt feared taking the lead only to later find that America was not behind him. Post Pearl Harbor, America was resolved for war. Roosevelt, whose natural inclination was always to lead, was finally ready to make the hard decisions.

After hearing out his visitors thoughts on MacArthur's request, Roosevelt replied: "We can't do this at all." Marshall later told his biographer, "*I immediately discarded everything in my mind I had held to his discredit ... I decided he was a great man.*"[17] After a brief discussion of the Philippines situation, Stimson and Marshall departed to work on a new message to MacArthur and a separate one to Quezon. Later that afternoon, Roosevelt authorized MacArthur to facilitate the surrender of the Filipino army, but ordered the American forces to continue the fight, while also demanding an end to further discussion of neutralizing the islands. That night a weary Stimson wrote in his diary: "It was a pretty hard day, for taking the decision which we reached was a difficult one, consigning as it did a brave garrison to a fight to the finish."[18]

There was no doubt that Roosevelt knew what he was asking, as his message to MacArthur concluded: "I therefore give you this most difficult mission in full understanding of the desperate situation to which you may shortly be reduced."[19] Roosevelt no longer wanted to hear MacArthur's plans on grand strategy or war winning combinations. What he wanted was for his commander in the Philippines to focus on the situation at hand conduct a dogged defense that would buy as much time as possible for the U.S. military to regroup. For the rest of the war no one was in any doubt who was in charge of the war.

Kent Roberts Greenfield, listing nearly two dozen times then Roosevelt overturned Marshall and the Joint Chiefs on major strategic matters, leaves no doubt that Roosevelt was the final arbiter of U.S. strategy throughout the war.[20] Many of these will be discussed in detail, but a few examples of FDR's influence in just the first year of the war demonstrates how involved the president was with wartime strategy. For instance, only upon FDR's insistence and a direct order did the U.S. military to provide massive and unstinting military aid, over Marshall's objections, to first Great Britain and then the Soviet Union. Marshall believed that both countries were be rapidly crushed under the German juggernaut, and pushed hard during policy meetings not to squander precious American armaments to aid lost causes. History, of course, proved Roosevelt's intuition correct. Later that year, FDR took both Marshall and King to task when he brutally thwarted their proposal to shift America's primary war effort to the Pacific. At almost the same time, FDR ordered the invasion of North Africa – Operation Torch – over the vociferous objections of Marshall.

Unlike Churchill, Roosevelt rarely bothered himself with the conduct of military operations, leaving that to the military professionals. Where FDR made his presence felt was in the strategic direction of the war, resolving interallied and interservice disputes, and in maintaining the public's support for selected strategic and operational courses of action. In doing so he was guided by a set of core principles[21]:

1. The Anglo-American coalition must be maintained, as well as the survival of Great Britain as a major power after the war.
2. Germany was enemy number one, and Atlantic operations took precedence over the Pacific.
3. The Soviet Union must be given all possible aid and kept in the war until the Axis powers were defeated
4. The Axis must be forced to accept unconditional surrender.
5. China must be kept in the war.
6. To assure a lasting post-war peace the world must have an international organization consisting of the wartime allies – the United States, the Soviet Union, Great Britain, and China.
7. The complete and unstinting support of the American people must be maintained throughout the conflict.

As long as Marshall and the Joint Chiefs were designing operations aimed at securing the Rooseveltian grand strategic objectives, FDR ruled with a light hand. But when Marshall and the Chiefs diverged from these core ideas, the president never hesitated to make his power felt and bring them up short. Throughout the war, Roosevelt was the strategic architect: Chairman of the Joint Chiefs Admiral William Leahy was the man who explained Roosevelt to the other Chiefs, and the Chiefs to Roosevelt; while the other three Joint Chiefs, including Marshall were mere draftsmen for FDR's vision.

Preparing and Waging War

Marshall was elevated to Chief of Staff on the day that the Germans unleashed their panzers on Poland. Shocked by the speed of Poland's collapse and how easily its large but obsolete military was pulverized, Marshall comprehended that the American military was not only pitifully small but also hopelessly antiquated. Fixing it required money and time, but most crucially political support. At this point in their relationship, Marshall was unsure how much influence he had with the President. Thus he first approached Hopkins and later Secretary of the Treasury Henry Morgenthau, men he knew had the President's ear, and who were already in Marshall's orbit.

But in early 1940, Marshall's major problem was Congress, which had taken a knife to FDR's budget request for more army funding. He took his problems to financier Bernard Baruch, who enlisted another Marshall friend, FDR political fixer, Jimmy Byrnes. Byrnes arranged a dinner for April 10, 1940, between Marshall and a dozen powerful senators. Marshall after hours of speaking without notes, could not read his audience. Disconsolately he said: "My job as Chief of Staff is to convince you of our needs, and I have utterly failed. I don't know what to do."[22] Senator Alva Adams from Colorado, laughed: "You came before us without even a piece of paper and you got everything you asked for."[23]

Baruch and Byrnes had come through for Marshall, Congress would not stymie the Army or Air Forces build-up. It was time to go to work on the President. As Hopkins was still recovering from his latest serious bout of illness Marshall turned to Morgenthau. Meeting on May 11, 1940, Marshall laid out in minute detail the Army's many needs. Morgenthau listened intently, plainly shocked at what he was hearing and repeatedly saying it was "all new to him."[24] When he was done, Marshall announced that the total bill was $640 million.

Morgenthau, after a brief pause, said, "I don't scare easily. I am not scared yet.

Marshall responded that "It makes me dizzy."

To which Morgenthau answered, "It makes me dizzy if we don't get it."[25]

Both men met with the President two days later. Also present were Budget Director Harold Smith, Secretary of War Woodring, and Assistant Secretary Johnson. From the start the meeting had fiasco written all over. Marshall just started making his points when Woodring and Johnson began bickering over what was required and the costs. Marshall was paying a price for not ensuring the confronted the president with a united front, as Roosevelt was able to take his preferred option for any major decision – postpone and see what developed. FDR was closing the meeting when Morgenthau leapt to Marshall's defense, begging Roosevelt to hear Marshall out. But Roosevelt, claiming he already knew what Marshall would say, refused. Marshall, taking heed of advice, earlier offered by Morgenthau, that very few ever stand up to the president, but that liked it when someone did, asked for a few moments. When Roosevelt graciously agreed to hear him out, Marshall unleashed an emotional torrent. When he was done, Roosevelt asked him to return the next day with a detailed list of his requirements. Morgenthau told Marshall that FDR would cut the list, but also that Marshall was convincing the president that preparedness involved a lot more than demanding more aircraft.

Marshall had won the first battle for preparedness. Later that year, France would fall to e German Blitzkrieg in a just a few weeks. After fighting the Germans to a standstill for four years in World War I, France's rapid defeat galvanized Congress, which suddenly open the money floodgates. Money, the crucial sinew of war, made everything else possible, still did not resolve the immediate issue, the Allies were losing the war and Marshall had no immediate answers. In fact, at this point in the war, there is evidence that Marshall could grasp the strategic dilemma before him. For example, when Grenville Clark, a lawyer and powerful behind the scene power player in Washington went to see Marshall to garner his support for a peacetime draft, he was dismayed at Marshall's hostile response.[26] Clark, to his amazed horror, discovered that Marshall was preoccupied with the idea that the Nazi's next move would be on South America. Clark, astonished at Marshall's strategic naiveté, tested the generals patience by ridiculing the notion that South America should be anywhere near the top of the War Department's concerns when France was verging on collapse.[27] Marshall, still growing into the job of Chief of Staff, was only slowly beginning to comprehend the magnitude of the tasks before him. He would later support the draft, once it had received Roosevelt's endorsement.

In the wake of Dunkirk, Roosevelt ordered every spare rifle, cannon, and round of ammunition be sent to Britain. At first, Marshall offered no objections. But soon thereafter, he asked Roosevelt to suspend further munitions transfers until army stocks had been replenished. Roosevelt refused the request. But the law forbid shipments of munitions unless Marshall and Chief of Naval Operations Admiral Stark certified it was surplus to U.S. military needs. Marshall was now in the untenable position of being able to countermand orders from Roosevelt – the Commander in Chief. On top of this, Churchill was requesting 50 aged U.S. destroyers, which Roosevelt wanted to give them, but Stark could not certify them as surplus. FDR's military advisors, stunned at German rapid conquest of France, agreed with French General Weygand's appraisal that Britain would in three weeks have its neck wrung like a chicken. Roosevelt, however, was sure that Britain would survive and use a finely crafted legal opinion, written by future Secretary of State, Dean Acheson, overruled Marshall and Stark and dared them to act contrary to his wishes. Both Chiefs suddenly discovered the munitions and ships were surplus after all.

It would take several more months for Roosevelt to push through bills relaxing the neutrality laws and then enact Lend Lease legislation. Both would give FDR substantially more room to aid the Allies with all aid short of war, while still promising the nation that the United States could stay out of the conflict. In the meantime, representatives of the British Combined Staff came to America to coordinate strategy, in the event America did enter the war. They came at an opportune time, as the U.S. military was in the midst of realigning its strategy, which for twenty years had placed fighting Japan at its core, to one based on defeating Germany before turning to engage Japan – the famous Plan Dog. Although Roosevelt never officially approved the Plan Dog memo, he also never disapproved it. For Marshall, silence was the same as approval, as he was beginning to recognize that Roosevelt had to weigh the political impact of every strategic decision. Having just won an election by promising to stay out of the war, Marshall understood that Roosevelt needed to be able to disown the plan if it was ever leaked to the press. Taking what he interpreted as the president's tacit approval, Marshall had his staff turn the foundational idea of Plan Dog into a full-fledged war plan – Rainbow-5. The new plan was sent to the Roosevelt on December 21, 1940, but Roosevelt re-fused, once again, refused to give it official approval, but did hint that it could be the basis for meetings with the British military staff.

The British arrived on January 29, 1941, for what was termed the American-British Conversations (ABC). Once the meetings commenced both sides found much to agree on. The British were particularly cheered by the American plans to place their emphasis on winning in the Atlantic first, as this accorded with the first two of the three priorities Churchill had given the Brit-ish representatives: stress the vital importance of the European Theater, and place a priority The British arrived on January 29, 1941, for the first of what was termed the ABC. The President did not meet with them, nor did any cabi-net secretary. In fact, after the initial welcoming talk from Marshall and Stark, no military chief took part in the discussions, although they paid close atten-tion to what was going on.[28] Once the meetings commenced both sides found much to agree on. The British were particularly cheered by the American plans to place their emphasis on winning in the Atlantic first, as this accorded with the first two of the three priorities Churchill had given the British representa-tives: underscore the vital importance of the European Theater. Only when the British stressed the defense of Singapore did the Americans balk. For the British, Singapore was the linchpin of the Empire in the Pacific and Indian Oceans. If it fell, there was a probability that much, if not all, of the Eastern British Empire would also be lost. The Americans could not care less, as the maintenance of the Empire was a political concern and not one they much cared about. The American negotiators agreed that losing Singapore would endanger the Empire, but they failed to comprehend what that had to do with winning the war. These opposing viewpoints would haunt Anglo-American councils for the remainder of the war, as British strategic conceptions were always put forth with an eye on ensuring Britain's hold on the Empire in the post-war years, while American leaders preferred a post-war world in which the British Empire no longer existed.

The American planners were also anxious to avoid any British attempts to scatter American troops throughout the Empire or regions the British thought vital to the Empire's security. But for the American negotiators the U.S. mili-tary was destined for only one thing – the invasion of Northern Europe. The British, haunted by visions of the Somme, did not give up the hope of avoiding such an invasion until 1944. As Churchill told Hopkins: "This war will never see great forces massed against each other."[29] Still, this difference of viewpoints did not get in the way of a final understanding. For the collision of massed armies was still a hypothetical for a later year. Until that time, the Americans saw nothing wrong with the British plan of weakening German by all possible means.. . "[30] So, despite some differences that would haunt Anglo-American strategic debates for the rest of the war, a final agreement was achieved. Plan Dog was restated as ABC-1, which was later integrated into Rainbow-5. This plan, with some modifications became the foundational plan for the remainder of the war. Once again, Roosevelt refused to sign off on the plan, but he did request it be resent to him in the event of war.

Roosevelt's hesitation stymied the military, as detailed planning and preparation needed to begin immediately, if the United States was going to meet its ABC-1 commitments. But was the military allowed to do so without presidential approval? The matter was resolved by Marshall calling together his private "war council"– Secretary of State Hull, Secretary of War Stimson, Secretary of the navy Knox and Admiral Stark – on June 10, 1941. Marshall started by telling the group that Roosevelt was asked noted with two options, either approve or disapprove the plans. There was no middle way. As he did not disapprove them, Marshall claimed that they were approved by default, reasoning that as he asked for their return in the event of war, he must have approved them. Stimson, Knox, and Stark were easily convinced, and after a few moments the always cautious Hull joined the cabal. It was full steam ahead.[31]

Even before Stark's removal, Marshall realized there was an imbalance within the Joint Chiefs that was bound to cause friction. With two army members (Marshall and Arnold) and only one navy member, the ever suspicious King would view every disagreement as "we-they" and continually get his back up defending the navy's turf. As Marshall well understood, each instance of such friction presented an opening for Roosevelt to interfere in the Chiefs' deliberations. To correct the unevenness Marshall, thinking that King could not possibly object, put forth having Admiral William D. Leahy appointed as chairman of the Chiefs of Staff. Marshall knew Leahy, but not well. He did, however, know enough about him to believe he would not make decisions based on the parochial navy interests. Marshall also knew that Roosevelt and Leahy had a long and close relationship dating from the President's days as Assistant Secretary of the Navy. Roosevelt, who loved to be at sea, often found an excuse to sail with the navy dispatch ship – *USS Dolphin*, commanded by then Captain Leahy. After his retirement from the navy, Roosevelt had first made him governor of Puerto Rico, and then America's ambassador to Vichy France. He was still doing tremendous services in this crucial position when Marshall began considering him for the Joint Chiefs.

At first, the President balked, telling Marshall "But you are the chief of staff." Marshall replied, "Butut there is no chief of staff of all the military services."

Well, Roosevelt said, "I'm the chief of staff. I'm the commander-In-chief."

Marshall went on with what he later said was great frankness that "it was impossible to conceive of one man with all of his duties as president being also, in effect, the chief of staff of all the military services; that it was a Superman job and I didn't think that even the exaggeration of the powers of Superman would quite go far enough for this." Roosevelt, unable to comprehend the role of the chief of staff, was not pleased with Marshall's analysis and for some time delayed his final decision.[32]

In early April 1942 a change of government in Vichy France precipitated a diplomatic crisis that forced Roosevelt to recall Leahy. Before he departed, however, his wife, Louise, had to have a hysterectomy that could not be postponed until they returned to the United States. Two days after the operation (21 April), she suffered an embolism and died with her husband at her side. For unknown reasons, Roosevelt had, by this time, changed his mind and agreed to appoint Leahy as Chairman of the Joint Chiefs.[33] He just never bothered to tell Leahy what he expected of him, what his role was, or even where his office was. Bewildered, Leahy went to see Marshall.

As King was out of town the Joint Chiefs could not meet until July 10. At that time, Marshall read the dispatch to his fellow Chiefs. According to the JCS minutes, Marshall read his own personal comments as to the British attitude, the gist of which was that Operation GYMNAST would be expensive and ineffectual, and that it was impossible to carry out SLEDGEHAMMER or ROUNDUP without full and aggressive British support. He then proposed that if the British position must be accepted, the United States should turn to the Pacific for decisive action against Japan. He added that this would help concentrate U.S. forces; that it would be highly popular throughout the United States, particularly on the west coast; and that, second only to BOLERO, it would be the operation that would have the greatest effect on relieving pressure on Russia. King expressed himself as being completely in agreement with Marshall's proposal, stating that he never considered that "the British were in wholehearted agreement with operations on the Continent."[34] Referring to GYMNAST, he said, "That it was impossible to fulfill naval commitments in other theatres and at the same time provide the shipping and escorts which would be essential should that operation be undertaken."[35] As a result the Joint Chiefs forwarded a memorandum to the President, who was at Hyde Park, asking permission to, as Stimson put it, "turn our backs on them [the British] and take up our war with Japan."[36] The memorandum pointed out that GYMNAST would be a heavy and indecisive drain on our resources, which would jeopardize our position in the Pacific while rendering no decisive support to any other theater of war. Marshall and King concluded by asking the President to send an ultimatum to Churchill warning him that "if the United States is to engage in any operations other than the forceful, unswerving adherence to full BOLERO plans ... we should turn to the Pacific."[37]

At Hyde Park Roosevelt, after carefully reading the memo, called Marshall and King's bluff. Telephoning the War Department, the President demanded that the Joint Chiefs dispatch to him "at once, by airplane, a comprehensive and detailed outline of the plans for redirecting the major effort of the United States to the war against Japan – including the effect of such a decision on the

Soviet and Middle East fronts during the balance of 1942." Roosevelt also demanded definite plans for the remainder of 1942 and tentative ones for 1943. He concluded by emphasizing that "it is of highest importance that U.S. ground troops be brought into action against the enemy in 1942."[38]

In as much as no one had foreseen any possibility of such a change of strategy, there were no detailed plans to send the President. Stimson had Marshall called back from Leesburg, where he was enjoying his first day off in some time. Both men arrived at their adjoining office at 3:00 PM, and immediately got to work. General Thomas Handy, who had taken over the operations position after Eisenhower's departure to Britain, had already produced a rough memorandum, which Marshall personally walked over to King at the Navy Department. After King had added "little more punch to it" Stimson approved sending it to the President, commenting that he hoped it would force the British to give up on their "fatuous defeatist position."[39] But he was not hopeful, writing in his diary: "The trouble is neither he[Churchill] nor the President has a methodical and careful mind. They do not implement their proposals with any careful study of the supporting facts upon which success of such expeditions must rest."[40]

Roosevelt received the memo while still at Hyde Park and rejected it out of hand. After briefly discussing it with Hopkins he laid the memo aside to meet with Queen Wilhelmina of the Netherlands for lunch. Roosevelt soon passed his hosting duties on to Eleanor and went to meet with Wendell Willkie. Willkie was there to request permission to visit Russia. Roosevelt, who apparently truly liked Willkie, readily agreed, and proposed he expand his trip to the Mid-East, India, and China, explaining that it would demonstrate national unity for the head of the opposition party to conduct a world-wide tour as a presidential emissary.

In the event, Roosevelt was not as solidly behind BOLERO as his military advisers supposed. By the end of what Stimson said was "a rough day," Roosevelt was sure of two things: that American troops must fight somewhere in 1942, and that the decision as to where must be resolved soon. That evening, Roosevelt had a long talk with Hopkins where he admitted that losing SLEDGEHAMMER was a blow, but that if "we cannot strike at SLEDGE-HAMMER we must stake the second best – and that is not the Pacific."[41] As a result of the day's conversations Roosevelt ordered Hopkins, King and Marshall to depart immediately for London for talks with Churchill and the British Chiefs.

To make sure he got what he wanted Roosevelt prepared a detailed letter of instruction for the three men.[42] In it, the President spelled out that he was unalterably opposed to an all-out effort in the Pacific against Japan, reminding all concerned that defeating Japan did nothing to help defeat Germany, while giving the Nazis time to complete their domination of Europe and Africa. Roosevelt also asked his representatives to keep three cardinal principles in mind – speed of decision on plans, unity of plans, and attack combined with defense but not defense alone. But it was the middle paragraph that ensured everyone knew what they had to come home with: "It is of the highest importance that U.S. ground forces to be brought into action against the enemy in 1942." In short, if SLEDGEHAMMER was out, don't come home without a new plan.

The three men left as part of a small party on July 16. Sherwood's biographer noted that Hopkins, who always loved these kind of trips, did not want to go on this one. Rather, he wanted to stay home with his fiancé, Louisa, and get married.[43] When they arrived, Churchill requested that the party stay at Chequers for the week, but Marshall and King insisted on going straight to London to meet with Eisenhower and Stark, and to then start meeting with their British counterparts as soon as possible. No sooner had the party checked into Claridge's than Churchill was on the phone with Hopkins. It took some time for Hopkins to convince the Prime Minister that no insult was intended, and the American Chiefs were not being rude. Hopkins later told Roosevelt that Churchill had thrown the entire British constitution at him, but since it was unwritten no damage was done.

Marshall and King fought hard for SLEDGEHAMMER, even at one point changing it from a sacrifice to help the Russians, to an all-out assault that would form a lodgment at Normandy or Brest and then dig in until reinforced by a larger ROUNDUP operation the following year. It was all useless. Churchill had sensed that the fight had gone out of Roosevelt, and that all the President wanted was American troops in the war, no matter where. Even Brooke realized they were facing a divided American party, writing in his Diary on 15 July: "It will be a queer party as Harry Hopkins is for operating in Africa, Marshall wants to operate in Europe, and King is determined to strike in the Pacific!"[44] The Americans were hooked. All the British had to do was hold tight and wrestle them into the boat.

The arguments raged for five days. By Tuesday night King and Marshall conceded that a 1942 invasion of Northern Europe was not in the cards. After a bit more discussion the Americans caved and agreed to GYMNAST. But at the last moment, Marshall insisted that the British also agree that GYMNAST would not be permitted to delay ROUNDUP in 1943. As he, and everyone else surely knew, an invasion of North Africa would consume so many resources as to make a 1943 invasion impossible; Marshall's hope was that the British would balk, making it possible for him to tell Roosevelt that he would have to wait until 1943 for Americans to get into the ground war. The British, however were more than happy to agree to Marshall's terms. They had what they wanted for 1942; they could argue about 1943 plans another day.[45]

In the event, Roosevelt was not as solidly behind BOLERO as his military advisers supposed. By the end of what Stimson said was "a rough day," Roosevelt was sure of two things: that American troops must fight somewhere in 1942, and that the decision as to where must be resolved soon. That evening, Roosevelt had a long talk with Hopkins where he admitted that losing SLEDGEHAMMER was a blow, but that if "we cannot strike at SLEDGE-HAMMER we must stake the second best – and that is not the Pacific."[46] As a result of the day's conversations Roosevelt ordered Hopkins, King and Marshall to depart immediately for London for talks with Churchill and the British Chiefs.

Despite having bowed to a presidential directive to get on with TORCH, Marshall remained convinced that the operation was fundamentally unsound. This was a conviction he shared with Stimson who, after discussing it with Marshall, recorded that the more he reflected on it the "more evil the President's decision appears to be."[47] As Stimson saw it the diagnosis for what was ailing the Allied cause was simple "British leaders have lost their nerve."[48] Together the two men spent much of the next few weeks covertly sabotaging the planning and preparation for the operation. Marshall, with King's support, told Leahy that as Roosevelt had not canceled ROUNDUP for 1943, he was justified in maintaining BOLERO (the build-up in Britain) until such time as Roosevelt canceled the 1943 invasion.[49] As there were not sufficient resources available to conduct TORCH and continue the BOLERO build-up, it is clear that Marshall was looking for loopholes that would allow him to postpone TORCH until it was no longer feasible in that year. Roosevelt put a quick end to this ploy when, during a meeting with the Joint Chiefs on July 30 he announced that he as Commander-in-Chief:

> Had made the decision that TORCH would be undertaken at the earliest possible date. He considered that this operation was now the principal objective and the assembling of means to carry it out should take precedence over other operations as, for instance, BOLERO.[50]

Inevitably the press picked up the split between Roosevelt and his military advisers, and began pounding the President about overriding the Joint Chiefs on military strategy. Incensed by the charges, at an August 6 cabinet meeting Roosevelt pointedly denied that he had ever overruled the Joint Chiefs on a military matter and made it clear that any further leaks to the press on this matter would not bode well for those concerned. Stimson, upset by FDR's claims that he had not overruled his Chiefs, wrote: "The President has the happy faculty of fooling himself and this was one of the most extreme cases of that I have ever seen."[51]

After further consultations with Marshall, Stimson prepared a memorandum to the President, intending to have it out once and for all. In the memo, Stimson detailed how Roosevelt had overrode all of his military advisers when he ordered the TORCH operation, in hopes the President would see the error of his ways. But when he showed the memo to Marshall on August 10, he found the Chief of Staff a changed man. He strongly advised Stimson to shelve the memo and let things play out.[52] From that point on Marshall began energetically pushing all obstacles to TORCH aside, so as to get on with the mission.

What accounts for this sudden change of heart? Of course, Roosevelt's firm declarations that TORCH was his first priority had much to do with it. But equal measure must be accorded a personal note Marshall received from Sir John Dill, an officer he truly respected:

> I am just a little disturbed about TORCH. For good or ill it has been ac-cepted and therefore I feel we should go at it with all possible enthusiasm and give it absolute priority. If we don't, it won't succeed …. Those playing a part in mounting the operation must be entirely whole-hearted about it, or they cannot give it all the help it should have and overcome all the dif-ficulties that will arise.[53]

The official army historians declared that Marshall was unimpressed by his friend's note, but this clearly was not the case. Marshall lived by a code, and a big part of the code, drummed into him since he had been a cadet at VMI, was that once a decision is made you do your best to make it a reality. The time for argument had passed, and the Commander-in-Chief had decided. As such, the code Marshall lived by left him only two options: make the decision his own and see it through to the end, or resign. For several weeks Marshall, with all the right intentions, had forgotten that code, and as a result endangered the success of TORCH. It took Dill's gentle reminder to snap him back to his duty. Stimson was worried that even Marshall was taking his eye off the prize, but he bowed to his Chief's desires.

Roosevelt was always determined to avoid letting electoral politics influence battlefield preparation, but in early October he weakened, just slightly. During one of General Marshall's TORCH briefings, the President held his hands up as if in prayer and said, "Please make it before Election Day."[54] According to Marshall, that was the only time the President allowed political concerns to enter into the wartime planning. Moreover, when Marshall later disappointed him with the news that the invasion could not possibly be launched before the elections, Roosevelt did not utter a word of complaint. On the other hand, Steve Early, the President's Press Secretary, who was told about the invasion just one hour before the landings, exploded in a hot anger over the delay that almost cost the Democrats their majorities on the Hill.

Back at home, Roosevelt was already looking ahead. On November 25, he had the Joint Chiefs over to the White House to discuss operations after North Africa was secured. Once again Roosevelt did not invite either Stimson or Knox, demonstrating his growing confidence in his own ability to run the war through his Chiefs. When Roosevelt opened the meeting by inquiring how long it would take to conclude current operations, Marshall optimistically said that he believed Tunisia would fall within two weeks, but possibly a few weeks longer if another division or two were required. In the event, and much to Marshall's chagrin, Tunisia was only declared secured after almost on May 6, 1943), after almost six months of hard slogging. Marshall went on to state that before any further operations were decided on he wanted "careful consideration of what it would cost to clear the Mediterranean ... and whether or not the large air and ground forces required for such a project could be justified."[55] Most of the remainder of the meeting was given over to matters of war production and allocation, concluding with Roosevelt alerting the Joint Chiefs that he and Churchill were discussing a planning meeting in North Africa at the earliest possible date. In fact, Roosevelt had cabled Churchill that morning with a suggestion for a conference of the big three (Roosevelt, Churchill, and Stalin) to be held in Cairo or Moscow in four to six weeks.[56]

If Marshall had intended during this meeting to reorient Roosevelt away from the Mediterranean in favor of future operations in Northern France, his approach was rather indifferent. If he still desired as early an invasion of Northern Europe as possible this was the time to forthrightly say so. Instead, Marshall pulled his punch. That he had reason to worry about a protracted conflict in the Mediterranean was made clear during a November 17, JCS Meeting. At that time, Leahy had told the other Chiefs that plans must be prepared for suitable activities in the Mediterranean, which could be discussed with the British when they put forward their own ideas on the subject.[57] Rather than come to an immediate conclusion, the matter was tabled, at Marshall's suggestion, and handed over to the Joint Strategic Survey Committee for further analysis.[58] What is notable is that when future operations in the Mediterranean were brought up, Marshall made no immediate objection. This was not the Marshall that had fought the invasion of North Africa every inch of the way.

The next day Roosevelt held a Thanksgiving at the White House. As 1942 drew to a close he finally had something to be thankful for – successful Allied offensives in the Pacific and Atlantic. Roosevelt himself had selected the hymns and designed the service, which was held in the East Room. Two hundred guests were invited, based on a list from an earlier occasion, and the Secret Service was ordered to stop the gate crashers who had been besieging the White House switchboard for days seeking invitations. Soon after his Thanksgiving dinner Roosevelt boarded the train for Hyde Park. During the ride, the President became indignant over how his service had been ruined because the orchestra had sped up the tempo, "making a two step out of the Battle Hymn of the Republic."[59]

Such idle concerns could not occupy him for long. On December 10, Roosevelt was once again sitting with his Joint Chiefs. This time Marshall was more explicit, saying that he "particularly opposed to dabbling in the Mediterranean in a wasteful way, and that ... he considered it important to be ready in March or April to launch operations against the Brest Peninsula, or Boulogne."[60] This is a remarkable comment giving that American troops were entering Britain at unimpressive 8,500 a month (in World War I the nations had send 10,000 men into France every single day).[61] As April was only four months off, one wonders how Marshall thought that the barely trained single division currently in Britain was going to make much of an impression on the Germans in Northern France. Moreover, to date no serious planning had been accomplished, all of the required transports were in the Mediterranean, and even if there was a rapid conclusion to the fighting in North Africa the divisions involved would need several months to refit. On this occasion, Marshall appears guilty of a lot more than just optimistic thinking.

But if one parses Marshall's language just a small bit, it become obvious that he was not calling for a full-blown invasion, lodgment, and breakout. Rather, he is recommending something much smaller. He had raised the idea for operations in the Brest Peninsula that summer, mostly as a face saving operation to show that the Anglo-Americans were doing something to open a true second front. Operations around Boulogne, in the teeth of the *Wehrmacht's* strongest defenses only made sense if Germany was crumbling. And this appears to be what Marshall was hoping for.[62] As he looked at the Red Army steamroller gathering steam in southern Russia, he saw a glimmer of a chance for a German crack-up that could be exploited by even a small number of American troops thrown onto the Continent. Failing that, even the preparations for such a thrust would work to his ultimate benefit, as troops and materiel would stop flowing to the Mediterranean and instead build-up in Britain to await the ultimate final offensive.[63]

On December 11, the Joint Strategic Survey Committee forwarded its recommendations for 1943 to the Joint Chiefs. Its main recommendations were to:

1. After Tunisia was secured, to cease further operations, except for strategic bombing, in the Mediterranean
2. Concentrate all efforts on BOLERO for a decisive assault on Northern Europe in 1943.
3. Stay on the defensive in the Pacific, conducting only enough offensive operations to keep open communications with Australia, and that operations in Burma should be remain limited.[64]

These recommendations were discussed in a closed JCS session on December 15.[65] Most of the discussion was dominated by King who was greatly offended by the idea that the Navy would stay on the defensive just when its forces were about to be vastly augmented. In a warm-up for his arguments at Casablanca, King stated that any let-up of pressure on the Japanese would greatly lengthen the war, and he therefore required that forces in the

Pacific keep going forward. Moreover, he considered operations in Burma as vital, as otherwise we could not keep China supplied and in the war. He agreed that Germany was currently the principal concern, but he was not certain that it was the "primary enemy," as Embick's the report stated. Nor was he convinced that making the primary effort against Germany in early 1943 was acceptable strategy given the critical situation in the Pacific. King also said that he thought the Pacific was only getting about 15 percent of the total forces and materiel produced for the war effort, and that to keep the Pacific offensives rolling he would need 25–30 percent. This was a bit ingenuous on King's part, as he was surely aware that over half the divisions deployed so far in the war had gone to the Pacific, along with most of the new war ships. Whether he was truly asking for a major increase in his share of the nation's resources, or setting a marker that would make it difficult to reduce what he already had, is difficult to tell. King, no doubt, thought he had a winning arguments and reiterated again at Casablanca.

Marshall, agreed that he report needed to be changed to reflect the requirement to maintain the pressure on the Japanese. His main concern, however, was to change the reports emphasis on a rather slow build-up in Britain so as to invade France in the fall of 1943, to a rapid buildup aimed at a Spring invasion target at Brest. He concluded that every effort should be made to have sufficient forces "in England for some quick, decisive, continental action."[66] Once the document was revised it was forwarded to the British Chiefs, who in turn sent their own plans for 1943 to the American. As everyone expected, the respective plans were strongly divergent, setting the stage for the next round of talks at the Casablanca Conference. On the morning of January 7, Roosevelt may have hoped to bring a united Joint Chiefs with him to Casablanca, but by the end of the day he knew that was impossible. His air Chief –Arnold – favored focusing entirely on bombing Germany into submission and thought there might be no need for a land invasion; his naval Chief – King – favored a massive reallocation of resources to the Pacific; and his land Chief – Marshall – wanted a focus on Northern Europe, but knew that was impossible in 1943.

Over the intervening decades a legend has grown up that the Americans were out-negotiated at Casablanca. According to myth, this unhappy result was due to the Americans arriving with too small a staff, and incomplete plans and position papers. In fact, after the meeting King had complained that "the British had a paper ready for every subject raised for discussion."[67] General Wedemeyer, who ran the American staff at Casablanca complained: "They swarmed down on us like locusts ... with prepared plans .... From a worm's eye's viewpoint it was apparent that we were confronted by generations and generations of experience in committee work, in diplomacy, and in rationalizing points of view. They had us on the defensive practically all the time."[68] After the event, Wedemeyer wrote: "We came, we listened, we were conquered."[69] Such an analysis severely distorts the reality of negotiations at the highest levels of government or the military. The American staff might have been embarrassed by their lack of preparation, and witnessing the JCS staff flounder may have annoyed King, but it was irrelevant. Marshall, King, and Arnold were without question strong-willed men. They were not about to be moved off of their positions because some staff officer had written a paper on the topic. While it may have been helpful to go tit-for-tat with position papers, as happened at subsequent conferences, there is no indication in the record of anyone ever changing their outlook based on a position paper. Both the British and American Chiefs were immersed in the war every moment of every day. They needed staff papers to inform them of certain technical details, not to guide them on strategic precepts.[70]

There is truly one reason why the British got almost everything they wanted at Casablanca – because the Americans agreed with them on all crucial points. The top menace remained the U-boats prowling the North Atlantic and they had to be destroyed. Strategic bombing was viewed by everyone as a potentially decisive weapon, so that remained on the priority list; as did supporting the Soviet Union, which was still killing 10 times the Germans that the Anglo-Americans were. King got what he wanted in the Pacific – permission to conduct further offensive operations – because he was King, and the British has no great interest in wrestling in the mud with him over a theater they were barely involved with. Where British interests were involved – Burma – they mostly got their way. In fact, one is struck when reading the minutes of the Casablanca discussions just how much time is given over to discussions of operations in Burma, and how relatively little is spent discussing invading the European continent. Of course, the debate of most significance revolved around whether 1943 would be dedicated to further operations in the Mediterranean, or would these be mostly shut down in favor of an invasion of Northern Europe. And it is in this debate that the Americans supposedly got their clocks cleaned by scheming and cunning British.[71] In reality, the Americans had surrendered to the British position before they arrived at Casablanca.

So where did the myth get started, and why does it persist? It began in one of the volumes of the Army's official history of the war – Maurice Matloff's and Edwin Snell's *Strategic Planning for Coalition Warfare: 1943–1944*. In it the author's write "At the Conference General Marshall led the JCS in a last stand for a major cross-Channel operation in 1943."[72] One would have look pretty hard at the minutes of the meetings to find any trace of this being true. What one finds instead is a few half-hearted attempts by Marshall and Arnold to secure a British commitment to an invasion of Northern Europe at some indeterminate date. Matloff and Snell build their case by some judicious cherry-picking of the minutes. For instance, they write "... he [Marshall] stated that the basic question was the extent to which the associated powers had to adhere to the general concept embodied in the BOLERO plan and the extent they could undertake diversions to help the USSR."[73] Matloff and Snell left out Marshall's words just before the section quoted by them: "Aid to Russia is regarded as being of paramount importance …. We must devise means to enable Russia to continue aggressively through 1943 by providing them with supplies."[74] From Matloff and Snell's account one could easily get the impression that Marshall was ready to curtail Lend-Lease to the Soviet Union so as to focus on BOLERO. Rather, the full quote demonstrates that continuing high levels of aid for Russia was one of his top priorities.

More egregiously, and in a quote repeated in almost every book dealing with Casablanca and the opening of a "second front" in France, Matloff and Snell write: "It is important for the American and British leaders to determine the main plot. 'Every diversion or side issue from the main plot, acts as a suction pump.'"[75] But, once again, they left out something important. The very next line of the minutes reads: "He [Marshall] stated that the operations against Sicily appeared to be advantageous because of the excess number of troops in North Africa."[76] So Marshall recognized that invading Sicily was a "suction pump" gobbling up resources that would make a 1943 invasion of France impossible, but he supported it anyway. This is a long way from the myth of a "last stand for a major cross-Channel invasion in 1943." Belief that Marshall, at Casablanca, strongly advocated a 1943 invasion is more a result of extrapolating from his previous stance on the matter than a reflection of his thinking by late 1942. Marshall remained convinced that invading Northern Europe was the quickest and most certain way to victory, but he also knew that would not happen until 1944. His arguments at Casablanca had nothing to do with an invasion of France in 1943, and everything to do with making sure the date did not slip past 1944.

As for Roosevelt, by the time he arrived the Combined Chiefs had been debating various plans and alternatives for three days. The President was whisked away from the airfield by the head of his Secret Service detail, Michael Reilly, to the Conference location at the Anfa Hotel on the outskirts of Casablanca. Besides the hotel itself, there were 14 associated two-story villas. The entire compound was surrounded by two massive lines of barbed wire, dozens of anti-aircraft guns, and hundreds of infantrymen were on constant patrol. General Patton was in charge of security, and the responsibility kept him in a state of constant agitation. Roosevelt was assigned Villa #2 "Dar es Saada," while Churchill was placed fifty yards away in Villa #3 "Mirador." Just moments after entering his room, Roosevelt sent Hopkins to get Churchill, who was at his door a minute later. The two men conferred for an hour before heading to dinner with the Combine Chiefs.

On the fourth day of the conference the Combined Chiefs presented their agreed proposals for 1943 to Roosevelt and Churchill. Both men had been kept up to date by their respective commanders, so there was little of surprise in the offerings. The Chiefs proposed to win the Battle of the North Atlantic, support Russia, continue the strategic air offensive against Germany, and invade Sicily (Operation Husky). When it came to the Pacific the British had for a time resisted any further offensive action, before bowing to the inevitable. King wanted to start rolling in the Pacific and Marshall and Arnold supported him. Faced with a united and unbreakable American front the British Chiefs caved, a lesson not lost on either Marshall or King. As such, the Chiefs proposed to start operations aimed at retaking Burma (Operation ANAKIM), capturing Rabaul, and an advance in the Central Pacific to the Marshall's and the Carolines.[77] Once approved by their political masters the Combined Chiefs had their agreement codified in a document titled CSS-155.[78]

But this was the day everything changed.[79] Before the Americans could even begin to press, the British suddenly agreed to stop focusing on what Stimson called "the little points" and said they would consider the "big point." Marshall then made an observation that he had not brought up in his earlier meeting with the American Chiefs. He mentioned that he had read a British planning paper that stated if Mediterranean operations were conducted post Sicily it would still be possible to conduct an invasion of Northern Europe on April 1, 1944. Brooke did not argue the point, only stating that such a date was possible only if further Mediterranean operations drew off German forces. He then amended the April 1 date to May or June, but that was close enough for the Americans.[80]

Sensing they were near an agreement, Marshall cleared the room, leaving only the Chiefs, Dill, and a secretary, who dared not pick up his pen. As one historian has said: "The Chief of Staff was going to squeeze an agreement and he wanted no witnesses."[81] When the British committed to May 1, 1944, as a firm date for the invasion of northern France, Marshall, suddenly a font of generosity, said that in the meantime he and the rest of the Joint Chiefs would agree to knocking Italy out of the war, assuming the invasion of Sicily was rapidly concluded. Brooke had not gotten a firm commitment to invade Italy, but it was close enough. As he wrote later, approving the unsatisfactory agreement was "far better than a break up of the conference."[82] But Marshall was elated. He had a firm date for the invasion of Europe, and though the British only agreed to invading France with 20 divisions – in effect, a super-SLEDGE-HAMMER – the scale of the operation could be adjusted later. Marshall had also gotten the British to commit to taking seven battle-hardened divisions out of the Mediterranean in the fall. This ensured that there was a clear path to shutting down the Mediterranean "suction pump." The reminder of the conference was mostly given over to securing bases in the Azores, and discussions over operations in Burma and assisting China. Though these prolonged debates often got heated, nothing of permanence was concluded. Moreover, the American preoccupation with China would soon come to an end, as China's centrality to America's Pacific calculations was about to dramatically change.

The final big decision made by Roosevelt was to choose a commander for OVERLORD. Hopkins, Stimson, Churchill, and even Stalin had wanted

Marshall to have the job. Even Roosevelt wanted to give the job to Marshall. They realized even if many Americans did not that while everyone remembered Pershing and Grant, few Americans could name the Chief-in-Staff back in Washington during the Civil War and World War I. Standing against Marshall's selection were the rest of the Joint Chiefs, particularly King, who thought Marshall was the indispensable man. On the other hand, the press had already made much of the perception that Marshall stepping down to take command of OVERLORD would be a punishment. But this the President could handle or explain. What really mattered was what Roosevelt thought, and though he believed Marshall deserved the command, he had grown used to having the general in Washington. Though they were never personally close, Roosevelt also considered him the indispensable man. Moreover, the Tehran Conference had put one major reason for giving Marshall the command behind him. Stimson had argued for months that only Marshall could see the project through against entrenched British opposition. But Stalin's firm support for OVERLORD, and the resulting British capitulation on the timing, made the invasion a certainty, with or without Marshall's presence in Britain.

Roosevelt still hesitated. He sent Hopkins to sound out Marshall as to his own desires. Marshall, despite having told his aide to prepare for a move and the fact that his wife was already moving personal furniture out of their official residence, told Hopkins that "he would go along wholeheartedly with whatever decision the President made."[83] Marshall's biographer, suspects that Roosevelt knew his man and expected he would reply as he did, thereby giving Roosevelt an open door to keep him in Washington. The next day Roosevelt met with Marshall in his villa, and repeated the question. Marshall then substantially gave the President the same answer he had given Hopkins. Roosevelt pondered the problem a bit more, before concluding the conversation, by stating: "I feel I could not sleep at night with you out of the country."[84] Hence Roosevelt selected Eisenhower as Supreme Commander for the invasion of Northern Europe.

Notes

1 James Lacey, *The Washington War* (New York: Bantam Press, 2019), p. 24. Much of this chapter directly draws upon what one will find in this book, as this exact subject matter was a crucial aspect of my earlier work.
2 Doris Kearns Godwin, No *Ordinary Time, Franklin & Eleanor Roosevelt: The Home Front in World War II* (Simon & Schuster, 1994), p. 23.
3 Conrad Black, *Franklin Delano Roosevelt: Champion of Freedom* (Public Affairs, 2003), p. 561.
4 Forrest C. Pogue, *George C. Marshall: Education of a General*, 1880–1939 (Penguin Books, 1991), p. 325.
5 Forrest C. Pogue, *George C. Marshall: Education of a General*, 1880–1939 (Penguin Books, 1991), p. 325. (Author's emphasis).
6 Forrest C. Pogue, *George C. Marshall: Education of a General*, 1880–1939 (Penguin Books, 1991), p. 122.

7 Thomas M. Coffey, *Hap* (The Viking Press, 1982), p. 80.

8 Jim Lacey, *Pershing* (Palgrave Macmillan, 2008), p. 158.

9 Ibid., p. 159.

10 Forrest C. Pogue, *George C. Marshall: Education of a General*, 1880–1939 (Penguin Books, 1991), pp. 223–224.

11 Mark Stoler, *George C Marshall: Soldier Statesman of the American Century* (Simon & Schuster Macmillan, 1989), p. 57.

12 See: *The Marshall Papers, Vol. 1*. (Johns Hopkins University Press, 1981), p. 407. There is a letter from Marshall to Senator Byrnes regretting the short time they had spent together and that his regret that he and Mrs. Marshall would have to forgo further fishing trips with the Senator and his wife.

13 Mark Stoler, *George C Marshall: Soldier Statesman of the American Century* (Simon & Schuster Macmillan, 1989), p. 62; and, Forrest C. Pogue, *George C. Marshall: Education of a General*, 1880-1939 (Penguin Books, 1991), pp. 318–319.

14 James Roosevelt, *My Parents: A Differing View*; as quoted in Susan Dunn, *1940: FDR, Wilkie, Lindbergh, Hitler—the Election Amid the Storm* (Yale University Press, 2013), p. 328.

15 Louis Morton, *Strategy and Command: The First Two Years* (Office of Chief of Military History Department of the Army, 1962), p. 190.

16 Stimson Diaries, Sunday, February 9, 1942.

17 Forrest C. Pogue, *George C. Marshall: Ordeal and Hope*, 1939–1942 (Viking Press, 1966), pp. 247–248.

18 Stimson Diaries, Monday, February 10, 1942.

19 MacArthur Papers, Record Group 2, Macarthur Memorial Archives and Library.

20 Kent Roberts Greenfield, *American Strategy in World War II: A Reconsideration* (Johns Hopkins Press, 1963). See the Appendix to Chapter III for a listing of every time Roosevelt overrules Marshall and the Joint Chiefs during the war years.

21 Ibid., p. 78. By the middle of 1943, FDR's interest in China waned, as Stalin promised to join the war against Japan after German was defeated, and the Capture of the Marianna Islands made it possible to bomb Japan without airbases in China. I have added the seventh point to Greenstein's original six.

22 Forrest C. Pogue, *George C. Marshall: Ordeal and Hope*, 1939–1942 (Viking Press, 1966), p. 28.

23 Ibid.

24 John Morton Blum, *The Morgenthau Diaries: Years of Urgency 1938–1941* (Houghton Mifflin Company, 1965), p. 139.

25 John Morton Blum, *The Morgenthau Diaries: Years of Urgency 1938–1941* (Houghton Mifflin Company, 1965), p. 139.

26 Mark S. Watson, *Chief of Staff: Prewar Planning and* Preparations (Historical Division of the United States Army, 1950), p. 190.

27 Kenneth S. Davis, *FDR: Into the Storm* (Random House, 1993), p. 507.

28 For a list of the discussion participants, see: Maurice Matloff and Edwin Snell, *Strategic Planning for Coalition Warfare: 1943–1944* (Center of Military History United States Army, 1953), pp. 33.

29 Lawrence Guyer, *The Joint Chiefs and the War in Europe, Section I*, p. 39.

30 Ibid.

31 Kenneth S. Davis, *FDR: The War President* (Random House, 2000), pp. 143–144; also: Louis Morton, *Strategy and Command: The First Two Years* (Office of Chief of Military History Department of the Army, 1962), p. 90.

32 All of the above information and conversation is drawn from transcripts of the Pogue interviews with Marshall, See: Tape 15: February 14, 1957, http://marshallfoundation.org/library/wp-content/uploads/sites/16/2014/05/Tape_15.pdf

33 One suspects that Congressman David Walsh's – Chairman of the Naval Committee – bill to improve unity of command in the military had much to do with Roosevelt's change of heart. As Roosevelt saw it, it was much better from him to choose a chief and outline his position, than to have Congress do it for him (Stimson Diaries, Friday, March 20, 1942).

34 24th mtg. of JCS, 10 July 1942, National Archives, Record Group 218.

35 24th mtg. of JCS, 10 July 1942, National Archives, Record Group 218. In *On Active Service in Peace and War*, McGeorge Bundy began a long-standing debate as to whether this was a serious proposal on Marshall and King's part. According to Bundy's interpretation of Secretary of War Stimson's biography, the proposal was: "… was designed mainly as a plan to bring the British into agreement with Bolero." However, this quote does not appear in the Stimson Diaries until July 15, three days after the memorandum was drafted, and only after Roosevelt had sharply rejected it. It is worth noting that Stimson had marked the quote, and much later, wrote in the margin "This shows how the Pacific argument for me was mainly a bluff." Prior to this the diary records: "I found Marshall very stirred up and emphatic over it [the British memo rejecting BOLERO]… As the British won't go through with what they agreed to, we will turn our backs on them and take up the war with Japan." A person planning a ploy is normally not as agitated as Marshall comes across. Moreover, if this plan was a ploy it would be critical to involve Stimson in it before it went to the President. However, there is no indication in the record of anyone thinking this plan was a ploy until after the President rejected it. In fact, the JCS minutes where it was discussed never mention that this was a ploy. The discussion revolves entirely around why this is a sound proposal and never once mentions that it was not a real proposal, but just a method to pressure the British. This event is covered in the Marshall Papers in detail, without any indication it was a ploy (*The Papers of George Catlett Marshall*, Vol. III, pp. 269–273). Moreover, when the President pushed back on this proposal, Marshall at first made an effort to defend his and King's position. This is an unusual approach to take for a ploy. One would assume that instead of defending his position, Marshall would just inform Roosevelt that it was designed to force Britain's hand and was not a serious proposal. One would also assume that the Joint Chief's would have brought the President into their thinking before forwarding such a radical proposal. As Roosevelt's reply makes it obvious he was not so informed, both Marshall and King were taking a severe risk the President would lose faith in their ability and judgment. One should also note that at this level of leadership this kind of game is not played, at least in this way. While the debate continues, all contemporary accounts indicate that both Marshall and King were serious about it. In fact Marshall's deputy, General Handy would return to this idea in November 1942. His unpublished memories (Handy File, Military History Institute; Carlisle, PA) demonstrates that this was a serious proposal on the eve of the Casablanca Conference, as was the early proposal discussed here.

36 Stimson Diaries, Friday, July 10, 1942. For a complete copy of the memorandum see: King and Whitehill, *Fleet Admiral King*, pp. 398–399.

37 Lawrence Guyer, *The Joint Chiefs and the War in Europe, Section III*, p. 122. The entire memo is reproduced in Appendix E to Chapter III.

38 Ibid.

39 Stimson Diaries, Sunday, July 12, 1942. The entire memorandum is reproduced in his dairies at this point.

40 Stimson Diaries, Sunday, July 12, 1942.

41 Robert Sherwood, *Roosevelt and Hopkins,* p. 602.

42 The entire memo is reproduced in Appendix F to Chapter III in Guyer's, *The Joint Chiefs and the War in Europe, Section III*. Another copy is available in: The President's Secretary's File (PSF), 1933–1945: Box 4. (FDR Library).

43 Robert Sherwood, *Roosevelt and Hopkins,* p. 607.
44 Alex Danchev and Daniel Todman, ed., *War Diaries 1939–1945: Field Marshall Lord Alan Brooke* (Weidenfeld & Nicolson, 2001), p. 280.
45 The entire memo is reproduced in Appendix G to Chapter III in Guyer's, *The Joint Chiefs and the War in Europe,* Section III.
46 Robert Sherwood, *Roosevelt and Hopkins,* p. 602.
47 Stimson Diary, Sunday, July 26, 1942.
48 Stimson Diary, Sunday, July 27, 1942.
49 Maurice Matloff and Edwin Snell, *Strategic Planning for Coalition Warfare: 1943–1944* (Center of Military History United States Army, 1953), pp. 283–284.
50 Maurice Matloff and Edwin Snell, *Strategic Planning for Coalition Warfare,* p. 284.
51 Stimson Diary, Wednesday, August 6, 1942.
52 A complete copy of the memorandum is reproduced in the Stimson Diary on July 10, 1942.
53 Maurice Matloff and Edwin Snell, *Strategic Planning for Coalition Warfare,* p. 295.
54 Pogue Interviews, October 5, 1956.
55 Notes taken at meeting in the Executive Office of the President, November 25, 1942; JCS Records, National Archives, Record Group 218.
56 FDR Library, Map Room Papers, 1941–1945: Box 3. Historians have made much of this exchange of messages, as Roosevelt was answering a cable from Churchill where the Prime Minister voiced his concerns about America's commitment to BOLERO and ROUNDUP. Churchill had taken note of an order to decrease construction of camps for arriving American troops, and wondered if Roosevelt was switching the nation's strategic emphasis. Many historians have used Churchill's cable to Roosevelt as evidence that he was fully behind an invasion of Northern Europe as early as 1943. It is much more accurate to state that Churchill was acutely sensitive to any indication that the United States was shifting its priority to the Pacific, and wanted to make sure the flow of troops to Europe would continue unabated. For Churchill, getting the troops into Britain was the crucial thing. What to do with them could be decided at a later date.
57 JCS Minutes, 10 July 1942, National Archives, Record Group 218.
58 The Joint Strategic Survey Committee, headed by retired General Stanley Embick, was formed in early November, 1942. It consisted of a limited number of flag-rank officer, and was charged with conducting deep examinations and making recommendations on future strategy, free from the daily pressures of dealing with immediate operations.
59 William D. Hassett, *Off the Record with FDR 1942–1945* (Rutgers University Press, 1958), p. 142.
60 Notes taken at meeting in the Executive Office of the President, December 10, 1942; JCS Records, National Archives, Record Group 218. The mention of attacking Brest or Boulogne is not in the original transcript. Rather, it is attached as a separate handwritten note, which was later added to the official record of the conversation.
61 There are two versions of this transcript in the JCS records. In the earlier one it says that "our rate of flow to the United Kingdom at this time is dangerously low." This is scratched out and what is found in the second version is penned in: "our monthly rate of flow to there being 8,500."
62 Several days before meeting with Roosevelt, Marshall had read the first report of the Combined Staff Planners (written on December 5, 1942), which had split opinion. But one thing both the American and British planners agreed on was that it would be impossible to launch a major operation in Northern Europe in 1943. What split them was whether further operations should still be conducted in the Mediterranean, while the build-up went on in Britain. See: Lawrence Guyer, *The Joint Chiefs and the War in Europe,* Section 3, pp. 154–155.

63 Guyer provides a detailed account of the search for a strategic plan in the aftermath of TORCH that greatly enhances that provided by Matloff and Snell. Sere: Matloff and Snell, *Strategic Planning for Coalition Warfare*, pp. 363–382); see: Lawrence Guyer, *The Joint Chiefs and the War in Europe*, Section III, p. 137.

64 Lawrence Guyer, *The Joint Chiefs and the War in Europe*, Section III, pp. 159–160.

65 Only four copies of the minutes of this meeting were made. I have not been able to find any of them. Guyer, however had a copy that he worked from to put together his account. There is a single page of these minutes in the JCS file in the National Archives. See: Lawrence Guyer, *The Joint Chiefs and the War in Europe*, Section III, pp. 159–163.

66 Lawrence Guyer, *The Joint Chiefs and the War in Europe*, Section III, p. 162.

67 JCS Minutes, May 8, 1943, National Archives, Record Group 218.

68 Albert Wedemeyer, *Wedemeyer Reports!* (New York, 1958). P. 192.

69 Ray S. Cline, Washington Command Post: The Operations Division (Center of Military History United States Army, 1959), pp. 236–237. Cline note that Wedemeyer greatly exaggerated the difference in the performance of the two staffs.

70 This does not mean that the Americans did not come without any position papers of their own. In fact, they had quite a number of them. Copies of these reports can be found in several locations, but the ones I reviewed can be found at FDR Library, Map Room Papers, 1941–1945: Box 26.

71 The complete minutes of every discussion during the Casablanca Conference are available at: FDR Library, Map Room Papers, 1941-1945: Box 26; and, Foreign Relations of the United States (FRUS), *The Conferences at Washington, 1941–1942, and Casablanca, 1943*. The FRUS documents include minutes of conversations between Churchill and Roosevelt that are not in the Map Room files.

72 Maurice Matloff and Edwin Snell, *Strategic Planning for Coalition Warfare: 1943–1944* (Center of Military History United States Army, 1959), p. 21.

73 Ibid., p. 21. NOTE: The phrase "embodied in the BOLERO plan" does not appear in the minutes of the meeting. This was added in by Matloff and Snell.

74 Minutes Combined Chiefs of Staff, January 16, 1943, FDR Library, Map Room Papers, 1941–1945: Box 26.

75 Matloff and Snell, *Strategic Planning for Coalition Warfare: 1943–1944*, p.21.

76 Minutes Combined Chiefs of Staff, January 16, 1943, FDR Library, Map Room Papers, 1941–1945: Box 26.

77 Lawrence Guyer, *The Joint Chiefs and the War in Europe*, Section III, p. 195.

78 For a full copy of CSS 155, see: Foreign Relations of the United States (FRUS), *The Conferences at Washington, 1941–1942, and Casablanca, 1943*, pp. 774–775.

79 Though this was a closed meeting, a detailed outline of the conversations is available in: The Foreign Relations of the United States: The Third Washington Conference, pp. 112–123.

80 The Foreign Relations of the United States: The Third Washington Conference, p. 101.

81 Ed Cray, *General of the Army: George C. Marshall, Soldier and Statesman* (W. W. Norton and Company, 1990), p. 396.

82 Alex Danchev and Daniel Todman, ed., *War Diaries 1939–1945: Field Marshall Lord Alanbrooke* (Weidenfeld & Nicolson, 2001), p. 407.

83 Robert Sherwood, *Roosevelt and Hopkins: An Intimate History* (Harper and Brothers, 1948), p. 803.

84 Ed Cray, *General of the Army: George C. Marshall, Soldier and Statesman* (W. W. Norton and Company, 1990), p. 13.

10

COULDN'T WINSTON TRUST HIS GENERALS?

Richard Toye

In November 1959, the poet and critic Hilary Corke reviewed a TV documentary featuring Viscount Alanbrooke. The programme, in which the Field Marshal was a somewhat reluctant participant, was occasioned by the publication of *Triumph in the West*. Billed as 'The Most Startling War Document Yet Published!' this was the second of two books about the Second World War by Arthur Bryant.[1] Like *The Turn of The Tide*, which appeared two years earlier, the book drew heavily on Alanbrooke's diaries. These were a sensation, because they revealed spectacular arguments between Churchill as Prime Minister and Sir Alan Brooke (as he then was) as Chief of the Imperial General Staff (CIGS) from 1941 onwards. This was damaging to the Churchillian legend, as bolstered by Churchill's own six volumes of war memoirs.[2] Alanbrooke (as he will be referred to here for convenience) described the Prime Minister's inconsiderate, thoughtless, and even bullying behaviour, and more seriously, consistently poured scorn on his military judgement. Corke, however, grumbled that, when in front of the cameras, Alanbrooke had pulled his punches, delivering a lucid but bland performance. 'At the very start he disclaimed all intentions towards controversy, and there ensued ten major strategic problems each potted down into a three-minute TV jelly-jar.' Corke wanted more spice, but not, he said, out of prurience. 'We are all aware that, generally speaking, the allies conducted the war according to a unified, consistent and highly successful policy. What is interesting to learn – what Lord Alanbrooke's memoirs tell us, but this programme did not – [is] how such a policy emerged in spite of, or even on occasions because of, violent differences of opinion.'[3]

Corke's insight was an important one. On the face of it, Churchill and Alanbrooke's blazing rows appear like the epitome of civil-military crisis – a seemingly deranged politician and a furious Brass Hat battling it out hammer

DOI: 10.4324/9781003375630-10

and tongs. 'Couldn't Winston Trust His Generals?' asked a *Daily Mail* headline when *The Turn of The Tide* was published.[4] Yet, this chapter argues, the true picture is both more complex and more interesting. Clearly, the differences between Churchill and Alanbrooke were real and substantial. They concerned not only the details of specific military operations but also broader strategy. At the same time, their shouting and fist-shaking should not distract attention from the many assumptions they in fact held in common. These are less easy for the historian to detect, precisely because they did not need to be articulated. In the end, the Churchill-Alanbrooke relationship was *difficult but functional*. Alanbrooke and the Chiefs of Staff, in the face of considerable provocation, offered robust responses to Churchill's excesses without ever straying into insubordination. Churchill, for his part, tested the ideas of his military advisers to destruction, but in the end bowed to their guidance, never overruling them on a point on which they had reached consensus. Within the context of severe geopolitical constraints, success emerged *in spite of, or even on occasions because of,* Alanbrooke and Churchill's tempestuous clashes. At the same time, those clashes may have been exacerbated by Churchill's determination to exert civilian control over the military, combined with his uncertainty, based on his past experience, of whether he could actually do so.

This chapter argues further that this relatively happy outcome was not merely the serendipitous product of two contrasting but complementary personalities. Moreover, effectively functioning civil-military relationships could not be taken for granted in the British context, as the period surrounding the First World War had demonstrated. Two things had changed. First, political circumstances had altered in such a way that leading soldiers no longer felt the desire or the need to test or challenge the government of the day. Second, institutional developments during the interwar period had created a framework for more effective communication and decision-making. The chapter begins with a discussion of the Alanbrooke diary, the fundamental source for studying its author's relationship with Churchill. It then discusses the civil-military crisis of c.1912–c.1922, its resolution, and the legacies that the interwar years left for the World War II. Next, it describes Alanbrooke's time as CIGH from the end of 1941 until the close of the war. The situation Britain faced after Pearl Harbor presented new challenges. On the one hand, the USA's entrance into the war guaranteed victory. On the other hand, it created new issues as Britain wrestled with its new status as a junior partner to the Americans and continued, at the same time, its recent and difficult alliance with the Soviets.

Alan Francis Brooke was born in 1883 to an Irish Protestant Ascendancy family, but in France, where he was raised to the age of eighteen. At that point he joined the army, serving first in Ireland and then in India. He served with distinction in World War I, by the end of which he had reached the rank of Lieutenant-Colonel. His interwar service included spells as an instructor at the Staff College in Camberley and at the Imperial Defence College. In 1938, reaching the rank of Lieutenant-General, he was given sweeping responsibilities for anti-aircraft defence. In August 1939, he was appointed Commander-in-Chief, Southern Command, and, upon mobilisation, took charge of the command of the 2nd corps of the British Expeditionary Force (BEF). He was a passionate ornithologist and maintained this interest even during the war. In 1925 his first wife died in an accident in a car in which he was driving. In 1929, he remarried – his diary was written to his second wife, Benita, to whom he poured out his feelings. The first entry was dated 28 September 1929, as Alanbrooke started for France. 'It is all too ghastly even to be a nightmare,' he wrote. 'The futility of it all, as proved by the last war! I am glad to say that it does not undermine my belief in an almighty and far seeing God, working toward one set purpose for the destiny of the human race.'[5]

As those words suggest, Alanbrooke was motivated by religious duty, but was no bloodthirsty warmonger.[6] Behind his composed and controlled façade, he felt things deeply, and sometimes broke out (not least with Churchill) into open expressions of anger. This explains the quality of the diary, which contained frequent denunciations of the follies of those who disagreed with him. It revealed him as 'a master of succinct but comprehensive condemnation.'[7] It was written in part to relieve his feelings, and he was capable of rectifying his criticisms in retrospect. In a series of post-war notes, he annotated his entries, sometimes taking the opportunity to correct injustices he had committed in the original. Consider this, on Churchill, from September 1944:

> He knows no details, has only got half the picture in his mind, talks absurdities and makes my blood boil to listen to his nonsense. I find it hard to remain civil. And the wonderful thing is that ¾ of the population of the world imagine Winston Churchill is one of the great Strategists of History, a second Marlborough, and the other ¼ have no conception what a public menace he is and has been throughout this war. [...] Without him England was lost for a certainty, with him England has been on the verge of disaster time and again. [...]
>
> Never have I admired and despised a man simultaneously to the same extent. Never have such opposite extremes been combined in the same human being.

Later he added: 'My criticisms of Winston's wrath on that day was obviously unnecessarily hard, it should however be remembered that they were written at a moment of exasperation due to his attitude during the meetings we had held, and desperation as to how I was to handle the conference in front of me with his continuous obstruction.' To another entry he added the words, 'I thank God I was given an opportunity of working alongside of such a man.'[8] But though Alanbrooke's admiration of Churchill was real, it was not for his *military* judgement. Interviewed on television in 1957, he happily took a prompt to describe him as 'the greatest war leader of modern times,' but glossed this by talking about his powers of inspiration rather than about his strategic judgement.[9] He was also impressed by Churchill's diplomatic skills, not least his handling of Stalin.[10]

Churchill, for his part, recognised Alanbrooke's capacity, but did not warm to him. Lord Moran, Churchill's doctor, described his patient's lukewarm relationship with the 'rather prim, self-contained, inscrutable' Alanbrooke. Churchill 'liked to do business with Alanbrooke – when they agreed – but he did not want to see too much of him out of school. If Winston did not like a man he would certainly not admire him.' Moran once asked Churchill if he agreed that Alanbrooke was good at his job. A lengthy pause followed. 'He has a flair for the business,' Churchill grunted, and would concede nothing more.[11] After the war, then, the two men's relations were not close – and Churchill disapproved when Alanbrooke, who stayed on until 1946 as CIGS, supported the new Labour government's policy towards Egypt.[12] Alanbrooke gave Churchill some help with his memoirs, but he may have resented the egocentric account that emerged from them.[13]

Alanbrooke was also in need of money. To the surprise of many who knew him, he teamed up with Arthur Bryant, a popular historian who had succeeded in covering up the memory of his pre-war fascist sympathies. His reputation as 'a supreme toady, fraudulent scholar and humbug' is not undeserved.[14] But although the version of the diaries that emerged was incomplete and somewhat corrupted (an authoritative edition was published in 2001), Bryant deserves some credit for bringing important new material into the public domain.[15] Prior to the publication of *The Turn of The Tide*, the two collaborators were aware that Churchill might take offence, and made some efforts (including an emollient preface by Alanbrooke) to soften the blow.[16] It was to little avail. Churchill privately called this first volume 'a bad book, a very bad book,' and took cheer from a hostile *Times Literary Supplement* review. Alanbrooke tried and failed to mend fences, though Clementine Churchill, who was initially shocked, resolved that she was not really angry. 'We must get used to criticism of Winston,' she acknowledged. 'I realize the poor darling cannot be a demi-god for ever.'[17]

The diaries cast different kinds of negative light on Churchill. It is indisputable that the Prime Minister imposed late-night conferences on his advisers, at which he would sometimes appear rambling, incoherent, and even a little drunk. His subordinates had to get up in the morning for an ordinary working day – but he did not. He often behaved in ways which could be described as bullying, though Alanbrooke was certainly not intimidated. '[W]hen I thump the table and push my face at him what does he do?' complained Churchill. 'Thumps the table harder and glares back at me.'[18] The facts of Churchill's behaviour are not in doubt but his manner could be defended. Arthur 'Bomber' Harris told Bryant: 'Winston blarnied, blustered and bullied with all the force of his incomparable oratorical powers. But in my view [...] he used those powers only as a flail with which to beat the good grain from the chaff.'[19] In this optimistic account, by constantly forcing the military chiefs to justify themselves, he could ensure that both his and their ideas received the necessary stress tests.

The most damaging charge in the diaries, though, was simply that Churchill's strategic ideas were generally lousy. In Alanbrooke's view, the Prime Minister lacked the capacity to grasp the entire strategic situation. 'Perhaps the most remarkable failing of his is that he can never see a whole strategical problem at once,' he wrote in 1943. 'His gaze always settles on some definite part of the canvas and the rest of the picture is lost.'[20] Churchill became obsessed, for example, with launching a second invasion of Norway, and, most notoriously, with capturing the Northern tip of Sumatra. Although he never insisted on going through with these projects in the face of the opposition of the Chiefs, an enormous amount of staff time was wasted on the scoping exercises necessary to prove to him that they were impracticable. Key aspects of Alanbrooke's account find confirmation in the papers of Admiral Cunningham, the First Sea Lord from 1943, with whom the CIGS enjoyed an effective rapport. Cunningham complained about 'the PM and his chorus of yes men,' as well as about Churchill's infantilism and bitter temper. At the same time, he regarded the Prime Minister, though infuriating, as indispensable – but not for his military thinking.[21] Later, he was asked if he shared Alanbrooke's assessment that Churchill's contribution to war strategy had been non-existent. 'Well, anyway,' replied Cunningham, 'it did not amount to much.'[22]

So although Alanbrooke's diaries can seem intemperate, even egotistical, he defied the predictions of some contemporaries that their publication would ruin, not Churchill's reputation, but rather his own. Before they appeared, their author was little known to the public, except through his occasional appearance on TV bird-watching programmes. Since then, he has rightly been considered to have made a major contribution to the war effort, and a series of important studies have given him no less than his due.[23] The Churchill-Alanbrooke relationship has even given inspiration in the field of Management Studies.[24] Indeed, although Alanbrooke, did attract some harsh criticism when Bryant's volumes were published, plenty of commentators succeeded in reaching even-handed judgements even then. Raymond Mortimer, writing in the *Sunday Times*, noted that, given the contrasts in Churchill's and Alanbrooke's characters, the remarkable thing was 'not that they often quarrelled but that they cooperated so long and so triumphantly.'[25] The *Economist* concluded that neither man could have achieved so much without the other. Alanbrooke had given a portrait that was not so much 'warts and all' as all warts. Nevertheless, this was 'a high-spirited, high-tempered, exhausting and astonishingly successful partnership: enriched by fun, growing dividends and a tremendous mutual respect.'[26]

Treated with sufficient caution, then, the diaries can reveal much, not least about the sheer exhaustion and frustration that were the almost inevitable product of high-level command. They supplement an official record which was intentionally kept bland.[27] We should not of course conclude from them that Alanbrooke was always right – after all, he made a series of pessimistic diary predictions which were happily falsified.[28] Nor should we conclude that Churchill was always wrong. And in fact, the two men were capable of being in agreement, and wrong, at the same time. The diaries present other dangers too. Alanbrooke saw only part of Churchill's activity (albeit this part was extremely important). The Prime Minister had to make not only military decisions but political and diplomatic ones. Arguably, if he was a poor strategist at the level of specific operations, he was much stronger (though not of course unimpeachable) in the geopolitical sphere.

Furthermore, Alanbrooke's diaries may, through their very richness, distract from the contributions of others who left dryer or less extensive records. One thinks here partly of P.J. Grigg, Secretary of State for War 1942–1945, with whom Alanbrooke developed a warm and effective partnership, but who has received little scholarly attention.[29] Archibald Nye, Vice-CIGS, to whom Alanbrooke delegated much of the running of the Army, an issue about which the diary is comparatively silent.[30] Nye himself emphasised that Alanbrooke's authority derived from the position that he held, 'literally, as the Chief of a Staff.' Calculating this required endless planning and replanning by now-forgotten officers. 'To my mind, Brookie's great achievement lay not so much in finding the right solutions (the less difficult part) but in getting his plans through – the more so that his natural qualities were those of an outspoken, forthright commander, and he was only able to adapt himself to the requirements of a Chief of Staff by a supreme and sustained exercise of self-control.'[31] Nye, incidentally, believed that Churchill 'had a totally wrong conception of the proper relation of a Prime Minister with his Chief of Staff.'[32]

Churchill and Alanbrooke's troubled but largely effective partnership should, moreover, be placed in longer-term perspective. Reviewing *The Turn of the Tide*, Lord Templewood (the former Cabinet minister Samuel Hoare) observed that there had never been a modern war in which the differences between the military and the politicians had not become acute:

The politicians are always inclined to think that the soldiers are prejudiced and unimaginative, the soldiers that the politicians are ignorant and irresponsible. In the First World War Lloyd George was always at issue with Haig and Robertson, although he never involved himself with them in a frontal battle. But in this latter case [World War II] their differences were finally settled by frank and often fierce disagreement, rather than by the devious expedients to which Lloyd George had such frequent recourse.[33]

Clement Attlee – who considered Alanbrooke a great man – was once asked about the lack of 'clash and intrigue' in the Second World War relative to the First. He replied: 'one thing was that a very large proportion of us in the Government had served in war, so we understood something about it; we understood the military mind.' He added: 'I think, also, we had much more intelligent Heads of the Services.'[34] Alanbrooke himself, when asked about the point said: 'I attribute that difference mainly to the fact that in the last war we had a Chiefs of Staff organisation functioning in war for the first time.'[35] These explanations have much merit, but there were also, other deeper factors at work.

The tensions between the army and the government pre-dated 1914. (Except in the special case of Admiral Fisher, relations with the navy were far less problematic.) There began a series of episodes, all of which are individually well-known, but which deserve reframing as a broader crisis of civil-military relations. (See also John Gooch's chapter in this volume.) A major cause of this crisis was the Liberal administration's policy of introducing Home Rule for Ireland; a Bill to this effect was introduced in 1912. That summer, the Conservative leader Andrew Bonar Law stated that 'I can imagine no length of resistance to which Ulster will go in which I shall not be ready to support them.'[36] This can only have encouraged dissidence amongst Protestant Unionist officers, many of whom had strong Irish connections, and who were congenitally distrustful of a Liberal Government. In March 1914, the Curragh 'incident' or 'mutiny' took place. This involved officers making clear that they would rather resign or be dismissed rather than take part in the 'coercion' of Ulster to accept Home Rule. The government rapidly backed away from confrontation. The outbreak of war put the Home Rule issue into temporary hibernation, but the problem had not been solved.

The appointment of Kitchener to the Cabinet in August 1914 must have seemed like a masterstroke. With this great military hero at the War Office, what Conservative would dare attack the government's handling of the fighting? It didn't work out like that, and not only because of Lord K.'s difficult personality and dubious competence in the role. When the war reached stalemate, and with the troops lacking the munitions they needed to make a breakthrough on the Western Front, leading military men were in a position to make a difficult political situation worse. On 14 May 1915, *The Times* published a shocking despatch by military correspondent Charles Repington. Contradicting a speech by the Prime Minister, H.H. Asquith, it blamed the recent British setback at Aubers Ridge on a shortage of high explosives. Repington denied colluding with Sir John French, Commander-in-Chief of the BEF, but the article certainly reflected his views.[37] French may have been searching for someone else to blame; perhaps he was seeking revenge for the fact that he had been pushed out as CIGS at the time of the Curragh incident. Anyhow, he seemed willing to play rough, without much concern for the consequences for the government. But it was neither the 'shell scandal' nor even the ongoing failure at the Dardanelles that was the direct cause of the crisis that forced Asquith to form a coalition government. Rather, it was the resignation of Fisher as First Sea Lord, after a clash with Churchill over naval dispositions, that triggered the end of the Liberal government. Churchill, however, was largely to blame, as he had himself insisted on recalling the aged and unbalanced Fisher to service after the outbreak of war.

This is not the place to review all of the conflicts between generals and politicians that occurred over the succeeding years, but we may note some key incidents. The government's failure to halt more quickly the executions of the Easter Rebels in Ireland was arguably a sign that the military were out of control. In 1918, Frederick Maurice, the former Director of Military operations and still a serving soldier, wrote to the press to charge the government with having starved the Western Front of troops prior to the Ludendorff offensive. Maurice may not have deliberately conspired to bring down the government (which at any rate survived) but such actions inevitably threatened to undermine it. Post-war, the 1920 debate over the previous year's massacre at Amritsar saw a clash between the supporters of its perpetrator, General Dyer, and those in the government who deplored his actions (but who did not actually punish him). Henry Wilson, CIGS from 1918 to 1922, was violently opposed to Lloyd George's decision to negotiate with Sinn Féin. After his retirement he was elected to Parliament; it is unclear how much trouble he might have caused had he not then been murdered by the IRA. During the Chanak crisis, which triggered the end of the Lloyd George coalition, Charles Harington, the commander of the Allied forces in Turkey, straightforwardly ignored government instructions to deliver an ultimatum to the Kemalists. In one sense, this was entirely sensible, as by this means war was averted. Yet it is still striking that, on such a vital issue, ministers could not get their orders obeyed.

How did Churchill perceive these events, and what was their legacy for World War II? It is not clear that he discerned a civil-military crisis in the systemic sense. Of Douglas Haig, who succeeded French as commander of the BEF, he wrote: 'Inflexible, rigorously pedantic in his assertion of the professional point of view, he nevertheless at all times treated the Civil Power with respect and loyalty. Even when he knew that his recall was debated amongst the War Cabinet, he neither sought to marshal the powerful political forces which would have come to his aid, nor failed at any time in faithfulness to the Ministers under whom he was serving.' Haig never threatened resignation even when he knew the government was weak. On the other hand: 'Amid patent ill-success he never in his own technical sphere deferred to their wishes, however strongly those wishes were supported by argument, by public opinion – such as it was – or by the terribly unfolding facts.'[38] More broadly, Churchill complained in his memoirs of how the public came to believe that generals and admirals were better suited than the politicians to deal with war issues.

> The foolish doctrine was preached to the public through innumerable agencies that Generals and Admirals must be right on war matters, and civilians of all kinds must be wrong. These erroneous conceptions were inculcated billion-fold by the newspapers under the crudest forms. The feeble or presumptuous politician is portrayed cowering in his office, intent in the crash of the world on Party intrigues or personal glorification, fearful of responsibility, incapable of aught save shallow phrase-making. To him enters the calm, noble, resolute figure of the great Commander by land or sea, resplendent in uniform, glittering with decorations, irradiated with the lustre of the hero, shod with the science and armed with the panoply of war. This sturdy figure, devoid of the slightest thought of self, offers his clear far-sighted guidance and counsel for vehement action – or artifice or wise delay. But his advice is rejected; his sound plans put aside; his courageous initiative baffled by political chatterboxes and incompetents.[39]

Churchill also disapproved of generals writing diaries. Wilson had kept one, referring dismissively to politicians as 'the Frocks,' and excerpts were published in a biography that appeared in 1927.[40] 'The reputation of the late Sir Henry Wilson was grievously affected by his devoted widow's ill-considered publication of his night-thoughts,' Churchill wrote.[41] One can well imagine his concern, on becoming Prime Minister in 1940, that the jealousies between soldiers and statesmen might recur. One can also guess his feelings had he known that Alanbrooke was keeping a somewhat intemperate journal.

Thus, Churchill's experience of civil-military tensions in the period surrounding the First World War likely influenced his expectations and conduct of the Second. At the same time, it is worth asking why the earlier crisis faded away, such that it did not blow up again after 1939. One might hazard that, if Liberal-led governments were distasteful to many high-ranking officers, the Conservative-dominated climate of the interwar years was much more congenial to them. The two, weak minority Labour governments did little to provoke conflict with the military. One significant civil-military dispute did occur during the Phoney War. Relations between Leslie Hore-Belisha, the Secretary of State for War, and the army's higher command collapsed. Hore-Belisha's behaviour was in truth very trying, though there have been allegations that some of his critics were motivated by anti-Semitism. Chamberlain dismissed him, effectively resolving the matter. However difficult Churchill's relations with his generals at times became, none of them offered any kind of subversive test of the kind that had repeatedly cropped up in the decade after 1912. Alanbrooke, for one, was not very interested in politics, but nor was there any obvious ideological divide between him and Churchill. He respected Attlee, but it seems he would have liked Churchill to hang on in Downing Street after 1945, if only for the sake of continuity.[42]

But what of the Chiefs of Staff, the organisation that Alanbrooke gave credit for the avoidance of the strife of the Great War? The failures of the Boer War seemed to demand efforts to rationalise planning. The Committee for Imperial Defence (CID) was created in 1902 and was given a permanent secretariat two years later. The position of Chief of the General Staff was created in 1904 (in place of the term Commander-in-Chief of the Forces) and the word 'Imperial' was added in 1909. The creation of the RAF in 1918 created a new factor. The embryo of a new system came into being during the Chanak Crisis, when the Chiefs of Staff began to meet informally to consider a coordinated response. A few months later, in mid-1923, the Chiefs of Staff Sub-Committee (COS) of the CID began meeting officially. However, the new organisation did not prove effective. The role of air-power was a particular point of controversy and during the 1935 Abyssinian Crisis, various tensions came out into the open.[43] During the Phoney War, though, Churchill, as First Lord of the Admiralty, challenged what he saw as the Committee's excessive power.[44] On becoming Prime Minister, he moved to centralise control in his own hands. He appointed himself Minister of Defence, to be serviced by the War Cabinet Secretariat's military section under Hastings Ismay, and created a new Defence Committee. In John Gooch's words, 'Churchill had created a combined battle headquarters under the direct supervision of the head of government, through which he could exercise continuous direct and personal control over the formulation of military policy and the conduct of military operations.'[45]

Alanbrooke – who was put in charge of in charge of UK home defence in the summer of 1940 – thought that these arrangements were perilous, at least insofar as resisting an invasion was concerned. He recalled that 'in the defensive organisation of this country, there was no form of combined command over the three services.' He feared that, had the Germans landed, Churchill would have attempted this coordination role himself. 'This would have been wrong and highly dangerous, with his impulsive nature and tendency to arrive at decisions through a process of intuition, as opposed to "logical" approach. Heaven knows where he might have led us!'[46] One might say that by this stage, Churchill had inherited the kernel of an effective organisation, and reformed it in fairly a sensible way, but that weaknesses remained, and that his own overbearing behaviour risked causing problems. In other words, the machine could be made to work – with the right personalities.

John Dill, who succeeded Edmund Ironside as CIGS in May 1940, was not the right man. Dill was a remarkable individual, and Alanbrooke rated him highly, but he failed to establish a good rapport with the Prime Minister. Dill contested Churchill's flights of fancy but did so on paper rather than in person, which did not go down well. He was further hampered by a strategic situation which left him little room for manoeuvre in response to Churchill's demands for action. Churchill, who unfairly nicknamed him 'Dilly-Dally,' soon concluded that he had made a mistaken appointment. Alex Danchev argues persuasively that Dill made a major contribution nevertheless. 'It was he, above all, who responded to the imperative of the moment and established the wearying but constructive adversarial relationship between Churchill and the chiefs of staff on which Brooke built so successfully for the duration of the war.'[47] Churchill's first choice for a replacement was Nye, who told him that Alanbrooke was the only conceivable candidate. [48] 'Yes, everyone thinks so,' replied Churchill, who nonetheless worried that Alanbrooke was 'very independent.'[49]

On 16 November 1941, at Chequers, Churchill told Alanbrooke that Dill would be standing down, and asked him to be his successor. After some hesitation, Alanbrooke accepted. He was wrenched, on account both of his feelings for Dill and of his appreciation of the dimensions of the task that faced him. Churchill 'then went on to explain the importance he attached to the appointment and the fact that the Chiefs of Staff Committee must be the body to direct military events over the whole world. He also stated that his relations with me must for now approximate those of a Prime Minister to one of his ministers.'[50] However, although Alanbrooke was appointed as CIGS, it was not until March 1942 that he took over the chairmanship of the COS, from Dudley Pound, the ailing First Sea Lord.

The attack at Pearl Harbor was, of course, a great relief to the British (though in the short term it triggered a series of stinging defeats in the Far East). Churchill seized the initiative by striking out for a conference with Roosevelt in Washington DC, codenamed Arcadia. Here the British and Americans agreed, in principle, a 'Germany First' strategy – but the practice was somewhat different, as the US Navy was determined to concentrate on Japan. Churchill had taken with him Dill (who was technically CIGS until 25 December) but not Alanbrooke, who was still bedding himself into his new role. After the conference, Dill stayed on in Washington as Churchill's personal representative. He fulfilled the role of diplomatic buffer effectively until his death in 1944. His tactful handling of the Americans involved making clear to them that he and Alanbrooke did not share the Prime Minister's more wayward notions.[51] On the other hand, he had to navigate the complexities of US Military politics. In January 1942, Dill wrote to Alanbrooke:

never have I seen a country so utterly unprepared for war – and so soft. […] The chief trouble in Washington is lack of organisation. There are no regular meetings of their Chiefs of Staff, and if they do meet there is no Secretariat to record their proceedings. They have no joint planners and no executive planning staff. […] Then there is the great difficulty of getting the stuff over to the President. He just sees the Chiefs of Staff at odd times, and, again, no record. There is no such thing as a cabinet meeting, and yet the Secretaries of War, Navy, etc., are supposed to function.'[52]

Things did improve, though considerable chaos remained, requiring in-
genious improvisation and the use of informal channels. George C. Marshall,
Chief of Staff of the US Army, created a new organisation, the Joint Chiefs
of Staff (JCS). He also initiated a further body, the Combined Chiefs of Staff
(CCS), which brought together the JCS and the British COS. This was over
the opposition of Alanbrooke, who feared that, being based in Washington,
the CCS would be dominated by the Americans.[53]

Marshall travelled to London in April 1942. Here, for the first time, he
met Alanbrooke, who was not much impressed. He found Marshall charming
but thought him no strategist: 'A big man, and a very great gentlemen, who
inspired trust, but did not impress me by the ability of his brain.'[54] According
to Harry Hopkins, FDR's éminence grise, who was also present: 'Brooke made
an unfavourable impression on Marshall, who thinks that although he may be
a good fighting man, he hasn't got Dill's brains.'[55] Though he rated Charles
Portal, Chief of The Air Staff, higher, Marshall's later assessment of Alanbrooke
was more generous: 'He had had a hard schooling in the battles of the Somme
in earlier years and had suffered the shock of the highly modernized Nazi Army.
This, for a year or more in our earlier negotiations, made it difficult for him to
meet our theory and battle inexperience with his practical and rather desperate
experience. All of this washed away as the War developed and we came more and
more into mutual understanding.'[56] But not, one might say, completely.

Marshall had not succeeded in selling the 'Germany First' strategy to Ernest
King, head of the US Navy, who continued to concentrate 'almost entirely
on the Pacific war.[57] But he now tried to sell to the British plans for a cross-
channel invasion as soon as the autumn of 1942. They thought this unrealistic,
given the shortage of available troops and the strength of the Germans. In the
words of Hopkins, at a dinner at 10 Downing Street, 'Churchill, displaying his
talents as a military historian, spent most of the evening discussing the Civil
War and the (First) World War and never really came to grips with our main
business, although General Brooke got into it enough to indicate that he had
a great many misgivings about our proposal.'[58] However, the British leadership
collectively failed to make clear to the Americans the extent of their concerns.
Albert C. Wedemeyer, one of Marshall's top planners, complained in his memoirs they had never expressed open opposition but had merely suggested that
there might be problems with particular aspects of what was proposed. 'I am
not suggesting that the will to deceive was a personal characteristic of any of
the participants,' he wrote, in rather jaundiced fashion. 'But when matters of
the state were involved, our British opposite numbers had elastic scruples. [...]
What I witnessed was the British power of diplomatic finesse in its finest hour,
a power that had been developed over centuries of successful international
intrigue, cajolery, and tacit compulsions.'[59]

One might rather suggest that, in addition to the familiar problem of
'two nations divided by a common language,' the British, rather than being

purposely duplicitous, were instead using the 'weapons of the weak.' Desperate to secure the commitment of US forces, they carefully avoided saying anything that might jeopardise that goal. Marshall's team went away believing that they had obtained a joint commitment to an attack across the Channel, definitely in 1943, and possibly in 1942.[60] When the true extent of British doubts became clear, the Americans felt betrayed. Garnering the support of Roosevelt, Alanbrooke and Churchill succeeded in deflecting the Americans away from an immediate Second Front in Europe and towards the November 1942 'Torch' landings in North Africa. Some top US soldiers became convinced that the British did not want to launch across the Channel at all. Eisenhower recorded Alanbrooke telling him, shortly before the invasion of Sicily, 'that he would be glad to reconsider the cross-Channel project, even to the extent of eliminating that bold concept from accepted Allied Strategy.'[61] Certainly the experience of the 1942 Dieppe Raid gave many grounds for caution.

Alanbrooke was slated to command Overlord, the invasion operation, and was looking forward to leading in the field. But in August 1943, at the start of the first Quebec conference ('Quadrant'), US War Secretary Henry L. Stimson wrote to the President:

> We cannot now rationally hope to be able to cross the Channel and come to grips with our German enemy under a British commander. His Prime Minister and his Chief of the Imperial Staff are frankly at variance with such a proposal. The shadows of Passchendaele and Dunkerque still hang too heavily over the imaginations of these leaders of his government. Though they have rendered lip service to the operation, their hearts are not in it and it will require more independence, more faith, and more vigor than it is reasonable to expect we can find in any British commander to overcome the natural difficulties of such an operation carried on in such an atmosphere of his government.[62]

A few days later, FDR and Churchill agreed that an American should take the command. Churchill broke the news to Alanbrooke as they looked down on the St. Lawrence river from the terrace of the Citadel. 'He had just returned from being with the President and Harry Hopkins,' recorded Alanbrooke. 'Apparently the latter pressed hard for the appointment of Marshall as Supreme Commander for the cross Channel operations and as far as I can gather Winston gave in, in spite of having previously promised me the job!'[63] (In due course it was Eisenhower, not Marshall, who was appointed Supreme Allied Commander of the Allied Expeditionary Force (SHAEF).) For Alanbrooke this was 'the bitterest pill he ever had to swallow.'[64] It was made harder by Churchill's failure to express any commiseration or remorse for the loss of 'what I had looked forward to as being something of a climax.'[65] Churchill may simply have been embarrassed.[66] Alanbrooke came to accept it was the right decision, which was a logical one given that the Americans were the ones providing the bulk of the forces.[67] However, the US desire to lead the operation was influenced not only by this *realpolitik* factor but by broader strategic differences amongst the two allies.[68]

The difficulties and conflicts persisted up until D-Day and well beyond, indeed into the very final phase of the war. Indeed, Alanbrooke's diary was quite restrained in comparison to that of Joseph Stilwell, aka 'Vinegar Joe,' who commanded US forces in the China-Burma-India theatre. A minor feature of the November 1943 Cairo conference there was a dispute with Admiral King over the possibility of landing craft being diverted from the far East to the Aegean. According to Alanbrooke, the meeting 'became somewhat heated.'[69] According to Stilwell, 'Brooke got nasty and King got good & sore. Brooke is an arrogant bastard.'[70] Alanbrooke recalled that his disagreements with Churchill made it harder to maintain a united front. The Prime Minister 'used to make matters rather difficult for me with Marshall with statements he would make, which Marshall would often think were inspired by me and they were not inspired by me at all.' This was especially the case with respect to Churchill's 'Balkan liking,' a geopolitical preference for operations there, which raised Marshall's hackles. 'And I couldn't go to him and say, I don't agree with a word my Prime Minister is saying.'[71]

Yet, in spite of their manifold differences and frequent contretemps Churchill and Alanbrooke shared some fundamental assumptions. W.G.F. Jackson argues: 'Like Churchill, Brooke was wedded to the traditional British maritime strategy of weakening Continental powers by blockade and peripheral operations, carried out in areas where the enemy found it most difficult to deploy and support large armies.'[72] From the side-lines at Quadrant, Canadian Prime Minister W.L. Mackenzie King noted the Americans' wish for an early stroke across the channel, matched by a desire not to press the invasion of Italy beyond the occupation of Sicily. 'They feel that attacking up in the North of Italy means that the Germans will be able to entrench themselves there as to make little headway.'[73] These differences of view explain the controversy over Operation Anvil, renamed Dragoon, the post-D-Day invasion of Southern France. This diverted effort from the Italian campaign – and thereby sacrificed the possibility of the allies strengthening their influence in Central Europe. Churchill cabled Roosevelt: 'Let us resolve not to wreck one great campaign for the sake of winning the other. Both can be won.'[74] It was in vain. Alanbrooke observed that the President's reply left his real reasons until the last paragraph: 'Then you find that owing to the coming presidential election it is impossible to contemplate any action with a Balkan flavour irrespective of its strategic merits.'[75]

The tensions diminished only slightly during the war's closing stages. The British secured a minor victory at the second Quebec conference ('Octagon') in September 1944. At a meeting of the CCS, King, over his violent objections, was forced to accept the participation of the British Fleet 'in the main operations against Japan in the Pacific.'[76] He resented intrusion onto his turf for, what he (rightly) regarded as political reasons, but was overruled by his own colleagues. The problems in directing the fighting in Europe were driven partly by personality issues. Alanbrooke doubted Eisenhower's capacity, and at the same time had to manage the considerable ego of his protégé Bernard Montgomery, now in charge of 21st Army Group. At the Malta conference in January 1945, Marshall, recalled, there was 'a very acid meeting' at which he and Alanbrooke presided for their respective countries.

> [Alanbrooke] said the British chiefs of staff were very much worried by the influence on General Eisenhower of General Bradley, and I think he mentioned General Patton. And I said. 'Well, Brooke, they are not nearly as much worried as the American chiefs of staff are worried about the immediate pressures and influence of Mr. Churchill on General Eisenhower. The president practically never sees Eisenhower, never writes to him – that is at my advice because he is an Allied commander – and we are deeply concerned by the pressures of the prime minister and the fact of the proximity of the British chiefs of staff, so I think your worries are on the wrong foot.'[77]

It should be no surprise that political-military relationships, and inter-Allied relationships, often flared up under the pressure of global war. 'I think it's extraordinary that they didn't flare up more than they did,' said Alanbrooke later.[78] The fights with the Americans were provoked in part by differences of culture. But they were also often triggered by the efforts of the British to punch above their weight, and were generally resolved by them bowing to the realities of their situation. Churchill and Alanbrooke's relationship should certainly not be idealised. The former's habit of writing to commanders behind the back of the CIGS was not merely infuriating but potentially dangerous.[79] But their strange manner of working, replete with bust-ups, was in many ways productive. On one occasion, Churchill told Ismay that Alanbrooke hated him and would have to be replaced. When told this, Alanbrooke replied: 'I don't hate him, I love him, but when the day comes that I tell him he is right when I believe him to be wrong, it will be time for him to get rid of me.'[80]

As we have seen, there was no repeat of the earlier crisis in civil-military relations. When trying to persuade Bryant to tone down the text of *The Turn of the Tide*, Cabinet Secretary Norman Brook admitted that 'Mr Churchill was sometimes critical of Commanders in discussions in Defence Committee and sometimes, perhaps, in the War Cabinet itself.' But, he argued, Mr Churchill had where possible reserved those criticisms for his smaller meetings with the COS. 'In any event [...] this sort of bickering between the "frocks" and the "brass hats" was very much less common in the Second War than in the First.'[81] Yet in a sense, the spectre of the First War continued to haunt the actors in Second. Some leading Americans believed that the memory of the slaughter made Churchill and Alanbrooke too cautious with respect to Overlord. Perhaps more significant was Churchill's memory of the struggles between the generals and the politicians in 1914–1918. Couldn't Winston trust his generals? In practice, yes, he could, but we can understand his behaviour better if we appreciate that he wasn't quite sure of the answer himself. He could not take the 'non-crisis' for granted. In 1942, Alanbrooke rejected a high-level field command. 'I had been offered the finest command I could hope for, and I had turned it down!,' he remembered later. 'I could not put the real reasons to Winston which were connected with the fact that, rightly or wrongly, I felt I could exercise some control over him.'[82] What Alanbrooke perhaps didn't realise was that, through the late nights, the shouting, and the banging of tables, Churchill was working through his anxiety that he might not be able to control *him*.

Notes

1 *Triumph in the West* publicity materials, Alanbrooke Papers, 12/6, Liddell Hart Centre, King's College, London. For Alanbrooke's dislike of appearing on TV, see Bryant's letters to Alanbrooke of 30 Aug. and 1 Sept. 1959, in the same file.
2 David Reynolds, *In Command of History: Churchill Fighting and Writing the Second World* War (Random House: New York, 2005), pp. 407–8, 518–22.
3 Hilary Corke, 'Critic on the Hearth: Documentary,' *The Listener*, 12 Nov. 1959.
4 George Murray, 'Couldn't Winston Trust His Generals?,' *Daily Mail*, 2 Nov. 1959.
5 Alex Danchev and Dan Todman (eds.), *War Diaries 1939–1945: Field Marshal Lord Alanbrooke* (Weidenfeld & Nicolson: London, 2001), p. 3 (entry for 28 Sept. 1939).
6 Alanbrooke gave permission for a series of religiously-themed extracts from his diary to be published in the May–June 1966 issue of the magazine *Practical Christianity*. Copy in Alanbrooke Papers, 12/7.
7 P.J. Grigg to Arthur Bryant, 16 Sept. 1956 (copy), Alanbrooke Papers, 12/4.
8 Danchev and Todman, *War Diaries*, pp. 590–1, 713 (entry for 10 Sept. 1944 and post-war notes).
9 'The Alanbrooke Diaries,' BBC Television, 8 Feb. 1957. Available on YouTube at https://www.youtube.com/watch?v=Qhx4z4jGroA&t=749s.
10 See his remarks in 'The Churchill Obituary,' 28 Jan. 2015, BBC2 England. https://learningonscreen.ac.uk/ondemand/index.php/prog/0892AE76?bcast= 114997939 (Accessed 15 Nov. 2021).
11 Lord Moran, *Churchill: Taken from the Diaries of Lord Moran: The Struggle for Survival, 1940–1965* (Houghton Mifflin: Boston, 1966), p. 765.
12 Winston Churchill to Lord Alanbrooke, 8 May 1946, Alanbrooke Papers, 6/4.
13 See the April 1951 exchange between the two: Churchill Papers, CHUR 4/322/137-143, Churchill Archives Centre, Cambridge (henceforward CAC).
14 Andrew Roberts, *Eminent Churchillians* (Phoenix: London, 1995), p. 288.
15 For the textual issues, see the Introduction to Danchev and Todman, *War Diaries*.
16 Arthur Bryant, 'The Making of The Turn of The Tide,' in David Fraser, *Alanbrooke* (Hamlyn Paperbacks: Feltham, Middlesex, 1983), pp. 540–63, at 558; Arthur Bryant, *The Turn of The Tide: A History of the War Years: Based on the Diaries of Field-Marshal Lord Alanbrooke, Chief of the Imperial General Staff* (Doubleday & Company: New York, 1957), ix.
17 Moran, *Winston Churchill*, pp. 762, 769.

18 Anthony Harrison, *Archie Nye: A Memoir* (privately published, 1980), p. 12. Copy in Cambridge University Library Rare Books Room, GBR/0115/RCS/RCMS 46.

19 Arthur Harris to Bryant, 19 Feb. 1957 (copy), Alanbrooke Papers, 12/9.

20 Danchev and Todman, *War Diaries*, p. 451 (entry for 30 Aug. 1943).

21 Andrew Cunningham to James Somerville, 19 Dec. 1943, in Michael Simpson (ed.), The Cunningham Papers: Selections from the Private and Official Correspondence of Admiral of the Fleet Viscount Cunningham of Hyndhope (Ashgate for the Naval Records Society: Aldershot, 1999), p. 157. See also the editorial comment at pp. 155–56, and Viscount Cunningham, *A Sailor's Odyssey* (Hutchinson & Co.: London, 1951).

22 Moran, *Churchill*, p. 761.

23 Fraser, *Alanbrooke*; Andrew Roberts, *Masters and Commanders: The Military Geniuses Who Led the West to Victory in World War II* (Penguin Books: London, 2008); Andrew Sangster, *Alan Brooke: Churchill's Right-Hand Critic: A Reappraisal of Lord Alanbrooke* (Casemate: Oxford & Philadelphia, 2021).

24 R.F. Grattan, 'A study in comparative strategy using the Alanbrooke diaries,' *Management Decision*, 42 (2004), pp. 1024–36.

25 Raymond Mortimer, 'Impetuous Titan,' *Sunday Times*, 17 Feb. 1957.

26 'Statesman and Solider,' *The Economist*, 23 Feb. 1957.

27 See L.C. Hollis to Brooke, 18 Dec. 1944, enclosing A.F. Brooke, C. Portal and Andrew Cunningham, 'Strategy in North West Europe,' 18 Dec. 1944, Alanbrooke Papers, Bryant Papers, N34. This minute to Churchill was not appended to the Chiefs of Staff records for reasons of secrecy, apparently because it was critical of Eisenhower's strategy. On the sensitivities of record-keeping and the opaque quality of many official documents, see also Arthur Bryant, *Triumph in the West 1943–1946* (Collins: London, 1959), p. 395, Fraser, *Alanbrooke*, pp. 35, 572, and Roberts, *Masters and Commanders*, pp. xxxiv–xxxvii.

28 B.H. Liddell Hart, 'Western War Strategy: A Critical Analysis of the Alanbrooke Diaries,' *Royal United Services Institution Journal*, 105 (1960), pp. 52–61, at 53.

29 Alanbrooke to P.J. Grigg, 23 Aug. 1945, P.J. Grigg Papers, PJGG/9/7, CAC; Danchev and Todman, *War Diaries*, p. 713 (post-war note); P.J. Grigg, *Prejudice and Judgement* (Jonathan Cape: London, 1948), pp. 417–20; H.F. Oxbury, 'Grigg, Sir (Percy) James (1890–1964), public servant,' *Oxford Dictionary of National Biography*. Retrieved 22 Nov. 2021, from https://www.oxforddnb.com/view/10.1093/ref:odnb/9780198614128.001.0001/odnb-9780198614128-e-33585.

30 Fraser, *Alanbrooke*, pp. 215–16.

31 Archibald Nye to Arthur Bryant, 29 Apr. 1957, with appended comments on *The Turn of The Tide*, Arthur Bryant Papers, F7, Liddell Hart Centre. A copy of the comments can also be found in the Alanbrooke Papers, 12/4.

32 Harrison, *Archie Nye*, p. 11.

33 Lord Templewood, 'Alanbrooke and Churchill,' *The Spectator*, 22 Feb. 1957.

34 'A Prime Minister Remembers,' *The Listener*, 22 Jan. 1959. Attlee's admiring review of *The Turn of The Tide* appeared in *World Books Broadsheet*, Aug. 1958, copy in Alanbrooke Papers, 12/5.

35 'The Alanbrooke Diaries.'

36 'Mr. Bonar Law,' *Sunday Times*, 28 July 1912.

37 A.J.A Morris, *Reporting the First World War: Charles Repington, 1914–1918* (Cambridge University Press: Cambridge, 2015), pp. 182–84.

38 Winston S. Churchill, *Great Contemporaries* (G.P. Puttnam's Sons: New York, 1937), pp. 193–94.

39 Winston S. Churchill, *The World Crisis 1916–1918 Part I* (Thornton Butterworth: London, 1927), p. 244.

40 C.E. Callwell, *Field-Marshal Sir Henry Wilson: His Life and Diaries*, 2 Vols. (Cassell & Co.: London, 1927).

41 Churchill, *Great Contemporaries*, p. 196.

42 Danchev and Todman, *War Diaries*, p. 712 (entry for 26 July 1945).

43 Stephen Roskill, *Hankey: Man of Secrets: Vol. II 1919–1931* (Collins: London, 1972), p. 290; John Gooch, 'The Chiefs of Staff and The Higher Organization for Defence in Britain, 1904–1984,' *Naval War College Review*, 39 (1986), pp. 53–65.

44 John Ehrman, *Grand Strategy Vol. V: August 1943–September 1944* (HMSO: London, 1956), p. 17.

45 Gooch, 'The Chiefs of Staff,' p. 58.

46 Danchev and Todman, *War Diaries*, p. 96 (post-war note).

47 Alex Danchev, 'Dill, Sir John Greer (1881–1944), army officer,' Oxford Dictionary of National Biography. Retrieved 29 Nov. 2021, from https://www.oxforddnb.com/view/10.1093/ref:odnb/9780198614128.001.0001/odnb-9780198614128-e-32826.

48 Harrison, *Archie Nye*, p. 12.

49 Letter from Nye, *Journal of the Royal United Service Institution*, 111 (1966), pp. 169–70. See also Nye's letter to Bryant (with enclosed cutting, 8 June 1966, Alanbrooke Papers, 12/15.

50 Danchev and Todman, *War Diaries*, p. 199 (entry for 16 Nov. 1941).

51 Alex Danchev, *Very Special Relationship: Field-Marshall Sir John Dill and the Anglo-American Alliance, 1941–44* (Brassey's Defence Publishers: London, 1986).

52 John Dill to Alanbrooke, 3 Jan. 1942, Alanbrooke Papers, 6/2. Extracts from the letter are quoted in Bryant, *Turn of the Tide*, pp. 239–40.

53 Roberts, *Masters and Commanders*, pp. 74–75.

54 Danchev and Todman, *War Diaries*, p. 247 (post-war note).

55 Robert Sherwood, *The White House Papers of Harry L. Hopkins: An Intimate History Vol. II: January 1942-July 1945* (Eyre & Spottiswoode: London, 1949), p. 528.

56 Bryant, *Turn of the Tide*, p. 301. On Portal, see Larry I. Bland and Joellen K. Bland (eds.), *George C. Marshall: Interviews and Reminiscences for Forrest C. Pogue* (George C. Marshall Research Foundation: Lexington, VA, 1991), p. 429.

57 Dill to Alanbrooke, 5 May 1942, Alanbrooke Papers, 6/2.

58 Sherwood, *White House Papers*, p. 528.

59 Albert C. Wedemeyer, *Wedemeyer Reports!* (Henry Holt & Co.: New York, 1958), pp. 105–6.

60 Roberts, *Masters and Commanders*, pp. 157–60.

61 Dwight D. Eisenhower, *Crusade in Europe* (William Heinemann Ltd.: London, 1948), p. 185.

62 Henry L. Stimson to Franklin D. Roosevelt, 10 Aug. 1943, *Foreign Relations of the United States: The Conferences at Washington and Quebec 1943* (United States Government Printing Office: Washington, DC, 1970), p. 496.

63 Danchev and Todman, *War Diaries*, p. 441 (entry for 15 Aug. 1943).

64 Hastings Ismay to Churchill, 25 Apr. 1946, Churchill Papers, CHUR/2/144/20.

65 Interview with Alanbrooke, 5 May 1961, George C. Marshall Foundation, https://www.marshallfoundation.org/library/wp-content/uploads/sites/16/2014/06/Alanbrooke_Final_59.pdf (consulted 2 Dec. 2021).

66 Mortimer, 'Impetuous Titan'; Bland and Bland, *George C. Marshall Interviews*, p. 344.

67 Interview with Alanbrooke, 5 May 1961.

68 Memorandum by Stimson enclosed with Stimson to Harry Hopkins, 4 Aug. 1943, *Foreign Relations of the United States: Washington and Quebec*, pp. 444–52.

69 Danchev and Todman, *War Diaries*, p. 478 (entry for 23 Nov. 1943 and post-war note).

70 Joseph Stilwell diary transcript, 23 Nov. 1943, Hoover Institution Archives, https://digitalcollections.hoover.org/internal/media/dispatcher/213318/full (consulted 1 Dec. 2021).

71 Interview with Alanbrooke, 5 May 1961.

72 W.G.F. Jackson, *'Overlord': Normandy 1944* (University of Delaware Press: Newark, DL, 1979), p. 46. See also Greg Smith, 'British Strategic Culture and General Sir Alan Brooke during the Second World War,' *Canadian Military Journal*, 18 (2018), pp. 23–44.

73 W.L. Mackenzie King diary, 10 Aug. 1943, https://www.bac-lac.gc.ca/eng/discover/politics-government/prime-ministers/william-lyon-mackenzie-king/Pages/diaries-william-lyon-mackenzie-king.aspx (consulted 2 Dec. 2021).

74 Churchill to Roosevelt, 28 June 1944, Warren F. Kimball (ed.) Churchill and Roosevelt: The Complete Correspondence Vol. III: Alliance Declining February 1944–April 1945 (Princeton University Press: Princeton, NJ, 1984), p. 219.

75 Danchev and Todman, *War Diaries*, p. 564 (entry for 30 June 1944).

76 Meeting of the Combined Chiefs of Staff, 14 Sept. 1944, *Foreign Relations of the United States: The Conference at Quebec 1944* (United States government Printing Office: Washington, DC, 1972), p. 335.

77 Bland and Bland, *George C. Marshall Interviews*, pp. 540–41.

78 Interview with Alanbrooke, 5 May 1961.

79 Fraser, *Alanbrooke*, p. 571.

80 Bryant, *Triumph in the West*, p. 19.

81 Comments on *The Turn of The Tide* enclosed with Norman Brook to Bryant, 18 Sept. 1956, copy in Alanbrooke Papers, 12/4.

82 Danchev and Todman, *War Diaries*, p. 294 (post-war note).

11

TRUMAN AND MACARTHUR

Rendezvous with History

Richard B. Frank

The relief of General of the Armies Douglas MacArthur by President Harry S. Truman in April 1951 ranks as one of the most—if not the most—dramatic episode in civil-military relations in the history of this nation. All discussions of this event pick up the story at least months before April 1951. MacArthur's esteemed biographer, D. Clayton James, offers July 8, 1950, when Truman appointed MacArthur to command United Nations (UN) forces in Korea as the date the countdown commenced to the relief.[1] This examination argues that the real countdown begins at least in 1941—and not with Truman as a principal. It had an ominous foreshadowing in 1932. Moreover, narratives of American history typically exhibit Truman's dismissal of MacArthur as the defining episode of their relationship. Here light will be cast over perhaps what should be recognized as at least as defining an episode in their relationship when they worked in cooperation to achieve one the most noble actions to grace this nation's history.

Bonus Army March

As to the first theme on the long route to Truman relieving MacArthur, we need to go far back, at least to 1941. Indeed, a case can be presented for still earlier dates that were clear milestones on the path to the events of April 1951. So how far back to we go? The first date to evaluate is May 1879. This is the month in which his parents conceived Douglas MacArthur. Would that we had then the possibility of applying modern medical technology to determine if in an embryonic state, we could identify markers warning that Douglas MacArthur was destined to violate his obligations to his civilian superiors.

DOI: 10.4324/9781003375630-11

While I may have suggested the date of May 1879 partly tongue in cheek, there can be no doubt that from an early age—and certainly by the time MacArthur graduated from West Point in 1901—he was imbued with a powerful sense that he was in the terms of that time a "Man of Destiny." Often such a creature by nature believes that many rules that govern others do not apply to him. MacArthur's predilections for distinctive dress in the field in World War I and World War II, and certain liberties he took with his uniform when the superintendent of West Point in the 1920s outwardly manifested a much more significant internal sense of greatness untethered to the norms applying to other mortals.[2]

American elites during his lifetime carried an overwhelmingly Eurocentric view of the world. MacArthur from youth learned to reject that view from his father Arthur. For heroic service at the Battle of Missionary Ridge in the Civil War, Arthur, then the "boy colonel" of his regiment, would eventually be awarded the Medal of Honor. Determination to emulate his father in this regard forms one braid among many of Douglas' his professional ambitions, but another stamped his worldview for life.

Former President Ulysses Grant returned from a world tour in 1879 convinced that the American future was in Asia. Grant's views encompassed not only the economic prospects of trade with Asia but also an American role as protector of peoples who would become free nations from outside aggressors as they emerged on the world stage. By happenstance, Grant first returned to American soil in San Francisco where then Captain Arthur MacArthur was then stationed. Grant conveyed his newfound vision to his former junior officer, who passed it on to Douglas. Inspired by Grant, Arthur wrote in a prescient paper that Western colonial rule over Asian peoples could not endure as those peoples naturally sought independence. At one level, Douglas' insistence on priority for this Southwest Pacific Theater in World War II and then for Korea in 1950–1951 fit perfectly with his colossal egocentric view that wherever he was, that was the center of gravity of American interests. But both also reflected his abiding Asia-centric view of American destiny radically at odds with the other elites with which he dealt.[3]

Arthur also established a family connection with the Philippines and the Filipinos. Arthur commanded American troops during the Philippine Insurrection, to mixed reviews. He clashed bitterly with William H. Taft, then civilian head of government and later president, over Philippine independence. His son served in the Philippines and by his account was enchanted. While both men were in their twenties, he established an enduring friendship with Manuel Quezon who became the paladin of Philippine Independence. But Quezon shrewdly concluded that independence would more likely accrue with the assistance of Americans like Douglas than armed rebellion. During his tours in the 1920s, Douglas passed an acid test with the Filipino elites, like Quezon. Most ex-patriots, however friendly they seemed in official settings, rigorously remained with other Whites in social settings after hours—with obvious racist implications. Douglas by contrast assiduously cultivated social relations with Filipino leaders like Quezon, where he treated them as intellectual and social equals—much to the resentment of other Whites who deemed him too close to the "Natives."[4]

The episode that forms a clear milestone on the path to April 1951 was the Bonus Army March in 1932. Very briefly, after World War I, Congress provided that a cash "bonus" would be paid to World War I veterans in 1945. The bonus amounted to about a thousand dollars which was a huge sum in 1932, particularly for a man with no job and perhaps a family at the height of the Great Depression. Hence, about 22,000 World War I veterans and family members came to Washington in the summer of 1932 to demonstrate in favor of legislation that authorized the government pay the "bonus" immediately. Congress defeated the bill and about half the marchers left. On July 27, President Herbert Hoover ordered the remaining Bonus Army Marchers cleared from public property in the District.

MacArthur was convinced that the marchers were puppets of communist agitation and that they posed a far graver danger to the government than later accounts credited. Hoover sent two orders to MacArthur expressly directing him to clear the marchers from the National Mall, but not to attempt to follow them across a bridge over the Anacostia River. MacArthur claimed not to have received the orders. The more likely facts are that the first message may not have reached MacArthur, but MacArthur deliberately refused to receive the officer with the second message, probably sensing it might prohibit him from doing what he believed was the right thing under the circumstances as he saw them. MacArthur sent the troops in the night to drive the marchers and families out of encampments in Anacostia. There were terrible scenes that seriously damaged Hoover and permanently blighted MacArthur's reputation in many quarters.

There are clearly ominous overtones to this episode for events in Korea. Although Hoover was probably the President MacArthur most esteemed, MacArthur effectively defied Hoover's orders. The implication of MacArthur's actions is that as the man on the spot, he thought he must be free to violate directives from his civilian superiors if he thought he knew better.[5]

The other part of the Bonus Army story is that it radically changed his image, at least in the more leftward precincts of America. He had been a dashing, valorous, charismatic combat leader in World War I, wounded and decorated multiple times. Then he was one of just two junior officers reaching general officer rank who retained a star. That rank gained him a posting as the Superintendent of West Point. MacArthur's war experience convinced him that West Point must prepare a different type of officer. Traditionally, West Point graduates entered a small regular army drawn from enlistees of very limited endowments who required strict discipline to become effective soldiers. MacArthur emerged from the war certain that he had seen the future: a mass army of

National Guardsmen, volunteers, or draftees. Such men possessed far higher attainments and could only be commanded effectively by officers who enjoyed their respect, not officers who ruled by fear. Around this vision, MacArthur attempted fundamental changes in scholastics, athletics, and a sharp curb on hazing. The academy's faculty fought a temporarily successful delaying campaign against MacArthur's reforms, but eventually MacArthur's reforms took hold for the better of the academy. Had MacArthur's career ended before the Bonus Army March, he would remain an ornament in the army's history, albeit of interest only to certain historians, of a courageous, effective World War I combat leader and reformer of West Point.[6]

But liberals, including Franklin Roosevelt, harbored the view that the Bonus Army March exposed MacArthur's barely veiled aspirations to become the "Man on Horseback." Roosevelt famously remarked to an aide that Huey Long was one of the two most dangerous men in America. When the aide asked the identity of the other individual, Roosevelt replied "Douglas MacArthur." (In the frequent retellings of this episode, Roosevelt's further comment that MacArthur's threat was merely latent is routinely omitted.) If it is correct to call MacArthur hysterical on the topic of communist influence in the United States at that time—and it is—it is likewise hysterical for his critics to charge that he harbored ambitions of becoming a dictator when no evidence of this exists in any known writing or saying he uttered.[7]

Trespasses Not Confronted

Truman inherited a fraught relationship between Washington and MacArthur from President Franklin D. Roosevelt and members of Roosevelt's administration, notably Secretary of War Henry Stimson and Chief of Staff General George C. Marshall. This situation developed in the months following Pearl Harbor. If you go back and look at those tumultuous months through the eyes of contemporaries, you see a very ugly picture of allied forces being almost uniformly defeated in places like Guam, Wake Island, Hong Kong, Malaya and Singapore, the Netherlands East Indies, and then Burma. Many of these defeats appeared humiliating.

This list followed in the wake of a parallel set of defeats in Europe militarily or morally between the Italian conquest of Ethiopia in October 1935 right up to the spring of 1942. By contrast, the sustained defense of the Bataan Peninsula until April 1942 seemed like a beacon of military effectiveness and heroism in a rolling nightmare. We know now it was not so simple, but that is the way it looked at the time. No small part of this apparent exemplar stemmed from MacArthur's communiqués, many authored by MacArthur himself. These communiqués were rife with exaggeration and falsehoods. Of the 142 communiqués issued by his command from December 1941 to March 1942, no fewer than 109 (77%) mentioned MacArthur.[8]

A combination of the appearance of MacArthur's brilliance as a general, the fact that he was a former chief of staff of the US Army–and thus his capture by the Japanese would be a propaganda bonanza for Tokyo—coupled with the regard Roosevelt and Marshall reposed in MacArthur at that time merged to produce Roosevelt's direct order for MacArthur to leave the Philippines. MacArthur stage managed his escape into a tremendous drama of a PT Boat run through Japanese-controlled waters and then a flight from Mindanao. On top of this, to preclude the Japanese from charging that MacArthur had abandoned his men in a cowardly manner, Marshall and Roosevelt bestowed the Medal of Honor on MacArthur, when objectively there was no basis for the award at that time.[9]

MacArthur's fame soared into stratospheric levels previously only touched by such public idols as Admiral George Dewey after the Battle of Manila Bay and Charles Lindberg after this famous flight. This fame, which would be further embroidered during the war by the Hearst Press and others who invested in MacArthur's greatness, shrouded MacArthur like an armored carapace that made him nearly invulnerable to the ordinary rules for handling senior officers.[10] In my reading, however, it would not be proper to charge that this idolatry went to MacArthur's head. The simple reason for this is that MacArthur probably viewed this as only the belated recognition by others of his manifest greatness!

From the time he reached Australia and for the rest of the war, MacArthur repeatedly showered Washington with messages carrying what can be fairly called provocations. Some reached the level of paranoid rants. Here is an example. During the preliminary negotiations between General Marshall and Admiral Ernest King, the Chief of Naval Operations, over what became the Guadalcanal operation in August 1942, King at one point threatened to conduct the operation without army support. He listed naval forces he would use which included the sparse naval forces then under MacArthur's command. At the same time, MacArthur learned that King had communicated directly with MacArthur's naval subordinate in violation of the chain of command. MacArthur fired a message off to Marshall claiming these actions demonstrated navy ambitions to the "general control of all operations in the Pacific theater." He said this was the product of a master plan which he had discovered "accidentally" when he was chief of staff of the army for the Navy to gain complete control over national defense and relegate the army to a training and supply organization. While petty service disputes littered the record of the American armed forces in the conflict, this burst through into the realm of unhinged paranoia.[11]

MacArthur sent other hysterical and paranoid messages to Washington predicting disaster if the national strategic priority for Europe was not reversed in his favor. These communications finally induced Secretary of War Stimson to secretly dispatch as a messenger Eddie Rickenbacker. He chose Rickenbacker because as the idolized top American ace of World War I, Rickenbacker's reputation cruised in the same orbits of public acclaim as MacArthur's. Stimson shrewdly recognized that MacArthur would far more likely regard Rickenbacker as a peer, far above the status of some staff colonel or general. But Rickenbacker's plane crashed into the Pacific on the trip out. He and the crew were presumed lost when miraculously twenty-four days later they were rescued. Rickenbacker delivered Stimson's orders for MacArthur to cease his campaign to generate more personal publicity for himself, to desist from his complaints that his theater was being starved of resources and to halt personal criticism of General Marshall.[12]

If Stimson's secret message abated MacArthur's behavior, it did so only temporarily. Further, no recitation of MacArthur's conduct far outside the perimeter of acceptable behavior in World War II would be complete without mention of his active nurturing, albeit episodic, of a bid to secure the Republican nomination for president in 1944. That MacArthur diverted even a minute of his attention to such actions is a gross manifestation of his flaunting of standards of behavior in an American army.[13]

There is another vital component to the loosening of control over MacArthur during World War II. This component is marked particularly by the deaths of Franklin Roosevelt and General John J. Pershing. The number of civilian or military superiors MacArthur respected was always small—assuming of course he did respect some. Of these, apart from Hoover who was out of power from 1933,[14] perhaps the three he probably held highest or at least some regards were Roosevelt, Pershing, and Stimson. All but Stimson were gone before Truman became president. When his mother died in 1935, another vital governor on his behavior dropped away.[15] MacArthur had been a general officer since 1918. He was a member of the generation of uniformed leaders who had with few exceptions passed out of active service and the public scene by World War II. Everyone else was junior by half a generation or more by age or several decades as a general officer by World War II. By the time of Korea, the senior uniformed leadership in Washington comprised exclusively men who had been junior officers when MacArthur was chief of staff.

Truman's Unlikely Rise

We need not ramble at length over Truman's background, but several points warrant note. If Douglas MacArthur's pedigree placed him in academy educated, army royalty, Harry S. Truman's originated from the mid-western, rural, and small-town middle class. His mother taught him to read by age five, but his formal education ended in high school, a mark of distinction in his environment and era. Truman's self-education was notable as a voracious reader, with many books on history and biography. As a National Guard officer, he knew combat firsthand commanding an artillery battery in World War I through several major battles. That battery excelled under his leadership. He bristled at the distain regular army officer radiated at National Guard officers. For good reason, he did not respect his West Point regimental commander. This colored his views of academy products whom he divided into great heroes, notably George C. Marshall, and detestable figures like George Armstrong Custer, George Patton, and Douglas MacArthur.[16]

While his comrades in the artillery battery produced the cornerstone of his political career, that career because linked to the corrupt Pendergast political machine of Kansas City, Missouri. This placed a cloud over his rise in politics. He shattered all reasonable expectations about a career ceiling by winning election as a US Senator. During World War II, he led what became known as the "Truman Committee" that exposed much waste and abuse in war contracts. This won him actual respect in Washington, and nation-wide but modest amount of public recognition.[17]

It also proved important that he remained in the army reserve during the interval between the wars. He attended camps for weeks at a time, listened to lectures by officers from the Command and General Staff College at nearby Fort Leavenworth, Kansas, and reached the rank of colonel. He met and immediately admired a regular officer named Jonathan Wainwright. When Roosevelt ordered MacArthur to leave the Philippines, he left Wainwright to face the ultimate humiliation of the surrender. This added a personal element to Truman's distaste for MacArthur. In sum, Truman's military background did not remotely match MacArthur's, but it was far greater than public figures who had no service, much less combat service.[18]

The Democratic Party establishment, mindful of Roosevelt's deteriorating health and profoundly worried that the then serving vice president, Henry Wallace, was too left wing and perhaps more than a bit unstable. As gimlet-eyed correspondent Allen Drury summed Wallace up: "He looks like a hayseed, talks like a prophet, and acts like an embarrassed school boy." On the first approach to see if Truman was interested in becoming Roosevelt's 1944 running mate, Truman delivered an emphatic and sincere no. He loved the Senate, glowed with newfound public respect over the work of the "Truman Committee," and understood how insignificant the vice president's role normally was. But the party regulars persevered. They secured Roosevelt's approval to make Truman the vice-presidential candidate on Roosevelt's successful 1944 reelection ticket.[19]

One anecdote provides insight into just how doubtful other senior Washington figures were of Truman's capacity for the job of president. With Foreign Service Officer Charles W. Yost standing beside him, Roosevelt's final Secretary of State, Edward Stettinius, remarked to the British Ambassador that if anything happened to President Roosevelt during his fourth term the "general feeling" in Washington was that Truman would have to be "poisoned." As Yost commented: "This facetious remark reflected the low repute in which an undistinguished product of the Kansas City 'Pendergast machine' was held in Washington at that time."[20]

When Roosevelt died, Truman became president in April 1945. Few Americans believed they knew Truman. On first impression, Truman seemed distinctly different from Roosevelt, much more modest, simple, and approachable. This won him early approval, but after a honeymoon, the impression began to cling to him that he was too common. Given the immense challenges he faced, the aura of being average harbored an insidious implication that maybe he was not fit for the presidency.[21]

Alas Truman made two serious errors in handling MacArthur. The first in 1945 transpired when Truman twice "invited" MacArthur to return to the states to receive the national ovation provided other top uniformed commanders like General of the Army Dwight D. Eisenhower and Fleet Admiral Chester W. Nimitz. MacArthur claimed he was too busy with his duties running the occupation of Japan. Truman permitted MacArthur to get away with this and it reinforced MacArthur's lack of respect.

Truman's second great error extended from 1945 to 1950. Except for a limited trip to Honolulu in July 1944, MacArthur had not been on US soil, much less to Washington, since 1937. Neither Truman nor any other major politician in Washington in 1950 personally knew MacArthur. The reverse was also true. Based on his secondhand knowledge, MacArthur regarded Truman as a "pure political hack."[22] MacArthur had served as a theater commander in World War II and then discharged huge responsibilities for the American government in Tokyo since 1945. Seldom fully emphasized, but of no small matter in the unfolding drama was MacArthur's extraordinary personal disconnect from his political superiors.

Only in August 1950 did Truman mount one extremely belated and indirect attempt to forge any type of personal relationship with MacArthur by sending a personal liaison officer.[23] He dispatched Maj. Gen. Frank E. Lowe to Tokyo. Notwithstanding his rank, Lowe not a career regular officer or even a reservist. He was "a successful fuel baron from Maine," among the business leaders recruited by George Marshall to manage the army's economic mobilization. In that role, he became a liaison officer with the Truman Committee. He and Truman bonded based on parallel service as artillery officers in World War I and active participation in the American Legion. When Lowe expressed interest to return to active duty for the Korean War, Truman obliged, but sent Lowe to become his "eyes and ears" in Korea with a specific task of assessing MacArthur. Unfortunately, MacArthur mesmerized Lowe, who returned glowing reports to Truman on MacArthur's mental and physical fitness. Lowe further asserted MacArthur had a plan to finish the war by the end of the year.[24]

Although Truman made many disparaging remarks in private about his egocentric subordinate (one classic was "Mr. Prima Donna, Brass Hat, Five

Star MacArthur"), Truman appears to have feared MacArthur as a political threat. Certainly, there was no comparison in the gravitas each man projected. Truman's typical clipped, flat speaking style compared badly to Roosevelt's regal majesty or MacArthur's Victorian pomp. Truman too often seemed not assured but daunted in his role and failed to project an overall resilient, sunny, optimism American expected of a president.[25]

The Collaboration That Saved Millions

The typical overall theme for narratives of relations between Truman and MacArthur is conflict. Yet, the two figures—without respecting or liking each other—cooperated to achieve a great and indeed noble end. Even more remarkably, it involved a humanitarian act for the Japanese people—immediately after a war fought with fury and hatred against Japan. But before we get to this story, MacArthur shares in the credit of one of his stellar subordinates ever: Col. (later Brig. Gen.) Crawford Sams.

Sams, a trained neurosurgeon and career medical corps officer, contributed to planning the invasion of Japan. He had no real contact with MacArthur before taking charge of the medical arm of the occupation of Japan. Sams immediately confronted multiple challenges as six million Japanese military personnel and civilians were repatriated from all over Japan's defunct empire, and tens of thousands of impressed (if not slave) laborers were being repatriated to their homelands from Japan. Many of them carried at least one from a medical textbook of lethal diseases like cholera and typhus. Sams sprang into frenetic action to halt then wipe out these diseases.

Sams then turned to a massive overhaul of standards and training of Japanese medical professionals. Eventually, he added a school lunch program to nurture millions of Japanese children. As the leading first-generation Japanese historian of the occupation, Eiji Takemae, noted cooperation between Americans and Japanese reached its zenith in the medical arenas of the occupation. Sams' work produced the stunning achievement that the annualized death rate in Japan more than halved from 18.7 per thousand in 1933–1940 to 8.1 in 1950–1951. Takemae estimated Sams probably saved three million Japanese lives. This amazingly was the lesser of the measures under MacArthur that saved millions of Japanese lives.[26]

American intelligence on Japan prior to the surrender had snatched a few indicators of problems with food supply but affirmed that Japan's food situation was nowhere near collapse.[27] Assuming Japan faced no food crisis, the initial directives issued to MacArthur provided for the Japanese government functioning under the US occupation to have total responsibility for Japan's economy, including feeding the population.[28] The directives additionally barred MacArthur from "gratuitous" distribution of American food to the Japanese.[29] The directives further granted MacArthur discretion to demand that the Japanese themselves feed the occupation forces, provided this did not lead to "starvation" of the Japanese population.[30] Demanding occupied areas to feed local Japanese forces had been a policy which heavily contributed to the deaths of millions of Asia. Estimates place starvation deaths just in Southeast Asia at 4.4 million, with the Japanese policies central to this toll.[31] MacArthur, however, ordered that the US feed its own occupation forces, an act that certainly helped save a great many Japanese lives.[32]

MacArthur became aware of the severe food crisis first anecdotally and then officially. From the outset, his headquarters, Supreme Commander Allied Powers (SCAP), questioned Japanese figures and insisted the Japanese government work on maximizing production. Even so, the basic problem of a food shortage was much aggravated by additional impediments like population dislocation, transportation disruption, hoarding, and diversion to the black market. In September 1945, MacArthur announced that only 200,000 US soldiers were needed for the occupation, an announcement very popular with the American public anxious to "Get the Boys Home." But this meant SCAP must absolutely rely upon the Japanese government for work in food collection and distribution.[33]

By October 1945, staff officers warned MacArthur that Japan's supply and distribution system might totally break down in the latter half of 1946 and that this could endanger the mission of the occupation.[34] MacArthur and his staff recognized that feeding the Japanese people was fundamental to achieving the goals of democratization and demilitarization set by Washington. The two could not be separated. As scholar Steven Fuchs stated, "no voice was louder than MacArthur's in insisting that the United States had an obligation to feed the Japanese."[35]

Two fundamental facts about the food situation dictated MacArthur's options. First, the urgent crisis involved the urban, not the rural population. The rural "self-suppliers" fared satisfactorily, if not well. Second, the lack of solid data on food being hoarded in rural areas and food diverted into the rampaging "black market" make it impossible to establish the actual total of food available in Japan, especially during the critical first year of the occupation.

The critical foodstuff in Japan was rice. It was harvested in September and October and November 1 commenced what the Japanese called the "Rice Year." In 1945, cold weather, a typhoon, lack of fertilizer (diverted to producing explosives), and floods devastated the rice harvest. The Japanese government reported the harvest totaled only 6.45 million metric tons, about 60 percent of the norm. Further, food imports had ceased. These had provided at least 30 percent of the food supply. The Japanese Minister of Finance in October 1945 publicly announced that ten million Japanese would die from starvation without food relief.[36]

It must be stressed that the official ration (1,042 calories per day in urban areas) was not enough to sustain life. In one of several well-publicized cases, a Japanese judge was profoundly disturbed by the fact that most persons brought before him were charged with economic crimes involving food. He instructed his wife to feed him only the official ration. He died.[37] Getting the average Japanese through this crisis required them to go beyond the official ration via home production, gifts from rural relatives, the black market, charitable organizations, emergency distributions, and imports.[38]

The government confronted a crisis over the collection of the rice harvest for the rationing system. The government typically held between 85 and 95 percent of the rice quota by the end of February, but in 1946, it held merely 60 percent—reflecting the farmers profoundly shaken confidence in the government. Additionally, social dislocation, hoarding, and fear of starvation before the next fall harvest all served to undermine quota collection. Further "black market" prices were "astonishingly higher" than official rates. By the first months of 1946, the rationing system teetered on verge of collapse.[39]

To equalize food distribution, SCAP started transfers from surplus to deficit areas. Getting some level of cooperation with local officials reluctant to transfer food required an appeal by the emperor himself and a warning by SCAP that imports would not be distributed until the deficit transfer program had been completed. In February 1946, the Japanese government enacted a measure to permit the expropriation of undelivered rice and stronger fines. In March, SCAP doubled the price of stable foods to reduce the disparity between the regular and the black market. These actions improved collection, but the delays in collection caused turmoil in the distribution system. In May, Tokyo residents received only 775 calories in the official daily ration. Food demonstrations erupted nationwide and on May 19, 1946, over 250,000 people demonstrated in the "Give Us Rice" rally in Tokyo at Imperial Palace.[40]

During the crisis, the Japanese government created 150,000 tons of "food substitutes" to feed the urban masses. These comprised:

> Stems and leaves of sweet potatoes, mulberry leaves, acorns, residue of starch manufacture, seaweeds, leaves of garden radishes, mugworts, residue from apple and grape presses, pumpkin seeds, water oats, arrowroot, silkworms, and locusts were dried, ground, and mixed with wheat flour.[41]

The evidence seems very clear, ultimately American food shipments proved crucial to heading off what could have been a mass famine. But the exact figures on American food aid remain murky. MacArthur had accumulated approximately 3.5 million tons of American foodstuffs stockpiled for the final campaigns against Japan. Some of this went to Korea and some was retained as a reserve against catastrophic supply failure at places in Japan. The precise total of the remaining tonnage distributed in Japan is not clear, but most of it was issued before May 1946.

Fuchs explained that MacArthur initially couched requests for American food mildly as necessary to "prevent disease and unrest." When this only produced a "lukewarm response," MacArthur turned to Plan B: "scare the hell out of them." He described rice harvest as the worse in 30 years (actually 35) and warned that the official urban ration of 1,042 calories per day could not be met from May 1946. He demanded 2.6 million metric tons of "rice equivalents" to sustain the rations. Failure he asserted would bring disaster, poverty, hunger, and disease, and would spark "uprisings of a major character." He said without food imports, he would need a massively increased occupation garrison which everyone knew was politically impossible in the United States. MacArthur's cables included the pointed comment that they should be shown to the president so that if food was not provided, "there may be no future question as to the chain of responsibility." Only MacArthur would have exhibited the effrontery to submit such a demand to Washington.[42]

MacArthur's dramatic messages did not immediately secure more food from Washington, but they did provoke a serious dialogue.[43] Washington dispatched a "food mission" in March 1946 under Col. Raymond Harrison to verify MacArthur's alarming portrait of the situation. Harrison reported quickly by cable (rather than waiting until the mission was back in Washington) that the situation was very perilous indeed. Then former President Hebert Hoover came through with a United Nations Relief and Rehabilitation Agency Mission. Hoover attested to the severity of the situation and provided a graphic picture that without food imports, the Japanese would be in conditions like "the Buchenwald and Belsen concentration camps." Maintaining order much less economic recovery would be impossible.[44]

Although the Harrison and Hoover report stirred Washington to accept that the food situation in Japan was indeed very critical and required US food imports, there remained factors that curbed Washington's willingness to ship large quantities of food. These included a worldwide food shortage, Japan's status as a particularly reviled former enemy nation, and the needs of Allied countries and liberated areas for food. Another consideration was a reluctance to offend Allies, particularly against charges of the US favoring the Japanese. This pushed the decision to meet MacArthur's calls to Truman.[45]

In the end, after initial skepticism, President Truman authorized the shipment of US food to Japan—just barely in time. Between May and October 1946, the most critical months of the food crisis, some 594,838 metric tons of "rice equivalents" of imported US cereals and canned goods were distributed. This may not sound like that much, but bear in mind that the dire crisis involved approximately 60 percent of the population, the urban dwellers, roughly about 43 million people. The height of the crisis fell in the second half of the "Rice Year." Assuming about half the total rice harvest went to the urban population, and that the crucial period was just half of the whole period, that means the regular rice distribution between May and October would have

TABLE 11.1 Japanese Population Feed May to October 1946 with Imported Us Food[46]

Month	Total population	Population feed with US food imports	Percentage of total population feed with US food imports	Percentage of US imported food issued as ration in Tokyo
May	74,024,000	1,878,000	2.5	–
June	74,679,707	5,307,000	7.1	74
July	75,322,946	18,630,000	24.7	100
August	75,683,324	20,353,000	26.8	100
September	75,904,563	15,243,000	20.1	62
October	76,155,553	5,319,000	7.0 (6.98)	–

been roughly 1.6 million metric tons. The imported US food alone would have added 37 percent to the total available food by weight during this period. Further complicating the math is that some types of US food contributed more to sustenance than an equal amount by weight of rice.

The following figures on the imports and their distribution to the population support this conclusion. Note that Tokyo held about 2.5 million people.

Japan's population remained without a fully adequate diet quantitatively in 1947 and 1948. Fortunately, the 1946 rice harvest cleared over 9 million tons, a vast improvement over 1945. From November 1946 steps commenced to address not only total caloric intake, but also nutritional deficiencies. One report prepared by occupation authorities declared that: "In view of the dependence of major urban areas on food imports for their existence during the most critical period of the food crisis, it is estimated that more than eleven million Japanese escaped possible starvation through food imports from the United States."[47] This statement and the available evidence are ambiguous as to whether eleven million Japanese were saved from severe food deprivation or from actual death. For one thing, the total available Japanese food stock remains unknown and the government by no means secured all available food beyond what rural populations required. Had the rationing system broken down, there would have been even more flight to the countryside where there was an additional supply of food beyond the tabulations of the government or the occupation authorities. On the other hand, without US food imports, it is likely that the rationing system would have collapsed creating a chaotic situation. Given all these considerations, a judicious estimate would be that without imported US food deaths from starvation would have numbered in the multiple millions, perhaps five or six million at least.

To place these numbers in context, total Japanese deaths in the Asia-Pacific War numbered roughly three million. Sams' exertions in the health field saved about 3 million lives and the defeat of a threatening famine by conservative estimate saved twice or perhaps even more lives. Thus, the American occupation of Japan easily saved several multiples of all the Japanese lives lost in the war. As one Japanese man who lived through this period observed, feeding the defeated Japanese was MacArthur's "most noble and perhaps his most important achievement during the occupation." Truman likewise deserves credit that he never has properly received.[48]

Korea

It was a quiet weekend in the United States when news broke that North Korea had launched an attack on South Korea on June 25, 1950. The possibility of the attack had been acknowledged, but the timing greatly surprised. In a later much-criticized speech ("Crisis in Asia") on January 12, 1950, Secretary of State Dean Acheson attempted to answer Truman administration critics raising cries about "Who Lost China." Acheson distinguished "strategic" (or "war-fighting" interests as historian Allan Millett aptly termed them) which ran along a line of Japan, Okinawa, and the Philippines, in contrast to "other forms of political interest." Here Acheson grouped Korea among other former colonial nations seeking to find their independent way deserving US support. Whatever Acheson intended his phrasing left the inference that Korea stood outside the perimeter of US "war fighting" interests. But news of the attack, however, revealed a fundamental conviction shared widely within the administration Stalin must have pre-approved the North Korean attack. This was only partly correct.[49]

Both North Korean leader Kim Il-sung and South Korean leader Syngman Rhee shared visions of a unified Korean—each under his rule. They differed in capability. The United States never outfitted the South Koreans with the heavy weapons to stage a cross bother attack, and as further insurance controlled the fuel and ammunition the South Koreans needed for such an endeavor. Kim convinced Stalin in 1949 to build-up his army ostensibly for defensive purposes. After earlier efforts failed, in March and April 1950, Kim secured Stalin's blessing for conquest of South Korea. Stalin, however, fixed two conditions: (1) Kim must swiftly (within about eight weeks) overrun South Korea before American intervention and (2) Mao must also approve. Mao approved the plan in May. Stalin, however, warned Kim he must not expect Soviet participation in the unlikely event the United States did intervene.[50]

Technically, Korea dangled in curious status under the US State Department (acting per UN auspices), but outside MacArthur's military Far Eastern Command. MacArthur's intelligence chief, Maj. Gen. Charles Willoughby, ran a conglomerate of intelligence organizations. These provided him with the best American reading of the situation in Korea. Willoughby's analysis forwarded to Washington detected the ominous shift of North Korea from a defensive to an offensive orientation. Willoughby's cables downplayed the imminence of a cross-border attack in the months prior to the actual attack, but still forwarded enough information to alert Washington. The urgency of the warning became hopelessly diluted during inner agency processing. Here as later when the Chinese intervened, the Central Intelligence Agency, created exactly to prevent "another Pearl Harbor," earned no laurels. The surprise of the attack represented an overall US "intelligence failure" in which both Washington and Tokyo shared culpability, though the former somewhat more so.[51]

Truman moved to intervene to defend South Korea. In the background loomed an ongoing intra-administration debate on overall foreign policy. Part of that involved the push for a greatly expanded defense budget. Secretary of Defense Louis Johnson had fought strenuously to limit defense spending for years. Truman supported Johnson with the result that his containment policy regarding the Soviet Union was richer in concept than means. Acheson became the prime advocate for a major defense spending surge.

But another policy issue had already been resolved, if not formally, in fact: conviction that any overt Soviet military action, even by a surrogate, must be countered. On the flash news from Seoul, Acheson secured from an outraged Truman authorization to set American policy. As they viewed the situation, this was about frontiers all around the globe, not just South Korea. By 30 June, with South Korean forces rapidly retreating with no prospect of halting, Truman made the fateful step of committing US ground forces to Korea. Properly understood, however, Truman's actions were not ad hoc or ill-thought-out. They were heavily foreshadowed by events going back years that powerfully predisposed him to take this action. The one special feature of the new policy was to seek and secure UN sanction as a benediction over the involvement.[52]

The North Korean attack across the 38th Parallel confronted MacArthur with his third war. From the opening hours and days of the war, MacArthur flaunted his willingness to act first and seek Washington sanction later. When MacArthur learned of the North Korean attack, he sent a ship loaded with ammunition under US air and naval escort to support South Korea and dispatched his air units to attack the invaders. He did all of this without higher authorization which only came later. Then during a real-time teletype "conversation" with Army Chief of Staff J. Lawton Collins, MacArthur insolently refused to respond to Collins' temporizing questions.[53]

Truman asked the Joint Chiefs of Staff (JCS) to recommend an officer to command the UN-authorized forces in Korea. MacArthur was then vastly invested in the occupation of Japan and Korea was not in his bailiwick. It would have been entirely reasonable to appoint some other officer under him or carve out an independent Korean command of UN forces under MacArthur. Further, he had just demonstrated again his willingness to take actions without prior approval. But the JCS gave Truman only MacArthur's name and on July 8 Truman made the appointment.[54] On a more positive note, Truman's rapid, decisive decision to defend South Korea astonished and pleased MacArthur.[55]

In July 1950, MacArthur flung parts of his Japanese army garrison piece-meal into Korea to delay the potent, tank fisted, North Korean attack. Though many were defeated piecemeal, sometimes in a humiliating fashion, they did slow the North Korean thrust. In August 1950, with UN forces now fighting desperately to hold a perimeter around Pusan at the southeastern end of the Korean peninsula, MacArthur answered a request for comments by a veterans' organization with a plea for American support for Chiang Kai-shek and his na-tionalists. Although Truman later stated he contemplated relieving MacArthur over this trespass into policy issues that are the prerogative of the president, he reduced his actual response to ordering MacArthur to publicly retract the comments. This MacArthur reluctantly did. The significance of this episode deserves more attention than MacArthur or later histories have accorded it. Truman eschewed the evasions and euphemisms of Washington since 1942 in response to MacArthur's numerous provocations and enforced MacArthur's subordination.[56]

Inchon

As early as mid-July, even as the United States and South Korean forces were being kicked back to an enclave around Pusan, MacArthur conceived a mas-ter stroke: an amphibious landing behind the North Koreans at Inchon. The strategic target would be Seoul; the timing is mid-September to mid-October. MacArthur never deviated from this vision. Further, while Washington dith-ered about whether a war aim should be reunification of Korea, MacArthur presumed this was manifest.[57]

Doubts about the basic feasibility of a landing ran rampant within the theater and Washington. They were exacerbated by MacArthur's appointment of Army Maj. Gen. Edward M. Almond, who lacked any amphibious experi-ence and whose ambition significantly exceeded his combat record, to com-mand the combined Marine and army troops for the landing. This was the X Corps, that MacArthur subordinated to himself, not Lt. Gen. Walton Walker's Eighth Army in overall charge of American and South Korean forces holding on at Pusan. The extraordinary challenge of Inchon was that it featured virtu-ally every conceivable obstacle to amphibious assault. The salt-water path to Inchon was a narrow winding channel, easily mined, dotted with islands, com-manded by high ground ideal for artillery. As everywhere on Korea's west coast, terrific tidal variances of thirty to thirty-four feet meant sharply restricted, well-separated periods where landing craft could operate. There was no real beach. The essential preliminary would be an assault on the main defensive redoubt of Wolmi-do Island, followed by a twelve-hour delay—a bountiful gift to the defenders—before the next tide permitted the main landing at Inchon proper.

MacArthur crushed the final opposition to the Inchon landing in a meeting on 23 August with Admiral Arthur W. Radford, Commander in Chief, Pacific and Pacific Fleet, Admiral Forrest P. Sherman, Chief of Naval Operations and Collins. Several staff officers spoke first, notably the highly experienced Amphibious Force Commander, Rear Admiral James H. Doyle. He delivered a pessimistic appraisal for the Inchon landing, punctuated with his ominous conclusion that "the best I can say is that Inchon is not impossible."[58]

MacArthur listened, smoking his pipe and making few comments through these presentations. Then he took the stage for his greatest performance: a 45-minute soliloquy. Pacing and gesturing with his oversized corncob pipe, MacArthur flipped all the intimidating reasons against the landing into his side by arguing they all would convince the North Koreans he would not dare land at Inchon. He ridiculed the timid alternatives and maintained Inchon was the only way for a quick, decisive, war-ending stroke. He taunted that his confidence in the navy exceeded the navy's self-confidence. After conceding Inchon was a 5,000 to one gamble ("but I am used to taking such odds") he intoned "We will land at Inchon, and I shall crush them." MacArthur had always been a force unto himself in conferences and never more so than here. He swayed the three men whose opposition could have canceled Inchon. Five days later, the JCS formally approved Inchon, attaching a wistful note that amounted to a feeble attempt to disavow responsibility if disaster ensued that MacArthur should continue to consider alternatives.[59]

The landing on 15 September unreeled as a typical sea-borne assault: a paralyzing pre-landing bombardment, followed by strong tempests of confusion and crowned with ugly friendly fire episodes. All this was redeemed by mostly intelligent and energetic interventions by subordinates. The surprised North Koreans nonetheless forced hard fighting before devastated Seoul was recaptured by 29 September. Meanwhile, Walker's Eight Army broke out of the Pusan Perimeter and thrust north meeting elements of Almond's X Corps on 26 September.[60]

The great triumph of the Inchon landing that reversed the tide of the Korean War seemed to be MacArthur's masterstroke as a strategist. It appeared to guarantee South Korea would be liberated. But what next? MacArthur believed all of Korea should now be liberated and brought under Syngman Rhee's government. Washington typically was divided. Broadly, the State Department feared Soviet or more likely Chinese intervention. It was also attuned to the views of US allies and neutrals like India who shared similar concerns and held no brief of Syngman Rhee's government. The state maintained that military operations to unify Korea required further UN sanctions which it believed (correctly) could be obtained. But State also insisted no United Nations Command (UNC) forces should approach the North Korean border with China.

Defense department officials, including the JCS, found the State Department's stance naïve. To destroy North Korean forces, MacArthur must be authorized to operate north of the Thirty-eighth Parallel. Reunification beckoned as the only logical way to preclude the repetition of a North Korean attack. Moreover, if Korea was to be liberated and unified after fair elections, the Eighth Army must be the occupation force, not Rhee's government bent first on bloody retaliation. On September 9, after meeting with Truman, the JCS sent MacArthur authorization to operate north of the Thirty-eight Parallel.

At the same time Truman effectively changed the nation's war aims to unifying Korea (blessed by a UN resolution on October 7), he also jettisoned Johnson as his secretary of defense. According to historian David McCullough, Johnson was "possibly the worst appointment Truman ever made." Privately, Truman thought Johnson was "mentally unbalanced." Press accounts about shortfalls in the equipment and performance of US troops placed blame on Johnson, though Truman and the Congress had supported policies leading to these failures. Truman secured the reluctant acceptance of George C. Marshall to return to government as Secretary of Defense following Johnson's resignation on September 19.[61]

In the flush of victory, on October 15 MacArthur and Truman met for the first time at Wake Island. Their encounter was supposed to be about policies, but the event reeked of politics as Truman sought to share in victory's glory as a resentful MacArthur noted. The conversations were amiable, disorganized, very broad, and very shallow. Two points stood out. MacArthur assured Truman that victory was won, and he rejected the prospect of Chinese intervention, noting that had it occurred in the first two months it might have been "decisive," but if attempted now, UNC air power would inflict "the greatest slaughter." In retrospect, as historian D. Clayton James emphasized the conference disposed of the huge Chinese intervention issue with one question by Truman, one response by MacArthur, and "absolutely no follow-up questions." Press coverage was glowing, though veteran newsman Robert Sherrod damned the meeting a "political grandstand play."[62]

UN forces drove north and crossed the 38th parallel into North Korea, first the South Koreans on October 1, then the Eighth Army on October 9. Between October 26 and November 7, Chinese forces conducted a surprise attack and inflicted severe losses upon four South Korean regiments and the US 8th Cavalry Regiment. A Marine regiment held its ground. Then the Chinese broke contact as suddenly as they attacked.

Though initially there were doubts about the identity of the enemy forces (North Koreans? Chinese? Even former Imperial Army soldiers?), intelligence officers of the 1st Marine Division and Almonds X Corps immediately identified these assailants as Chinese. Over the next three weeks. intelligence officials in Eighth Army, MacArthur's headquarters, and Washington (including the Pentagon, State Department, and the CIA) all concurred that a huge number of Chinese soldiers stood massed across the Yalu River international boundary in Manchuria. But they all found reasons to discount Chinese intentions to seek a big war.[63]

MacArthur planned an "end the war offensive" to drive to the Yalu to begin on November 24. Air power would isolate the battlefield in North Korea. The Eighth Army on the western side of the Korean peninsula and the X Corps on the eastern side would drive to the Yalu. A final top-level review in Washington on November 21 by State and Defense looked at intelligence placing massive Chinese forces in Manchuria but denying Chinese intent to intervene. Truman would not halt MacArthur noted historian Allan Millett "unless someone convinced him the United Nations Command faced disaster," but "no one felt defeat beckoned."[64]

From the moment Truman committed US ground troops to Korea, Mao, and others in the leadership began to contemplate intervention in the war. Initially, they adopted a defensive posture. Over 500,000 men were mustered to guard the Korean border. This took considerable time, during which the command of a potential intervention was established. Planning advanced on operations and logistics, but this demonstrated no intervention on this huge scale was feasible before October. The Chinese warned Kim about the Inchon landing, but no effective measures were taken before the landing.[65]

As his armed forces reeled in defeat, Kim pleaded for Soviet and Chinese intervention. Stalin promised limited air cover, some munitions, but not troops. Mao determined to intervene. His first effort on October 1 to secure the blessing of other top party bosses failed. On October 3, Zhou Enlai told the Indian Ambassador that China would enter the war if UN troops crossed the Thirty-eighth Parallel. Over October 4–5, Mao believed he had secured sanctions for intervention from the other leaders. On October 8, Mao advised Kim that Chinese forces would intervene. But Zhou went to Moscow to bargain for Soviet support over October 11–12, as though intervention itself, not the terms, remained unresolved. Mao ordered the movement into Korea of four armies with 120,000 men that commenced on the night of 19–20 October. These forces inflicted a stinging reverse on UN forces from November 7, gaining valuable insight into how to fight the Americans and South Koreans. The Chinese broke contact, but far larger forces crossed the Yalu. They maintained strict discipline on concealment, with no campfires permitted despite the extreme cold and inadequate uniforms and boots.[66]

Peng Dehuai, the overall Chinese commander, overall faced about 342,000 men in UN forces with his 388,000 men. Dehuai found MacArthur's offensive provided superb operational and tactical vulnerabilities he could exploit. Further, he prioritized as targets the much less well-armed and thus vulnerable South Korean divisions, particularly three with Eighth Army, but he also sought to destroy the 1st Marine Division with X Corps. He deployed the Thirteenth Army Group against the Eighth Army and the 9th Army Group against X Corps. Because his logistical "tail" was so thin, his numerical strength translated into a much greater superiority in maneuver combat line battalions (infantry, artillery, armor, and combat engineers) 456 to 204.[67]

During the night of November 25–26, the Chinese storm broke. The grim details are beyond the scope here. They crushed four South Korean divisions and severely mauled the US 2nd Infantry Division. This compelled a rapid UN exit from most of North Korea. There were only two positive notes for the UN forces. First, the effort to crush the 1st Marine Division failed at great cost (though one nearby army infantry regiment was smashed). Second, Walker abandoned guidance from MacArthur and rapidly withdrew from Peng Dehuai's trap, which saved the bulk of his army. [68]

As the enormous magnitude of the defeat gradually dawned. MacArthur was stunned as was Washington. As MacArthur declared, it was "an entirely new war."[69] The British government became bluntly defeatist and looked not only to abandon Korea but also to accept Chinese demands that the United States get out of Asia.

MacArthur became so bleak he argued that unless the restrictions on attacking targets in Manchuria were lifted, he would have to abandon Korea. Washington wobbled but regained its senses far sooner. Truman declared he would not abandon the South Koreans to be murdered. Secretary of Defense Marshall set the course: the UN would hold South Korea and maybe part of North Korea, but would do so with the forces at hand, subject to a stream of replacements. There would be no wider war with China.[70]

There was an awkward moment on November 30. A reporter's series of leading questions at a press conference nudged Truman down a route that seemed to imply that not only was the use of nuclear weapons being contemplated but that he had released authority to use them to MacArthur. That brought British Prime Minister Clement Atlee scurrying across the Atlantic. After consultations, the British concerns about use of atomic weapons were quelled, but the United States intent to remain in Korea was affirmed.[71]

Walker was killed in a vehicle accident on December 23. Lt. Gen. Mathew B. Ridgeway was appointed to replace him. Ridgeway's revitalization of the UN forces in Korea over the next five months became legendary, and properly so. After the successful evacuation of X Corps from North Korea, UN forces withdrew south of the Thirty-eighth Parallel, abandoning Seoul. But Ridgeway then stabilized the front and defeated the fourth iteration of a Chinese offensive. Then, beginning in February, Ridgeway launched a series of counterattacks that retook Seoul and by April 22 pushed the UN line well north of the Thirty-eighth parallel in the center and east of the front. The end of this process was overshadowed by Truman's decision to relieve MacArthur.[72]

Countdown to Relief

This countdown began in December. MacArthur reacted to this humiliating defeat by casting aside all restraint and making numerous statements trying to justify his prior actions and seeking to reverse the national strategy that favored

Europe. In early December, Truman issued directives ordering all US officials, uniformed and civilian, to clear any statement on foreign policy through the State Department.[73]

On March 7, 1951, as the Eighth Army began an offensive called Operation Ripper, MacArthur stated in front of journalists that without reinforcements for the Eighth Army and a lifting of restrictions on his air and sea forces, the Korean War was headed for a strategic stalemate. This appeared to violate the December 1950 order not to make policy statements without prior clearance in Washington.[74]

This incident paled before the next. On March 20, the JCS sent MacArthur an advanced draft of a speech by Truman aiming for the pursuit of peace discussions. As historian Allan Millett phrased it, MacArthur saw this "as appeasement at best and a treacherous sellout at worst."[75] On March 24, MacArthur issued a communiqué in Tokyo that "widely exceeded his past record of direct challenges to his superiors."[76] He taunted the Chinese Communists as lacking the industrial backing to support air and naval forces or to provide ground forces with first-class firepower. He called on the Chinese to admit publicly defeat in Korea and approach him as a supplicant to secure a cease fire. This communiqué seems unmistakably designed to sabotage Truman's diplomatic strategy for seeking a settlement in Korea. MacArthur may even have entertained the idea that he could force a fundamental reorientation of American foreign policy to embrace Chiang and emphasize Asia over Europe.[77] Truman later reported that he resolved to relieve MacArthur that very day, March 24. If so, the first visible manifestation of such presidential ire appears strange. The JCS sent a message to MacArthur merely "reminding" him of the prior directive requiring officials to clear foreign policy statements.[78]

But within days, another shoe dropped. For that story, we much go back. Congressman Joseph Martin had sent MacArthur a copy of a speech he gave urging the Chiang be permitted to open a "second Asiatic front" in the war. Martin asked for MacArthur's views. On March 20 MacArthur replied by letter. He did not ask Martin to keep the letter private. MacArthur declared that he had advised Washington without effect that Asia was decisive front in war against communism and that if Asia fell "the fall of Europe is inevitable" and that "There is no substitute for victory."[79]

On April 5, less than two weeks after the March 24 communiqué that provoked Truman's anger, Martin read MacArthur's letter into the Congressional Record. The very next day, April 6, Truman assembled the men he called his "Big four": Dean Acheson, Averell Harriman, George C. Marshall, and Omar Bradley to discuss what Truman damned in his diary as MacArthur's "rank insubordination." Truman, however, did not divulge his resolve to relief MacArthur.

It bears emphasis that Truman's advisers by no means immediately endorsed MacArthur's relief. In this session, Acheson firmly supported MacArthur's relief, but warned that this stroke would produce the "biggest fight of your administration." Sources differ, but apparently, Harriman also urged MacArthur's relief and may even have suggested a possible court martial. But Marshall and Bradley disagreed and recommended a very stern rebuke but not relief. They warned of likely public outcry against the administration over outright relief.[80]

The four officials requested more time to study the issue. Truman granted the request as he clearly understood the gravity of the action he was contemplating and the importance of securing endorsement of the relief from other key civilian and uniformed leaders in Washington. Truman detailed Bradley to poll the members of the JCS on their views of MacArthur's competence. On April 6 and 7, during separate meetings of the "Big Four" Acheson and Harriman renewed their recommendations for MacArthur's relief. Marshall and Bradley still baulked asserting they still did not see legal insubordination.[81]

During a Sunday, April 8 meeting of Bradley with the three other members of the JCS, J. Lawton Collins, Forrest Sherman, and Hoyt S. Vandenberg, the service heads acknowledged that they all had come to doubt MacArthur's judgment and his willingness to follow the administration strategic priorities. Meanwhile, Truman consulted members of the Democratic Party and particularly congressional leaders to get them behind his action.[82]

When Truman met again with his Big Four advisers on April 9, Marshall and Bradley had been won over by the JCS to support MacArthur's relief. The issues they believed were civilian control and the constitutional powers of the president. Truman then announced his decision to relieve MacArthur. Mathew Ridgeway would replace him in Tokyo and General James Van Fleet would take charge of the Eighth Army.[83]

To this point Truman had navigated well some serious rip tides in getting his main subordinates to endorse his firing of MacArthur, but the actual handling of the relief was a fiasco.

The plan was for Secretary of the Army Frank Pace to personally hand the relief order to MacArthur at 10:00 AM local, April 12 in Tokyo. This was 8:00 PM, April 11 in Washington. This would let the administration get out its story before MacArthur could speak to the press and get it broadcast or published in the United States.[84]

But by the evening of April 10, Truman believed his plan was about to be preempted by the arch-anti-administration *Chicago Tribune*. Reporters for that publication had begun questioning Pentagon officials about a reported rumor in Tokyo that MacArthur was going to be relieved. They further offered that denied or not, the *Tribune* would publish the story the next day. It is conceivable that this threat was a ploy to panic Truman into canceling the relief. Moreover, Acheson reported earlier on April 10 that a leak about the action had reached two senators who had warned that MacArthur's relief might jeopardize delicate budget negotiations.

Truman then directed his press secretary to release the news. Joseph H. Short called a 1:00 AM White House press conference and released the news. MacArthur learned about it via a radio broadcast. Truman had labored since FDR's death under perceptions by many that he was not a large enough man for the job of president. The handling of this appeared drenched in a pettiness and meanness of spirit that unfortunately seemed to reinforce such doubts. It also damaged Truman's actual case and made MacArthur seem a martyr.[85] Truman spoke by radio to the nation on the evening of April 11 to explain his decision. The broadcast noted one historian was "a complete flop."[86]

MacArthur handled the details of his relief with an aristocratic grace and dignity. He returned to the United States for the first time since 1937. His receptions from the West Coast to Washington were tumultuous. His ticker tape parade in New York City set a record for debris.[87] As MacArthur's biographer D. Clayton James described it, the relief "set off a nationwide cacophony of howls of indignation, shrieks of hysteria, and screams of anger that at first created such a racket that the quieter sounds of sorrow and reason were barely heard."[88] A Gallup poll of April 14 found only twenty-five percent of Americans supported Truman; sixty-six percent supported MacArthur. [89]

On April 19, MacArthur spoke before a joint session of congress. The 37-minute address was broadcast live on television and radio. It was a rhetorical triumph, if your taste runs to MacArthur's style. Senate hearings began on May 3 with MacArthur as the first witness. Seven administration witnesses appeared from May 7 to June 9, followed by six more witnesses, more or less supporting MacArthur, through June 25.[90]

Details of the hearings need not detain us. One senator compared the hearings meandering path to the Korean War as "vague, indefinite and purposeless,"[91] One arresting point is that MacArthur rejected the notion that the Chinese Communists were subservient tools of Moscow. While MacArthur displayed what one account called an "Olympian manner and finely turned phrases" and he also never appeared tired or ruffled in three days of testimony, the subsequent Administration witnesses undermined his assertions that he had always been properly subordinate to his superiors, that his views on Korean war and strategy were shared by the JCS, that he had always been dutifully subordinate to his superiors and that he had never raised any challenge to civilian control. Public attention waned and insofar as available measures show, public opinion at least shifted away from lop-sided support for MacArthur.[92]

In summary, the road to MacArthur's relief by President Truman was very long. Its earliest clear mile markers involved actions or inactions by the Roosevelt administration which participated in making MacArthur into a towering public hero and then failing to respond with vigor and clarity to MacArthur's frequent ill-considered outbursts and outrageous provocations. Even allowing that the administration had to make some leeway for

MacArthur's exceptional public and political standing, MacArthur's enormous ego was inflated to still more gargantuan size by this treatment.

President Truman made two serious errors in his handling of the extremely difficult hand he was dealt. He failed to enforce subordination from MacArthur in 1945 over Truman's request cum order for MacArthur to return to the United States for a suitable public recognition. Truman then failed to take any measure until too late to establish some reasonable personal relationship with the figure exercising such vital duties. When Truman did enforce MacArthur's subordination over his provocative public statement in August 1950, MacArthur's long acclimation to steering his own course from 1942 to 1950 undercut the effectiveness of Truman's decisive action.

The JCS shares in blame. The decision to make MacArthur the UN commander was not nearly so foreordained as apparently, they saw it. Then they were intimidated by the spell of Inchon. He seemed to be proven brilliantly right and they wrong. Though they would not then or later admit it, they were in awe of him in the weeks before Chinese intervention.

This is not to suggest that MacArthur does not bear the greatest responsibility as author of his own fall. But we should recognize that it is entirely possible that stern action between 1941 and 1945 might have installed curbs on MacArthur that would have avoided the dramatic confrontation of April 1951.

Finally, it is a great pity for both leaders that their collaboration in 1946 to save millions of Japanese from starvation has been omitted or not properly acknowledged by the narratives of the occupation of Japan as well as their personal biographies. While accounts of the occupation never fail to mention the severe degree of the food shortage, especially in the first year, the role of US food in staving off mass death has as far as this writer can determine, never received the coverage it warrants.[93]

Notes

1 D. Clayton James, *The Years of MacArthur, Vol. 3: Triumph & Disaster 1945–64* (Boston: Houghton Mifflin Company, 1985), 438 [hereafter James, *The Years of MacArthur, Vol. 3*].

2 Richard B. Frank, *MacArthur: A Biography* (New York: Palgrave McMillan, 2007), 4, 8, 12-3 [hereafter Frank, *MacArthur*].

3 Arthur Herman, *Douglas MacArthur: American Warrior* (New York: Random House, 2016) XIII, 16–22.

4 Brian McAllister Linn, *The Philippine War 1899–1902* (Lawrence, KS: University Press of Kansas, 2000), 209–18; D. Clayton James, *The Years of MacArthur, Vol. 1, 1980 to 1941* (Boston: Houghton, Mifflin Company, 1970), 295–97, 320 [hereafter James, *The Years of MacArthur, Vol. 1*].

5 James, *The Years of MacArthur, Vol. 1*, 400–11; Paul Dickson and Thomas B. Allen, *The Bonus Army: An American Epic* (New York: Walker & Company, 2004) 179–80; Carlo D'Este, *Eisenhower: A Soldier's Life* (Henry Holt and Company, 2002), 221–23.

6 Geoffrey Perret, *Old Soldiers Never Die* (New York: Random House, 1996), 114–24 [hereafter Perret, *Old Soldiers Never Die*]; James, *The Years of MacArthur, Vol. 1*, 259–94.

7 Rexford G. Tugwell, *The Democratic Roosevelt: A Biography of Franklin D. Roosevelt* (Garden City: Doubleday and Company, 1957), 348–51.

8 D. Clayton James, *The Years of MacArthur, Vol. 2, 1941–1945* (Boston: Houghton, Mifflin Company, 1975), 89–90 [hereafter James, *The Years of MacArthur, Vol. 2*].

9 James, *The Years of MacArthur, Vol. 2*, 98–100, 129–32.

10 Ibid., 133–40.

11 Richard B. Frank, *Guadalcanal* (New York: Random House, Inc., 1990), 33–4.

12 Forrest C. Pogue, *George C. Marshall, Ordeal and Hope, 1939–1942* (New York: The Viking Press, 1966), 374–75, Frank, *MacArthur*, 59–60.

13 James, *The Years of MacArthur, Vol. 2*, 403–40.

14 James, *The Years of MacArthur, Vol. 3*, 618.

15 James, *The Years of MacArthur, Vol. 1*, 494–95.

16 Alonzo Hamby, *Man of the People: A Life of Harry S. Truman* (New York: Oxford University Press, 1995), 7–17, 57–82, 89–92 [hereafter Hamby, *Man of the People*]; D. M. Giangreco, *The Soldier From Independence: A Military Biography of Harry Truman* (Minneapolis, MN: Zenith Press, 2009), 24–5, 203; David McCullough, *Truman* (New York: Simon & Schuster, 1992), 109, 399–400 [hereafter McCullough, *Truman*].

17 Hamby, *Man of the People*, Hamby, *Man of the People*, 108–14, 117–20, 124–26, 145–47, 157–59, 182–84, 192–98, 249–60, 203–4.

18 Hamby, *Man of the People*, 89–92.

19 Ibid., 278–84.

20 Charles W. Yost, *History and Memory: A Statesman's Perceptions of the Twentieth Century* (New York: W. W. Norton & Company, 1980), 115–16.

21 Hamby, *Man of the People*, 293–98.

22 Allan R. Millett, *The Korean War 1950–1951: They Came From the North* (Manhattan: University Press of Kansas, 2010), 67 ("political hack") [hereafter, Millett, *They Came From the North*]. Millet's books on the Korea War now tower above earlier works not only with respect to the American perspective, but also the Korean and Chinese. James, however, remains fundamental on MacArthur.

23 Frank, *MacArthur*, 172.

24 Millett, *They Came From the North*, 167–68.

25 McCullough, *Truman*, 399 ("Mr. Prima Donna, Brass Hat, Five Star MacArthur"); Hamby, *Man of the People*, 483–86.

26 Eiji Takemae, *Inside GHQ: The Allied Occupation and its Legacy* (New York: Continuum, 2002) 192, 425; James, *The Years of MacArthur, Vol. 3*, 47, 276–79.

27 Richard B. Frank, *Downfall: The End of the Japanese Empire* (New York: Random House, Inc., 1999), 353–54 [hereafter Frank, *Downfall*].

28 Steven J. Fuchs, "Feeding the Japanese: Food Policy, land reform and Japan's economic recovery," 26–7, in Mark E. Caprio and Yoneyuki Sugita, *Democracy in Occupied Japan: The U.S. occupation and Japanese politics and society* (London and New York: Routledge, 2007) citing JCS1380/15 [hereafter Fuchs, "Feeding the Japanese"].

29 Takemae, *Inside GHQ*, 406 citing JCS-1534, 25 October 1945.

30 Fuchs, "Feeding the Japanese," 26–7; Aaron William Moore, "An Insatiable Parasite: Eating and Drinking in WWII Armies in the Asia-Pacific Theaters (1937–1945)," 109–30, Toby Lincoln, "From Riots to Relief: Rice, Local Government and Charities in Occupied Central China," 11–28; Kyoung-Hee Park, "Food Rationing and the Black Market in Wartime Korea," 29–52, Moore, Lincoln and Park in Katarzyna J. Cwiertka, *Food and War in Mid-Twentieth Century East Asia*

(Burlington, VT: Ashgate Publishing Company, 2013) [hereafter Cwiertka, *Food and War*].

31 Greg Huff, *World War II and Southeast Asia: Economy and Society Under Japanese Occupation* (Cambridge; Cambridge University Press, 2020), Ch. 7, 382.

32 Takemae, *Inside GHQ,* 72.

33 Fuchs, "Feeding the Japanese," 28–9.

34 Takemae, *Inside GHQ,* 406.

35 Fuchs, "Feeding the Japanese," 31.

36 Fuchs, "Feeding the Japanese," 28; Christopher Aldous, "A Dearth of Animal Protein: Reforming Nutrition in Occupied Japan (1945–1952)," Cwiertka, *Food and War* [hereafter Aldous, "A Dearth of Animal Protein"]; John W. Dower, *Embracing Defeat: Japan in the Wake of World War II* (New York: W. W. Norton & Company/The New Press, 1999) 93 [hereafter Dower, *Embracing Defeat*].

37 Dower, *Embracing Defeat*, 99–100.

38 Ibid., 29.

39 Ibid., 29–30.

40 Ibid., 30–31; Dower, *Embracing Defeat*, 262–24.

41 Frank, *Downfall*, 351.

42 Fuchs, "Feeding the Japanese," 32.

43 Aldous, "Contesting Famine," 240–41.

44 Fuchs, "Feeding the Japanese," 33.

45 Aldous, "Contesting Famine," 240, 242.

46 General Headquarters, Supreme Commander for the Allied Powers, Economic and Scientific Section Price Control and Rationing Section, Food Situation During the First Year of Occupation, 20 and Table 4, RG-31, Papers of E. G. Skoglund, MacArthur Memorial and Library, Norfolk, VA [hereafter "Food Situation During the First Year of Occupation"]; General Headquarters, Supreme Commander for the Allied Powers, Economic and Scientific Section, Natural Resources Section, Public Health and Welfare Section; Food Situation During the Second Year of Occupation, Table 1: Monthly Population of Japan Proper with Natural Increase and Migration Changes Each Month Since 1 October 1945, RG-31, Papers of E. G. Skoglund, MacArthur Memorial and Library, Norfolk, VA.

47 "Food Situation During the First Year of Occupation," 20–20a.

48 James, *The Years of MacArthur, Vol. 3*, 156.

49 Millett, *They Came from the North*, 63–64, 109–11.

50 Ibid., 46–49, 109–11.

51 Ibid., 41–45.

52 Ibid., 109–29.

53 James, *The Years of MacArthur, Vol. 3*, 420–21, 425, 431.

54 Ibid., 436–38.

55 Millett, *They Came From the North*, 118.

56 James, *The Years of MacArthur, Vol. 3*, 460–64.

57 Millett, *They Came From the North*, 168–69, 206–8.

58 Ibid., 212 ("the best I can say … ").

59 Ibid., 210–12; James, *The Years of MacArthur, Vol. 3*, 468–71.

60 Millett, *The Came From the North*, 249–53.

61 Millett, *They Came From the North*, 236–39; McCullough, *Truman*, 741–42 ("possibly the worst appointment … " and "mentally unbalanced"), 798; James, *The Years of MacArthur, Vol. 3*, 501–2.

62 Millett, *They Came From the North*, 282–83; James, *The Years of MacArthur, Vol. 3*, 502–17 ("absolutely no follow-up questions" at 508 and "political grandstand play" at 515).

63 Millett, *They Came From the North*, 301–3.

64 Ibid., 314–15, 334.
65 Ibid., 233–35.
66 Ibid., 290–97.
67 Ibid., 317–20, 335.
68 Millett, *They Came From the North*, 334–46.
69 Ibid., 291 ("an entirely new war").
70 Ibid., 351, 362.
71 Ibid., 357, 361–64; Hamby, *Man of the People*, 552–53.
72 Millett, *They Came From the North*, 373–74, Ch 11 (376–416).
73 James, *The Years of MacArthur, Vol. 3*, 540–42.
74 Millett, *They Came From the North*, 414.
75 Ibid.
76 Frank, *MacArthur*, 161 ("widely exceeded his past record ... ").
77 Millett, *They Came From the North*, 414–15; Frank, *MacArthur*, 161.
78 Millett, *They Came From the North*, 415.
79 Ibid., 414.
80 James, *The Years of MacArthur, Vol. 3*, 590–92; Millett, *They Came From the North*, 420–21.
81 James, *The Years of MacArthur, Vol. 3*, 592–93; 421.
82 James, *The Years of MacArthur, Vol. 3*, 593–96.
83 James, *The Years of MacArthur, Vol. 3*, 596; Millett, *They Came From the North*, 421.
84 James, *The Years of MacArthur, Vol. 3*, 597.
85 Ibid., 597–600.
86 Ibid., 602.
87 Ibid., 611, 617, 620.
88 "set off a nationwide cacophony of howls ... ": Ibid., 607 ("set off a nationwide cacophony of howls ... ").
89 Ibid., 608.
90 Ibid., 612–16, 623.
91 Ibid., 638 ("vague, indefinite and purposeless"). The comment was by Senator Ralph E. Flanders (R Vermont).
92 Ibid., 625–40.
93 A review of some of the most significant published sources on the threat of mass starvation in Japan relieved by US food imports reflects the following. James records MacArthur's support for the importation of US food but does not provide figures. He does include a comment by a Japanese man that getting US food for the Japanese people was "the general's most noble and perhaps his most important achievement during the occupation." Ibid., 155–56. Takemae provides similar coverage, again without total figures on the quantity of imported food and the number of Japanese being sustained on that food. Takemae, *Inside GHQ*, 76–79, 105, 405–9. Neither the Hamby, *Man of the People*, nor McCulloch, *Truman* biographies address Truman's key role in critical food relief to Japan. Dower, *Embracing Defeat*, is the most interesting case. It contains many references to food and hunger during the occupation's early years (48, 56, 58–59, 64, 72, 74–76, 93–97, 89–103, 105, 118, 121, 146, 169–70, 209, 231, 263, 265–66, 268, 279, 529), and contains numerous references to US food aid (74–76, 93–97, 169–70, 231, 265–66, 268, 529). It does not, however, in my view accord clear and fair recognition overall to the role of US food. The lack of reliability of food supply data in 1945 and 1946 ("unreliably or simply nonexistent") is emphasized (p. 95). This is an important fact, but the magnitude of the peril was immense no matter the exact figures. The statement by the minister of finance in 1945 that ten million Japanese would die of starvation in the next year without food imports is called

"huge (and exaggerated)" (p. 93). The same page goes on the state mildly that "[f]ood shipments from the United States helped avert the anticipated disaster" (p. 93). The narrative further notes that "[a]lthough US food shipments averted the calamitous shortages of basic staples anticipated in mid-May (1946)." (p. 268). But this comment is not connected to other more extensive comments on the food situation. The phrasing that US food "helped avert an anticipated disaster" and that it averted "calamitous shortages," combined with describing as "exaggerated" the statement from the minister of finance about the likelihood of ten million starvation deaths seem unfortunately to understate the peril. The text also acknowledged that the bulk of the two billion dollars in US aid "took the form of critical food-stuffs and material deemed essential just to keep the economy afloat and stave off social unrest" (p. 529). In sum, from these sources a reader: (1) would understand US food aid went to Japan; (2) but not clearly the role of MacArthur and Truman; (3) not the total amount of the US food aid; or (4) figures on how much of the population was being sustained by US food during the critical period from July to September 1946.

12

MAO AND HIS GENERALS

The War to Resist America and Aid Korea

Christopher D. Yung

Introduction

Any discussion of Chairman Mao's management and command of the Chinese war effort in Korea must inevitably involve Mao's relationship with the commander of the Chinese People's Volunteers (CPV)—Peng Dehuai. Curiously Western scholarship as well as American intelligence missed the fact that Peng had been given command by Mao and the Politburo in the fall of 1950 just before the Chinese intervention. Instead, Western scholars and military observers believed that another of Mao's civil war generals—Lin Biao, had initially been given command and then was subsequently replaced with Peng.[1] But an essay solely focused on Mao's relationship with Peng misses a key element of how Mao managed modern China's largest extraterritorial conflict. The Chinese Communist Party had, in fact, emplace a system, worked out after years of trial in the Chinese civil war, to manage war planning and execution. Mao managed this system through a Military-Party bureaucracy made up of those military commanders or commissars with whom he had developed a close relationship through the civil war, and it is these individuals as the principal actors of the Chinese national security system who helped Mao manage the Korean conflict.

China's Party-Military-State Apparatus on the Eve of War

When the Communist Chinese defeated the Nationalists in 1949—Chiang Kai-shek having fled to the island of Taiwan, the Communist leadership had to immediately turn to governing China's 500 million people. Mao and the CCP leadership decided to leave the military forces which had just previously defeated the Nationalists largely in place and created civilian-administrative

DOI: 10.4324/9781003375630-12

organs around these existing forces. Thus, the peculiar governing arrangement of a military region commander, a senior Party chairman, and a military-governor were all put in place in the six-key geographic regions in the new country. Over time the CCP dissolved the military-state apparatus and inserted civilian governors of provinces but in 1949 these state posts were occupied by PLA senior commanders or commissars.[2] As a key example, the Southwest Region had Deng Xiaoping as the Southwest Region Party Chairman, Liu Bocheng (a future PLA Marshal) as Southwest Region Military Commander, and He Long (another future Marshal of the PLA) as the region's Military-governor.[3] All three of these individuals were known personally by Mao, and the fact that three of his most senior commanders and commissars were co-located in one region of the country suggests that the Party still had serious national security threats to contend with, but also that Party central did not want to concentrate too much power in the hands of a single military strong-man.[4]

This pattern of putting Mao's key allies in places of authority throughout the country is consistent throughout the country: Ye Jianying (a future Marshal of the PLA) was made governor of the Southeast Region and Mayor of Guangzhou[5]; Chen Yi (a future Marshal of the PLA) was made military-governor of the South Central Region of the country and mayor of Shanghai[6]; Lin Biao (a future Marshal and eventual anointed successor to Mao) was given command of the South Central Military Region[7]; and Gao Gang (a close ally of Mao's during the Civil War, but who subsequently fell afoul of the Party Central for anti-Party activities and subsequently stripped of his authority) was given command of the Northeast Military Region.[8]

A similar pattern is observed when it comes to the staffing of the military bureaucracy on the eve of the Korean conflict. Zhu De, one of Mao's oldest comrades in the PLA enjoyed the title of the PLA's Commander-in-Chief.[9] The aforementioned Peng Dehuai (a future Marshal) was made Minister of Defense but was also the Vice Chairman of the Revolutionary Military Committee of the Central Government, and concurrently as Commander of the Northwest Military Region; Luo Ronghuan (again a future Marshal) was given the post of the Director of the General Political Department[10]—the organization responsible for ensuring loyalty of PLA personnel, propaganda for the armed forces, political warfare, and mobilizing the masses to support the war effort; and Nie Rongzhen (a future PLA Marshal) was made acting Director of the General Staff Department—the organization most responsible for operational planning, intelligence, training and equipping PLA forces in the field.[11]

The Absence of a Civilian-Military Divide

Another characteristic of national security and military decision-making in Maoist China is the apparent absence of a civil-military divide. At the outset of the creation of the People's Republic governance was characterized by concentration of power by the Chinese Communist Party elite who had been either military commanders or political commissars in the PLA. No civil-military division of labor existed during the Chinese Civil War and that pattern continued following the establishment of the PRC. As a result a powerful figure like Zhou Enlai, one of Mao's closest confidants throughout the Civil War, served at one time or another, and sometimes concurrently, as China's foreign minister, prime minister, head of the Organization Department of the Central Committee of the CCP, and Ex Officio member of the Central Military Commission.[12] The historical record uncovers evidence of Zhou interacting with the Indian Ambassador, attempting to signal to the United States not to approach the Yalu and China's borders, while at the same time Zhou personally oversaw some of the logistical support to the troops during the conflict, worked on the operational outline for PLA intervention into the Korean conflict,[13] and even engaged with Mao on specific operational and tactical decisions pertaining to Chinese forces in Korea.[14] While it makes sense for Liu Shaoqi, the President of the PRC and the second highest ranking member of the CCP, to go to Moscow in 1950 to personally ask Stalin for needed Soviet military assistance and equipment; a similar follow-up function is played by Lin Biao and Zhu De none of whom have foreign affairs bona fides.

The Maoist Philosophy on Military Strategy

Another factor shaping the Chinese decision-making environment was Mao's thinking on how to formulate a military strategy for the war. As early as the 1930s when Mao first espoused his thoughts on how best to defeat the Party's enemies—the Nationalists in the late 1920s and early to mid-1930s; the Japanese in the mid-1930s to mid-1940s—it is clear that Mao believed that military effectiveness and political effect were intertwined. Mao's opening assessment on the strategic situation with Japan in "On Protracted War" mixes a net assessment of the military capabilities of the combatants with the political situations the Japanese and Chinese find themselves in.[15] He, in fact, concludes that Japan's favorable military-strategic situation could not last long because its political situation—occupying a large hostile territory with world opinion increasingly turning against it—was slowly but inevitably worsening. Mao engages in similar politico-military strategy formulation when he contemplates war in "Problems of Strategy in China's Revolution."[16] As we will see this had a profound impact on Mao's disagreements with Peng Dehuai—the commander in the field.

The Role of Political Commissars

Because of the importance Mao placed on political effect and military strategy, the role of political commissars evolved and became a permanent feature of how the PLA fought its wars. Originally a Soviet innovation, the Chinese fully embraced the concept and integrated commissars in the tactical, operational, and strategic decision-making process. There is historical evidence that the dual command relationship between military commanders and commissars produced tensions in command and control during China's civil war.[17] Yet the CCP stuck with the concept because the commissar's primary function—ensuring the loyalty of the troops and command elements—was essential when dealing with a military culture prone to defections by commanders and their subordinates. Commissars also played a very useful function in winning over popular support—an essential element of CCP success during the civil war.[18]

At the strategic level, Mao and the CCP ensured the continued bureaucratic influence of the political commissar by creating in 1931 a general headquarters for the commissar function—the General Political Department, which was the counterpart to the aforementioned General Staff Department. Here the Party concentrated functions associated with maintaining the morale of the fighting forces; ensuring the loyalty of not only the frontline troops but also of the most senior military commanders; the formulation and distribution of propaganda; the ideological training of the military; the evaluation of the performance of military personnel; and an investigatory function related to the misconduct of military personnel.[19] Mao placed his old colleague—Luo Ronghuan—as the Director of the GPD. Luo's running of the GPD during the Korean conflict meant that Mao did not have to worry about the details of conceptualizing a large-scale propaganda campaign (The War to Resist America and Aid Korea), plan recruit enlistment campaigns, or scrutinize the loyalty of commanders in the field.

Curiously the PLA high command elected to dual-hat Peng Dehuai as both the military commander of the CPV and the political commissar.[20] A deputy political commissar, General Du Ping dutifully played that role for the duration of the Korean conflict, but the decision not to counterbalance Peng's authority with an equal is a curious historical anomaly.[21]

The Civil War Performances of Lin Biao and Peng Dehuai

A major consideration for Mao's thinking on who should lead Chinese forces in a Korean conflict was the wartime records of the prospective commanders. As we will see below Su Yu was an early candidate identified by the Central Military Commission to command the troops; but it is possible that Mao's only two serious considerations were Lin Biao and Peng Dehuai. Although Su Yu's record during the Civil War is impeccable and his significant role in the operational planning for the 3rd Field Army is largely responsible for some of the Communists' major victories—the Huai Hai campaign in particular—Su was still junior to both Lin and Peng and in fact, Lin was his superior for the last two years of the civil war.[22] Another reason it was unlikely that Su would be selected to command the CPV was that he was at the end of 1949 and a good part of 1950 elbow deep in the planning for a Taiwan invasion and all of the frustrations that went with that endeavor.[23]

A strong argument can be made that Mao could only consider a military commander with the seniority and stature of a Lin Biao or a Peng Dehuai: both military men had been with Mao from the beginning of the civil war, Peng Dehuai bringing his troops with Zhu De to the Jinggang mountains following the abortive Nanchang uprising, and Lin Biao's company even being assigned to guard Zhou Enlai, who, at that time, was one of the highest ranking Party members.[24] Both also participated in the Long March, Lin Biao again given the tough assignment of guarding the Party leadership as it criss-crossed the country.[25] Both also sided with Mao during the intra-Party struggle settled at the Zunyi conference in 1934, and were senior military leaders at Yenan, with Lin leading troops against the Japanese during this period, and Peng engaging in the "Hundred Regiments Campaign"—one of the best known PLA campaigns against the Japanese[26]; Finally, both men commanded field armies during the second phase of the civil war with the Kuomintang (1946–1949), with Lin Biao largely credited with victories in the Liao-Shen, Ping Jin, and Huai Hai campaigns and Peng largely credited with the successful campaigns of the west and central parts of the country.[27]

Objectively the two future Marshals can be said to have had equal performances during the civil war. Another consideration which may have crossed Mao's mind was whether the two had been loyal to Mao throughout the civil war and anti-Japanese war periods. Both had sided with Mao during a significant Party split during the Long March and settled at Zunyi in Sichuan province. Even Zhu De, Mao's long-time military partner during the civil war sided with Mao's rival Zhang Guotao at this time, and later had to reconcile with Mao.[28] Lin and Mao do suffer a break in relations in 1936 when Lin disagreed with Mao's decision to break up Lin's 1st Corps and distribute the units to other forces; Lin was relieved of his command and assigned to be the head of the newly established Workers and Peasants Red Army Academy. Although this apparent demotion did see Lin's career to fall behind those of his peers, his subsequent assignments during the anti-Japanese war and the Second phase of the Civil War mitigated these setbacks. Lin also managed to miss the next major intra-Party struggle—the Yenan Rectification campaign—owing to illness and medical treatment in Russia from 1939 to 1942.[29] Peng Dehuai on the other hand was not so fortunate. As his memoirs reveal Peng had taken an equivocal line between two contending ways forward for the CCP—those of Mao who advocated for a continuing of CCP anti-KMT activities while allied with the Nationalists and his then major competitor, Wang Ming, who argued for setting aside the expansion of Party activities to concentrate on strengthening the united front with the Nationalists in the cause of the war with Japan.[30] Mao was to remember Peng's position during the Rectification campaign and this would haunt Peng later during the Cultural Revolution; however, at the time of the civil war and anti-Japanese war Peng was not overtly criticized by the Party center.[31]

Mao's Relationship with Stalin and His Perception of His Role in International Communism

Finally, Mao's motivations for intervention and the strategic objectives for that intervention were significantly influenced by Mao's desire to impress Stalin and to demonstrate the contribution the People's Republic of China could make toward the cause of international communism. The perception that China has an outsized role in the Cold War contest applies to other Chinese leaders, such as Zhou Enlai.[32] As we will see, however, Mao repeatedly came back to the logic of the effect Chinese intervention in Korea would have on American designs in Asia; on the nascent communist movements globally; and on the viability of the Nationalists on Taiwan.[33] Mao was careful to not take action which was at cross-purposes with Stalin's overall assessment of the situation and to adhere to the Soviet leader's larger strategy on Korea.[34]

The Korean Conflict and the Chinese Decision to Intervene

Another major shortcoming of Western analysis of the Chinese decision to intervene in Korea was the timing of the decision. Alan Whiting and a whole host of American scholars sets the decision at late September and early October.[35] It is universally agreed now that new Chinese archival materials have been made available since the 1990s that the decision came much earlier in the summer of 1950. Initial American scholarship gives the impression that Mao hurriedly convened a meeting of the politburo to decide on intervention. Peng Dehuai's memoirs made available in the mid-1980s reinforces this impression since he was hurriedly called to Beijing to take part in a politburo meeting to discuss intervention and was given command at that moment.[36]

We now know that the Chinese decision on intervention was much more deliberative and analytical and took place well before the American intervention. The historian Chen Jian's meticulous examination of the archives shows that the timeline for consideration of the impact of conflict on the Korean Peninsula came as early as June 1950. This is because Mao and Stalin were both notified of the possibility of a North Korean attack much earlier than has been recorded by Western historians. Chen Jian notes that as early as April 1950 Kim Il-sung secretly visited Moscow to get Stalin's approval for a DPRK invasion of the ROK. Chen's research shows that Kim did not ask Mao's permission until May of 1950; and Chen has found that Kim did not provide any operational details or precise timelines.[37] Mao knew of Kim's intentions but he did not know the "when" or the "how" of what Kim was proposing to do. Chen notes that Kim most likely received Mao's blessing at that meeting, which led to a speeding up of preparations for the invasion.[38]

When the North Korean invasion took place in June of 1950 Chen notes that the fact of the invasion did not surprise China's leaders, and, as later reinforced by Western scholarship the Chinese were surprised by the American decision to intervene in the conflict after the Truman administration had signaled strongly that they did not consider Korea a part of America's vital national interest. The most recent scholarship related to Chinese discussions on intervention, however, moves some distance from what American historians have believed to be the case for decades.[39] Chinese American historians—Chen Jian, Zhang Shuguang, Li Xiaobing—with access to the CCP and governmental archives in the 1990s and early 2000s started publishing new details of the CCP leadership's response to events in Korea.[40] This later scholarship displays a much more deliberative and analytical process than was thought to be the case.

Following the passage of a UN resolution in late June giving the United States the authority to assist South Korea following the DPRK invasion, the United States and its allies began operations on the Korean Peninsula. At roughly the same time in early July, Zhou Enlai convened two conferences in Beijing attended by key leaders of the Central Military Commission, the heads of the PLA's different services, and the heads of the Military Regions (MRs). At this conference, Zhou revealed that Mao had already made the decision to create a Northeast Border Defense Army (NEBDA) so that "in case we need to enter the war we would be prepared."[41] This decision precedes the American action at Inchon. The conferees decided to move the 38th, 39th, and 40th Armies (13th Army Corps) to the NEBDA. According to Chen the conference appointed Su Yu, then Commander of the East China Military Region as the prospective commander and Xiao Jingguang, the then Commander of the newly formed PLA Navy as Political Commissar. Li Jukui, then Deputy Chief of Staff for the South-Central Military region was to serve as the NEBDA's logistics commander. The conference directed the General Logistics Department to begin planning for recruitment of additional personnel since China had undergone a massive demobilization following the end of the Civil War. The conference presented its work to Mao and the Politburo Standing Committee who approved the plan; of note Mao specifically approved of Su Yu as the prospective commander of the NEBDA. This approval manifested itself in the formal orders issued by the CMC on 13 July 1950 "Orders to defend the Northeast Borders."[42]

After the CMC orders, the Chinese military-bureaucratic apparatus then went into full gear preparing the PLA for potential mobilization and participation in a Korean conflict. Nie Rongzhen, then Acting Chief of General Staff advised Mao and Zhou on 2nd of August to dispatch anti-aircraft artillery units to the Northeast Military Region to protect bridges over the Yalu River.[43] Zhou Enlai directed the Northeast People's Government Headquarters, the

Northeast Military Region, and the Headquarters of the Central-southern Military Region to which the 13th Army Corps belonged before being transferred to NEBDA, to provide logistical support and set guidelines for combat service supply. By mid-July the General Logistics Department had already directed the other military regions of China to provide massive stocks of clothing, gloves, socks, and footwear to be shipped to the NEBDA.[44] In early August the full Politburo met to discuss the implications of a Chinese intervention in Korea. The records of that meeting show that the CCP leadership was immediately taken up with the wider negative implications of having the US intervene so strongly on the side of the ROK. The CCP leadership consensus at this time, then, appears to have been of the view that China must intervene or else face the possibility of world peace being threatened by American hegemonism.[45] This is a curious new finding since we will see the Politburo much more hesitant in a subsequent meeting to advocate for intervention.

Between late August and early October 1950 events rapidly changed on the ground in Korea that forced the CCP leadership to convene an enlarged meeting of the Politburo for the purposes of immediate intervention. No decision to deploy had been made in August because the NEBDA's assessment of their situation indicated that it was not yet ready to move into Korea. Moreover, Mao was reluctant to authorize the intervention until he had secured Stalin's cooperation which Chen argues came in August. Kim Il-sung had also been reluctant to approve Chinese interference owing to domestic political issues of his own. But he suddenly changed his position when the North Korean People's Army suffered a sudden reversal of fortune with the successful landing of US forces at Inchon.[46] This development prompted the enlarged Politburo meeting of 1–2 October to discuss China's immediate intervention.

The enlarged Politburo meeting is a good lens to examine supreme command in the Chinese Communist decision-making system. Between June and October 1950, the system worked as most observers have assessed as typical of the process. The Party-Military bureaucracy convened working groups or conferences to study a particular problem, the views of the relevant players were aired, and broad outlines for action were put forward for the Chairman to approve or disapprove. The Central Military Commission then took the broad outlines of the plan and issued orders to be carried out with the General Staff Department, which fleshed out the specifics of how the orders were to be executed. The sudden reversals suffered in Korea forced the CCP leadership to make some snap judgments and to act without delay.

Mao convened the meeting and Chen argues that it was clear from the opening remarks from the chairman that he favored intervention.[47] Interestingly the historical record shows that unlike the Politburo meeting of August, Mao faced near unanimous objection to intervention by his military advisors. The thrust of their objections according to the record was that China was significantly inferior to the United States in terms of military capability, the country had just been formed and therefore the CCP had not sufficiently consolidated power, and Soviet military aid had been slow in coming. Mao continued to argue for the intervention and kept pressing his colleagues to reconsider their objections. A particular surprise in this exchange is the apparent objection to intervention by Lin Biao.[48]

Mao had additionally opened the proceedings by stating that one of the first orders of business was to identify a commander for the Chinese forces. Since the CMC order of 13 July 1950 had explicitly named Su Yu as commander of the NEBDA, the decision on who would command the invasion force had obviously changed since then. Part of the historical record seems to suggest that Su was suffering from some kind of ailment and therefore was not medically fit to command the forces. The dispatch of so many forces from the Fourth Field Army to the NEBDA, however, suggests that within this time-frame Mao had elected to go with Lin Biao (the former Fourth Field Army Commander during the Civil War) as the commander instead of Su.[49] Lin's reluctance, if not refusal to command the troops, complicated this plan. Peng's late arrival to the Politburo meeting and subsequent agreement with Mao that China's intervention was necessary and led to his agreement to command the invasion forces. This sealed both the decision for China to intervene and for Peng to serve as the commander of the invasion.[50]

China Crosses the Yalu

Conventional scholarship in thinking that the Chinese skillfully employed lessons that they had learned from the Chinese civil war—superiority in numbers, concentration of forces at the point of attack, mobility, tactical surprise—as they prepared to intervene in Korea. By moving at night, resting by day, and camouflaging the large number of troops on the march the Chinese People's Volunteers were able to move some 300,000 troops into Korea with American intelligence oblivious to their presence.[51] Recent scholarship illustrates a pattern of interference from Mao which would prove highly disruptive for the on-scene field commanders. On October 9, the day after Peng arrived in Shenyang to organize his command and get operations underway, Peng conferred with Deng Hua and Hong Xuezhi, his two deputy commanders. The original CMC plan called for two armies to cross the Yalu into North Korea and to hold two armies in reserve, preparing to cross at a subsequent date. Peng's subordinates advised him that this was unrealistic. They believed that without strong artillery and air support, two armies were insufficient to develop a defensive base area in North Korea against UN Forces. Additionally, they said, the US Air Force was engaging in relentless air attacks against roads and bridges. It would be very likely that the two armies waiting to cross into Korea would find it extremely difficult, if not impossible, to do so with most of the bridges and roads relentlessly bombed and strafed. Peng sent a request to the CMC to change the original order to one involving all four armies crossing the Yalu simultaneously along with three artillery divisions. Mao agreed to the request, informing Peng on 11 October.[52]

This would prove to be one of the rare instances of the Korean conflict in which Mao listened to his subordinates and acted on their advice. Shortly after this exchange, however, Mao began agitating for an earlier entry into Korea. He sent a cable to CPV headquarters directing that one army should head out by October 17 as an advanced party in order to arrive at Tokchon by 23 October. The advanced party would rest for a day and then begin construction of defensive works. The second army would depart China by 18 October followed by the remaining two armies shortly thereafter. Mao ordered that all armies should have crossed the Yalu within ten days of the 17 October start of the operation. As Shu Guang Zhang has written Mao changed his mind several times, urging different combinations of armies deploying into Korea and varying the different measures to be employed to ensure secrecy.[53]

Peng was unable to fully comply with Mao's orders. As Zhang has written the establishment of CPV command in Korea had fits and starts and Peng, for a time, even lost contact with 13th Army Group Headquarters. In a cable dated 22 October Peng asked that Mao amend his orders to allow for the establishment of a defensive base area to include Changjin, Huichon, and Kusong and to provide specific air defenses for ferry points along the Yalu. Peng even asked that the CPV be relieved of the requirement to defend certain North Korean cities because it would not be able to defend against UN naval, air, and armored forces. Peng assured Mao that, at a subsequent date, the CPV would attack ROK forces if such an opportunity arose. In his reply on the 23rd of October Mao acquiesced to Peng's request but as Zhang has observed "he was evidently not pleased with Peng's caution," arguing that from a military perspective combat decisions should be instructed by "whether we can take advantage of the enemy's complete unawareness [of our entry] so as to wipe out three or even four [ROK] puppet divisions with a surprise attack."[54] Mao's larger rationale, which incidentally would be a theme of Mao's throughout the war, was that a major battlefield triumph would force the US/UN forces to reconsider their campaign objectives. Failing to achieve a major victory, Mao reasoned, would move the overall situation toward one favorable to the ROK, the United States, and the UN forces.[55]

As it turned out, despite Peng's caution, the CPV was able to accomplish major battlefield successes in that first encounter with ROK and US troops. As the 39th Army was attacking Unsan on November 1, they accidentally engaged with American units of the 1st Cavalry Division and completely took them by surprise, wiping out one US battalion, and overwhelming two additional battalions.[56] The first campaign accomplished what Mao and Peng had set out to do—stabilize the situation in North Korea, give the North Korean regime strategic breathing room to recover, and pushed American forces south. At the same time, the First Campaign failed to accomplish the original objective of destroying several American divisions.

The Second Offensive

Encouraged by the success of its initial encounter with the US/UN forces, Peng and his subordinates planned on a feigned withdrawal in order to lure UN forces north into a group of pre-set traps.[57] After Peng Dehuai's plan was approved by Mao, all four CPV armies withdraw north but left one division to conduct "mobile" and "guerilla warfare" to wipe out smaller enemy units and to lure additional UN forces north.[58] MacArthur obligingly launched his "home by Christmas" campaign using Eighth Army units in the west and X Corps units attacking in the East. The Chinese Second Offensive began when the CPV counter-attacked in force with the 39th, 40th, 50th, and 66th armies attacking in a frontal assault against Eighth Army, the 38th Army maneuvering between the ROK's 7th and 8th Divisions at Tokchon and the 113th Division ultimately occupying the strategically vital Samso-ri which threatened the US Army's Second Division and potentially trapping a good proportion of the US Eighth Army.[59]

Between the 4th and 8th of December, faced with the large-scale CPV Second Offensive, UN Forces gave up the Ch'ongch'on River bridgehead along the western front and withdrew. The forces on the eastern front in the meantime retreated to Hamhung.[60] This large-scale withdrawal included the abandonment of Pyongyang. On December 8th, the Commanding General of the UNC ordered his forces to establish defensive positions on the 38th Parallel as part of a larger defense strategy.[61]

At this point, further encouraged by the successful operations of the CPV, Mao began to agitate for further operations to press the US and UN forces even further south and off the Peninsula. Realities on the ground, however, kept Peng cautious about the prospects for a continued offensive south. A large number of his troops had suffered from the severe winter conditions, with many deaths attributed to frostbite. Intelligence was also starting to come in that US forces had ceased retreating and were possibly preparing for a counter-attack possibly along the same lines as an amphibious flanking attack not unlike at Inchon. Peng at this moment decided to cease the offensive and ordered each of his armies back to the 38th Parallel for rest and refit.[62]

The Third Offensive

Despite CPV successes at the end of the year 1950, United Nations forces began an aggressive counter-offensive in early December. The offensive took the Chinese by surprise and Peng sent a message to Mao asking that he either be permitted to accept "neutral countries" calls for a "limited cease fire" or be allowed to withdraw his forces "15 to 30 kilometers north."[63] Peng reasoned that if the CPV and NKA could not hold UN forces the defense of "bridge-head positions" would be in doubt making it difficult to accomplish Mao's objective of wiping out a large enemy force for the purpose of driving the US/ UN forces out of Korea. Given the exhaustion of Peng's troops and the need for replenishment and refit following the last offensive, Peng saw such a counter-offensive as unrealistic. Concerned that the proposal for a ceasefire was a trick to freeze the conflict at the 38th Parallel, Mao responded the following day with a telegram to Peng indicating that he felt it "inappropriate" to retreat north or to accept a limited cease-fire. He called for an immediate counterattack.[64] Mao argued in his telegram that it is "not a great difficulty even if our forces have not been resupplied with munitions; we still possess the capability of ... destroying some U.S. units and four or five ROK divisions if we try our best." Mao would not permit a retreat north; in fact, he ordered the CPV to advance south sixty miles to the 36th parallel. On December 13th, 1950, Mao issued the order for the CPV to begin planning for the Third Offensive.[65] The order directed Peng to envelop and destroy both ROK and UN forces south of the 38th Parallel, with another objective being the recapture of Seoul.[66]

Sensing that a scaled-down version of Mao's all-out counterattack order would be criticized in Beijing, Peng asked for flexibility in his objectives and the right to disengage if necessary. According to Yu Bin, Mao conceded to Peng's request and "granted him the tactical flexibility to disengage and stop the operation whenever necessary," but Mao insisted that "political agitation work be stepped up and [the CPV] won't be withdrawn from Korea until all enemy forces are destroyed."[67]

On January 1, 1951, the Communists initiated its Third ("New Year") Offensive.[68] The campaign did accomplish some tactical surprise. In eight days CPV forces were able to cross the 38th Parallel from their defensive positions, recapture Seoul, and push UN forces down to the 37th Parallel. UN forces conducted an orderly retreat and casualties were minimal.[69] Owing to the insufficient rest and refit time for CPV units, Chinese forces quickly became exhausted after marching long distances and incessant combat. Additionally, the CPV suffered huge losses—85,000 KIA or WIA. For these reasons, in addition to the suspicion that UN forces were deliberately attempting to lure Communist forces south with a feigned retreat, Peng, following the capture of Seoul, ordered the third offensive halted, effectively ending the pursuit of retreating UN forces.[70]

The Fourth Offensive

The "petering out" of the third offensive was a serious reversal for the Chinese on Korea. However, Mao was uninterested in scaling back his plans. He was still very much invested in another large-scale offensive. The relative success of the first three Chinese offensives (the first two more than the third) convinced Mao that Chinese forces must continue to press south until they had driven US/UN forces off of the Peninsula.[71] The CPV's February Offensive began in earnest when UN forces initiated a counteroffensive on the western front, attacking toward the Han River. Despite CPV forces not having been resupplied or received reinforcements, Peng ordered a hasty counteroffensive attacking UN forces on the central front.

In early March 1951 Mao cabled Peng that UN forces would subsequently do one of the following: continue to attack north in an effort to take advantage of CPV exhaustion, halt at the 38th parallel for about ten to twenty days, or remain at the 38th Parallel for a period of two to three months before resuming attacks.[72] He concluded that the first two options would initially be the more likely option; however, "once the enemy discovers the arrival of our reinforcements in large numbers, the third possibility will become reality, that is, [the enemy] will lock us in a stalemate along the 38th Parallel."[73] In order to avoid this possibility Mao called for Peng to concentrate his forces along the 38th Parallel in order to prepare for yet another counterattack. Peng's objectives should be to "wipe out another ten thousand American troops and completely destroy Syngman Rhee's forces around the 38th Parallel and then advance south to the South Han River."[74]

Peng read Mao's orders to his disbelieving subordinates and the North Korean representatives at his joint headquarters. Yu Bin's account of this period is instructive. Peng's subordinates began to question "Mao's judgement, and some even raised the question of how far political considerations should dictate military operations."[75] According to Shu Guang Zhang Peng sought to "split the difference" by seeking to "minimize CPV losses while at the same time meeting the intent of Mao's guidance." He ordered his planners to develop operational plans to conduct a counter-offensive. As Zhang has described it, "given that the U.S./UN forces were advancing side by side, an all-out frontal counterattack would be disastrous. Peng thus decided to employ the 38th and 50th Armies on the southern bank of the Han River to delay the enemy advance on Seoul, have the CPV/NKPA forces pull back in the east to allow the ROK forces to move ahead of the other U.S./UN columns, and assemble the 39th, 40th, 42nd and 66th Armies in the Hoengsong area to attack overextended ROK forward elements."[76]

CPV forces ultimately were forced to abandon Seoul by mid-March 1951 and withdraw forces north of the 38th Parallel. A number of factors explained UN/US successes here; but the most apparent factor was superior US firepower and mobility. The other factor explaining US/UN success was the ability of US forces to flexibly adapt tactics to past Chinese operations. One such successful tactic was the "magnet" tactic in which US tacticians figured out that Chinese units could only sustain their frontline troops for one week at a time and would then have to withdraw owing to exhaustion and poor supply.[77] Thus, Small US and UN tactical units would constantly engage larger Chinese units until they became combat ineffective. According to Yu Bin, US forces also abandoned "the fast advance strategy along highways and tried to advance in close ranks so that their flanks would not be exposed."[78] According to Yu, "these more disciplined tactics allowed UN forces to take advantage of their superior firepower. Ubiquitous US observation aircraft also increased considerably the accuracy of US artillery firepower."[79] In the end, relentless pressure from UN forces led to a steady worsening of the Chinese tactical situation forcing Peng to recognize that earlier gains were in jeopardy.

The General Staff and Logistics Departments in Support of the War Effort

One of the enduring problems experienced by Chinese forces in Korea was the poor supply of food, clothing and other equipment. Commanders also reported that, in a number of instances, they had to halt offensives and stop the pursuit of retreating UN forces because they had run out of ammunition or fuel.[80] Additionally, some reports noted that the UN forces had surmised the Chinese weakness and had sought to take tactical advantage of the situation, by withdrawing under cover of fire and then after the CPV had exhausted its ammunition they would launch a large scale counter-offensive.[81]

Zhou Enlai had been approached by Mao to oversee the overall preparations for a potential conflict in Korea.[82] By default, the Chairman thus placed Zhou in charge of the logistical support for the Korean conflict. Although he had no specific position within the CCP national security system, he was tapped by the Chairman to oversee its management. In the run up to the Korean conflict, Zhou issued guidance on logistics support and continued to do so throughout the war. The General Staff Department and General Logistics Department worked with the Central Military Commission to develop such innovations as motorized kitchens, and improved canned foods for frontline troops; the General Staff Department eased the slow supply to the front lines by increasing protection to the PLA's rail service, constructing alternative railway and highway lines, increasing the number of air raid shelters along transportation routes, deploying an increased number of anti-aircraft observation posts, storing repair materials ahead of time to locations likely to be attacked by enemy aircraft, and in some cases constructing underwater bridges.[83] Hong Xuezhi, Peng's Deputy Commander recalled making a special trip to Beijing in order to meet with Premier Zhou for the purpose of relaying logistics lessons learned and to advocate for the creation of a special CPV logistics headquarters.[84] Both Hong and Nie Rongzhen report that the creation of this headquarters markedly improved the PLA's logistics problems in Korea.[85]

The Last CPV Offensive

Convinced that one final effort would successfully push UN forces off of the Peninsula, Mao continued to agitate for another offensive. In a series of cables to the Chairman, Peng insisted that another campaign at that moment would prove futile. Unable to convince Mao otherwise, Peng asked his subordinates to begin planning for a Fifth offensive. His commanders' skepticism was beginning to show and so Peng felt the need to speak with them collectively. On April 6 he spoke at an enlarged CPV command meeting that included the commanders and political commissars of the 9th Army Group, the 19th Army Group, and the 3rd Army Group. At that meeting, he pointed out that "the United States is determined to carry on the war with us and peace is by no means likely in the near future … considerable evidence indicates that the enemy is prepared to fight a larger scale war. Any illusions regarding peace and wishful thinking about winning the war by a fluke will soon be smashed." From Peng's point of view it would be better to fight now than later because as Shu Guang Zhang quotes the CPV commander "the enemy is tired, its troops have not been replenished, its reinforcements have yet to gather on the front, and its military strength is relatively weak at this point."[86] Since this is the case, "if the enemy advances fast, we will begin the counteroffensive around April 20; if the enemy moves slowly, we will act in early May."[87] Zhang notes in his work that Peng next stated that the purpose of this next campaign was to "destroy a few more U.S./UN divisions and crush the enemy plan for a major attack."[88] In doing so, Peng observed, the CPV would retain the initiative and be able to "carve up the enemy forces into many pockets and wipe them out one by one."[89]

Peng spoke with confidence to his commanders because over a number of weeks in early 1951 the CPV had been receiving reinforcements and resupply. Over twenty infantry divisions had joined the 13th Army Group at the front. The 19th and 3rd Army Groups were now considered fully combat ready. Some of the other Army groups, particularly the 9th Army Group had been rested for a number of months and its casualties had been evacuated and replaced.[90] Field artillery divisions were also beginning to arrive at the front, significantly enhancing CPV firepower. Owing to the efforts of Deputy Commander Hong Xuezhi, the creation of a CPV logistics headquarters, and the renewed focus of the Central Military Commission on the problem of supply, the CPV rear services support improved markedly.[91]

Surprisingly, the initial results of the CPV attack were not promising. Instead of retreating US/UN forces were able to mount a vigorous, tactically disciplined defense. Despite the large size of the offensive the CPV proved unable to cut UN forces into pieces and individually wipe them out.[92] In a telegram to Mao on April 26 Peng asked Mao to consider calling off the offensive. He explained that the CPV have proven incapable of exploiting any gaps in the enemy defenses.[93] He also worried that after four days of heavy fighting, it might be possible for the enemy to mount a second amphibious flanking movement leading to a military disaster for the CPV. Fearful of a two-front battlefield engagement, Peng suggested to Mao that he send three CPV armies and two NKPA corps to tie up US/UN forces near the 37th parallel around the Han River, while the remainder of the CPV force would retreat to the 38th parallel.

Mao shared Peng's concern that UN forces could conceivably launch an amphibious flanking attack; however, he refused to allow Peng to withdraw his forces north and urged him to continue pressing the attack. In contrast to previous instances in the war, Peng's commanders did not share Peng's conservative view of what should happen next. They were not in favor of a retreat and agreed with Mao that the CPV should continue pressing the attack.[94] Peng cautioned them to examine the military situation more realistically, but he gave in to their demands to continue the offensive. In looking over the military situation in the spring of 1951 Peng believed that the best course of action would be to shift offensive operations to the east.[95] He planned on a 9th and 3rd Army Group shift of forces to the east in order to launch a secret attack on ROK forces and then to move west to outflank US/UN forces there.[96]

Owing to poor command, control, and coordination, the planned CPV counteroffensive did not succeed. CPV forces failed to destroy the initial ROK troops who subsequently conducted an orderly retreat into the mountainous terrain.[97] The effort to outflank UN/US forces in the west also failed as the CPV met fierce resistance from Army and Marine divisions positioned near Hongchon.[98] As UN/US reinforcements entered the battle, the Chinese offensive stalemated and the old problem of CPV resupply then set in. Fearing a rout, Peng halted the offensive and directed his Army Groups to begin retreating north.[99] But poor communications and command and control led to a disorderly and uncoordinated retreat leading to large losses. The 180th Division for instance lost over 7,000 troops—5,000 of whom were captured by US forces. Peng immediately called for the 63rd, 64th, 15th, 26th, and 20th armies as well as several corps of the NKPA to form a defense in depth along the 38th Parallel.[100]

Stalemate and Exit Strategy

Following the failure of the Fifth Offensive, Mao now realized that his aspiration to use large-scale military offensives to drive UN forces off of the Peninsula was unrealistic.[101] Thus, he now acquiesced to Peng and his subordinates' suggestions for more cautious and deliberative military operations. As a result, CPV operations were designed to avoid direct confrontation and large-scale battles with UN/US forces. Rather, military operations were designed to give leverage to Chinese and North Korean representatives at the peace talks at

Kaesong and eventually at Panmunjom. In some cases, CPV military operations even sought to communicate to their UN/US adversaries the willingness to cease fighting along the 38th Parallel.[102]

Conclusion: Mao and Supreme Command

There is every reason to conclude that on the eve of the Korean conflict, Mao had firm control over the decision-making process and appeared to quickly formulate a strategy to address what appeared to be an inevitable Chinese intervention. At least at this stage in Mao's leadership of the Party, he gives off an air of collegiality, even though, as we have seen Mao did not rely on collectivist leadership. As mentioned above, the Chinese system had emplaced a Party-Military bureaucracy to manage strategic and operational decision-making. Mao appears to have allowed the principals of the organizations designed to address these kinds of issues, to work out how best to manage the issue at hand, and then largely agreed with the decisions or suggested ways to revise policy. The major exceptions to this were the Politburo meeting of October 1950, when Mao's military advisors advocated against intervention; and the disagreements Mao had with Peng Dehuai over how best to prosecute the war following the initial intervention.

In many respects Mao's behavior during China's involvement in the Korean conflict was typical of a totalitarian dictator formulating and communicating military strategy with his military commanders. Mao allowed his views on the importance of political objectives to eclipse realistic military planning on the ground. Despite views to the contrary issued by his hand-selected commander-in-chief of Chinese People's Volunteers—Peng Dehuai—Mao continually pushed for large-scale ground offensives or counter-offensives whether realistic or not. Mao's motives in this regard have been attributed largely to his driving need to get Stalin's approval and acknowledgment that China had an important role to play in the global struggle with Hegemonism. In any case, it is curious behavior considering that the Chinese Communists appeared to have a winning military formula coming out of the civil war, only to have that formula pushed to the side as a sacrificial lamb to Mao's ambitions.

At the same time, Mao's management of the Korean conflict also reflects the unique Chinese Communist system of governance and administration. In the run-up to the initiation of Chinese involvement in the war, we can see the Chinese administrative system at work. As trouble was beginning to brew on the Peninsula all the bureaucratic organizations responsible for discussing, planning, staffing, and executing a Chinese military response to a potential conflict had begun to convene months before actual Chinese involvement. Two conferences convened by the Central Military Commission and chaired by Zhou Enlai had already met and discussed command relations and the units to be involved in a potential conflict. The later decision to intervene was made at enlarged meetings of the Politburo, involving the PLA high command as well as the top CCP leadership, a historic fact which makes complete sense from a Chinese Communist governance perspective. Three of the most significant bureaucratic players of Chinese administrative-military power, the General Staff Department, the General Politics Department, and the General Logistics Department each played prominent roles in the planning and execution of military strategy, manpower and recruitment, morale and propaganda, morale building, supply and services support, transportation, and force protection for the war.

A curious feature of the Chinese Communist administrative apparatus at the beginning of the creation of the People's Republic is the personalized nature of management of a highly bureaucratized system. Whereas the bureaucratic administrative structures were in place to manage the major issues of the war as illustrated with examples above, the system was still characterized by a highly personalized network. On the eve of conflict on the Korean Peninsula Mao had in place military commanders, Party chiefs, and military-state governors who were personally loyal to the chairman. Each of the major Party and military administrative organs were headed by CCP leaders who had personal connections to Mao. Thus, a consequential feature of the management of the war led to a real blurring of civilian-military lines of authority. Why, for instance, was Zhou Enlai, then Prime Minister also doing work of the Central Military Commission, in charge of the major military support issues of the war as an ex officio member? We have accounts of Zhou meeting with Peng Dehuai's deputy to discuss what the Beijing leadership could do to improve logistics support for the war effort. While it makes sense for Liu Shaoqi, the President of the PRC to visit Moscow to ask for Soviet aid for the war effort; it makes less sense for Lin Biao, the Commander of a large military region in north China to play the same role later on in the war.

The personalized nature of the Military-Party apparatus also led to some curious manning and command and control decisions early in the conflict. Once the decision had been made to send specific units to Korea, the Chinese high command went through extensive and prolonged efforts to make sure the leadership of those troops had some past connection with them. Thus, the eventual deputy commander of the Chinese People's Volunteers—Hong Xuezhi, was ordered up to Beijing and then dispatched to Korea for the explicit purpose of serving as Peng Dehuai's executive officer because Peng had had no personal connection to the 13th Group Army which would be the first troops to go into Korea. The effort to move Hong up to north China and into Korea meant taking him from his original post in Southern China in support of Chinese forces still waging a mopping-up campaign against Nationalist troops there.

Only remnants of the institutionalized bureaucratic system evident in the run-up to and during the Korean conflict survive today.[103] There is no evidence of the kind of personalized control of the war that Mao enjoyed for the Korean conflict. It might be argued that a personalized system continued through Mao's lifetime and presented itself in the decision-making process of the Sino-Indian border clash, the Jinmen and Mazu shelling, the Sino-Soviet border clash, and the seizing of the Paracels. It might even be argued that elements of the Maoist system survived in the early years of Deng Xiaoping's reign as paramount leader as manifested in the Sino-Vietnam border clash. However, even Deng Xiaoping did not possess the sheer charisma and reputational power as Mao in his heyday. No General Secretary of the Party or paramount Party leader including even Deng has enjoyed the level of stature, military experience, personal network both within the Party and within the military as Mao Zedong did prior to his later missteps in the 1950s and 1960s. Thus, we can expect no repeat of the kind of Party-military decision-making that took place at Korea. The Party's management of a military crisis or campaign would look like something quite different regardless of the increasingly personalized nature of Xi Jinping's tenure as China's leader.

Consequently, it is not surprising that the story of the Chinese supreme command during the Korean conflict is largely a story of Mao's interactions both with the field commanders on the ground—primarily Peng Dehuai—and the leaders of the Chinese institutionalized bureaucratic system all of whom were personally connected to Mao during the Chinese Civil War. It is not surprising that the bureaucracy put in place to manage national security and large-scale war was still a bureaucracy of personalities and networks reaching out informally to manage the Korean War. It is even less of a surprise to find that individuals high up in the Party who officially had civilian administration positions, nevertheless were still heavily involved in managing military-related issues owing to the informal, personalized nature of the then new Chinese system.

Notes

1 William Whitson, The Chinese High Command: A History of Communist Military Politics, 1927–71 (New York: Praeger, 1973), 328.
2 Alexander Pantsov and Steven Levine, *Deng Xiaoping: A Revolutionary Life* (New York: Oxford University Press, 2015), 143.
3 Ibid.
4 William Whitson, The Chinese High Command: A History of Communist Military Politics, 1927–71 (New York: Praeger, 1973), 190–91.
5 Ibid., 324.
6 Ibid., 245.
7 Ibid., 324.
8 Ibid., 328.
9 There is some question over how much authority Zhu enjoyed as the PLA C-in-C. He is unquestionably at important meetings discussing matters of important national security and he is the recipient of numerous PLA reports on the state of the Korean conflict and the status of PLA modernization. It appears however that the

title is largely honorific, involving a great deal of time in diplomatic engagements, making speeches, and meeting with Korean war generals and veterans.

10 Shu Guang Zhang, *Mao's Military Romanticism: China and the Korean War, 1950–3* (Lawrence, KS: University Press of Kansas, 1995), 58.

11 Marshal Nie Rongzhen, "Beijing's Decision to Intervene," in Li, Millet, and Yu, eds., *Mao's Generals Remember Korea* (Lawrence, KS: University Press of Kansas, 2001), 38.

12 Xiaobing Li, Allan R. Millett, Bin Yu, See, for example, the wide range of roles Zhou played in the Party, State and Military bureaucracies as illustrated in his writings in Zhou Enlai, *Selected Works of Zhou Enlai, Volume I* (Beijing, PRC: Foreign Language Press), 1981, in entirety.

13 Chen, "China's Road," 163.

14 See, for example, Hong Xuezhi, "The CPVF's Combat and Logistics," in Li, Millet, and Yu, eds., *Mao's Generals Remember Korea* (Lawrence, KS: University Press of Kansas, 2001), 122–30; Chen, "China's Road," 169.

15 Mao Zedong, "On Protracted War," Selected Works of Mao Tse-tung (Beijing: Foreign Language Press, 1975),.

16 Mao Zedong, "Problems of Strategic in China's Civil War," Selected Works of Mao Tse-tung (Beijing: Foreign Language Press, 1975).

17 William Whitson, The Chinese High Command: A History of Communist Military Politics, 1927–71 (New York: Praeger, 1973), 439–57.

18 Ibid., 436–44.

19 Ibid., 452–54.

20 Marshal Nie Rongzhen, "Beijing's Decision to Intervene," in Li, Millet, and Yu, eds., *Mao's Generals Remember Korea* (Lawrence, KS: University Press of Kansas, 2001), 42.

21 Lt. Gen. (Ret.) Du Ping, "Political Mobilization and Control," in Li, Millet, and Yu, eds., *Mao's Generals Remember Korea* (Lawrence, KS: University Press of Kansas, 2001), 61–105.

22 William Whitson, The Chinese High Command: A History of Communist Military Politics, 1927–71 (New York: Praeger, 1973), 240–43.

23 Although, a counter argument is that by the summer of 1950 it was clear that Korea would be the focus and not Taiwan. Su Yu informed the Third Field Army in mid-July that in order to focus on Korea, the Taiwan campaign, which he had been spending most of the end of 1949 and the first half of 1950 planning for, was to be postponed. See Chen, "China's Road," 131.

24 Thomas Robinson, *A Politico-Military Biography of Lin Piao, Part I, 1907–1949* (Santa Monica, CA: RAND), 10.

25 Ibid., 23–32.

26 Peng Dehuai, *Memoirs of a Chinese Marshal* (Beijing: Foreign Language Press, 1984), 434–47; Thomas Robinson, *A Politico-Military Biography of Lin Piao, Part I, 1907–1949* (Santa Monica, CA: RAND), 23–32.

27 Larry Wortzel, "The Beiping-tianjin Campaign of 1948–1949," in Finkelstein, et al., eds., *Chinese Warfighting: The PLA Experience Since 1949* (Armonk, NY: M.E. Sharpe, 2003), 57–67, and William Whitson, *The Chinese High Command: A History of Communist Military Politics*, 1927–71 (New York: Praeger, 1973), 111–14.

28 Thomas Robinson, *A Politico-Military Biography of Lin Piao, Part I, 1907–1949* (Santa Monica, CA: RAND), 21.

29 Ibid., 17–23.

30 Peng Dehuai, Memoirs of a Chinese Marshal (Beijing: Foreign Language Press, 1984), 415–25.

31 Ibid.

32 Chen, "China's Road," 143.

33 Ibid., 142–43.
34 This is best illustrated by the telegram Mao dispatches to Stalin immediately after the October Politburo meeting in which the CCP leadership decides to intervene in Korea. In this telegram Mao lays out specifically what the Chinese will be doing; what expectations he has for Soviet support to the effort; what the war aims are for the People's Republic of China; and what Mao's expectations are for the outcome of the conflict. See Chen, "China's Road," 175–80.
35 Alan Whiting, China Crosses the Yalu: The Decision to Enter the Korean War (Stanford, CA: Stanford University Press, 1960), 47–116.
36 Peng Dehuai, *Memoirs of a Chinese Marshal* (Beijing: Foreign Language Press, 1984), 472–74.
37 Chen Jian, China's Road to the Korean War: The Making of the Sino-American Confrontation (New York: Columbia University Press, 1994), 85–91.
38 Ibid.
39 Ibid., 112–57.
40 See Chen Jian, China's Road to the Korean War: The Making of the Sino-American Confrontation (New York: Columbia University Press, 1994); Shu Guang Zhang, *Mao's Military Romanticism: China and the Korean War, 1950–3*, (Lawrence, KS: University Press of Kansas, 1995); and Li Xiaobing, *A History of the Modern Chinese Army* (Lexington, KY: University Press of Kentucky, 2007).
41 Ibid., 135–37.
42 Ibid.
43 Ibid., 137.
44 Ibid., 137–57. See also Marshal Nie Rongzhen, "Beijing's Decision to Intervene," in Li, Millet, and Yu, eds., *Mao's Generals Remember Korea* (Lawrence, KS: University Press of Kansas, 2001), 40.
45 Chen Jian, *China's Road to the Korean War*, 142–45.
46 Ibid., 146–71.
47 Ibid., 173.
48 Ibid., 173–75. See also Shu Guang Zhang, *Mao's Military Romanticism: China and the Korean War, 1950–3* (Lawrence, KS: University Press of Kansas, 1995), 80–81.
49 It is for this reason, the deployment of large numbers of Fourth F.A. units to the Northeast Military Region and the planned NEBDA that Western scholars believed Lin Biao had been given command of the CPV.
50 Chen Jian, China's Road, 173–85; Shu Guang Zhang, Mao's Military Romanticism, 80–83; and Peng Dehuai, *Memoirs of a Chinese Marshal*, 472–74.
51 Alan Whiting, *China Crosses the Yalu: The Decision to Enter the Korean War* (Stanford, CA: Stanford University Press, 1960), 116–51.
52 Shu Guang Zhang, *Mao's Military Romanticism: China and the Korean War, 1950–3* (Lawrence, KS: University Press of Kansas, 1995), 86–94.
53 Ibid.
54 Ibid., 99.
55 Ibid., 99–100.
56 Yu Bin, "What China Learned from its 'Forgotten War' in Korea," in Finkelstein et al., eds., *Chinese Warfighting: The PLA Experience Since 1949* (Armonk, NY: M.E. Sharpe, 2003), 127.
57 Peng Dehuai, *Memoirs of a Chinese Marshal* (Beijing: Foreign Language Press, 1984), 476.
58 Yu, "What China Learned," 128.
59 Yu Bin, "What China Learned from its 'Forgotten War' in Korea," in Finkelstein et al., eds., *Chinese Warfighting: The PLA Experience Since 1949* (Armonk, NY: M.E. Sharpe, 2003), 128.

60 Korea Institute of Military History, the Korean War, Vol. 2 (Lincoln, NE: University of Nebraska Press, 1998), 282.
61 Ibid., p. 299.
62 Yu, "What China Learned," 130; also see Shu Guang Zhang, "Command, Control, and the PLA's Offensive Campaigns in Korea, 1950–1," in Finkelstein et al., eds., *Chinese Warfighting: The PLA Experience Since 1949* (Armonk, NY: M.E. Sharpe, 2003), 104.
63 Ibid., 130–31.
64 Yu, "What China Learned," 131; also see Peng Dehuai, *Memoirs of a Chinese Marshal* (Beijing: Foreign Language Press, 1984), 477–79.
65 P. 410, Korean War, Vol. 2.
66 Ibid.
67 Yu, "What China Learned," 131.
68 The Korean War, Vol. 2, 410.
69 Yu, "What China Learned," 131.
70 Ibid., p. 424.
71 Zhang, "Command, Control and the PLA's Offensive Campaigns," 108; also see Peng Dehuai, *Memoirs of a Chinese Marshal* (Beijing: Foreign Language Press, 1984), 479.
72 Ibid.
73 Ibid.
74 Ibid.
75 Yu, "What China Learned," 131.
76 Zhang, "Command, Control and the PLA's Offensive Campaigns," 106.
77 Yu, "What China Learned," 133.
78 Ibid.
79 Ibid.
80 Marshal Nie Rongzhen, "Beijing's Decision to Intervene," in Li, Millet, and Yu, eds., *Mao's Generals Remember Korea* (Lawrence, KS: University Press of Kansas, 2001), 52.
81 Ibid.
82 Chen, "China's Road," 135.
83 Ibid., 56–57.
84 Hong Xuezhi, "The CPVF's Combat and Logistics," in Li, Millet, and Yu, eds., *Mao's Generals Remember Korea*, (Lawrence, KS: University Press of Kansas, 2001), 122–29.
85 Ibid., 129–38; Marshal Nie Rongzhen, "Beijing's Decision to Intervene," in Li, Millet, and Yu, eds., *Mao's Generals Remember Korea* (Lawrence, KS: University Press of Kansas, 2001), 53.
86 Zhang, "Command, Control and the PLA's Offensive Campaigns," 109.
87 Ibid.
88 Ibid.
89 Ibid.
90 Ibid.
91 Hong Xuezhi, "The CPVF's Combat and Logistics," in Li, Millet, and Yu, eds., *Mao's Generals Remember Korea* (Lawrence, KS: University Press of Kansas, 2001), 122–30.
92 Zhang, "Command, Control and the PLA's Offensive Campaigns," 111–12.
93 Ibid., 110.
94 Zhang, "Command, Control and the PLA's Offensive Campaigns," 110.
95 Ibid., 111.
96 Ibid.
97 Ibid., 111–12.

98 Ibid.
99 Ibid.
100 Ibid.
101 Yu, "What China Learned," 135.
102 Maj. Gen. (Ret.) Chai Chengwen, "the Korean Truce Negotiations," in Li, Millet, and Yu, eds., *Mao's Generals Remember Korea* (Lawrence, KS: University Press of Kansas, 2001), 184–232.
103 The GSD, GPD, and GLD persisted within the Chinese system until the 2016 Joint Military Reforms. The functions of these three organizations were subsumed by the Central Military Commission into the Joint Staff Department, the Political Warfare Department and the Joint Logistics Department.

CONCLUSION

The Complexities of High Command

Williamson Murray

It is not surprising that the issues involved in the political and military control of the government should represent an important indicator of successful or unsuccessful strategic effectiveness. After all, they are intimately intertwined in the beginning, conduct, and ending of wars. If we can paraphrase Clausewitz, war is a continuation of politics by other means.[1] And therein lies the rub.

War itself, to an even greater extent than peace, throws a fog of chance, ambiguity, and uncertainty over its conduct. Those who conduct either the political or military side of conflict find themselves confronting General James Wolfe's comment, when facing the difficulties raised by the siege of Quebec, that "war is an option of difficulties."[2]

And here lies the conundrum. The political leader confronts issues that may well impinge on the conduct of military operations. Yet, in many cases, he or she may have no clear idea of the issues and possibilities that his commanders in the field may confront, while on the other side, the latter will often want to pursue a course that opposes or undermines political needs. Thus, in the summer 1942, Roosevelt and his chiefs found themselves contesting a crucial issue confronting the Allied grand strategy. His military advisers strongly argued for a major operation to be launched against Northern France, which the British strongly opposed. Marshall and King felt so strongly opposed to what they believed to be a subsidiary operation in North Africa, which the British were urging, that they suggested a radical change in the American effort. What they failed to understand, and Franklin Roosevelt did, was that there were political factors that demanded the commitment of American forces to the war against Germany, even if it meant commitment to a landing in North Africa.

But perhaps the greatest difficulty that statesmen and military leaders confront is the fact that war takes place in a world of constant change and flux.

DOI: 10.4324/9781003375630-13

They inevitably discover that their prewar assumptions and beliefs are often fundamentally flawed and that they must adapt to a very different world from their conceptions. As Michael Howard has suggested, military organizations inevitably get the next war wrong. Military effectiveness then demands that they adapt to the real world, which means they must alter many of their prewar assumptions. The same applies to statesmen.

Unfortunately, the past suggests that most are unwilling to adapt and instead meander along their misplaced course. The result, more often than not, has been military and strategic disasters. Adding to the difficulties of marrying up a successful political strategy with the conduct of military operations is the fact that the enemy too has a vote, which he will exercise at the most inopportune moments. As we adapt, he too will adapt, and in most cases in a fashion that we have not expected or prepared to meet. Thus, perhaps the most important quality in strategic and military effectiveness lies in the willingness and ability to adapt.

Learning on the Fly: The American Civil War[3]

The American Civil War presents the most idiosyncratic case studies, because as Lincoln noted in his 1864 inaugural speech: "And then the war came." With a background as a West Point graduate, veteran of the Mexican War, and secretary of war, Jefferson Davis believed he had all the answers. He did not and his interference in the choice of senior commanders and strategy was mediocre to say the least. In the case of Abraham Lincoln, the new president possessed no illusion about his ignorance about things military. Early in his presidency, as he began to grapple with the problems of the war, he would request that the Library of Congress send over to him a selection of works dealing with war and military history.

In 1861 both men held the illusion that the great majority of their countrymen held. The putative threat was minimal. For White Southerners, Northerners were little more than a collection of mudsills who would run away at the opening shots of artillery and gunfire. Southern gallantry and agricultural backgrounds would sweep the Yankee trash away. Northerners, on the other hand, believed that the great mass of Southerners were supporters of the Union whom a corrupt and dishonest planter class had misled into supporting succession.

At the beginning, strategic thinking, military knowledge, and the supporting bureaucratic structure for a great war did not exist. Everything had to be built out of whole cloth, while it took a considerable period time for the prewar illusions to dissipate. As Grant noted in his memoirs, up until the battle of Shiloh, a full year after the beginning of the war, he had believed that a major victory over Confederate arms would bring sense to white Southerners, but Shiloh, coming only a couple of months after the destruction of a whole Confederate Army at Forts Donelson and Henry disabused him of that notion.

It took Lincoln until the defeats at the First Bull Run and then the troubles he confronted with the pusillanimous military leadership of George McClellan to recognize that the Union was now engaged in a long war, but it was not until the Army of the Potomac achieved a draw at the killing battle of Antietam that he was able to turn that recognition into a full-fledged war against not only the Confederacy's military but its economy as well with the Emancipation Proclamation, which by freeing the slaves undercut the South's economic structure.

The relationship between the Army of the Potomac and the president represented a low point in civil-military relations in the history of the United States. While the replacement of McClellan may have improved those relations, it did little to improve the military effectiveness of the Army of the Potomac, the culture of which had been poisoned by McClellan's brand of leadership. Lincoln was eventually able to bring Grant to the East, where he finally found a general able to grasp the larger framework of total war, where political and economic factors were as important as the conduct of campaigns.

While the Army of the Potomac was floundering from one defeat to another, Grant was learning the larger business of strategy and wide-spreading military operations. He also possessed a clear political sense, so that when Lincoln sent directed telescopes out to the Western armies in the spring 1863 to get a better idea of what was happening, Grant welcomed them with open arms, rather than as spies, which they.

Lincoln's eventual appointment of Grant as commander in chief of Union armies in February created for the first time a high command with as clear a relationship between the military and civilian world as could be expected. The operational strategy that Grant proposed for 1864, a movement of all the Union armies into the center of the Confederacy, was quite similar to what Lincoln had proposed to McClellan in 1862 and which the self-proclaimed military genius had contemptuously dismissed.

That strategy should have won the war in 1864. It did not because the subsidiary theaters were commanded by politicians important to Lincoln's re-election in the fall 1864 but who possessed not an iota of military competence. Grant never complained because he understood the political necessity of leaving Banks, Siegel, and Butler in crucial command positions. In terms of executing the strategy, Grant discovered that the command culture of the Army of the Potomac remained firmly mired in McClellan's approach of moving at a snail's pace, displaying no willingness to show initiative, and fear of what Lee was going to do to them, rather than what they could do to Lee. But whatever the occasional differences between the president and his general, both understood that war means fighting. And so Lincoln accepted Grant's military strategy that led to the Wilderness, Spotsylvania Court House, and Cold Harbor, which pinned Lee and the Army of Northern Virginia to Richmond, but which resulted in a terrible casualty bill. Meanwhile, in the West, Sherman would break into the heartland of the Confederacy, capture Atlanta, and in the March to the Sea underline that no sanctuary remained for the successionists.

The situation in the Confederacy was quite different. Jefferson Davis displayed little military sense and even less political understanding. Above all, he believed that he should be the Confederate high command in charge of national military and political strategy with little input from others. He also focused excessively on the Eastern theater. Nevertheless, he did recognize after Chancellorsville that matters were not going well in the West and that it made strategic sense for Lee to transfer Longstreet's corps from Virginia to reinforce Pemberton and the defense of Vicksburg. But Lee, who paid no attention to what was happening in the West, urged that the Army of Northern Virginia with its full strength invade the North to seek a decisive victory that would win the Confederacy its independence. The decisive strategic meeting occurred among Davis, his Secretary of War, and Lee on the same day that Grant was crushing Pemberton's army at Champion's Hill, making the siege of Vicksburg inevitable.

If Davis generally followed Lee's advice in the East, he constantly meddled in operational and strategic matters in the Western Theater of Operations both in urging particular courses of operation and his disastrous interference in personnel matters of the generals in command. In 1862, he selected Albert Sydney Johnson, one of the most over-rated generals in the war, to command in the West. He and Johnson made a series of disastrous mistakes: first in attempting to defend everything; then in emphasizing the Mississippi River over that of the Cumberland and Tennessee Rivers; and finally in concentrating Confederate forces in Corinth, Mississippi for the attack on Shiloh, which opened up New Orleans to the Union seizure by an amphibious force.

In particular, with the exception of Lee, the Confederate president proved a disastrous chooser of military talent. His constant quarreling with General Joe Johnston led to a series of mistakes in the Western Theater of Operations that doomed the Confederacy to defeat. His appointment of Braxton Bragg to command of the Army of the Tennessee was an understandable mistake, but his keeping Bragg in command, even after that army's corps commanders mutinied, represented an appalling piece of stupidity. Yet his greatest error was his decision to fire Johnston in July 1864 and replace him with John Bell Hood, who not only lost Atlanta at a crucial political point in late summer 1864 with Lincoln's re-election hanging in the balance but then proceeded to open all of Georgia to the ravages of Sherman's Army. It was only with Hood's campaign into Tennessee that Davis finally relieved him after the disastrous defeats at Franklin and Nashville.

The French High Command in World War I: Clemenceau and Foch

No two leaders in war responsible for the military and political leadership would seem to have had less potential to work together in running a nation confronting a desperate military situation than Georges Clemenceau, premier of France from 1917 to 1920, and Ferdinand Foch situation, the Supreme Commander of Allied Armies from March 1918 through to the end of the war. The former was a radical politician, who spent much of his political career in supporting left-wing politics, particularly in efforts to remove the influence of the Catholic Church from French politics. Undoubtedly influenced by the four years that he spent in the United States in the aftermath of the American Civil War, he was a strong advocate of the efforts to separate Church and state. Not surprisingly, he was one of the leading advocates who attempted to rectify the appalling miscarriage of justice perpetrated by the army against Captain Alfred Dreyfus.

Foch, on the other hand, was a deeply religious man, educated by the Jesuits and marked by his experiences in the disastrous defeat French armies had suffered in the Franco-Prussian War. The Dreyfus affair did not harm his rise in the army, except that his brother was a Jesuit priest. But both he and Clemenceau shared a deep antipathy to Germany and a desire to overthrow the peace Bismarck had imposed on France as a result of the Franco-Prussian War. Thus, whatever their political and religious differences, they were firmly united in their desire to bring the Germans down.

Nevertheless, at the start of the war both held important positions but were not in a position to drive France's strategic policy. Foch, along with Pètain, adapted far more quickly to the tactical realities of the war than did most other French generals. Simply put, Foch understood that the search after great Napoleonic victories was no longer in the cards, but in fact was causing inordinately high casualty rates. He understood that war now had to be one of attrition, industrial production, and the mobilization of political will, Clausewitzian perceptions that reflected Foch's experiences as commandant of the *Écoe Supérieur de Guerre* in the period before the war.

In November 1917, like Churchill in 1940, Clemenceau assumed control of the ramshackle French government, which now felt the hard hand of a politician who knew how to get things done. The new premier carried out an extensive purge of the fifth column who were disturbing France's internal stability, desired to make peace with the Germans, who were from the highest levels of French political life. At the same time, he provided an added push to French armament production, particularly important because the French were going to have to provide much of the heavy armaments the ill-equipped Americans would require.

Both Foch and Clemenceau were critics of how the war was being pursued by the innumerable French governments and the army's chief of staff, General Joseph Joffre. That general's mishandling of the Verdun battle finally led to his replacement in December 1916, but his successor proved even more incapable and the disastrous defeat of the Nivelle offensive in spring 1917 came close to breaking the French Army. Pétain replaced him, and while he would restore order in the army, he was hardly possessed the imagination or drive to handle a major crisis in military affairs.

That crisis came in March 1918 when Ludendorff launched Operational Michael, a massive assault, based on a new offensive doctrine of decentralized command and control that aimed to drive the French and British out of the war before the Americans arrived in strength. The main focus of the German offensive was General Julian Byng's Fifth Army, but Byng's troops held. The real problem came farther south where Herbert Gough's Third Army collapsed. In this desperate situation, with Haig and the British Army falling back on the Channel Ports and Pétain proposing to fall back on Paris, the Allies, largely under Clemenceau's influence, created a supreme command under Foch. The new commander made it clear to Pétain that there would be no retreat to Paris and that he would support Haig. There would be continuing tension between Clemenceau and Foch through to the end of the war, but the general fully subscribed the premier's statement that "he made war."

There would be considerable squabbing between the two over the course of the war's last month. In some respects, their relationship would resemble that between Churchill and his chiefs of staff in the next war. But those very arguments were essential to working out a French strategy that would contribute significantly to victory by its combination of political necessity with military reality. And in the postwar period, the connection between Clemenceau and Foch collapsed. Clemenceau would very much have liked to impose a harsher peace on the Germans than what transpired at Versailles but recognized the importance of the political relations among the allies trumped military concerns. On the other hand, Foch understood the potential strategic consequences of not crushing the Germans permanently. As he noted shortly after the signing of the Versailles Treaty, France had only gained a twenty-year truce.

The British High Command in World War I: Haig and Lloyd-George

The first two years of the war saw the British political leadership flounder in its attempts to deal with a multitude of problems for which there were no obvious solutions. One might characterize their efforts as a great muddling through. It was not that Asquith ran a loose ship – he ran no ship at all. By spring 1915 it was clear that things had to change. The crisis came in May 1915 with the failure of the British offensive at Gallipoli and at the same time severe criticism in the newspapers about the supposed lack of shells, particularly in France. Sir John French commander of the BEF (British Expeditionary Force) in France fed the reports on army difficulties directly to reporters. French's difficulties reflected a breakdown in relations between the army in France and the War Office in London, which would characterize much of the rest of the war; the names changed but not the conflict.

The second part of the crisis also came that month with the formation of a coalition government: the price of the Conservatives to join the government was the removal of Winston Churchill, First Lord of the Admiralty, on whom the failure of Gallipoli had largely fallen. That personnel change with the firing of Churchill meant that there was no one in London in the government who understood war and strategy. The one improvement in the government came with the creation of the Ministry of Munitions, to which David Lloyd George received appointment. In that position, Lloyd George, using his powers of intelligence, drive, and ruthlessness, would bring order out of chaos. But matters hardly improved between those responsible for running British grand strategy in London and those in command on the Continent. Asquith was simply not up to the business of running a great war, on which the survival of the nation depended.

The major problem that the British high command confronted in the waging of the war lay in the fact that there were deep divisions between those who wanted the major focus of the war on defeating the Germans on the Western Front and those who that the major military efforts should focus on strategic areas, such as the Balkans, Turkey, and the Mediterranean. The soldiers supplied much of the support for the BEF's efforts, but they received support from a considerable number of Conservative leaders and the great press lords. To all intents and purposes that political statement would remain in place through Ludendorff's Offensive in March 1918 threatened the Allies with defeat on the battlefield.

By the end of 1916, Britain's position appeared dismal indeed. The struggle over conscription had used up much of Asquith's capital; the Easter Rebellion in Ireland underlined the weakness at home; the Somme offensive had made only minimal gains at the cost of horrendous casualties; the Germans were about to resume unrestricted submarine warfare; and on the Eastern Front, the Russians were in serious trouble, while in late summer the Germans had conquered Romania. All of these accumulated troubles only added to the dissatisfaction with the government. Under great pressure, Asquith resigned from office to be replaced by Lloyd George.

Unlike Neville Chamberlain who would go into the political darkness in May 1940 while supporting his successor, Asquith split the Liberal Party, which placed the new prime minister in a difficult political position; Lloyd George had to depend on the Conservatives to continue in office, and they enjoyed close relations with Haig in France and Robertson in France. Moreover, Lloyd George possessed considerable contempt for the generals. As he once commented about Haig, the general was brilliant to the top of his boots. The result was that the new prime minister had to tread carefully with Haig, not only because of the general's close relations with the Conservatives but with the newspaper proprietors, who were in Haig's pockets.

The great summer offensive of 1916 on the Somme showed the British Army at its best and worst. It displayed a considerable ability to adapt to the conditions, but the casualties were horrendous. Lloyd George, and most of the politicians in London were horrified. But there was little the prime minister could do. The politics of his coalition government had thoroughly boxed him in. But it was also the very nature of modern war, supported by great populations and massive industrial and technological developments that made attrition war inevitable. As Robertson had noted to the new prime minister, war was about killing. And that harsh reality represented a truth that Lloyd George was unwilling to recognize even after the war.

However, Lloyd George's first major conflict with the military came with the obdurate refusal of the First Sea Lord, Admiral John Jellicoe to countenance the introduction of merchant shipping in spite of the threat that U-boats represented. By the summer 1917, the attacks by German U-boats on Allied and neutral vessels had reached a point where it appeared the Germans might win the war. At that point, at Haig's urging, Lloyd George brought in Erich Geddes as First Lord of the Admiralty. Geddes had no naval experience, but he was a magnificent organizer, who eventually forced the Admiralty to utilize the convoy system, which largely ended the U-boat threat. By December 1917, supported by Lloyd George, he was able to end Jellicoe's tenure as First Sea Lord.

While the quarrel with the admirals over the utility of convoys was occurring, the prime minister confronted several major crises from the near collapse of the French army in May 1917 and that of the Italians in November, difficulties in maintaining the coalition government in Britain, and some degree of cooperation from the prickly Americans. But the greatest difficulty came with Haig's Passchendaele Offensive that began in August 1917. In the bloody fields of Flanders, soaked in blood, the BEF fought the Germans to a standstill. But the carnage was horrendous. Significantly, Lloyd George made no effort to force Haig to call off the offensive that was steadily sinking in the Flanders mud. As recent scholarship has indicated, Lloyd George bears considerable responsibility for the bloodletting caused by his failure to reign Haig in.

Lloyd George determined that he would prevent the generals from launching another bloody offensive in the coming year. But he confronted the same conundrum that he had faced in early1917; he could not fire Haig, even if there were a more suitable general available, due to the weakness of the political coalition that he headed as well as the excellent connection the BEF's commander enjoyed with the political elite back in London. In response, he settled on preventing the BEF from receiving sufficient manpower allocation of reinforcements from the United Kingdom to carry out major military operations.

So how to prevent Haig from launching another Passchendaele? First, given the difficulties that the French Army was in, he agreed that the BEF would take over a substantial portion of the front line that his allies held, diluting the numbers Haig possessed for a great offensive. Second Lloyd George insured that the army would receive only a small percentage of those drafted. And third, the prime minister held 120,000 soldiers as a general reserve in the United Kingdom. The result was that the BEF was desperately short of manpower when Ludendorff struck. Nevertheless, it is worth noting that with a major German offensive in the offing, BEF allowed nearly 100,000 soldiers to go on leave.

The result was a near collapse of the BEF. But the order came out of disorder. Foch received command of Allied armies, which forced real cooperation on the British and French and now the Americans for the first time. But the crucial element in the lowering of the temperature in civil-military relations was clearly the fact that the losses the Germans suffered in its spring offensives created a situation where they were no longer able to stand up against the hammer blows the Allies launched against them. If anything, the British high command had devolved into those in Britain supplying the ammunition, manpower, and other accruements of war, while the BEF had become an effective army which with the other Allied armies accomplished the German defeat.

The German High Command in World War I: The Kaiser Against the Rest

It is difficult to envision a more dysfunctional approach to the running of a war than what the Germans possessed over the course of the First World War. The root of the failure initially lay with the system of government Bismarck had created in the aftermath of the Franco-Prussian War. It was one that only the "iron chancellor" could have followed with any degree success; those who followed in his footsteps had little hope of understanding, much less running a government in which confusion and competing authorities were the order of the day.

At the top of a contending group of power centers was the Kaiser. Beset by psychological problems resulting from possessing a withered arm and an upbringing that combined the worst of the nineteenth century's British and German educational systems, Wilhelm assumed the position of monarch, largely unprepared for the position. One of his first acts was to fire the "Iron Chancellor" and with the help of those who supposedly made policy in the Reich proceeded to disassemble Bismarck's foreign policy. By the time the war broke out, Wilhelm had been on the throne for a quarter of century. In that period, he had displayed none of the qualities that a stateman requires: a diligence to work at the head of the government, a knowledge of foreign and military affairs, and an understanding of the state's internal politics.

The problem was that no one else did either. With no one guiding the government, the system was chaotic. No less than forty senior military officers had the right of access to the Kaiser. The army and the navy simply refused to coordinate on any strategic issues. Even within the army, there was a considerable split between the Great General Staff and the Prussian War Ministry. The former designed a plan, today known as the Schlieffen Plan, that aimed for a great outflanking movement through the Low Countries into northern France to destroy the French Army at the war's start.

Until shortly before the war the War Ministry refused to supply the manpower for such a great offensive due to a belief that a newly enlarged army would require too many middle-class officers and thus dilute the percentage of noble officers in the officer corps. At least the General Staff did make clear to the foreign office the outline of the Schlieffen plan, but the bureaucrats in the Wilhelmstrasse simply filed the memorandum away without bothering to examine the plan's political or strategic implications.

The failure to discuss either the political or strategic implications of the Schlieffen Plan reflected a general acceptance among the Reich's military and political leaders that "military necessity" should overrule all concerns about strategy, politics, or morale issues. The result was a series of decisions throughout the war that harmed the Reich's political and strategic situations. In April 1915 the army launched an experiment with gas war; on the tactical level it proved immensely successful, but there were no reserves available, largely because there was no operational goal. Moreover, there appears to have been no discussion at the higher levels of its political impact on the attitude of the neutral powers by Germany's introduction of the gas war. Similarly, there was no examination of the strategic implications of the decision to launch a submarine blockade against Britain – a decision that failed to examine even whether there were sufficient U-boats for such a campaign. There weren't.

The failure of the Schlieffen Plan led to a considerable argument between the new chief of the General Staff and the generals in charge of the war in the east, Hindenburg, and Ludendorff. In the end, the former over-ruled the arguments for a great drive into Russia on the thoroughly reasonable basis that the Russians possessed almost unlimited space with the implication that the German Army could not overcome the logistical problems such an invasion would raise. Instead, Falkenhayn agreed to a defensive war in the west and a limited offensive in the east and Balkans for 1915.

At least Falkenhayn recognized that the Reich had involved itself in a great war of attrition, but then at the end of the year, he convinced Kaiser that the best solution was a battle of attrition that would bleed the French army white and force the Allies to make peace. The result was the disastrous battle of Verdun, during which the German Army suffered as heavy casualties as did the French. The defeat saw Falkenhayn replaced by Hindenburg and Ludendorff with the latter in charge. At least Ludendorff addressed the tactical problems the war in the West had raised. And the pressure the Germans were able to place on Tsarist Russia finally led to the collapse of that corrupt and incompetent regime.

Faced with a difficult strategic situation, the Germans now proceeded to make it worse. At the end of 1916 the navy, using totally bogus figures, brought forward a proposal to end the war by resuming unrestricted submarine warfare. In early January 1917 at one of the few meetings of the senior political and military leaders, the Germans decided to resume the U-boat war, even though they fully recognized that it was almost certain to bring the United States into the war with its financial strength. It could not have come at a better time for the Allies, who were on the brink of bankruptcy. Ludendorff summed up the consensus among the military officers participating in the discussions with the comment that "I don't give a damn about the Americans." The flood of Americans arriving in France in the summer 1918 put paid to German assumptions.

Faced with overwhelming Allied strength in manpower and material, the Germans attempted one last throw of the dice. Beginning in March 1918 with the Michael Offensive, they launched a series of tactical breakthrough battles that possessed no operational, much less strategic goals. As Ludendorff commented when asked what the operational goal of the Michael Offensive was, Hindenburg's partner commented, "we shall punch a hole in their line and see what turns up." What turned up were nearly a million casualties and an army that would collapse at the end of 1918."

It is hard to speak of a German high command in the First World. The senior leaders consistently confused tactics with strategy. The fact that the leaders of the Reichstag were not informed about the difficulties the army was confronting until September 1918 suggests the level of disfunction in the system. But then the army and the navy hardly ever talked to each other. Germany had only a small chance of escaping the consequences of strategic policies based on arrogance and ignorance and a belief that "military necessity" should always overrule political and strategic concerns.

The German High Command in World War II: Hitler Versus the OKW

What can say about a national political leadership that managed to repeat every major strategic mistake that its predecessors had made in the last conflict. To a considerable extent, the disastrous course the Germans followed was a result of their overemphasis on the sharp end of war, on the tactics of frontline fighting. It also reflected a desire to have a political leadership that would handle the messy side of war, namely the politicians, while the army handled the business of war. There was never a real high command in Hitler's system of military governance even when Hitler assumed control of the *Wehrmacht*. Each service ran its own organization. The navy under Admiral Erich Raeder remained an independent force because Hitler had little interest in naval matters. As the war proceeded, Hitler increasingly interfered with the air war, but Göring's political position allowed the *Luftwaffe* to sail on its own course with little interference from the other services.

The most serious political-military clash came at the end of 1937 with the Fritz-Blomberg crisis. In November 1937 at the Hossbach meeting, Hitler made clear that he had decided on war, and war in the near future. He received considerable pushback from his minister of war, Werner von Blomberg, the army's commander, Werner von Fritsch, and the foreign minister, Konstantin von Neurath. Hitler was furious at what he believed the pusillanimous behavior of his senior advisors. He did not immediately strike, but when a scandal broke in early 1938 – Blomberg had married a woman with a dubious past – he moved.

He fired Blomerg, Fritsch, and Neurath – Frisch on the basis of a trumped-up charge of homosexuality. The result was a political crisis, during which a substantial number of army generals turned against Hitler. What matters to us is the organizational outcome of the crisis. Hitler replaced Blomberg with himself, while he renamed the War Ministry as the High Command of the *Wehrmacht* (OKW). As his chief military adviser, he appointed Wilhelm Keitel, whose nickname soon became "lackey" for his complete subservience to what he believed was Hitler's genius. The hard-nosed Fritsch, he replaced with Walter von Brauchitsch, a weak reed, whose position Hitler further weakened by providing the general with a large donative to enable him to pay for his divorce settlement. Hitler picked both Brauchitsch and Keitel because he recognized correctly that neither one of them would oppose his aggressive policies.

Embolden by the success of the Anschluss (the seizure of Austria) and angered by the recalcitrant Czechs who, alarmed by the increasingly antagonism, had mobilized their army in late May 1938, Hitler determined to crush Czechoslovakia in the fall. For the first and only time in the history of the Third Reich, he ran into significant opposition from several senior military leaders. The most important of these was the chief of the Greater General Staff, General Ludwig Beck. Beginning in late 1938 Beck wrote a series of strategic memorandum the warned that the Western Powers would not stand idly by and watch the *Wehrmacht* destroy Czechoslovakia. Moreover, he stressed that Germany, with its weak economic and financial position, had no chance against the military power that Britain and France would be able to assemble.

The resulting argument over the viability of a military campaign to destroy Czechoslovakia was the only time that discussions over strategic issues appeared in the German high command. Neither Brauchitsch nor Keitel displayed the slightest willingness to stand up against Hitler and his argument that there was little chance that the Western Powers would support the Czechs. Without any support from the other generals, Beck resigned as head of the Great General Staff. Erich von Manstein, who gained the reputation as one of masters of operational art in the upcoming war, wrote his mentor that he should not resign: after all, Hitler had proven himself to be a political genius, who had been correct in each of his judgments; so better to follow the course the *Führer* had laid out.

From this point on, Hitler would increasingly dominate the German higher levels of military decision-making. With the Polish campaign, Hitler allowed the *Oberkommando des Heeres, OKH,* the army high command) to make most of the planning and operational decisions, but it was another matter with the upcoming French campaign. At the beginning of planning in the fall there was a furious row between Hitler and the *OKH*. Driven by serious economic difficulties, Hitler demanded an immediate offensive against the Low Countries and France. Brauchitsch and Franz Halder, the latter Beck' replacement, argued that serious problems had appeared in Poland and that they needed until the spring to sort matters out. In the end, bad weather forced the Germans to postpone the offensive until the spring, thereby preventing a serious military setback. Unlike the Polish campaign, Hitler would interfere with both the planning and conduct of operations. After the war, a number of generals complained that Hitler had been responsible for the stop order at Dunkirk, but in retrospect, it is clear that the army generals were also responsible. After the successful campaign, Keitel saluted Hitler as "the greatest field commander in history."

Within slightly more than a month Hitler was discussing a possible invasion of the Soviet Union in the spring of 1941. The *Führer* was, of course, the driving force behind what was soon codenamed Operation Barbarossa. From the beginning Hitler in combination with the generals was responsible for the egregious mistakes that were made: no attention to logistics, compete ignorance of Soviet industrial strength, and a general underestimation of the Red Army's capabilities.

As the campaign proceeded, the *Wehrmacht* gained a series of impressive victories but was no closer to overthrowing Stalin's regime than at the start. In November, largely as a result of the urging of the generals, the Germans resumed their advance on Moscow in spite of the distinct possibility that winter was about out to arrive. As Halder commented to a group of army chiefs of staff, cold weather would freeze the mud, while the snow would not arrive until January – an astonishing weather forecast. The leadership paid no attention to the reality that a continuation of the advance on Moscow by the exhausted panzer divisions would prevent the establishment of fuel and ammunition dumps as well as winter clothing for the troops.

The result of the smashup in front of Moscow. Hitler fired Brauchitsch, all of his army group commanders, most of his army commanders and various other generals. He then decided that would assume Brauchitsch's position as commander in chief of the army. The difficulties within the army continued into the next year's campaign. The winter fighting saw the armies in the east barely hanging on. Operation Blue, the summer 1942 campaign, aimed at divergent aims: the first the city of Stalingrad; the second the oil wells of the Caucasus.

Halder, still the army's chief of staff was as responsible for a campaign that paid as little attention to logistics and even less to the correlation of forces as Hitler. Immediately at the beginning of Operation Blue, Hitler fired Field Marshal Fedor von Bock, Blue's commander; Halder went in September, his replacement, General Kurt Zeitzler; other generals followed. The army's strategic decision-making by the fall of 1942 had reached the point where no one in either the *OKH* or *OKW* were willing to take crucial decisions about the Allied invasion of North Africa because Hitler was on a train proceeding from Munich to Berlin. From this point, army leaders found themselves in a position where Field Marshal Gerd von Rundstedt commented: "I cannot move the guard in front of my headquarters without permission from Berlin." By 1943 the *OKW* and *OKH* were running entirely separate campaigns. The former in charge of the west and Mediterranean; the latter in charge of the Eastern Front under the control of the latter.

The relations between Hitler and the *Luftwaffe* mirrored those of the army because he was never willing to part ways with *"der Dicke* (the fat one)" because of the close political leadership the two shared in driving the Nazi Party to its seizure of power in January 1933. The general collapse of the *Luftwaffe* reflected the fact that Hitler understood even less about air power than he did about ground operations. Especially damaging to the German conduct of the air war was Göring's unwillingness to stand up to Hitler's disastrous penchant for making faulty decisions about the conduct of the air war. In 1943 and 1944, this showed particularly in his demand that *Luftwaffe* production priorities remain focused on bombers and anti-aircraft artillery, rather than on day and night fighters. The disastrous results showed clearly in the spring1943 in the RAF's Bomber Command's Battle of Ruhr and in the following year's Operation Pointblank, waged by the American Eighth Airforce. The former severely impeded the German economy, while the latter won air superiority over Europe for the Allies.

One of the earliest decisions Hitler made with the outbreak of war was his command that the German military would execute no research and development programs unless they were immediately relevant to the conduct of military operations. When that edict finally was altered in 1942: it was too late. The Anglo-Americans were well on the road to victory in the war over technology. But here the German high command proved as unwilling to recognize how far behind they were. Supposedly, Göring remarked that he had seen Allied technology and it was no more than a bunch of wires. Roosevelt and Churchill would have displayed no greater knowledge of wires and vacuum tubes. But they were willing to accept their ignorance and allow the scientists and technologists get on with the business of war.

Stalin and Zhukov

There were a number of similarities between how Stalin and Hitler interacted with the high commands that they supposedly directed. Ironically those similarities were reversed. On one hand in the early years of the war, the latter displayed a considerable willingness to listen to the advice that his generals and admirals passed along to him as the German campaigns succeeded in destroy much of the opposition that the *Wehrmacht* confronted. Admittedly, there were serious arguments, such as the one that occurred in the fall 1939 over whether to move against Moscow or Kiev in August 1938. But the smashup between Hitler and his generals did not come until the December defeat across the entire Eastern Front. And here Hitler every reason for his anger. His generals had provided him with extraordinarily bad advice.

The case with Stalin and his generals had been the opposite. Nothing better underlines Stalin's distrust of his military than the great purges that savaged the Red Army's senior officer corps beginning in May 1937. By the time the purges came to their dismal end in 1940, Stalin had ordered 50 percent of the officer corps shot (35,000 out of 70,000). Ninety percent of the generals went before firing squads or disappeared into the gulag. Of colonels, 50 percent suffered the same fate. The impact of the purges reduced the officer corps to incompetents or imbeciles, capable only of spouting Stalin's slogans.

The Finnish Winter War and then the 1940 catastrophe that destroyed the French Army did partially put an end to the illusions, but it was too late to repair the deficiencies. Beginning on June 22, 1941, the *Wehrmacht* savaged the Red Army during Operation Barbarossa – 300,000 prisoners at Minsk, 300,000 at Smolensk, 600,000 at Kiev, and another 600,000 at Vyazma and Bryansk. Nevertheless, the desperate efforts of the Red Army took a terrible toll of the Germans. The casualties the Soviets suffered were a direct reflection of Stalin's penchant for appointing the politically loyal, but military incompetents to command positions. In the crushing defeat at Kiev in September 1941, Stalin failed to listen to his senior military advisers that the Germans were creating a dangerous salient around Kiev, and Soviet troops should pull back. The Red Army suffered its worst defeat of the war.

The initial weeks of Barbarossa were so disastrous to those defending in front of Minsk found themselves before firing squads. General Dimity Pavlov was the first to go, but others soon followed. The political commissar, Lev Mekhils, one of Stalin's foremost flunkies, played a major role in Pavlov's fate. Interestingly Mekhils would be responsible for a major defeat by Soviet armies in the Crimea in spring 1942 but suffered no penalties except for demotion and a vicious letter from Stalin, highly critical of his performance.

In the terrible defeats of summer and fall of 1941, Stalin maintained a deep belief that he knew better than his generals. Despite Zhukov' advise that the Soviet counter offensive in front that had rocked the Germans back on their heels should remain focused on destroying the forces in front of Moscow, Stalin ordered the Red Army to go on the offensive across the broad front of the entire Eastern Front. As a result, the Soviets only gained a marginal success and allowed the *Wehrmacht* to escape the full extent of the predicament in which it found itself. Shortly after in May 1942 came a disastrous defeat in front of Kursk. Again, Stalin refused to listen to his military advisers, who warned that the Germans had substantial reserves in the area of the southern front and that the Soviet spearheads were in danger of being surrounded.

It was this point that Stalin gained a modicum of military common sense. He accepted Zhukov's and Boris Shaposhnikov's advice that the Red Army trade space and time, while building up its reserves. At the same time, Hitler's relations with his senior military went in the opposite direction as he fired Bock, List, and Halder among others, while assuming the position for a time as commander of Army Group A during the drive to the Caucasus. In November 1942, the stunning Soviet offensive that trapped the Sixth Army in front of Stalingrad caught Hitler returning from Munich to Berlin by train, and thus incapable of making crucial operational decisions. And by this point in the war, neither Zeitzler nor Jodl, the two key figures in the *OKW*, were willing to make independent decisions. They and the commanders in the field slavishly followed the *Führer's* instructions.

On the other hand, Stalin was now willing to listen to his advisers, who were given considerable latitude. Nevertheless, the dictator maintained close control over his commanders, so that no one was a political threat. Moreover, he ensured that no single marshal dominated the Army. Thus, one sees the rise of other marshals who possessed Zhukov's character without his personality. Two of the new marshals, Konstantin Rokessovsky and Nikolai Vatutin would be responsible for much of the planning for Kursk in July 1943. From this point, we can date the steady improvement of the Red Army over its German opponents. Paraphrasing Erich von Manstein, one might characterize the war's last twenty-one months as being "less disastrous defeats" rather than "lost victories." From the Soviet perspective, the Red Army won increasingly impressive operational victories, while Stalin guided a national strategic approach to the war in the East that ensured that the Soviet Union gained its political objectives.

The British High Command in World War II: Churchill Versus the Chiefs of Staff

The British high command possessed three important advantages in the Second World War. First, it possessed strong, knowledgeable leadership with Winston Churchill combining the positions of prime minister and minister of defense. There would be no quibbling over who was in charge. Second, as a result of their experiences in World War I, the British had created the Joint Chiefs of Staff, an effective bureaucratic system to examine strategic issues in a political framework which considered political, military, and economic factors in their broad context of national strategy. Third, unlike their opponents, the British included scientists and technologists in their examination of the factors impinging on the conduct of the war.

The result was that the British punched well above their weight. With far fewer resources than what the Third Reich possessed, British military forces played the major role in winning the Battle of the Atlantic, were a crucial factor in the waging of the strategic air campaign against the Third Reich, and contributed to the land campaigns in Burma, the Mediterranean, and Northwestern Europe. Here American support was a major factor. The Churchill – Roosevelt relationship kept the alliance together. But the British were crucial in the day-to-day management of what was one of the most successful alliances in history. The invention of the cavity magnetron in 1939 by British physicists represented one of the most important inventions of the war. It gave the Anglo-Americans an important advantage in radar over the Germans. But it is most important contribution came when British scientists at Churchill's instruction in 1940 shared its secrets with their American colleagues. It opened up a level of trust between the Anglo-American Allies that was quite extraordinary in the history of alliances. Here, Churchill's direction that his military advisers *would* cooperate with their American allies, no matter how often the Americans strained their sensibilities.

Churchill deserves much of the credit for these successes as well as some significant failures. His most important contribution came in the first six weeks of the war when he outmaneuvered a portion of the Conservative Party's leaders to keep Britain in the war, even given what appeared to be Britain's desperate military situation. At this critical juncture with Fighter Command confronting what appeared to be the *Luftwaffe*'s overwhelming strength, he kept Air Marshal Hugh Dowding in his position. It was to prove a wise decision.

Recent histories of the war have made much of Churchill's bullying of his military advisers, and they have some justification in their criticism. Yet, the performance of British military forces, particularly that of the army was less than impressive in the opening years of the war. Churchill's frustrations appear understandable, if not justified at all times. After all, in the interwar period, the military had been living off the meager fare that British politicians had served up for the defense of the Britain and its far-flung imperial possessions – a period that Churchill accurately summed up as "the locust years." No doubt, the prime minister was a difficult person to work for, but given the extent of his responsibilities and the extent of the threats, it is not surprising that there would be substantial disagreements.

The crucial point, however, is that Churchill never overruled his chiefs when they took a firm position. The exchanges at such times led to furious rows, during which he tested the patience of his military advisers. Nevertheless, on the larger strategic issues, the chiefs and the prime minister were in substantial agreement. In 1940 and 1941 there was no choice but to support Fighter Command and the war against the U-boats in the North Atlantic to protect the SLOCs on which Britain's survival depended. The war in the Mediterranean remained a significant commitment on which both the chiefs and prime minister were in full agreement because that area held the crucial SLOCs to the Middle East and India. Not until 1944 did the British Army reach a strength sufficient to take on the Germans in Northwestern Europe with the aid of their American allies.

Part of the problem Churchill confronted in working with the Army lay in the fractious nature of the Chief of the Imperial General Staff (CIGS), Field Marshal Alan Brooke. The CIGS is often credited with being a great strategist, but the fact that he agreed with Churchill in believing that a drive through northern Italy into Austria and southern Germany represent a preferable alternative to the Normandy landings raises serious doubts in that regard. But the real weakness in Alan Brooke's conduct of the war lay in his failure to choose first-class officers to command the armies in the field.

The difficulties between Churchill and Alan Brook also reflected the fact that Britain confronted economic and manpower difficulties to an extraordinary extent. There were simply not enough resources to meet the commitments the British confronted. In effect, they were fighting a poor man's war to an even greater extent than was the case with Nazi Germany. Max Hastings judgment on the importance of the Churchill-Brooke combination is that "they created the most efficient machine for the higher direction of war possessed by any combatant nation even if its judgements were sometimes flawed and its ability to enforce its wishes increasingly constrained." That is a fair judgment. While the British Empire was on the verge of collapse by the end of the war, Britain had survived.

The American High Command

With the Japanese attack on Pearl Harbor, the United States exploded on the international scene as it moved from great power to superpower. The maximization of its economic, political, and military reflected to a considerable extent the fact that America's high command worked almost flawlessly. And in this regard, the relationship between President Franklin Delano Roosevelt and his high command seemingly stands in stark contrast to what was occurring in Britain. Among the considerable differences was the fact that while Churchill met with his military leaders almost every day, Roosevelt rarely if ever troubled their time. He would only see them when necessary, but only when necessary. The difficulty in working with Roosevelt was that virtually nothing was written down. He played his cards closely to his chest but on crucial issues, he made his intentions clear.

The president hardly, if ever, quarreled with his chiefs. Yet on several occasions, he directly overruled them, a factor which never occurred in Britain. Nevertheless, he allowed them considerable latitude to get on with the war. And his interventions came in matters only of the greatest importance. The first came immediately before the war. In 1940 Roosevelt ordered that the battle fleet be moved from San Diego to Pearl Harbor – a decision that Admiral James Richardson, commander in chief US fleet (CinCUS), strongly disagreed with to the point that in October 1940 he told Roosevelt the navy lacked confidence in the country's civilian leadership. As result the president removed the admiral from his position in early February 1941.

The second major argument between Roosevelt and his military advisers came in the summer 1942. Marshal and King believed that the United States should mount a great invasion of Northwest Europe. Opposite in their strategic attitude were the British, who already had extensive experience with the Germans not only in World War I but in North Africa over the past year against Erwin Rommel's Afrika Korps. They made clear their refusal to support such a landing. In its place, they suggested that it would be far more reasonable for Anglo-American amphibious forces to strike at the Vichy French colonial possessions in North Africa. The seizure of Morocco, Algeria, and Tunisia would put Rommel in the bag and represent the first step for opening up the Mediterranean to Allied shipping, which would save upwards of 4,000,000 tons of shipping.

At the high point in the quarrel King and Marshall proposed to the president that the Americans switch their war effort from the Germans to the Japanese. Their proposal represented a fundamental change in American strategy. Roosevelt's push back to their suggestion was immediate and decisive. What the president recognized, and the service chiefs did not, was the fact that for political reasons, it was necessary to keep the focus of the American people on the war in Europe. In a letter to Marshall and King, he made clear that the landings in North Africa were going to occur, soon to receive the codename of Operation Torch, and there would be no shifting of the war from Europe to Asia.

Like Churchill, Roosevelt had had considerable experience in the last war. The president did not forget the ineptness of Woodrow Wilson's doctrinaire refusal to prepare the nation for war. In the interwar period, Congress and the American people placed considerable restrictions on providing the necessary funding, but the military prepared ruthlessly in its planning for the massive appropriations that eventually took place in the aftermath of Pearl Harbor. So great were its demands that by late summer 1942, the army had reached the point where its proposed force structure threatened to overthrow the entire armament program. In the end, the New Deal economists won out. While the historical record is not entirely clear who was supporting the downsizing of the proposed army, the president is a real possibility.

Truman and MacArthur

The contest between President Harry Truman and General of the Armies Douglas MacArthur for control of America's grand strategy represents one of the great civil military clashes in American history. On one hand, the president had assumed his position only through Roosevelt's death, while MacArthur had made general in 1917, had served as the theater commander the Western

Pacific for the course of the conflict, and had found himself as America's pro-consul during the occupation of Japan after the surrender of that nation in August 1945.

Not surprisingly, the Truman – MacArthur breakup was very much the result of two men who had little understanding of each other. Moreover, while Truman had spent the past two decades deeply imbued with Washington politics, MacArthur had spent the past fourteen years in the Philippines, Australia, and Japan, never once visiting the continental United States. In almost every sense he was out of touch with his native country.

Underlying the quarrel was a fundamental disagreement over America's strategic interests. For Truman and his advisers in Washington, they lay in repairing the politics and economies of Western Europe, which to them were more threatened strategically than the situation in Western Asia. Thus, the additional deployment of substantial American forces to expand the Korean War to China at MacArthur's urging was something the United States could not afford, given the Soviet military threat to Western Europe. General of the Armies Omar Bradley, chairman of the JCS, put the administration's position about extending the Korean War in testimony to Congress; it would commit the United States to "the wrong war, at the wrong place, at the wrong time, and with the wrong enemy." In this view of the strategic world, the high command in Washington and the president were in almost complete agreement.

MacArthur took a quite different view of the importance of Asia to the United States. His world was an entirely an Asian-centric view of the strategic landscape. And it was largely in disagreement with that of the American elites running American strategy in Washington. Nevertheless, one should not forget that there was considerable support among Republicans who had been/isolationists before Pearl Harbor for an American strategy that would support Asia over the ongoing effort in Europe.

From the onset of the invasion if South Korea, MacArthur acted as if he were an independent actor, free to make decisions on his own. That was a road already well-traveled by the general. Thus, even before Washington had decided on which road it would take in regard to the war, MacArthur had authorized the shipping of weapons and ammunition to the South Koreans. Ironically unlike the other case studies in this book, he did not represent a national military high command. The insulting letters and comments he had made over the years, and not just to Truman, make extraordinary reading. He must have thought himself invulnerable when he sent his disastrous letter to Joe Martin. But he was not. He now joined the long gray line of retired West Pointers.

Mao and His Generals

One of the reviewers of this work suggested that we should have included more studies by non-Western examples of the interplay political leaders and their high command. To examine more, one supposes, would elucidate the differences between Western practices and those of other polities as being considerable. The examination of the relations between Mao and his generals suggests why that is not so. Mao ran a murderous regime, but at least during the Korean War the relations with his generals were reasonable. In fact to all intents, he was both the high command and the political leader.

Unlike our other examples, it is hard to describe the situation in China as involving tensions between a military high command and the politicians. Mao and his generals had run the great civil war against the Chinese Nationalists Chiang Kai-shek – a war that had lasted for two decades. Thus, they embraced the military and political as a single whole. Mao might well be considered as the *primus inter pares*, but the ties between the chairman and the generals who worked with him in running the war against the Americans and the UN were far closer than in any of the others among our case studies. Moreover, virtually all of them possessed civilian assignments along with their military positions.

Nevertheless, there were tensions, largely between Mao and Peng Dehuai, but those represented the troubles inherent between those far from the battle front and those close up against an opponent who possessed military powers far beyond the comprehension of anything the Chinese had experienced during the civil war. Admittedly, they had seen the arrival of B-29s on Chinese airfields, but that had been a relatively short period before the Americans had left for the Marianas. While the Chinese Communists had gotten a quick view, it is doubtful they had recognized the implications.

What is particularly impressive is how quickly the Chinese adapted to the new experiences of war against the Americans. With their intervention, the Chinese believed they could achieve their aims with the kind of ruthless blows that had destroyed Chiang's Nationalist armies. In North Korea, it worked quite well against the ill-prepared Americans and South Koreans. But the further south Chinese armies advanced the greater became their logistic lifelines. Adding to their problems were the poundings that USAF, navy, and marine aircraft inflicted on them. By the time the Chinese army reached the 38th Parallel, the balance between Chinese numbers and American firepower were almost equal with US air gaining an advantage as increasingly favorable weather enabled American air power to inflict ever greater damage on Chinese logistics.

On 5 January 1951 the PLA retook Seoul, but the push south had already lost momentum. There now occurred a series of murderous battles, where UN forces at times gave ground, but their firepower was such that they soon regained what they had lost. The casualty ratios were increasingly in the UN favor, but Mao, far away in Beijing refused to recognize that Communist armies were facing a losing proposition. Heavier and heavier losses were showing no results, while UN forces were steadily improving. Moreover, the logistic situation was reaching catastrophic proportions. By mid-May UN forces were on the brink of creating a major breakthrough. Mao finally recognized reality and agreed to begin armistice talks and the advance of UN forces halted.

Conclusion

And so, what are we to make of the divergent approaches to the problems involved between high commands and the political leadership. The first category is the easiest to examine, namely examples where the relationship is one where chaos exists that prevents any coherent examination of strategic issues. Here, the Germans in World War I presents a dismal example of how issues of strategy and even operations can disappear in a welter of confusion, exacerbated by the fact that no one is in charge.

The second category is clearly an approach to building effective relationship between the political leadership at the top and the high command responsible for running the war. The German solution reflected their experiences in the last war. In response to the myth that the Reich's defeat in World War I had been caused by a fifth column stabbing an unbeaten army in the back, it became popular for many Germans to argue that a strong political leadership at the top would be able to keep matters at home in order. At the same time, the military would wage a "pure" war that would exclude concerns about politics and economics from the conduct of military operations. That was certainly the message of generals like Manstein and Guderian in their memoirs written after the war.

The irony, of course, lay in the fact they, and most of their colleagues, had been enthusiastic, ideologically motivated supporters of the Nazi regime and even the final solution, in some cases ordering their troops to participate in war crimes, including the massacre of Jews and other undesirables. But the deal the office corps had made with the devil came back to haunt its members. Beginning in 1943 the Nazi regime inserted specialized, highly motivated officers throughout the army to ensure soldiers of the proper ideological motivation against the Bolshevik and plutocratic enemies of the Reich. They were the Nazi equivalent of the Soviet commissars. As such they were responsible to ensure that the officer in charge was obeying his orders to the letter.

As suggested above, the Soviets resembled their Nazi brothers in major ways, particularly in how ideology motivated the decision-making processes except that Hitler refused to learn from his defeats. The catastrophe of the summer and fall 1941 helped to push Stalin toward a more realistic view of the relationship between himself and his high command, but it was not until the summer of 1942 that Stalin was willing to take the advice of his generals. By 1943 we are talking about a system based on tyranny where the tyrant was willing to cooperate with his generals in a highly effective fashion. Even Zhukov, one of the war's most effective generals, found himself forced to admit to Stalin's increasing sophistication in military matters. But the cost had been enormous with millions of dead, spread from Stalingrad to Berlin.

The case studies dealing with the democracies reflect Churchill's well-known comment that democracy is the worst form of government except all the others. In the end, democracies force their leaders to learn and adapt, because if they fail to do so, they will find themselves on the outside looking in.

That was certainly the case with Asquith. Unwilling, or incapable, of adapting, the prime minister found himself floundering in a sea of military and economic challenges that not at all resembled the peacetime flow of British politics. The surprising element in his story is that he lasted as long as he did. Asquith's replacement, Lloyd George brought order and coherence to the home and industrial fronts, but because of the dynamics of Britain's internal politics, he was never able to control Haig and the generals.

Churchill and Roosevelt displayed enormous differences in their personalities, but their underlying understanding of the world and the political arena in which they operated was outstanding. Churchill was openly combative, but more than willing to listen to others. The president was anything but confrontational in his dealings with others, but he too was willing to listen. But in the end, it did not matter. It was the openness and an ability to grasp the essential that mattered. Thus, when presented with reasonable arguments both were willing to alter their positions.

But perhaps the most interesting case of the effectiveness of democratic regimes is that of Lincoln and Grant. Both knew little about the business grand strategy much less war in 1861. But by early 1864, they had developed the most successful integration of the high command with the political leadership in American history. But it had taken them two long years of failures to reach that point, and the cost of learning and adaptation was high. In contrast, Jefferson Davis displayed little interest in changing or adapting, and the results speak for themselves.

The bottom line in thinking through the issue involved in grand strategy is the stark reality that it is a crapshoot. Political and strategic issues change over time. There are always internal political problems that stand in the way of a coherent strategic approach. The enemy always gets a vote, while our understanding of him and the evolving situation are faulty. In the end, the relationships between the military high command and the political leadership are driven by uncertainties and ambiguities – a reality that makes the relationship so difficult.

Notes

1 Carl von Clausewitz, *On War*, trans., and ed. by Michael Howard and Peter Paret (Princeton, NJ: Princeton University Press, 1976).
2 Quoted in Williamson Murray, *War, Strategy, and Military Effectiveness* (Cambridge: Cambridge University Press 2011), p. 58.
3 For the American Civil War, see particularly: James McPherson, *Battle Cry of Freedom: The Civil War Era* (Oxford: Oxford University Press, 1988); and Williamson Murray and Wayne Hsieh, *A Savage War: A Military History of the Civil War* (Princeton, NJ: Princeton University Press, 2016).

INDEX

Note: Page numbers followed by "n" refer to end notes.